SELECTED SPIRITUAL WRITINGS OF ANNE DUTTON

EIGHTEENTH-CENTURY, BRITISH-BAPTIST, WOMAN THEOLOGIAN

BAPTISTS
HISTORY, LITERATURE, THEOLOGY, HYMNS

General Editor: Walter B. Shurden, Mercer University

John Taylor, *Baptists on the American Frontier: A History of Ten Baptist Churches*
Edited by Chester Young

Thomas Helwys, *A Short Declaration of the Mystery of Iniquity*
Edited by Richard Groves

Roger Williams, *The Bloody Tenant of Persecution for Cause of Conscience*
Edited by Richard Groves; Edwin Gaustad, Historical Introduction

James A. Rogers†, *Richard Furman: Life and Legacy*

Lottie Moon, *Send the Light: Lottie Moon's Letters and Other Writings*
Edited by Keith Harper

James Byrd, *The Challenges of Roger Williams: Religious Liberty, Violent Persecution, and the Bible*

Anne Dutton, *The Influential Spiritual Writings of Anne Dutton: Volume 1: Letters*
Edited by JoAnn Ford Watson (Fall 2003)

David T. Morgan, *Southern Baptist Sisters: In Search of Status, 1845-2000*
(Fall 2003)

William E. Ellis, *"A Man of Books and a Man of the People":*
E. Y. Mullins and the Crisis of Moderate Southern Baptist Leadership
(paperback Fall 2003; hardback 1985)

Jarrett Burch, *Adiel Sherwood: Baptist Antebellum Pioneer in Georgia* (Winter 2003)

Anthony Chute, *A Piety Above the Common Standard: Jesse Mercer and the Defense of Evangelistic Calvinism* (Spring 2004)

Annie Armstrong, *Rescue the Perishing: Selected Correspondence of Annie W. Armstrong*
Edited by Keith Harper (Spring 2004)

William H. Brackney, *A Genetic History of Baptist Thought* (Fall 2004)

Henlee Hulix Barnette, *A Pilgrimmage of Faith: My Story* (Fall 2004)

Anne Dutton, *The Influential Spiritual Writings of Anne Dutton: Volume 2: Discourses, Poetry, Hymns, Memoir*
Edited by JoAnn Ford Watson (Fall 2004)

Walter B. Shurden, *Not an Easy Journey: Some Transitions in Baptist Life* (Spring 2005)

Marc A. Jolley, editor, *Distinctively Baptist: Essays on Baptist History: Festschrift Walter B. Shurden* (Spring 2005)

Keith Harper and C. Martin Jacumin, Esteemed Reproach: The Lives of Rev. James Ireland and Rev. Joseph Craig (2005)

Charles Deweese, Women Deacons and Deaconesses: 400 Years of Baptist Service (BH&HS, 2005)

Pam Durso and Keith Durso, Courage and Hope: The Stories of Ten Baptist Women Ministers (BH&HS, 2005)

Anne Dutton, *The Influential Spiritual Writings of Anne Dutton: Volume 3: Autobiography*, Edited by JoAnn Ford Watson (Spring 2006)

SELECTED SPIRITUAL WRITINGS OF ANNE DUTTON

EIGHTEENTH-CENTURY, BRITISH-BAPTIST, WOMAN THEOLOGIAN

Volume 3
THE AUTOBIOGRAPHY

compiled and with an introduction by
JOANN FORD WATSON

MERCER UNIVERSITY PRESS
MACON, GEORGIA USA
MAY 2006

ISBN 0-86554-908-7   MUP/H670

Selected Spiritual Writings of Anne Dutton.
Eighteenth-Century, British-Baptist, Woman Theologian.
Volume 3. *The Autobiography*
Copyright ©2006
Mercer University Press
All rights reserved
Printed in the United States of America
First edition, May 2006

Library of Congress Cataloging-in-Publication Data

[CIP data is available from the Library of Congress]

CONTENTS

Volume 3. THE AUTOBIOGRAPHY

ANNE DUTTON
from the frontispiece to
Selections from Letters on Spiritual Subjects /etc./ (1884)

PREFACE

The manuscript, *A Brief Account of the Gracious Dealings of God, with a Poor, Sinful, Unworthy Creature, in Three Parts* is held in the British Library, London, England. The microfilm of the British Library copy used here comes from the Gale Group's Eighteenth Century Collection, reel 8837, location no. 2 on the reel ID no. 01D006160-001. I thank Mr. Mark Holland, publisher and vice-president, Gale United Kingdom, Reading, for permission to publish this transcription of the manuscript. I also thank Mr. Martin Zonis of Gale Group, Primary Source Microfilms, Research Publications, Woodbridge, Connecticut, for his assistance in obtaining permission to publish the manuscript and for obtaining the microfilm of the manuscript.

I thank Dr. Russell Morton, research librarian at Ashland Theological Seminary, and Ms. Sylvia Locher, head librarian at Ashland Theological Seminary, for their wonderful assistance in obtaining the manuscript. I thank Ms. Kathleen Slusser, Ashland Theological Seminary graduate assistant, for her assistance in keying the manuscript for publication, and Dr. Dawn Morton for her assistance in compiling the index. I would like to thank my husband, Duane F. Watson, for his kind support and editorial expertise. The work is dedicated with love to my daughter, Christina Lucille Watson, a precious daughter of God.

The photograph below is of the Baptist Chapel at Great Gransden that was built by Anne and Benjamin Dutton. It was the meetinghouse they built between 1731 and 1733. It still stands today in the church yard by the cemetery in Great Gransden near Anne Dutton's tombstone. It is orange stucco with a thatched roof. I took this photograph in July 1997.

The manuscripts are here transcribed with the original spellings, except the so-called "long s" (*f*) becomes a regular "s." The page numbers in Dutton's work cited in the introduction are to those of the original manuscript. Errata corrections in the original appear here in the running text as bracketed notes.

JoAnn Ford Watson

BAPTIST CHAPEL AT GREAT GRANSDEN
built by Benjamin and Anne Dutton, 1731–1733.
Photograph by JoAnn Ford Watson.

INTRODUCTION

Anne Dutton[1] begins the completed version of her spiritual autobiography in three parts (1750) with an "Epistle to the Reader":

Dear Reader,
THE First *and* Second *Parts of my Brief Account, were printed some Years ago, as appears by their Date. And the* Third *Part, which is now added, perhaps might not have been printed till after my Decease, but for special Reasons which induc'd me to it. I have sincerely aim'd in the Whole, so far as I know my own Heart, at the* Glory *of* GOD, *and the* Good *of Souls: And not at my* own Honour, *that any Man should* think of me, *more highly than is* meet: *Or any otherwise, than as a* chief Sinner, *on whom the* LORD *hath* shewed great Mercy. . . . Oh,* Not *unto* me, Not *unto* me, *unto vile unworthy me; but unto the* LORD *alone, be* all the Glory! *If* GOD's *Ways of Grace, may be made* known, *by any Thing I have written: To the* Praise *of his great Name, the Joy of his dear Children. . . .*[2]

Dutton introduces the autobiography and then arranges it in three parts with an appendix and an attached letter. I will introduce each part, covering important events and publications related to each. I will offer summaries of the three parts, the appendix, and the letter. These will assist the reader in understanding the contents of the autobiography of Dutton's life, work, and ministry, and enable a clearer reading of the text.

Part I

A Brief Account of the Gracious Dealings of God, with a Poor, Sinful, Unworthy Creature, Relating to the Work of Divine Grace on the Heart, in a saving Conversion to Christ, and to some Establishment in Him. Part I. By A.D. Come all ye that fear God, and I will declare what He hath done for my Soul, Psa. lxvi. 6. London: Printed by J. Hart, in Poppings-

---

[1] A general introduction to the life and work of Anne Dutton appears in vol. 1, pp. xi-xliv.

[2] Anne Dutton, "Epistle to the Reader" found at the beginning of *A Brief Account of the Gracious Dealings of God, with a Poor, Sinful, Unworthy Creature, Relating to the Work of Divine Grace on the Heart, in a Saving Conversion to Christ, and to Some Establishment in Him*, part I (London: J. Hart, 1743) i-ii. Hereafter abbreviated as *A Brief Account*.

Court, Fleet-street: And Sold by J. Lewis, in Bartholomew-Close, near West-Smithfield; and E. Gardner, at Milton's-Head, in Gracechurch-Street MDCCXLIII [1743].

Part I begins with a preface addressed to *"Christian Reader"*:

MY *Design in the following Sheets, was to bear a* Testimony, *as one of God's* Witnesses, *to the exceeding Riches of his* Grace, *in the* Salvation *of my Soul. But yet, when I first began to think about it, (having been requested to engage in this Work) I could not, for some Time, find my Heart inclined hereto: As being under a prevailing Sense of my own Weakness, to say any Thing that might tend to the Advancement of God's Free-Grace, and the Edification of his People. So that thou hadst never had the following Narrative, if the Lord himself had not encourag'd me to attempt this Work. And he sweetly drew my Heart, as being one of his Witnesses, to bear this Testimony for* Him, *and his* Way *of saving poor Sinners, of whom I am Chief. . . .* [See 1 Timothy 1:15.][3]

Dutton concludes the preface:

> *And now, That God's Free Grace, which hath saved me, may further extend its Riches, in owning this weak Attempt; that the God of all Grace may be glorify'd, and his People reap some Advantage; is the earnest Desire of,*
> *The Least of* CHRIST's,
>   A. D.[4]

In part I, Dutton offers an explanation of the design of her tract in four sections:

MY Design in this little Tract, being to give a brief Account of the Lord's Loving-kindness to my Soul; I shall in Order hereto, give some Hints, *First*, Of my Manner of Life from my Childhood. *Secondly*, Of the Work of Divine Grace on my Heart, in a saving Conversion to CHRIST. *Thirdly*, of my being brought to some Establishment in HIM. And, *Fourthly*, Something by Way of Reflection.[5]

Dutton begins the first major section with an account of her religious education as a child. She states that "It pleas'd the Lord to order it so, that

---

[3] *A Brief Account* I:3.
[4] *A Brief Account* I:4.
[5] *A Brief Account* I: 5.

I had the Advantage of a Religious Education; my Parents being both Gracious By Means of whose Care and Diligence, I was train'd up in the Ways of God: Being early instructed into the Doctrines and Worship of the Gospel, so far as my tender Years were capable of."[6] She describes her church training as a child:

> I attended with my Parents upon the Ministry of the late Mr. *Hunt*, who was then Pastor of a Church of Christ at *Northampton*; which was the Place of my *first*, and also of my *second* Birth. I kept up private Prayer frequently, but not constantly. From a Child I was acquainted with the Holy Scriptures and took Pleasure in reading them, with other good Books; especially Hymn-Books, which I greatly delighted to learn, and commit to Memory.[7]

Dutton continues with her second major section, "Of the Work of Divine Grace upon my Heart, in a saving Conversion to CHRIST," stating that, "It pleas'd the Lord to work savingly upon my Heart, when I was about thirteen Years of Age; tho' I can't fix the precise Time of its Beginning."[8] Dutton speaks of being convicted of her own sinfulness:

> Again, I was convinc'd, that I had been doing nothing else but *sinning against God*, ever since I had a Being . . . . I now, no longer thought myself to be *better* than others; but one of the *vilest* Creatures the Earth bore. Yea, I thought myself to be the very *Chief* of Sinners.[9]

Dutton quotes two lines of a hymn from Mr. Shepherd: "Sure I'm More *Vile* than any one / Of wretched *Adam's* Race!"[10] and writes of her reception of Christ's grace:

> Again, it pleas'd the Lord to convince me, that *Salvation* was alone by God's *Free-Grace*, thro' what Christ had *done*, as the Redeemer of

---

[6] *A Brief Account* I:5-6.

[7] *A Brief Account* I:6.

[8] *A Brief Account* I:9.

[9] *A Brief Account* I:12—with rather obvious reference to 1 Tim 1:15.

[10] John Mason, *Spiritual songs, or, Songs of praise to Almighty God upon several occasions, together with the Song of songs, which is Solomon's; first turn'd, then paraphrased in English verse, with an addition of a sacred poem on Dives and Lazarus*, begun by John Mason and completed by Thomas Shepherd (London: printed for T. Parkhurst, [7]1701, [10]1708) in *A Brief Account* I:12.

Sinners. And that it was impossible for me to be sav'd, without *Faith in Christ*, of the special Operation of God. Further, I was fully convinc'd of the *Sufficiency* of Christ to save even the *worst* of Sinners.[11]

Dutton questions the concept of election when she continues: "About this Time I was put upon some Doubt about Election, whether there was any such Thing. And received full Satisfaction from *Rom*. xi. 5."[12]

Dutton provides an understanding of Christ's grace and the work of the Holy Spirit upon her troubled soul, which had been seeking grace. She writes of the assurance of God's saving work in her soul:

> There was, I remember, an Expression dropp'd in Company, where I was, that did very much affect me: It was this, "the least Dram of *Saving Grace* will land a Soul safe in Glory, when they which have Abundance of *common Grace* may go to Hell with it." And, oh, how I long'd for one Dram of this *Saving Grace*![13]

Dutton refers to a book that was helpful to her as "a Book that was cast into my Hands, which treated of the Happiness and Glory of the Saints in Heaven; as it consists in a perfect Enjoyment of God, and Conformity to him: (its Author I know not, the Title-Page being rent out). . . . "[14] Dutton also indicates that "Mr. *Shepherd's Penitential Cries* were also of great Use to me."[15] She includes a hymn from Mr. Shepherd in her autobiography because of its great use to her heart. She also includes lines from from Mr. Mason's hymn.[16] She claimed that these "were exceeding precious to my Soul at that Time"[17] when she found Christ's grace in her soul in the new birth. She quotes Mr. Mason: "O, was I born first from Beneath! And then born from Above!"[18]

Dutton tells of her conversion and healing on her sickbed: "The Lord rais'd me up from a *Sick-Bed*, From *Death to Life*, both in Soul and Body. I was as it were brought forth into a *New World*: All Things apprear'd *new*

---

[11]*A Brief Account* I:13.
[12]*A Brief Account* I:14.
[13]*A Brief Account* I:24.
[14]*A Brief Account* I:24.
[15]*A Brief* Account I:24.
[16]*A Brief Account* I:24-27.
[17]*A Brief Account* I:31.
[18]*A Brief Account* I:31.

to *me*."[19] She writes of her longing for Christ and her desire to know him more deeply in her soul. She writes:

> I remember I was once so pained for the Discoveries of Christ's Love, that I thought, if he did not speedily manifest himself to me, I could not live. . . . I breath'd out my Desires in the following Lines of Mr. *Mason's* Paraphrase on Song viii. 6.
>
> "Love me, my Lord, or else I die! . . . "[20]

Dutton continues with the third section of her autobiography of "being brought to some Establishment in Christ."[21] She joined Mr. Hunt's church at Northampton when she was 15 years old. She writes:

> And by the Word of the Gospel was I nourish'd up in Faith, and my new-born Soul strengthened. It pleased the Lord, in the Fifteenth Year of my Age, to incline my Heart to join with a Church of Christ, in *N---n*, over which the late Mr. *H---t* was Pastor. Under his Ministry, I was often laid to the Breasts of Consolation, and being fed with the Milk of the Word, which was suited to my present State, I grew thereby.[22]

Dutton concludes part 1 with the fourth section, one of reflection concerning the people of God.

> Fourthly, Somewhat by Way of Reflection. And,
> 1*st* To the People of God, under two Ranks.
> 1. To such of the Saints, who have a comfortable *Knowledge* of the Work of Grace in their own Souls. . . . You have heard something of the Lord's loving Kindness to my Soul. . . .

---

[19] *A Brief Account* I:34.

[20] Mason, *Spiritual songs*, in *A Brief Account* I:40.

[21] *A Brief Account* I:42.

[22] *A Brief Account* I:42. In his *The Life and Faith of the Baptists* (London: Kingsgate Press, 1946) 51, H. Wheeler Robinson records that Dutton was "brought up in a religious home and attended the Independent Church at Castle Hill under the Rev. John Hunt (1698–1709)." John Whitebrook (*Ann Dutton: A Life and Bibliography* [London: A. W. Cannon and Co., 1921] 4n.1) notes that "John Hunt (son of a minister ejected in 1662 from Sutton, Lambs) was minister of Castle Hill Meetinghouse from 1698 to 1709. He was a paedobaptist and a keen controversialist. He died at Tunstead, Norfolk on September 15, 1725."

2. To such of God's People, that have not, as yet, a full *Persuasion* of a special *Work* of Grace in their Hearts.[23]

Dutton calls people to come and see the grace in Christ Jesus.[24]

Part II

A Brief Account of the Gracious Dealings of God, with a Poor, Sinful, Unworthy Creature, Relating to a Train of special Providences attending Life, by which the Work of Faith was carried on with Power. Part II. By A. D. *Come and hear all ye that fear God, and I will declare what he hath done for my Soul*, Psa. lxvi. 16. *One Generation shall praise thy Works to another, and so all declare thy mighty Acts. I will speak of the glorious Honour of thy Majesty, and of thy wondrous Works. And Men shall speak of the Might of thy terrible Acts: and I will declare thy Greatness. They shall abundantly utter the Memory of thy great Goodness, and shall sing of thy Righteousness*, Psa. cxlv. 4, 5, 6, 7. London: Printed by J. Hart in Poppings Court, Fleet-street: And sold by J. Lewis, in Bartholomew-Close, near West-Smithfield; and E. Gardner, at Milton's Head, in Gracechurch-Street. 1743. [Price One Shilling.]

Dutton sets forth the emphasis for part II when she writes:

I shall now in *this* give some further Account of the LORD's gracious Dealings with me, relating to a Train of special Providences, attending my Life, by which the Work of Faith was carried on with Power. And as enabled I shall give some Hints,
    First, Of these special Providences of *God* towards me. And,
    Secondly, Make some Improvement.[25]

She then begins the first part, "With Providences," by stating that, "The Providences I chiefly intend to take notice of, are such that relate to my being *planted in the House of the* LORD, in order to my *Flourishing in the Courts of our* GOD."[26] She focuses on the removal of her first pastor, Mr. Hunt, from one church to. She leaves this church when she does not like his

---

[23] *A Brief Account* I:54.
[24] *A Brief Account* I:72.
[25] *A Brief Account* II:3.
[26] *A Brief Account* II:3.

replacement. She goes to Mr. Moore's church in Northampton where she grows in the knowledge of the Lord. She writes: "The Providence I shall first mention, and take a little Notice of, relates to my Removal from that Church of Christ in *N---n*, where I first join'd, to another Church in the same Town, of which the late Mr. *M---re*, was Pastor."[27]

Dutton tells the story of the loss of Mr. Hunt and the change of churches to Mr. Moore's pastorate:

> Mr. *H---t*, my first Pastor, was removed, and another Minister succeeded him. The Ministry of this Servant of Christ was of Use to me in some Respects; tho' I did not fall in with his Judgment in several Points. . . . --- But some Time after this, not finding myself edify'd under his Ministry, and my Dissatisfaction increasing, I thought it my Duty to acquaint him with it. . . . I thought I should meet with Opposition if I attempted it; and much indeed came on. . . . --- Upon which I intreated the Lord to tell me what was my Duty in the present Case. And having receiv'd full Satisfaction, That it was his Mind I should remove my Communion from that Church to which I then related, to that over which Mr. *M---re* was Pastor; I accordingly did it.[28]

Dutton states that the move to Mr. Moore's Church was very beneficial to her spiritual growth:

> The Lord Jesus, my chief Shepherd, led me, by the Ministry of his Servant, Mr. *M---re*, into fat, green Pastures. The Doctrines of the Gospel

---

[27] *A Brief Account* II:4. Robinson (*Life and Faith*, 52) records that in 1709 the Rev. John Hunt was removed as her pastor and that the Rev. Thomas Tingey succeeded him (1709–1729). However, Tingey's ministry did not edify Dutton. Therefore she moved her membership to the open-membership Baptist Church in College Lane under the ministry of the Rev. John Moore. Whitebrook (*Ann Dutton*, 6n.2) notes: "John Moore was from Rauden, Yorkshire, and elder of the Church of Rossendale, Lancashire. . . . [He] was minister at College Lane from December 1700 till his death in 1726. He was a Baptist; but the Church admitted 'open communion.' The meetinghouse was built in 1714: a hired room having formerly been occupied."

[28] *A Brief Account* II:4-5. Robinson (*Life and Faith*, 52) refers to Dutton's *Brief Hints Concerning Baptism* ([London, 1746] 27) to state that it was not until she was a member of College Lane that she was baptized on profession of faith.

were clearly stated, and much insisted on in his Ministry. The Sanctuary-Streams ran clearly; and the Sun Shone gloriously.[29]

Dutton continues her autobiography with a second important event. In 1714 she marries at twenty-two years of age a Mr. Cole(s) (or Catle, Cattell, or Cattle).[30] She then moves from Northampton to London with her new husband and joins Mr Skepp's church. She writes: "The next Providence I shall give some Hints of, relates to the Lord's removing my Habitation from *N---n*, to *L---n*: Which was occasion'd by my entring into a Marriage-State, when I was 22 Years of Age."[31]

Concerning her church membership at this time, she continues: "Upon my Removal to *L---n*, I had *transient* Communion with the Church of Christ under the pastoral Care of Mr. *Sk---p*. But after I had walked with 'em thus for some Time, it was thought proper, my Abode being *fixed*, that my Communion should be so too."[32] It was at this time that Dutton joined Mr. Skepp's church, regarding which she says, "My Fellowship herewith was sweet. . . . "[33]

---

[29]*A Brief Account* II:5.

[30]For a discussion of marriages, ages, and name, see *Selected Spiritual Writings of Anne Dutton: Eighteenth-Century, British-Baptist, Woman Theologian*, vol. 1, *Letters*, ed. JoAnn Ford Watson (Macon GA: Mercer University Press, 2003) xv-xvi. Whitebrook (*Ann Dutton*, 6) states "At the age of 22 she married Mr. *Coles*. . . . With Mr. *Coles* she lived about five years, in London, then at Warwick, then again in London" (italics added). Arthur Wallington states that Dutton "was married first at the age of 22 to a Mr. *Cole*" ("Wesley and Anne Dutton." *Proceedings of the Wesley Historical Society* 11/2 [June 1917]): 44; italics added). Michael Haykin ("The Celebrated Mrs. Anne Dutton," *Evangelical Times* [April 2001]: 19) states that "when she was twenty-two she married a Cattell (his first name does not appear to be known) and moved to London."

[31]*A Brief Account* II:10.

[32]*A Brief Account* II:11.

[33]*A Brief Account* I:12. Robinson (*Life and Faith*, 53) records that at age 22 (1714) Dutton married her first husband and they moved to London where she had communion with the church at Cripplegate under the Rev. John Skepp. In a 1715 entry, the Cripplegate Church Book Register of Letters states "No. 18 Ann Catle from Northampton for Transient." Dutton was not fully transferred, but did receive temporary communion. Two years later, about 1718, the Church Book Register further records that "Ms. Ann Cattle" made a full transfer. Robinson further notes the College Lane Church Book entry for August 18, 1715: that "Ann Cattell [was]

Dutton speaks of a brief further move from London to Warwick due to her husband's business and of her distress there. She includes a letter she wrote during this time to her pastor, Mr. Skepp.

> In the next Place, I shall take a little Notice of my being remov'd to *W---k*. After I had been some Time at *L---n*, the Providence of God so order'd it, that there was a far greater Prospect of Advantage, with respect to my Husband's Business at *W---k*: Upon which he thought it best for us to go down thither for that Season.[34]

Dutton finds the worship in this new place lacking and writes about it to Mr. Skepp:

> But when I came to *W---k*, I found a strange Alteration: I was got into another *Climate*, much further off the Sun. I thought, when I came first, "Surely, this People worship *without* the Blood of Jesus." . . . in this Place, being expressed in a Letter, that I wrote to Mr. *Sk---p* from thence, I think it may not be amiss to insert it.[35]

The letter appears on pages 17-23 in the original manuscript and is signed: "*Your unworthy sister, A. C.*"[36]—for Anne Cole(s), being in her first marriage.

Dutton then moves again and returns to London, from Warwick. She writes: "Thus kindly the Lord dealt with me during my Stay at *W---k*; and in a little Time he gave me the Desire of my Heart, in fixing my Abode again at *L---n*."[37] This time she and her husband lived in London for 5 years.

Dutton speaks of the illness of her body at this time: "Another Time I was under Illness of Body, and other Trials: And having a tender Mother, such Thought sprang up in my Mind, 'If I was with *her* she would pity

---

dismissed to Mr. Skepp's Church near Cripplegate in London" (*Life and Faith*, 53n.1).

[34]*A Brief Account* II:14. Robinson (*Life and Faith*, 53) notes that Dutton's business called them away for some time from London to Warwick.

[35]*A Brief Account* II:17.

[36]*A Brief Account* II:23. Robinson, *Life and Faith*, 53; Whitebrook, *Ann Dutton*, 6.

[37]*A Brief Account* II:23. Robinson, *Life and Faith*, 54.

me.' "[38] Dutton states that in her trials, God comforted her. She quotes a verse of Mr. Bunyan's, thus:

If Gall and Wormword they give me,
Then God doth Sweetness cast,
So much thereto, that they can't think
How bravely it doth taste![39]

Dutton writes of the death of her first husband, Mr. Cole(s), about 1719–1720, after they had returned to London for about five years:

During my Abode at L---n, I was highly favoured with the Enjoyment of God, both in publick and private. But after I had been there near five Years, it pleased the Lord to take away my Yokefellow by Death. And some Circumstances attended, which made it very trying. But my kind Lord comforted me.[40]

Dutton continues that she moved again back to Northampton, after her first husband died: "Upon the Death of my Husband, the Lord removed me to N---n, and again fix'd my Abode there."[41] She then writes that she marries a second time here at Northampton, to Mr. Benjamin Dutton, a clothier turned Baptist Minister:

In the next Place, after I had been at N---n some Time, I was again married; And the Lord gave me that Word, concerning it, *Gen*. xxii. 17. *In Blessing, I will bless thee.* . . . Upon this Change, I had a Mind to return to L---n; for my Heart was *there*, because I enjoy'd so much of GOD, under the Ministry of Mr. Sk---p. But the all-wise Providence of God, so over-ruled Things, so to fix our Abode at N---n.[42]

---

[38]*A Brief Account* II:25.

[39]John Bunyan, "Prison Meditations," in *The Works of John Bunyan*, vol. 1. (repr.: Carlisle PA: Banner of Truth Trust, 1991; Glasgow: Blackie, 1854) 64, verse 22, original 1665 poem, quoted in *A Brief Account* II:27. Dutton's quotation does not correspond exactly with Bunyan's 1854 edition, the first two lines of which read: "If they give me gall to drink, / Then God doth sweet'ning cast." Whether Dutton paraphrased or quoted a textual variant cannot be determined.

[40]*A Brief Account* II:29.

[41]*A Brief Account* II:29.

[42]*A Brief Account* II:32. Haykin ("Anne Dutton," 2) records that, following the death of her first husband, Dutton returned to her family in Northampton. "She was not long single. Her second marriage in the early 1720s was to Benjamin Dutton

Dutton further records that at this time, her beloved pastor, Mr. Skepp, died in 1721: "After I had been married a little Time, Mr. *Sk---p* died, which was a great Grief to me."[43] After Skepp's death, and in the same year, Dutton turns her attention to the preaching of the Rev. William Grant of Wellingborough. She wants to move from Northampton to Wellingborough to be part of his church and grow under his preaching.[44] The move took a long time.

Dutton records the preaching of her new pastor, Mr. Grant, at her new church at Wellingborough that she hears at Northampton prior to moving to Wellingborough. It will be spiritually uplifting for her. She writes:

> But here I may take Notice, that before this, Mr. *G---t*, of *W---h*, had preach'd several Times at *N---n*, and I had heard him with Pleasure. And once, in particular, he was so filled with the Spirit, in Prayer, that I saw a very great Glory of the divine Presence in him.[45]

Dutton reports that the worship directed by this pastor was spiritual. She looks forward to experience it when she and her husband move. "And my poor Soul was brought *nigh*, to worship with him in the Fellowship of the same Spirit."[46]

In preparing to move from Northampton to Wellingborough, there were delays. Dutton struggles with the economic necessities and avails herself of the Lord's providence. She writes:

(1691–1747), a clothier who had studied for vocational ministry in various places, among them Glasgow University." Robinson (*Life and Faith*, 54) records that Anne married Benjamin Dutton within a year or so of returning to Northampton. Benjamin had apprenticed with a clothier and draper and then studied for the ministry. After their marriage he returned to the ministry. Whitebrook (*Ann Dutton*, 7) records that "She married Mr. Benjamin Dutton the youngest of many children of Matthew Dutton." Records show he was born 12 February 1691 or 1692. Benjamin had been converted "at the age of 17" and became "apprenticed to a clothier."

[43]*A Brief Account* II:33. Skepp died in 1721. Robinson, *Life and Faith*, 54; Whitebrook, *Ann Dutton* 7; Haykin, "Anne Dutton," 1.

[44]*A Brief Account* II:33.

[45]*A Brief Account* II:40.

[46]*A Brief Account* II:40.

The House being sold, where we liv'd, and we to remove, I was loth to go into another at *N---n*. Whereupon, I intreated the Lord that he would not suffer me. And some Hopes I had, that I should have my Request. But the Lord was pleased to disappoint me in this: and to exercise me further, by bringing a great *Death* upon the *Promise*, for about a Year.[47]

Dutton's delay of about a year before their removal from Northampton to Wellingborough is evident here. This is her spiritual winter of discontent and trial. Dutton resigns herself to God's will and the sureness of his mercy: "Thus, being satisfied about the *Sureness* of the promis'd Mercy: I was resign'd into *God's Will*, as to the *Time* of it; believing that he would bring it forth in its proper Season, in which it should appear most beautiful."[48] Dutton agrees to move to temporary housing in Northampton while awaiting the move to Wellingborough: "And by this Time I was made willing to go into another House; which I did, in Obedience to divine Providence. And I dwelt in it, much like a Stranger, or Pilgrim in a Tent, or Tabernacle that was shortly to be taken down."[49]

Dutton records that during this time her future pastor, Mr. Grant at Wellingborough, was near death but recovered. She writes, "Thus I went on, between Faith and Fear, until I received the welcome News of his Recovery."[50] Dutton includes a letter to a Christian Friend she wrote about the state of her soul at this time of Mr. Grant's recovery:

And a little of the Frame of my Soul at this Time, may be seen in a Letter which I then wrote, with Design to send it to a Christian Friend: Which is as follows.
    Beloved Brother,
I Am willing to let you know, that the Lord has brought me to his Foot. I trust, as an Answer of our Prayers.[51]

The letter is signed: " . . . Is the earnest Desire of, *Yours in Him*, A. D."[52]— "A. D." of course standing for Anne Dutton.

---

[47] *A Brief Account* II:46.
[48] *A Brief Account* II:48.
[49] *A Brief Account* II:48.
[50] *A Brief Account* II:54.
[51] *A Brief Account* II:56.
[52] *A Brief Account* II:57.

Knowing that Mr.Grant's life was spared by God, Dutton requests God to send them to Wellingborough to live and hear his preaching. It was not to be so just yet. Dutton has to wait a while longer. It is the continuing winter season of her in her spiritual life: "[W]e did again enquire, whether there was any *Door* open'd yet for our outward Supply in that Place. . . . That as it was *Winter* with the *Garden*; so now it was the *Winter-season* with respect to the *Promise*."[53]

Dutton includes a hymn she wrote during this period of trial: "And then, in the Joy of Faith, trusting the LORD in the dark, I compos'd the following Lines, as expressive of my Case."[54] This first hymn is two stanzas of four lines each. The first two lines of the hymn state:

> The LORD makes *Darkness*; and it's *Night*,
> And HE doth make the Darkness *Light*.[55]

Several pages later, she includes a second hymn she has composed concerning the triumph of faith in darkness. She writes:

> And with a holy Scorn, as being far above the Reach of any Enemy, in the Triumph of Faith, I compos'd and sung the following Lines.
> JEHOVAH's *Name*, A *Tower* is:
> Thither the *Righteous* fly: . . .[56]

This hymn has four stanzas of four lines each, a total of sixteen lines.

Dutton speaks of continued difficulty when she writes, "And further, another Method of Employ came into our Minds; which we attempted to make some Trial of: But lo, it *fail'd*."[57] Writing again of trial, she states, "A little before my Deliverance came, I met with a very great *Trial*. My Husband being gone [on] a Journey on Account of some Business, sent me Word when to expect him Home: And he, being prevented, stay'd three Days longer than he design'd."[58]

---

[53] *A Brief Account* II:61.
[54] *A Brief Account* II:65.
[55] *A Brief Account* II:65.
[56] *A Brief Account* II:70.
[57] *A Brief Account* II:76.
[58] *A Brief Account* II:77. Robinson (*Life and Faith*, 54) records that Anne "gave her husband no peace until they removed to Wellingborough, though this was long delayed for business reasons. . . . She was greatly upset when business kept him

Dutton describes her situation as being delivered from trial into *Canaan*, the land of God's mercies. She is finally able to make her move from Northampton to go to her new home, Wellingborough and her new pastor Mr. Grant. She writes: "Being now got into *Canaan*, I may give a Hint of the *Goodness* of the Land."[59] She continues:

> And the several *Graces* I was instructed into, which, like so many *Pair of Horses*, should *run together*, or be *jointly exercis'd*, in drawing the *Chariots* of God's gracious *Promises*, and special *Providences*, were *these*:

Faith,		Love.
Hope,		Joy.
Humility,	and	Patience.
Self-Denial,		Godly Fear.
Zeal for God's Glory,		Gospel Repentance.[60]

Finally, after Dutton arrives to her promised land, her home in Wellingborough, she is only to move, again on account of her husband's business, to Whittlesey near Peterborough. She writes, "Thus I have given a large Account of my being brought to *W---h*. But after I had been there some Time, Things seem'd to work as if the Lord was about to remove me from *thence*: Which prov'd a *great Trial* to me."[61] Dutton then writes: "The next Step of Providence, I shall take some Notice of, is, The Lord's Removing me from *W---h*, to *W---*."[62]

Dutton at first is unwilling to move again, not having been in Wellingborough a full year, but God's mercy suffices.[63] Dutton states: "And down I went to *W---*, before I had been at *W---h* a full Year."[64] In a letter to Mr.

---

away three days beyond time."

[59] *A Brief Account* II:84.

[60] *A Brief Account* II:87.

[61] *A Brief Account* II:89.

[62] *A Brief Account* II:95. Whitebrook's biography records that the Duttons first lived in Northampton, then in Wellingborough, then Whittlesey, and then again for a second time for two years at Wellingborough while Anne "enjoyed the friendship of a Baptist minister, Mr. William Grant" (*Ann Dutton*, 7). This seems to be accurate according to Dutton here.

[63] *A Brief Account* II:95.

[64] *A Brief Account* I:96. Robinson, *Life and Faith*, 54.

Grant, her pastor, after having been at Whittlesey for only two months, she writes:

> But something of the kind Succours I received from the Lord under *this*
> Temptation, may be seen in a Letter that I wrote to Mr. *G---t*, when I had
> been at *W---*, near two Months: Which was as follows,
>   *Dear and honour'd Brother*,
> I Received your Letter with Gladness, and thankfully own your Kindness
> therein. I bless the Lord, I was refreshed by what you wrote. . . .[65]

The letter to Mr. Grant is signed

> With dear Love to your whole self, I rest
>   Your unworthy Sister in Christ,
>   *A. D.*[66]

Dutton is consoled that "the Lord was with me amidst Distresses."[67]

She includes a second letter she wrote to Mr. Grant, her pastor, and describes his friendship. She states in this second letter, "I thank you for your Letter, I take it kindly, and look upon it as a Part of Christian Friendship, that you will hold this Kind of Communion. . . ."[68]

Dutton continues to record her trial of ill health at Whittlesey. Her time of spiritual waiting upon the Lord and spiritual exile is Whittlesey. It brought suffering for her. She writes: "But while the Mercy was *delay'd*, I often had my *Fainting-Fits*; in which the Lord sweetly reviv'd me, by some Promise or other, and encourag'd my Soul to *wait on*."[69]

During this time of waiting on the Lord when Dutton desires to return from the spiritual exile of Whittlesey back to Wellingborough, she writes two "little Tracts": *Meditations and Observations upon the 11th and 12th Verses of the 6th Chapter of Solomon's Song*, and *Brief Hints concerning God's Fatherly Chastisements, &c.*[70] Regarding these writings, she says:

> And therefore that I might the better *retain* what the Lord had taught me,
> in order to direct my Soul in its Duty of waiting for him, I *wrote it down*.

---

[65] *A Brief Account* II:97.
[66] *A Brief Account* II:106.
[67] *A Brief Account* II:106.
[68] *A Brief Account* II:107.
[69] *A Brief Account* II:113.
[70] *A Brief Account* II:114n.

But what I then wrote for my own Use, being since design'd for publick Good, I have put, with small Additions, into two little Tracts.[71]

Dutton then includes a third letter to Mr. Grant, regarding which she says:

But some further Account of the low Estate I was in at *W---*, and how the Lord help'd me to exercise Faith on Christ for Deliverance, may be seen in the following Letter, I wrote to Mr. *G---t* from thence.
  Much honoured and beloved Brother, . . .[72]

She concludes this third letter

  With endeared Love, I rest
      Yours in Christ,
        A. D.[73]

Dutton's faith is exercised as she seeks deliverance from Whittlesey. She wants to go back to Wellingborough, but it is not to be. She remains at Whittlesey and becomes even more ill. She writes: "Instead of the Lord's Appearance to bring me again to *W---h*, which I expected, I was visited with an Ague and Fever, which being continued long upon me, threatned no less than my Death in *this Place.* . . . But, blessed be his Name, *his Grace was sufficient for me.*"[74] Thus she states triumphantly: "But the Lord's Design was to *raise* me from a sick Bed, and give me to *see* his promised *Goodness*, in the *Land of the living.*"[75]

Dutton continues to suffer with ill health at Whittlesey. She writes a poem of words from the Lord during this time of illness and distress:

At this Time I was extremely weak in Body, and the Lord was exceeding near to my Spirit. I lay as it were at the Mouth of the LORD, in the Bosom of GOD. And some Verses were dictated to my Mind, which were very precious to me. . . . The two first were as follow:
  Now I'll contend *no more*;
    In *Anger* I'll not *smite*:
  Because of *Love* that was *before*,

---

[71]*A Brief Account* II:113-14.
[72]*A Brief Account* II:114.
[73]*A Brief Account* II:120.
[74]*A Brief Account* II:120.
[75]*A Brief Account* II:122.

> In which I do *delight.*
> *My Kindness* on *thee fixt. . . .*[76]

Dutton remembers the Lord's deliverance at this point: "He *remember'd* that I was but Dust; and *spared me,* that I might recover Strength. And this Affliction which seem'd to me to militate *against* the Promises, the Lord made the *Means* of their Fulfilment."[77] She continues that she needs to return to Wellingborough to restore her health in a better environment, "For by Reason of its long Continuance, my Nature was so weakned, that it was *necessary* for me, for the Recovery of my Health, to return again into my own Air."[78]

At this point the Lord delivers Dutton from Whittlesey back to Wellingborough for about three more years. The Lord restores her health when she returns home to Wellingborough. She writes: "[T]he Lord's bringing me back from *W---,* and fixing my Abode again at *W---h.*"[79] Then: "Thus the Lord restored me to the Enjoyment of all those Privileges which for a Time had been suspended."[80]

Dutton wishes to rejoin the church at Wellingborough: "But yet I had some Hopes, notwithstanding, that the Lord would bring me back again to *W---h,* and that then, upon this recommendatory Letter, I should enjoy the desired Blessing of dwelling in that House of God. Which accordingly came to pass."[81]

Dutton, however, falls ill again, even in Wellingborough. She longs to serve the Lord anyway, and states: "I *longed,* even to *Fainting,* to do something for his Glory, before I went home to the full Enjoyment of him. . . . Quickly after this, it pleased the Lord to lay his afflicting Hand upon me, and bring me near to the Gates of Death."[82] Regarding her present affliction, Dutton continues: "Under this Affliction, I was confined nine Lord's Days from publick Worship: And my Soul *longed* exceedingly, for the Privileges of God's House."[83]

---

[76] *A Brief Account* II:126.
[77] *A Brief Account* II:127.
[78] *A Brief Account* II:127.
[79] *A Brief Account* II:127. Robinson, *Life and Faith,* 54.
[80] *A Brief Account* II:130.
[81] *A Brief Account* II:131.
[82] *A Brief Account* II:133.
[83] *A Brief Account* II:136.

Scriptural metaphors help Dutton describe the delights of heaven that await her. She writes:

> It was with great Delight, I beheld the Inheritance reserved for me in Heaven, set forth, in this Text, under three Metaphors; 1. That of *white Robes*, Rev. iii. 4, 5. As Tokens of Victory, Purity and Honour. . . . 2. I view'd the Glory prepar'd for me, under the Similitude of *a Feast*. . . . 3. I saw the Glory reserved for me, set forth under the Metaphor of the *Spring*, the Spring-Season of the Year. . . .
>
> Thus my kind Lord, made this Affliction a fair *Seeds-time*, from whence I expected a *joyful Harvest.*[84]

Dutton focuses next on her move from Wellingborough to Great Gransden in Huntingtonshire. This is where her husband takes up the pastorate. Mr. Benjamin Dutton is to be the pastor of the Baptist Chapel at Great Gransden. She writes: "To the last Step of Providence I shall take Notice of, *viz*. the Lord's removing my Habitation from *W---h*, to *Great Gransden*, in *Huntingtonshire*, the Place of my present Abode."[85]

Dutton recounts the call of her husband, Mr. Benjamin Dutton, to the ministry:

> It pleased the Lord, some considerable Time before, to call my Husband to the Work of the Ministry. From the Time that the Lord wrought upon his Heart, in a saving Conversion to Christ, which was about the seventeenth Year of his Age, he had a very strong Desire after the Ministry of the Gospel. And tho' he was then an Apprentice to a Clothier and Draper, yet this Desire after the Ministry prevail'd so far, that

---

[84]*A Brief Account* II:138-39, 141.

[85]*A Brief Account* II:141. Haykin ("Anne Dutton," 3) records that ministry took the couple to such towns as Whittlesey and Wisbech in Cambridgeshire before leading them finally in 1731 to Great Gransden, Huntingdonshire. Robinson (*Life and Faith*, 54). records that the Duttons "lived in Wellingborough for about three years, till in 1732 they removed to Great Gransden in Huntingdonshire." Wallington states that the Duttons settled in "Great Gransden Hunts," and that this removal was not for business reasons ("Wesley and Anne Dutton," 44). Whitebrook (*Ann Dutton*, 7) records that "in June 1732 the couple removed from Eversholt to Great Gransden, a Huntingdonshire village, where Mr. David Evans had long been minister." Whitebrook (p. 7) also states that a new chapel and an adjoining house were built in 1732. This was partly funded at the expense of Anne and Benjamin Dutton.

he requested his Father to buy out his Time, and bestow that Money which he design'd to set him up for a Tradesman, in giving him Learning for the Ministry, that so he might be more fully qualify'd for this great Work, which he so much desired.[86]

Dutton continues to tell about her husband's preparation for ministry:

And thus from a Desire after the Ministry, he went on in the Pursuit of his Studies. But after we were marry'd, for our present Subsistence, he did something at his Trade: As I hinted before, in the Account I gave of our being brought to *W---h*. And thro' several trying Things that fell out, it was some Time e'er the Desire of his Heart was given him, in his being statedly employ'd in the Work of the Ministry.[87]

Dutton gives a brief account of her husband's call to the pastorate at Great Gransden—where she goes to live for the rest of her life. Her husband had been preaching there sporadically for some time, but was now called to Great Gransden as pastor.

But having been call'd to the Work, by a Church to which he join'd, he preach'd occasionally for a while at several Places. And thus he preach'd during great Part of the Time of our last Abode at *W---h*, which was about three Years, at several Places, some of which were pretty far distant. And he having heard of a poor People at *Great Gransden*, which wanted Supply, the Lord laid it upon his Heart to give them a Visit. Which accordingly he did, was kindly received, and invited to assist them as often as he could. Soon after my dear Yokefellow had preach'd at *Gransden*, he was invited likewise to preach at *Croyden*, four Miles distant. The People at both those Places made but one Church; and were used to keep up their Meetings (when they had a Pastor, or stated Minister) at both Towns; one Lord's Day at *Gransden*, and another at *Croyden*, successively. And as the People wanted Supply for both these Places, and our Habitation was far distant, it was their Desire, that we should in a little Time remove the Place of our Abode to reside amongst them, in order to serve them wholly.[88]

---

[86]*A Brief Account* II:142.
[87]*A Brief Account* II:142.
[88]*A Brief Account* II:142-43.

Dutton recounts that at first, this move to Great Gransden seemed to be a *"great Trial"* for her.[89] But then she states that God's "own Hand made my Heart willing to *give* whatever HE *call'd for*."[90] Dutton writes favorably of the call to Great Grandsden:

> But after a while, there was an Appearance of a fresh Call to *G---n*. My Husband having visited them according to their Desire and his Promise, he found their Hearts much knit to him; and upon their Request he went and preach'd to them once a Fortnight. And after a little Time, they were very desirous to have him come to settle among them, if we could take up with what they could do towards our Subsistence. And the Lord engag'd the Heart of my Yokefellow to trust him, and made him desirous to go, to serve this little Handful of his People.[91]

And she recounts her own feelings at this time:

> And as for myself, tho' I had for some Time laid aside Thoughts of removing; yet when the Lord renew'd the Call of Providence. . . . I was, thro' his Hand holding my Heart, still of the same Mind; *willing* to resign whatever HE call'd for, and to go at his Bidding. And as for the People, the Lord having put 'em into my Heart, I found Bowels of Compassion afresh working in me towards 'em, a Desire to serve them, and a Kind of natural Care for their Good. Which made me *willing* to venture a Remove, with my dear Yoke-fellow, to dwell among them:[92]

---

[89]*A Brief Account* II:143.

[90]*A Brief Account* II:149. Robinson (*Life and Faith*, 54) states: "Mr. Dutton had been preaching for some time, and was now called to become minister of the church there—a struggling cause. Her [Anne's] long debate as to whether she ought to go makes it plain that she regarded the call as one to herself even more than to her husband." Haykin ("Anne Dutton," 3) says of Dutton's ministry at Great Gransden that "under Dutton's preaching the church flourished. On any given Sunday the congregation numbered between 250 and 350, of whom roughly 50 were members. This growth led to the building of a new meetinghouse, which can still be seen in the village." (See in this volume the photograph of the Baptist Chapel at Great Gransdon, p. viii.)

[91]*A Brief Account* II:149.

[92]*A Brief Account* II:149-50.

Dutton writes a letter of request to be dismissed from her church at Wellingborough, to join her husband's church and ministry at Great Gransden.

> I wrote for my Dismission, as before hinted. ----- And this Church having desir'd my Husband to join with them, he requested his Dismission from the Church to which he related, and was received into *this*. And they being desirous to get into Order, gave him a Call to the Pastoral Office. Which he declaring his Willingness to accept, a Day was appointed to set him apart thereto. And *Oct.* 10, 1732. he was solemnly set apart to the Pastoral Office in this Church, in the Presence of Messengers from several Churches. ---- And I also, upon my Dismission from the Church I belong'd to, was received into this Church.[93]

Moving to Great Gransden, Dutton joins the work of her husband in ministry. She finds her usefulness for the Lord in correspondence and letter writing for the encouragement of Christian souls. Of her purpose in ministry, she writes:

> And as to myself, in particular, the LORD has greatly blest me with respect to personal Usefulness, since my Abode at *G---n*. I would humbly hope, yea, I know thro' Grace, that the Lord has made me of some Use to his People *here*, in Converse with them.[94]

Particularly of her letter-writing ability, ministry, and vocation, Dutton writes:

> And *here* has the Lord employ'd me to write many Letters to his dear Children in divers Parts; which thro' his Blessing upon them, have refresh'd their Souls. Yea, *here* has the Lord given me a Heart, and Opportunity, an outward Call, and inward Inclination, to write and publish many little Tracts: Which thro' his gracious Assistance, and kind Providence, have been brought out, and dispersed abroad in divers Places and Nations. And blessed be his Name, HE has given me to hear, that he has us'd most of them for the Good of his People.[95]

Dutton concludes part II "With a few Words to the People of GOD, by Way of Improvement."[96] She offers four main points.

---

[93] *A Brief Account* II:159.
[94] *A Brief Account* II:161.
[95] *A Brief Account* II:161.
[96] *A Brief Account* II:163.

"1. To *seek* the Lord in your Distresses. . . . "

"2. Beware of *limiting* the holy One of *Israel*; as to the exact Time, or Manner of fulfilling the Promises which HE gives you. . . . "

"3. Learn to *wait* patiently, for the Time of God's fulfilling his Promises. . . . "

"4. Let us learn to put a high *Estimate* upon the Glory reserved for us in the compleat Fulfillment of *all* the Promises."[97]

Part III

A Brief Account of the Gracious Dealings of God, with a Poor, Sinful, Unworthy Creature, Relating to Some particular Experiences of the Lord's Goodness, in bringing out several little Tracts, to the Furtherance and Joy of Faith. With an Appendix, and a Letter prefix'd on the Lawfulness of a Woman's appearing in Print. Part III. By A. D. *Come and hear all ye that fear* GOD, *and I will declare what He hath done for my Soul,* Psal. lxvi. 16. *And Things which are despised, hath God chosen,—That no Flesh should glory in his Presence,* 1 Cor. i. 28, 29. *When the Lord shall build up Zion, He shall appear in his Glory. He will regard the Prayer of the Destitute, and not despise their Prayer. This shall be written for the Generation to come: And the People which shall be created, shall praise the* LORD, *Psal. cii. 16, 17, 18.* London: Printed by J. Hart, in Popping's Court, Fleet-street; and sold by J. Lewis, in Pater-noster-row, near Cheapside. 1750.

In part 3, Dutton offers two sections:

First. Some particular *Experiences* of the LORD's *great Goodness*, in bringing out several of my little *Tracts.* And

Secondly. The *Answer* of my *Desire* and *Prayer*, in the LORD's sending some of my *Books* into *America*: To my *Furtherance and Joy of Faith.*[98]

In the first part devoted to her publishing, Dutton discusses her writing as "aim'd at the Glory of God and the Good of Souls, in all the little Pieces I have written and publish'd."[99] She continues:

---

[97]*A Brief Account* II:164, 164, 165, 166.

[98]*A Brief Account* III:4.

[99]*A Brief Account* III:4-5.

Volume 3. The Autobiography

> My Design, in those Particulars which I penned, was, To take some Account for *myself*, of what the Lord said unto me about my Books, *&c.* when He appear'd in his kind Providence, to bring out several of them, and to open a Door for my desired Usefulness.[100]

She further states that

> Not with a View to *publish* what I wrote, did I engage in this Work; it was only design'd for my own *private Use*. But now the Lord inclines my Heart to prepare it for the *Press*, and graciously acquaints me, that HE will use it to *others*.[101]

Dutton discusses in detail several of her published works:

> And as in the following Particulars, I begin the Account with my *Three Books*, which came out together; and soon after mention, in telling of the great Things which the Lord shew'd me He had done for me, That He had brought out my poor Books, unto *Sevenfold*: I think it best just to give a Hint or two about the first *Four*. Which were these: *A Narration of the Wonders of Grace: In Verse*, &c. *A Discourse on Walking with* GOD, *&c. A Discourse Concerning* GOD's *Act of Adoption*. With, *A Discourse on the Inheritance of the adopted Sons of God*. And, *A Sight of* CHRIST, *necessary for all true Christians, and Gospel-Ministers*.[102]

Dutton goes on to discuss "those particular *Experiences* of the LORD's *Goodness*, in bringing out others of my little Tracts: Which I wrote for my own *private Use*."[103]

Dutton continues: "In *October*, 1740, my *Three Books* were printed: *viz. New-Birth, Justification* and *Letters*."[104] She further indicates that the works were delayed somewhat in publication, but then God's Providence turned:

---

[100] *A Brief Account* III:6. Robinson (*Life and Faith*, 55) writes, "Her activity as a writer, already begun, formed her dominant interest in Great Gransden, to judge from the third part of her autobiography. This consists of a long and detailed account of the publication of her successive books."

[101] *A Brief Account* III:6.

[102] *A Brief Account* III:6-7. Most of these pieces are included in the bibliography in this volume, below, XXX-XX.

[103] *A Brief Account* III:12.

[104] *A Brief Account* III:12.

All on a sudden as it were, he gave a mighty Turn, a Call of Providence, as we judg'd it, for their Publication; and mightily wrought upon the Heart of my dear Yokefellow to bring them out; and with them a Book of Letters.[105]

This 1740 *Book of Letters* published by her husband, her "dear Yoke-fellow," is probably *Letters on Spiritual Subjects Sent to Relatives and Friends* (1740).[106] Dutton comments that the Lord used her to write to the Methodists:

> Another Instance of God's kindness to me, in raising me up as it were from the Dead, unto a Life of Fruitfulness, in some Degree, is *this*: He opened a Door for me to write many *Letters* to the *Methodists*; and likewise *blest them* to *many Souls*.[107]

These are her *Letters to the Reverend Mr. John Wesley against Perfection As Not Attainable in This Life* and *A Letter to the Reverend Mr. John Wesley In Vindication of the Doctrine of Absolute, Unconditional Election, Particular Redemption, Special Vocation, and Final Perseverance, etc.* Dutton confirms that her books were sent to America: "When some in *England* slighted my Books, and would *None of me*: God sent 'em *beyond the Seas*: Wrought Marvels by his mighty Hand. . . ."[108]
Dutton further comments on her publications:

> The Lord shew'd me, That in his great Grace, he had pardon'd all my great Sins, and brought forth my poor Books, unto Seven-fold, notwith-standing my great Unworthiness! And these last, in the Exuberance of his Love, *Three at once!*[109]

---

[105] *A Brief Account* III:13.

[106] *A Brief Account* III:12-13. This book of letters could be No. 5: *Occasional Letters on Spiritual Subjects* (7 vols., 1740–1749) (Whitebrook, *Ann Dutton*, 16). Or it may be the *Letters of Spiritual Subjects and Divers Occasions sent to Relatives and Friends* (8 vols., 1740–1750) that are housed at Speer Library, Princeton Theological Seminary. (Speer has volumes I, IV, VI, and VIII.)

[107] *A Brief Account* III:16-17.

[108] *A Brief Account* III:17. See the discussion of Dutton's correspondence with Wesley in Watson, ed., *Anne Dutton*, vol. 1, xxvi-xxiii.

[109] *A Brief Account* III:18-19.

She defines herself: "I was a *Sinner*, a *chief* Sinner."[110] And continues: "I scarce know which was greatest, whether the *Refreshment* to my fainting Spirit, that was ready to faint with Longing to serve Jesus, or the *Surprize* at his Grace, in regard to my Vileness."[111] Thus: "Upon the whole I was persuaded, That I had Christ's *Heart*, and should have his *Hand*."[112]

In diary entries for August 5, 1741, Dutton records her seeking the Lord about being useful to him: "As I was seeking the Lord for personal Favours, and relative Usefulness; that Word was precious to my Soul."[113] In a diary entry for September 1, 1741, she quotes a letter from a friend. Dutton here refers to Song of Solomon 7:10 seeing that "I was Christ's *own*."[114] In a subsequent diary entry, for October 17, Dutton refers to another difficult letter from a friend, and writes: "I was somewhat oppressed in Spirit for a Time."[115] She concludes about God here, "that he would make me *fruitful*."[116]

Dutton speaks of her distress of moving from Northampton to Wellingborough; and from Whittlesey, again to Wellingborough.[117] This has been discussed previously. She speaks of God's kindness to her. In the entry for October 24, 1741, she refers to "A Letter from a Friend" and of humble rejoicing for "God's Kindness"[118] to her. Dutton then writes on October 29, 1741, that God opens the "Way for my farther [*sic*] *Usefulness*."[119] In the next entry, October 31, 1741, she again feels "some Stirrings of *Sin* in my *Soul*."[120] Yet again following this, she receives the favor of the Lord and his usefulness of her. She writes for November 12, 1741:

> As I was seeking the Lord, that Word dropt upon my Heart, *Then was I in his Eyes as one that found* Favour, Song vii. 10. In which I heard an

---

[110]*A Brief Account* III:22.
[111]*A Brief Account* III:23.
[112]*A Brief Account* III:25.
[113]*A Brief Account* III:27.
[114]*A Brief Account* III:35.
[115]*A Brief Account* III:36.
[116]*A Brief Account* III:38.
[117]*A Brief Account* III:44.
[118]*A Brief Account* III:44.
[119]*A Brief Account* III:46.
[120]*A Brief Account* III:48.

encouraging Sound of Free-Grace, That *I* should find *Favour* with the Lord, with regard to *Usefulness*.[121]

In the following entry, November 16, 1741, She references her further publishing: "writing my *Letter to the Saints, on the Duty of Love*."[122] In the entry for November 20, 1741, Dutton further delineates her publications and correspondence, and refers to the fact that her labor for the Lord should not be done in vain or for vanity. She specifically speaks of this in reference to her "beginning to transcribe my Letter, *Hints of the Glory of Christ*: &c."[123] Further, she records God's positive use of her in her letter-writing ministry.

On December 6, 1741, Dutton speaks of receiving a delightful letter from a friend, "That the Lord had made me of *Use* to comfort and strengthen *his Soul*."[124] In the following entry, for December 7, 1741, Dutton speaks of God's "Word dropt sweetly on my Heart."[125] In the December 10, 1741 entry, she writes of "a painful *Feeling* of the Working of *Sin* in my soul, . . . and a delightful *View* of GOD's boundless *Love*, thro' a crucify'd JESUS."[126]

Dutton continues delineating her publications. In the October 18, 1742 entry, she records her writing of a "*Letter to the believing Negroes*."[127] On February 9, 1743,[128] she records, "My *Second Volume of Letters* was put to the Press."[129] This is probably volume II on *Spiritual Subjects Sent to Relatives and Friends*. Dutton continues:

> And as when my *Second* Volume of Letters, last mention'd, was to be printed; and other of my Books soon to follow, which were to be sent into *America*; I had some *Fears* of the Difficulties, Dangers, and Trials, that might attend their Publication: I thence sought the Lord, to give me some Encouragement from Himself about them, and as to this Book in

---

[121]*A Brief Account* III:51-52.

[122]*A Brief Account* III:54.

[123]*A Brief Account* III:57.

[124]*A Brief Account* III:61.

[125]*A Brief Account* III:65.

[126]*A Brief Account* III:69.

[127]*A Brief Account* III:76.

[128]The text reads "1742-3." The dates before (18 October 1742) and after (29 April 1743) this entry suggest the year is 1743.

[129]*A Brief Account* III:82.

particular, that was just *then* coming out. And He was pleas'd to say to me, *Fear not ye. . . .*[130]

And concludes with an earnest petition: "*Prosper thou*, O LORD, *this Work of my Hands!*"[131]

On April 29, 1743, Dutton writes concerning the publication of this spiritual autobiography:

> *The* last Week, My Pamphlet, *A brief Account of the gracious Dealings of* GOD *with a poor, sinful, unworthy Creature, Relating to the Work of Grace on the Heart, in a saving Conversion to* CHRIST, &c. Part I. was put to the Press. As was soon after the IId Part. I had much Work, much Writing, &c. upon Hand the last Week; by which I was in some Sort diverted from that particular *Seeking of the Lord*, for some Intimation of his Mind, about the Publication of this little Tract, which I had been wont to observe with respect to my others already published.[132]

Dutton comments that she sought the Lord about this further publication. She receives the verses from Rev. 12:6, 14, and states: "From which the Lord gave me a sweet Hint, *Where* my poor Books were to be *us'd*, even in the *American* Wilderness; that there I had a *Place* prepared of God."[133] Concerning part II of this publication, she writes:

> A Hint I would just give, as to the 2d Part of my *Brief Account of the gracious Dealings of* GOD, *Relating to a Train of special Providences attending Life*. This, as I said, was not put to Press quite so soon as the others. I wanted Time to revise it, *&c*. But as both are but one continued Account of the Lord's Dealings with me; which were both as it were coming out together; I take that gracious Promise which the Lord gave me for the 1st Part, *Thou art my Servant—in whom I will be glorify'd*: to extend also to the 2d Part.[134]

A list of twenty-one of Dutton's publications appears in part III.[135] Dutton states that

---

[130]*A Brief Account* III:84.

[131]*A Brief Account* III:85.

[132]*A Brief Account* III:85.

[133]*A Brief Account* III:87.

[134]*A Brief Account* III:91.

[135]The list is continued in the appendix, below. See also the bibliography in this volume, XXX-XX.

sweetly has He encourag'd me to write and publish them *all*. And the Number of my little Pieces, which the great Grace of my God has brought out for me, are as follow.

I. *A Narration of the Wonders of Grace, in Verse*, &c.

II. *A Discourse on Walking with* GOD: *&c.*

III. *A Discourse concerning* GOD's *Act of Adoption: And another on the Inheritance of the Adopted Sons of* GOD.

IV. *A Sight of* CHRIST, *absolutely necessary for all true Christians, and Gospel-Ministers*: &c.

V. *A Discourse on Justification*: &c.

VI. *A Discourse concerning the New-Birth*: &c.

VII. *Letters on spiritual Subjects, and divers Occasions*: &c. VOL. I.

VIII. *A Letter to all the Saints, on the general Duty of Love.*

IX. *A Letter to the Reverend Mr John Wesley: In Vindication of the Doctrines of Absolute Election, Particular Redemption, Special Vocation, and, Final Perseverance.*

X. *Some Thoughts about Faith in* CHRIST. *Whether it be requir'd of all Men under the Gospel? To prove that it is.*

XI. *A Letter to the Negroes, lately converted to* CHRIST *in America.*

XII. *Letters on spiritual Subjects, and divers Occasions*: &c. VOL. II.

XIII. *Letters sent to an Honourable Gentleman, for the Encouragement of Faith.* VOL. I.

XIV. *A Letter to such of the Servants of* CHRIST, *who may have any Scruple about the Lawfulness of printing any Thing written by a Woman*: &c.

XV. *Letters to the Rev. Mr. J. Wesley: Against Perfection.*

XVI. *Meditations and Observations upon the eleventh and twelfth Verses of the sixth Chapter of Solomon's Song.*

XVII. *Brief Hints concerning God's Fatherly Chastisements: Shewing their Nature, Necessity, and Usefulness; and the Saints Duty to wait upon God for Deliverance, when under his Fatherly Corrections.*

XVIII. *The Hurt that Sin doth to Believers*: &c.

XIX. *A Brief Account of the gracious Dealings of* GOD, *with a poor, sinful, unworthy Creature. Relating to the Work of Divine Grace on the Heart, in a saving Conversion to* CHRISTS, *and to some Establishment in Him.* Part I.

XX. *A Brief Account of the gracious Dealings of* GOD, *with a poor, sinful, unworthy Creature. Relating to a Train of Special Providences attending Life, by which the Work of Faith was carried on with Power.* Part II.

> XXI. *A Letter to all Those that love* CHRIST *in Philadelphia: To excite them to adhere to, and appear for, the Truths of the Gospel.*[136]

Specifically, Dutton mentions the particular usefulness of three publications:

> *First*, The *Letter to the Rev. Mr John Wesley: In Vindication of the Doctrines of Absolute Election*, &c. . . .
> *Secondly, Thoughts about Faith in* CHRIST: *&c.* . . .
> . . . And,
> *Thirdly.* The *Letter to those that love* CHRIST *in Philadelphia, to excite them to adhere to, and appear for, the Truths of the Gospel.*[137]

Then, concerning the publication of this part III, Dutton states that "even this *Third* Part, which was at first design'd for *my own Use*; He hath inclin'd my Heart, and greatly encourag'd me to prepare it for the *Press*."[138]

An Appendix

Dutton follows part III with an appendix. She seeks to accomplish three things in the appendix:

> *First*, Some *farther Account* of the *Lord's Goodness*, in bringing out divers *other* of my poor *Manuscripts*; and also some Hints of that great *Encouragement* which the Lord gave me to present them to *publick View*.
> *Secondly, Answer* to an *Objection* that may be made against the Lord's Grant of my Desire in *special Favour*, in sending my Books into *America*: From that great *Trial* which followed upon it in the *Loss of my dear Husband by Sea*. And
> *Thirdly, Close*, with a Word or two of *Use*.[139]

Dutton begins the first part of the appendix by focusing on her husband's taking her books to America:

> I *begin* this farther Account, with my *Husband's* going into *America*. . . .
> As my dear Husband, apprehending it his Duty to go thither on another Account, brought out *all my Books*, I then had by me in MS. and took with

---

[136]*A Brief Account* III:92-94.
[137]*A Brief Account* III:94-95, 96.
[138]*A Brief Account* III:98.
[139]*A Brief Account*, appendix, 103.

him a great *Number* of them; which the Lord *blest* to *many Souls.—Praise* to my good GOD, who in this Regard heard my *Prayer!*[140]

Dutton states that on August 17, 1743, her husband, Benjamin Dutton, traveled by ship to America, that "My dear *Husband* went from Home, in order to embark for *America.*"[141] Dutton continues writing after her husband goes to America. She states, "Some Time after my Husband was gone, the Lord gave me Opportunity to write many *Letters* to his dear Lambs, who desir'd to hear from me. And I found my Heart inclin'd to take the *Copies* of them."[142]

On October 1, 1744, Dutton writes, "I sought the Lord, about bringing out a *Third* Book of *Letters.* And He satisty'd me that it was his Mind it should come out, by this Word."[143] She previously had published a "Collection of Letters, sent to the Reverend Mr. *Whitefield* and his *Friends,*"[144] regarding which she says, "those Letters sent [to] that dear Servant of Christ, Mr *Whitefield,* and to several of his *Brethren* in the *Ministry;* who were as *Princes* among God's People."[145]

Continuing to date her publications, Dutton offers the results of her fruitful writing career.

> *June* 12, 1745. THE Lord brought out my *Third* Book of *Letters:* At the Close of which He inclin'd me to add a *Letter on the Being and Working of Sin in a justified Man,* &c. and another *Letter on the Duty and Privilege of a Believer to live by Faith; and to improve his Faith unto Holiness.*[146]

This "*Third* Book *of Letters*" is probably volume III of *Letters on Spiritual Subjects Sent to Relatives and Friends.* Dutton records on July 7, 1746 that God had blessed her publication: "BEFORE this Time, the Lord gave me to

---

[140]*A Brief Account,* appendix, 104.

[141]*A Brief Account,* appendix, 104. Haykin ("Anne Dutton," 3) records that Benjamin Dutton "had gone to America to help raise funds to pay off the debt incurred in the building of the meetinghouse."

[142]*A Brief Account,* appendix, 104.

[143]*A Brief Account,* appendix, 106.

[144]*A Brief Account,* appendix, 106.

[145]*A Brief Account,* appendix, 107.

[146]*A Brief Account,* appendix, 109.

hear, that He *had blest* my *last Book*, to some Souls in several Places."[147] Dutton is confident of her fruitful productivity for the Lord. Of her further publishing activity she writes:

> And now the Lord inclin'd my *Heart*, and gave me *Ability* to put to the Press *Two* other *Books*, viz. *A Postscript to a Letter on the Duty and Privilege of a Believer to live by Faith*, &c. (which was at the End of the Book published last Year) To which was added, *A Caution against Error, when it springs up together with Truth; in a Letter to a Friend*; and *Some of the Mistakes of the* Moravian Brethren, *in a Letter to another Friend*.[148]

Dutton then mentions additional works: "He inclin'd my Heart to bring out a *Fourth* Book of *Letters*."[149] This is probably volume IV of *Letters on Spiritual Subjects Sent to Relatives and Friends*. Dutton stirs up controversy with her work: "And as to the other *Letter* added, *Some of the Mistakes of the Moravian Brethren*; It was written at first, in answer to the Request of a particular Person, who desir'd me to inform him, 'Wherein I thought the *Moravians* were *mistaken*.' "[150]

During the writing of these tracts, Dutton had put off writing the postscript but now decided to do so.[151] Also, during this work, she "fell *sick*, and was laid aside for some *Weeks*"[152]

Dutton continues to recount her prolific publishing career: "With these Two Books, the Postscript and 4th Book of Letters, the Lord brought out also my *Two Letters on Baptism*."[153] On "April 19, 1747," she records: "My *Letters on Baptism, Postscript*, and both my last *Letter-books*, the Lord hath now given me to hear, That he hath *blest them* for the *Good of Souls*."[154] She again stirs controversy by writing Mr. Cudworth: "*April 23, 1747*. I sent my Letter to Mr. *Cudworth* to the Press, which is a *Reply* to his *Answer* to my *Postscript*."[155] Then she notes: "*June 21, 1747*. I sent my *Fifth*

---

[147]*A Brief Account*, appendix, 109.

[148]*A Brief Account*, appendix, 109-10. For a discussion of Dutton's refutation of the Moravian Brethren, see Watson, ed., *Anne Dutton*, vol. 1, xxxiv-xxxv.

[149]*A Brief Account*, appendix, 110.

[150]*A Brief Account*, appendix, 114.

[151]*A Brief Account*, appendix, 116.

[152]*A Brief Account*, appendix, 113.

[153]*A Brief Account*, appendix, 120.

[154]*A Brief Account*, appendix, 121.

[155]*A Brief Account*, appendix, 122. For a discussion of Dutton's controversy

Volume of *Letters* to the Press"[156]—probably volume V of *Letters on Spiritual Subjects Sent to Relatives and Friends.*

Dutton continues to record her publishing work: "*May* 9, 1748. Having Thoughts of sending my little Piece to the Press, *Hints of the Glory of Christ, as the Friend and Bridegroom of the Church*; and *Thoughts on the Lord's Supper.*"[157] She adds: "*June* 6, 1748. I sent my *Sixth* Volume of *Letters* to the Press."[158] This is probably volume VI of *Letters on Spiritual Subjects Sent to Relatives and Friends.* She continues: "*Aug.* 12. I sought the Lord, to know if he would please to have the *Appendix* I had written to my Pamphlet, [*Some Thoughts about Faith in Christ:* &c.] published."[159] She concludes that the Lord does desire her further work for him. She writes: "So that *I*, his poor *Worm*, after the Example of my great *Lord*, should be faithful in declaring to my *Brethren*, the Things which he had given unto *me.*"[160]

On August 13, 1748, Dutton records that she should have sought the Lord before sending her sixth volume of letters to the press: "I was troubled, that thro' Hurry I had not so fully sought the Lord, as I should, before I sent my *Sixth* Volume of *Letters* to the Press."[161] Dutton repents before the Lord and discovers his mercy. Dutton prays to "the God of all Grace, that he would *bless* this poor *Book*, to his dear Children. . . . to bless it to his *tender Lambs.*"[162] Already she has prayed to be a positive witness for the Lord: "And that he should herein do so *much* for me, give me so *many* little Pieces to bring out for Him, and then in his infinite Condescension, account me therein, as an *Heap of Witness* unto HIM!"[163]

On May 10, 1749, Dutton says she "sought the Lord" to publish her seventh volume of Letters, and that "He was pleas'd to say to me, with

---

with William Cudworth, see Watson, ed., *Anne Dutton*, vol. 1, xxxiv-xxxv.

[156]*A Brief Account*, appendix, 124.

[157]*A Brief Account*, appendix, 127.

[158]*A Brief Account*, appendix, 130.

[159]*A Brief Account*, appendix, 131. Bracketed material is in the original, that is, it is not an editorial insert.

[160]*A Brief Account*, appendix, 131.

[161]*A Brief Account*, appendix, 133.

[162]*A Brief Account*, appendix, 135.

[163]*A Brief Account*, appendix, 133.

respect to this Service, I *have* chosen thee."[164] Dutton refers to her volume VII of *Letters on Spiritual Subjects Sent to Relatives and Friends*. She continues: "And I intreated my dear Lord, to grant his *Blessing* upon this little *Piece*, for the *Feeding of his tender Lambs*, and the *Conversion of Souls*."[165]

On June 29, 1749, Dutton refers to her thinking about sending to the press her second volume of letters to an honourable gentleman. She speaks of a desire to "feed his Lambs, . . . that the Lord would *feed* them by my poor *Book*."[166]

Dutton seeks the Lord about her continued work and her usefulness to him. On July 17, 1749, Dutton writes: "I sought the Lord about copying for the Press *Short Notes on the Love of Christ*, from Eph. iii. 19."[167] Then on August 3, 1749, she speaks of her work, *The Hurt That Sin Doth to Believers*.[168]

> Having copied my *Notes on the Love of Christ*, as above, and Thoughts of adding them to my little Piece, *The Hurt that Sin doth to Believers*, which I had a Desire to Re-print; as when first printed, I chiefly design'd it for *England*, and almost all the Copies were, by Mistake, sent into *America*, when my dear Husband went: I sought the Lord for his Direction and Blessing.[169]

Dutton further explains that "for the former Part, *The Hurt of Sin*, and *The Word of Intreaty*, at the End of it, He was graciously pleas'd to hint both my Duty and Privilege in its Publication."[170]

In the appendix, Dutton continues the list of publications from part III. She writes: "And to shew the complete Number of my Books now extant, I shall add the latter to the former, with their Names, as they came out in

---

[164]*A Brief Account*, appendix, 137.

[165]*A Brief Account*, appendix, 137.

[166]*A Brief Account*, appendix, 141. Whitebrook (*Ann Dutton*, 16n.10) records three volumes of *Letters to an Honourable Gentleman* (vol. 1, 1743; vol.2, 1749; vol. 3, later). Edward Starr (*A Baptist Bibliography* [Rochester NY: American Baptist Historical Society, 1959] 202) also records the three volumes, with the third volume dated 1761.

[167]*A Brief Account*, appendix, 143-44.

[168]Whitebrook (*Ann Dutton*, 18n.30) gives 1733 for the first edtion and 1749 for the second edition.

[169]*A Brief Account*, appendix, 145.

[170]*A Brief Account*, appendix, 146.

Order."[171] This updates the list to 1750. She gives twenty-one titles in part III and here she begins with number XXII.[172]

>XXII. *Letters on Spiritual Subjects, and divers Occasions: sent to the Rev. Mr. George Whitefield, and others*, &c. VOL. III.
>
>XXIII. *A Postscript to a Letter lately published, on the Duty and Privilege of a Believer, To live by Faith, and to improve his Faith unto Holiness*: &c.
>
>XXIV. *Letters on Spiritual Subjects, and divers Occasions*: &c. Vol. IV.
>
>XXV. *Brief Hints concerning Baptism*: &c.
>
>XXVI. *A Letter to Mr William Cudworth: In Vindication of the Truth, from his Misrepresentations:--Being a Reply to his Answer to the Postscript of a Letter lately published*: &c.
>
>XXVII. *Letters on Spiritual Subjects, and divers Occasions*: &c. VOL. V.
>
>XXVIII. *Hints of the Glory of Christ, as the Friend and Bridegroom of the Church: From the Seven last Verses of the Fifth Chapter of Solomon's Song*: &c.
>
>XXIX. *Thoughts on the Lord's Supper*: &c.
>
>XXX. *Letters on Spiritual Subjects, and divers Occasions*: &c. VOL. VI.
>
>XXXI *An Appendix to a Pamphlet, entitled, Some Thoughts about Faith in Christ*: &c.
>
>XXXII. *Letters on Spiritual Subjects, and divers Occasions*: &c. VOL. VII.
>
>XXXIII. *Letters sent to an Honourable Gentleman, for the Encouragement of Faith*. VOL. II.[173]

Dutton notes that these works were read in England and sent to America: they "were dispersed in England . . . and . . . dispersed abroad."[174] She is assured of the usefulness of her publications: "Even in *England*, my good GOD, had greatly blest my poor Writings, before any of my Books were sent into *America*."[175] She adds:

---

[171]*A Brief Account*, appendix, 148.

[172]Also see the bibliography in this volume, XXX-XX.

[173]*A Brief Account*, appendix, 148-49.

[174]*A Brief Account*, appendix, 149.

[175]*A Brief Account*, appendix, 150.

> I have no Doubt, of God's sending my Books into *America*, as an
> *Answer* of my *Prayer*, nor that he did this of *Special Favour*. And in that
> he did it by Means of my dear *Husband's* going thither, who dispers'd
> them abroad in such *Numbers*, as no other Person either could or would.
> . . .[176]

Dutton receives a letter from her husband telling her of the success her
tracts and books have had in America. She writes of the letter and quotes
from it:

> Great was the Goodness of my GOD towards me, in sending my Books by
> my dear *Husband*, in that unthought of, undesired *Way*; in carrying him
> and them safe over the great Waters; in preserving his Life till they were
> spread abroad, and till he could inform me, "That many dear Friends
> desir'd to be remembred to me most kindly, and that he would acquaint
> me, that the Books had been *blest to their Souls*, and they made to *bless*
> GOD, that they ever saw them."[177]

Dutton further records her husband's words from his letter: "That *his
Labours* in the *Gospel of Christ*, were *blest* for the Edification of *Saints*, and
for the Conversion of some *Sinners*, not less than *Eleven* or *Twelve
Souls*."[178]

While joyful about her husband's success, Dutton misses him terribly.
He has been gone for quite a long time. She states that knowing of his
success was "a very great *Joy*; and made the Pain of Absence more easy."[179]
Her husband's absence has been a great difficulty for her and for the
church. She writes, "But notwithstanding this, my *Trial* was very *great*; not
only *personally*, but *relatively* consider'd, with respect to the *Church*. I had
not only lost my dear *Husband*, but the Church also had lost its *Pastor*."[180]
Dutton's husband has been gone to America for several years. She writes:

> Thus for several Years was I carried on. Promises supported me,
> Providences try'd me. . . . I cry'd to him, believ'd in him, lov'd him,

---

[176]*A Brief Account*, appendix, 154.

[177]*A Brief Account*, appendix, 155.

[178]*A Brief Account*, appendix, 155.

[179]*A Brief Account*, appendix, 156.

[180]*A Brief Account*, appendix, 156.

long'd for him. . . . And every Spring and Fall, when I had Hopes of my Husband's Return, my Trial was renewed by repeated Disappointments.[181]

Dutton recounts that the ship fleet she expected her husband to be returning with, came back. However, there is no word from her husband. For six months after the ship fleet's return, still there is no word. She writes: "The *Fleet* came, with which I expected my *Husband*, but *He* was not with it; nor any *Letter* from him, (as I us'd to have when he was prevented coming) nor *Account* of him, had I by it.—This *try'd me exceedingly*."[182] She continues hopefully writing, "as from that Time I waited earnestly and constantly, in hopes to see, or hear from him, or of him, and could hear Nothing, for near *Six Months* afterwards."[183]

Finally, Dutton learns of her husband's ship foundering at sea and her husband's drowning and death in 1747. She writes:

> At length, it pleas'd my kind Lord, to grant my Desire of a *Letter*.— But oh! the *News* it brought: Instead of my dear Husband's safe *Return*, I heard of his *Death*, and that he was *cast away* in his Passage home, by the *foundering of the Ship!* How *grieving* was this to Nature! How *trying* to my Faith and Hope! The real *Loss* of my *dear Yokefellow*; the seeming *Denial* of my *earnest Prayers*; and the *Failure* of my *Expectation*, as to his Return.[184]

She seeks to find God's promise of glory at the death and loss of her husband: "And mean while, To give my GOD a *little Glory* by the *Trial*, Oh, it was Joy in Sorrow, Ease in Pain, Life in Death, to my Spirit!"[185]

Dutton concludes that God has brought hopeful promise beyond her husband's death:

> For tho' the Lord did not give me the main *Thing* I desir'd, by my Husband's *Return*, he gave it me in another *Way*, which HE thought *better*, by another *Minister*, brought to reside amongst us, and dispense his *Gospel* to us; and some *Reviving* by his Ministry he blest us with. The Lord *lov'd* my dear Husband into his own Bosom, *lov'd* the Trial of his Death to me and the Church, and *lov'd* another Minister to us in his Room:

---

[181]*A Brief Account*, appendix, 158-59.
[182]*A Brief Account*, appendix, 160.
[183]*A Brief Account*, appendix, 160.
[184]*A Brief Account*, appendix, 161.
[185]*A Brief Account*, appendix, 162.

All which, infinite Wisdom and Goodness saw *better*, more for God's Glory and our Advantage, than if Things had been as I *wish'd*, and *hop'd for*.[186]

Letter

Attached to the appendix is

A Letter to Such of the Servants of Christ, who May have any Scruple about the Lawfulness of Printing any Thing written by a Woman: to shew, That Book-Teaching is private, with Respect to the Church, and permitted to private Christians; yea, commanded to Those, of either Sex, who are Gifted for, and Inclin'd to engage in this Service. By A. D. London: Printed by J. Hart in Poppings-court, Fleetstreet; and Sold by J. Lewis, in Bartholomew-Close, near West-Smithfield; and E. Gardner, at Milton's-Head, in Gracechurch-Street, 1743. [Price One Penny]

This letter was first published separately in 1743 and then added to the 1750 edition of all three parts of the autobiography with appendix that is being reprinted here. The letter begins as follows.

A LETTER to Such of the Servants of *CHRIST*, who have any Scruple about the Lawfulness of PRINTING any Thing written by a Woman: A Friend and Servant of Theirs, sendeth Greeting.

> *Honour'd Brethren,*
> Having heard that some of you have objected against my appearing in *Print*; as if it was [*sic*] contrary to the revealed *Will* of God: I thought it my Duty, meekly and humbly to offer to your Consideration, what is satisfactory to my own Soul in this regard. . . .[187]

---

[186]*A Brief Account*, appendix, 168. Robinson (*Life and Faith*, 55) states that Benjamin Dutton was in America from 1743 to 1747. Wallington ("Wesley and Anne Dutton," 44) records that Dutton went to America to help raise money for the Great Gransden Church and drowned upon return. Haykin ("Anne Dutton," 3) writes that Dutton "perished at sea" in 1747. The ship on which he was returning foundered not far from "the British coast." Wallington ("Wesley and Anne Dutton," 13) records that Whitefield wrote Anne Dutton on 25 October 1747 and stated, "Mr. Dutton, I believe, is lost in his return to England. The ship foundered."

[187]"A Letter," 3.

In the letter, Dutton makes four main points in her defense. "First [she says], I beg Leave to assure you, that my Design in publishing what I have written; was only the Glory of God, and the Good of Souls. . . . Secondly [she continues], That my appearing in Print, is not *against* any of the Laws of Christ in the sacred Records."[188]

Dutton refers to 1 Timothy 2:12 and 1 Corinthians 14:34-35, and states:

> It is plain from these *Texts*, that it is a Publick Authoritative Teaching in the Church, that is here forbidden unto *Women*: And that it is in this regard only, they are commanded to be in Silence. And *Printing* is a Thing of a very different Consideration.[189]

That is, she validates her ministry of publication as being for the *private* use of the church:

> For tho' what is printed is published to the *World*, and the Instruction thereby given, is in this regard *Publick*, in that it is presented to every ones View: Yet it is *Private* with respect to the *Church*. *Books* are not Read, and the Instruction by them given in the *public Assemblies* of the Saints: But visit every one, and converse with them in their own *private Houses*. And therefore the Teaching, or Instruction thereby given is *private*: and of no other Consideration than that of Writing a private *Letter* to a Friend, or of having private *Conference* with him for his Edification. And this is not only permitted to all the Saints, of whatever Sex they be.[190]

Dutton bases her third point on Romans 14:19:

> Thirdly, It is *commanded*, Rom. xiv. 19. *Let us therefore follow after the Things which make for Peace, and Things wherewith one* (any one, Male or Female) *may edify another.* If it is the Duty of *Women* to seek the *Edification* of their Brethren and Sisters; then is it their Duty to use the *Means* of it, whether it be in speaking, writing, or printing: Since all these are *private*, and proper to the *Sphere* which the Lord has allotted them. . . .

---

[188]"A Letter," 3. Haykin ("Anne Dutton," 3) notes that Anne Dutton wrote not for fame but for the good of souls and the glory of God.

[189]"A Letter," 4. In reference to the accusation of violating 1 Tim 2:12, Haykin ("Anne Dutton," 3) notes that Dutton's position was that her books were for private use, not for public worship and address. According to Dutton, 1 Timothy referred to public worship.

[190]"A Letter," 4-5.

And unless *Women* were excluded from being *Members* of Christ's mystical Body, *their Usefulness*, in all due Means, ought not to be hindered.[191]

Dutton's fourth point is that her books were made for use in private homes:

> Fourthly, As private Instruction is the *Duty of Women* as well as Men; so we have an *Example* thereof, *Acts* xviii. 26. Where we are inform'd that *Aquila and Priscilla took unto them*, even an *eloquent Apollos, a Man mighty in the Scriptures, and Expounded unto him the Way of God more perfectly*. And *this* of communicating ones Mind in *Print*, is as *private*, with respect to particular *Persons*, as if one did it particularly unto every one by *himself* in ones own *House*. There is only this *Difference*: The one is communicating ones Mind by *Speech*, in ones *own* private House: The other is doing it by *Writing*, in the private House of *another* Person. Both are still *private*.[192]

Dutton places the controversy about her publications within the context of the work of the Devil raging against Christ's work. The Lord's servants should not oppose one another in the Lord's work. To make her point, Dutton cites the story in Matthew 26:7 of the woman anointing Jesus, from which she concludes that

> the Disciples had *Indignation* against the Woman who pour'd the Box of precious Ointment upon Christ's Head; and said unto her. *To what purpose is this Waste? . . .* To whom our Lord reply'd: —*Why trouble ye the Woman? For she hath wrought a good Work upon me.*[193]

Dutton speaks of herself as God's instrument. She offers the words of God as infant's words to be patiently listened to:

> Imagine then, my dear Friends, when my *Books* come to your *Houses*, that I am come to give you a *Visit*; (for indeed by *them* I do) and patiently attend to the Lispings of a *Babe*: Who knows but the Lord may ordain *Strength* out of the Babe's Mouth? And give you a Visit *Himself*, by so weak a *Worm*, to your strong Consolation? It is all one to Omnipotence, to work by Worms, as by Angels. And remember, that the more contempt-

---

[191]"A Letter," 5. And see Haykin, "Anne Dutton," 3.
[192]"A Letter," 6-7.
[193]"A Letter," 9.

ible and weak the *Instrument* is that the Lord *works* by, the more it commands the Glory of his *Grace*, and the Excellency of his *Power*.[194]

Dutton concludes her letter, that her purpose in writing is to advance the Redeemer:

And this is by *Prayer* unto God for you. For as *for me to live is Christ*; so while I live in the Flesh, it is my earnest Desire, some Way or other, to serve *Him*, his *Interest and People.* . . .[195]

and then signs:

—Thus wishing all Peace and Prosperity: I am,
   Gentlemen and Brethren,
      Your most affectionate,
         Humble Servant,
            In our Glorious L O R D,
               A. D.[196]

---

[194]"A Letter," 11.

[195]"A Letter," 11-12.

[196]"A Letter," 12. Haykin ("Anne Dutton," 3) notes that Dutton's position is that she writes to advance the Redeemer and tell of his love for the good of souls. In conclusion Haykin wrote: "Though most of Anne's works survive now in only a few copies, they are well worth the effort of finding and reading . . . . Hopefully, this brief introduction to her life [that is, Haykin's journal article, and now the present introduction and her own autobiography] will prompt a renewed appreciation of her legacy and spirituality."

BIBLIOGRAPHY

Primary Sources: Anne Dutton[197]

A Brief Account of the Gracious Dealings of God, with a Poor, Sinful, Unworthy Creature, in Three Parts . . . With an Appendix. And a Letter Prefixed, on the Lawfulness of a Woman's Appearing in Print. London: John Hart, 1750.

This autobiography was published in three parts over a period of years. Part 1 and part 2 were originally published together with separate titles as *A Brief Account of the Gracious Dealings of God, with a Poor, Sinful, Unworthy Creature, Relating to the Work of Divine Grace on the Heart, in a Saving Conversion to Christ, and to Some Establishment in Him* and *A Brief Account of the Gracious Dealings of God, with a Poor, Sinful, Unworthy Creature, Relating to a Train of Special Providences Attending Life, by which the Work of Faith was Carried on with Power.* London: John Hart, 1743. Part 3 and the "Letter" were included with the 1750 publication (see above). Part 3 is entitled *A Brief Account of the Gracious Dealings of God, with a Poor, Sinful, Unworthy Creature, Relating to Some Particular Experiences of the Lord's Goodness, in Bringing Out Several Little Tracts, to the Furtherance and Joy of Faith.*

The publications referred to in the title ("Several Little Tracts") are pamphlets published by John Hart before 1750.

(Parts 1 and 2 [1743] are available in the United States at Harvard University and Baylor University. The complete work [1750] is in the British Library, London.)

Brief Hints Concerning Baptism. London, 1746. May be identical to *Letters on the Ordinance of Baptism* (1746). (Whitebrook, 18 no. 25.)

Brief Hints on God's Fatherly Chastisements, Showing Their Nature, Necessity and Usefulness, and the Saints' Duty to Wait upon God for Deliverance When under His Fatherly Corrections. 1743. (Whitebrook, 17 no. 14.)

A Caution against Error When It Springs Up together with the Truth, in a Letter to a Friend. 1746. (Whitebrook, 17 no. 24.)

A Discourse Concerning God's Act of Adoption. To Which is Added a Discourse upon the Inheritance of the Adopted Sons of God. London: E. Gardner, 1737. (British Library, London.)

---

[197]"Whitebrook" refers to the bibliography of John Cudworth Whitebrook, in his *Ann Dutton: A Life and Bibliography*, 15-20, as offprinted from "The Life and Works of Mrs. Ann Dutton," in *Transactions of the Baptist Historical Society* 7:129-46.

A Discourse Concerning the New-Birth: To Which Are Added Sixty-Four Hymns; Compos'd on Several Subjects; with an Epistle Recommendatory, by the Reverend Mr. Jacob Rogers, B.A. London: John Hart, 1743. (Yale University Beinecke Rare Books Library.)

A Discourse Concerning the New-Birth: To Which Are Added Two Poems: The One on Salvation in Christ, by Free-Grace, for the Chief of Sinners: The Other on a Believer's Safety and Duty: with an Epistle Recommendatory, by the Reverend Mr. Jacob Rogers, B.A. London: John Oswald and Ebenezer Gardner, 1740. (British Library, London.)

A Discourse upon Justification: Shewing the Matter, Manner, Time and Effects of it. To Which are Added Three Poems: I. On the Special Work of the Spirit in the Hearts of the Elect. . . . III. On a Believer's Safety and Duty. London: printed by John Hart and sold by J. Lewis and E. Gardner, 1740, 1743. (The 1743 edition is at Harvard University Libraries.)

A Discourse upon Walking with God: In a Letter to a Friend. Together with Some Hints upon Joseph's Blessing, Deut. 33.13, &c. As Also a Brief Account How the Author Was Brought into Gospel-Liberty. London: printed for the author and sold by E. Gardner, 1735. (Gale Group.)

Divine, Moral, and Historical Miscellanies in Prose and Verse. Edited by A. Dutton. 1761. (British Library.)

Five Letters to a Newly Married Pair. 1759. (Whitebrook, 18 no. 33.)

Hints of the Glory of Christ: As the Friend and Bridgroom of the Church: From the Seven Last Verses of the Fifth Chaper of Solomon's Song: In a Letter to a Friend. London: printed by John Hart and sold by J. Lewis, 1748. (British Library, London.)

 Originally published as *Meditations and Observations upon the Eleventh and Twelfth Verses of the Sixth Chapter of Solomon's Song.* 1743. (Whitebrook, 16 no. 13; 18 no. 27.)

The Hurt that Sin Doth to Believers, etc. 1733. Second edition, 1749. (Whitebrook, 18 no. 30.)

A Letter from Mrs. Anne Dutton to the Reverend Mr. G. Whitefield. Philadelphia: printed and sold by William Bradford, 1743. (Library Company of Philadelphia.)

A Letter on the Application of the Holy Scriptures. Poppings Court: printed by John Hart and sold by J. Lewis, 1754. (Whitebrook, 18 no. 31.)

A Letter on the Divine Eternal Sonship of Jesus Christ: . . . Occasioned by the Perusal of Mr. Romaine's Sermon . . . Entitled, A Discourse Upon the Self-Existence of Jesus Christ. With Three Letters on Assurance of Interest in Christ: . . . Written as the Author's Thoughts, on Part of Mr. Marshal's . . . The Gospel-Mystery of Sanctification. And Two Letters on the Gift of the Holy Spirit to Believers . . . By One Who Has Tasted that the Lord is Gracious.

London: printed by John Hart and sold by G. Keith, 1757. (Oxford University Bodleian Library.)

A Letter on the Duty and Privilege of a Believer to Live by Faith, and to Improve His Faith unto Holiness. 1745. (Whitebrook, 17 n. 21.)

A Letter on Perseverance, against Mr. Wesley. 1747. (Whitebrook, 18 no. 38.)

A Letter to All Men on the General Duty of Love among Christians. 1742. (Whitebrook, 16 no. 7.)

A Letter to all the Saints on the General Duty of Love: Humbly Presented, by One That is Less Than the Least of Them All, and Unworthy to be of Their Happy Number. London: printed by John Hart and sold by Samuel Mason, 1742; printed by John Hart and sold by J. Lewis and E. Gardner, 1743. Philadelphia: Joseph Crukshank, 1774. (Harvard University Andover; Harvard Theological Library has the 1743 edition.)

A Letter to All Those That Love Christ in Philadelphia. To Excite Them to Adhere to, and Appear for, the Truths of the Gospel. 1743(?). (Whitebrook, 17 no. 19.)

A Letter to the Believing Negroes, lately Converted to Christ in America. 1742. (Whitebrook, 16 no. 9.)

A Letter to Christians at the Tabernacle. 1744(?). (Whitebrook, 18 no. 37.)

A Letter to Mr. William Cudworth, In Vindication of the Truth from his Misrepresentations: With Respect to the Work of the Spirit in Faith, Holiness, The New Birth &c. Being a Reply to his Answer to the Postscript of a Letter Lately Published, &c. 1747. (Whitebrook, 18 no. 26.)

A Letter to the Reverend Mr. John Wesley. In Vindication of the Doctrines of Absolute, Unconditional Election, Particular Redemption, Special Vocation, and Final Perseverance. Occasioned Chiefly by Some Things in His Dialogue between a Predestinarian and His Friend; and In His Hymns on God's Everlasting Love. London: printed by John Hart and sold by Samuel Mason, 1742. (Pitts Theology Library, Emory University.)

A Letter to Such of the Servants of Christ Who May Have Any Scruple about the Lawfulness of Printing Anything Written by a Woman. 1743. (Whitebrook, 17 no. 18.)

Letters against Sanddemanianism and with a Letter on Reconciliation. (Whitebrook, 18 no. 36.)

Letters on the Being and Working of Sin in a Justified Man. 1745. (Whitebrook, 17 no. 20.)

Letters on the Ordinance of Baptism. 1746. May be identical to *Brief Hints Concerning Baptism.* London, 1746. (Whitebrook, 18 no. 25.)

Letters to the Reverend Mr. John Westley [sic] *against Perfection as Not Attainable in This Life.* London: John Hart, 1743. (Pitts Theological Library, Emory University; John Rylands Library, University of Manchester.)

Letters on Spiritual and Divers Occasions. London: G. Keith, 1749. (Whitebrook,
    18 no. 29.)
Letters on Spiritual Subjects, and Divers Occasions, Sent to Relatives and Friends.
    London: printed and sold by John Oswald and Ebenenzer Gardner, 1740.
    London: printed by John Hart and sold by J. Lewis, 1748.
*Letters on Spiritual Subjects and Divers Occasions, Sent to the Reverend Mr.
    George Whitefield And others of his Friends and Acquaintance. To Which is
    Added, A Letter on the Being and Working of Sin, in the Soul of justify'd Man,
    as Consistent with His State of Justification in Christ, and Sanctification
    Through Him: With the Nature of His Obedience, and of His Comfort,
    Consider'd: As the One is from God, and the other to Him; notwithstanding his
    Corruptions may be great, and His Graces Small in His Own Sight. As Also,
    A Letter on the Duty and Privilege of a Believer, To Live by Faith, and to
    Improve his Faith unto Holiness. By One Who Has Tasted that the Lord is
    Gracious.* London: John Hart, 1745. (Pitts Theology Library, Emory
    University. Incomplete copy.)
Letters on Spiritual Subjects Sent to Relations and Friends. Two parts. Second
    revised edition. Edited by Christopher Goulding. London: T. Bensley,
    1823–1824. (Duke University Library.)
*Letters Sent to an Honourable Gentleman, for the Encouragement of Faith. By One
    Who Has Tasted that the Lord is Gracious.* London: printed by John Hart and
    sold by J. Lewis and E. Gardner, 1743. (Boston Athenaeum.)
*Meditations and Observations upon the Eleventh and Twelfth Verses of the Sixth
    Chapter of Solomon's Song.* 1743. Published later as a pamphlet entitled *Hints
    of the Glory of Christ as the Friend and Bridegroom of the Church: From the
    Seven Last Verses of the Fifth Chapter of Solomon's Song, &c.* 1748.
    (Whitebrook, 16 no. 13; 18 no. 27.)
*Mr. Sanddeman Refuted by an Old Woman: or Thoughts on His Letters to the
    Author of Theron and Aspasio. In a Letter from a Friend in the Country to a
    Friend in Town.* London: John Hart, 1761. (Brown University Library.)
*A Narration of the Wonders of Grace, in Six Parts. I. Of Christ the Mediator, as Set
    Up from Everlasting in All the Glory of Headship. II. Of God's Election and
    Covenant—Transactions Concerning a Remnant in His Son. III. Of Christ's
    Incarnation and Redemption. IV. Of the Work of the Spirit, Respecting the
    Church in General, throughout the New Testament Dispensation, from Christ's
    Ascension to His Second Coming. V. Of Christ's Glorious Appearing and
    Kingdom. VI. Of Gog and Magog; Together with the Last Judgment. To Which
    Is Added, A Poem on the Special Work of the Spirit in the Hearts of the Elect,
    also, Sixty One Hymns Composed on Several Subjects.* A new edition. Revised,
    with a preface and collected memoir of the author, by John Andrews Jones.

London: John Bennett, 1833. Pages xxxii + 115. (Covenant Theological
Seminary, St. Louis.)
Second edition. "Corrected by the author, with additions." London: printed for
the author and sold by John Oswald, 1734. Pages viii + [9-]143.
First edition. London: printed for and sold by the author, 1734. Pages viii +
139.

Occasional Letters on Spiritual Subjects. Seven volumes. Popping's Court: John
Hart and Bartholomew Close: J. Lewis, 1740–1749.

*A Postcript to a Letter Lately Published, on the Duty and Privilege of a Believer to
Live by Faith, &c . . . Directed to the Society at the Tabernacle in London. . . .
As Also, Some of the Mistakes of the Moravian Brethren. . . . By One Who Has
Tasted that the Lord is Gracious.* London: printed by John Hart and sold by
J. Lewis and E. Gardner, 1746. (Union Theological Seminary, New York.)

*Selections from [Occasional] Letters on Spiritual Subjects: Addressed to Relatives
and Friends.* Compiled by James Knight. London: John Gadsby, 1884. (Turpin
Library, Dallas Theological Seminary.)

A Sight of Christ Necessary for All True Christians and Gospel Ministers. 1743.
(Whitebrook, 16 no. 11.)

Thoughts on the Lord's Supper. London, 1748. (Whitebrook, 18 no. 28.)

*Three Letters on I. The Marks of a Child of God. II. The Soul-Diseases of God's
Children; . . . III. God's Prohibition of His Peoples Unbelieving Fear: . . . By
One Who Has Tasted that the Lord is Gracious.* London: printed by John Hart
and sold by G. Keith and J. Fuller, 1761. (Oxford University Bodleian
Library.)

A Treatise on Justification: Showing the Matter, Manner, Time, and Effects of It.
Third edition. Glasgow: printed by William Smith for Archibald Coubrough,
1778. The author is listed as "the Rev. Mr. Thomas Dutton," presumably one
of Anne Dutton's pseudonymns. (British Library, London.)

Primary Sources: Dutton's Contemporaries

B. D. [Benjamin Dutton]. *The Superaboundings of the Exceeding Riches of God's
Free Grace, towards the Chief of the Chief of Sinners, &c.* No publisher, no
date.

Baker, Frank, ed. *The Works of John Wesley.* Volume 26. *Letters II (1740–1755).*
Oxford: Clarendon Press, 1982.

Bunyan, John. *The Holy War.* London: printed for Dorman Newman and Benjamin
Alsop, 1682.

_____. *Pilgrim's Progress.* 1678. Repr.: Ulrichsville OH: Barbour Publish-
ing, 1985.

_____. *The Works of John Bunyan: With an Introduction to Each Treatise, Notes, and a Sketch of His Life, Times, and Contemporaries*. Three volumes. Edited by George Offor. Repr.: Edinburgh and Carlisle PA: Banner of Truth Trust, 1991. Original: Glasgow: W. G. Blackie and Son, 1854.

Cudworth, William, *Truth Defended and Cleared from Mistakes and Misrepresentations*. See Arthur Wallington, "Wesley and Ann Dutton," 48.

Middleton, Erasmus. *A Letter from the Reverend Mr. [Erasmus Middleton] to A[nne] D[utton]*. 1735. (British Library, London.)

Wesley, John. *A Dialogue Between a Predestinarian and His Friend*. London: W. Stratan, 1741.

_____. *Wesley's Standard Sermons*. Two volumes. Edited by Edward H. Sugden. Fifth edition. London: Epworth, 1961.

_____. *The Works of John Wesley*. Fourteen volumes. Third edition. Edited by Thomas Jackson et al. London: Wesleyan Conference Office, 1873–1893. Repr.: Grand Rapids: Zondervan, 1958-1959.

_____. *The Works of John Wesley*. Volume 19. *Journal and Diaries II (1738–1743)*. Edited by W. Reginald Ward and Richard P. Heitzenrater. Nashville: Abingdon Press, 1990.

Wesley, John and Charles. *Hymns of God's Everlasting Love*. Bristol: S. and F. Farley, 1741.

_____. *The Poetical Works of John and Charles Wesley*. Thirteen volumes. Edited by George Osborn. London: Wesleyan-Methodist Conference Office, 1868–1872.

Whitefield, George. "A Letter to the Rev. Mr. John Wesley in Answer to His Sermon Entitled 'Free Grace' " (24 December 1740). In [Whitefield's] *Journals*, 571-88. London: Banner of Truth Trust, 1960.

_____. *The Works of the Reverend George Whitefield*. Six volumes. London: Edward and Charles Dilley, 1771–1772.

Secondary Sources

Austin, Roland. "The Weekly History." *Proceedings of the Wesley Historical Society* 11/2 (June 1917): 239-43.

Burder, Samuel. See under Thomas Gibbons.

Dana, Daniel. See under Thomas Gibbons.

A Dictionary of Hymnology. Edited by John Julian. New York: Scribner's, 1892.

Gibbons, Thomas. *Memoirs of Eminently Pious Women, Who Were Ornaments to Their Sex, Blessings to Their Families, and Edifying Examples to the Church and World*. Two volumes. London: printed for J. Buckland, 1777.

(2) Dana's abridged edition: "Abridged from the large work of Dr. Gibbons, London, by Daniel Dana." Women and the Church in America 9. Newburyport MA: printed for the subscribers by Angier March, 1803.

(3) Jerment's expanded edition: "Republished [with some omissions] in 1804, with an additional volume by George Jerment." Two volumes. (Volume 1 contained all of Gibbons's material, originally in two volumes; volume 2 contained additional material by Jerment.) London: printed by W. Nicholson for R. Ogles, 1804.

(4) Burder's new and further expanded edition: "A new edition, embellished with eighteen portraits, corrected and enlarged by Samuel Burder." Three volumes. (Volume 1 comprises the original material of Gibbons; volume 2 is Jerment's 1804 addition; volume 3 adds Burder's new material.) London: Ogles, Duncan, and Cochran, 1815.

(Gibbons's *Memoirs* is most readily available today in the following Burder edition. Consequently, *Memoirs* is routinely cited in the literature under "Burder" as author.)

(5) Reprint of the Burder expanded edition: "From a late London edition, in three volumes; now complete in one volume." One volume. Philadelphia: J. J. Woodward, 1834ff. (This is the edition routinely cited herein, and that in its 1836 reprinting.)

Green, Richard. *Anti-Methodist Publications: Issued during the Eighteenth Century: A Chronologically Arranged and Annotated Bibliography of All Known Books and Pamphlets Written in Opposition to the Methodist Revival during the Life of Wesley; Together with an Account of Replies to Them, and of Some Other Publications. A Contribution to Methodist History.* London: C. H. Kelly, 1902. Repr.: New York: Burt Franklin, 1973.

Haykin, Michael. "The Celebrated Mrs. Anne Dutton." *Evangelical Times* (April 2001). (The third in an extended series of articles under the general title "A Cloud of Witnesses.")

Heitzenrater, Richard P. *Wesley and the People Called Methodists.* Nashville: Abingdon, 1995.

Herbert, George. *The English Poems of George Herbert.* Edited by C. A. Patrides. London: S. M. Dent and Sons, 1991.

Jerment, George. See under Thomas Gibbons.

Johnson, Dale A. *Women and Religion in Britain and Ireland: An Annotated Bibliography from The Reformation to 1993.* ATLA Bibliography Series 39. Lanham MD: Scarecrow Press, 1995.

MacHaffie, Barbara J. *Her Story: Women in Christian Tradition.* Philadelphia: Fortress, 1986.

The Oxford Dictionary of the Christian Church. Second edition. Edited by F. L. Cross and E. A. Livingstone. Oxford: Oxford University Press, 1974. Third edition. 1997.

Robinson, H. Wheeler. *The Life and Faith of the Baptists.* Revised edition. London: Kingsgate Press, 1946; first edition, 1927; repr.: Wake Forest NC: Chanticleer, 1985. The section on Anne Dutton appears on pp. 50-56: "Studies in Baptist Personality: (6) A Baptist Writer (Ann Dutton)."

Starr, Edward, editor. *A Baptist Bibliography.* Rochester NY: American Baptist Historical Society, 1959. (Section D, 201-204, lists about seventy works by Anne Dutton.)

Stein, Stephen. "A Note on Anne Dutton, Eighteenth-Century Evangelical." *Church History* 44 (1975): 485-91.

Wallington, Arthur. "Wesley and Anne Dutton." *Proceedings of the Wesley Historical Society* 11/2 (June 1917): 43-48.

Watson, JoAnn Ford, "Anne Dutton: An 18th Century British Evangelical Woman." *Ashland Theological Journal* 30 (1998): 51-56.

Whitebrook, John Cudworth. *Ann Dutton: A Life and Bibliography.* London: A. W. Cannon and Co., 1921. Also appears as "The Life and Works of Mrs. Ann Dutton," *Transactions of the Baptist Historical Society* 7 (1920–1921): 129-46. (*Transactions*, 1908–1921, became the *Baptist Quarterly*, 1922 to date.)

Whitley, William Thomas. *A Baptist Bibliography: Being a Register of the Chief Materials for Baptist History, Whether in Manuscript or in Print, Preserved in Great Britain, Ireland, and the Colonies.* Two volumes. London: Kingsgate Press, 1916, 1922. Repr.: Two volumes in one: Hildesheim: Georg Olms, 1984.

A Brief

A C C O U N T

OF THE

Gracious Dealings of *God*,

WITH A

Poor, Sinful, Unworthy CREATURE,

IN THREE PARTS.

Relating to PART I.
The WORK of Divine Grace on the Heart, in a Saving
Conversion to CHRIST, and to some Establishment in
HIM.

PART II.
A Train of Special PROVIDENCES attending *Life*, by which
the Work of Faith was carried on with Power.

PART III.
Some particular EXPERIENCES of the LORD's Goodness in
bringing out several little TRACTS, to the Furtherance
and Joy of Faith.

WITH AN

A P P E N D I X.

AND A

LETTER *prefix'd* on the *Lawfulness* of a WOMAN's appearing in PRINT.

By *A. D.*

*Come all ye that fear GOD, and I will declare what HE hath
done for my Soul.* Psal lxvi. 6.

L O N D O N:
Printed by J. HART in *Popping's Court, Fleet-Street*. And sold
by J. LEWIS, in *Pater-noster-Row*, near *Cheap-side*. 1750.

EPISTLE

TO THE

READER.

Dear Reader,

*T*HE First *and* Second *Parts of my Brief Account, were printed some Years ago, as appears by their Date. And the* Third *Part, which is now added, perhaps might not have been printed till after my Decase, but for Special Reasons which induc'd me to it. I have sincerely aim'd in the Whole, so far as I know my own Heart, at the* Glory of GOD, *and the* Good of Souls: *And not at my* own Honour, *that any Man should* think of me, *more* highly *than is* meet: *Or any otherwise, than as a* chief Sinner, *on whom the* LORD *hath* shewed great Mercy. *I desire forever to be deeply* humbled *for my* Unworthiness *and* Vileness, *and that* GOD's Free Grace *alone, may be highly and eternally* exalted, *in the Whole of my* Salvation, *in my present and future* Bliss. *Oh,* Not *unto* me, Not *unto* me, *unto vile unworthy me; but unto the* LORD *alone, be* all the Glory! *If* GOD's *Ways of* Grace, *may be made* known, *by any Thing I have written: To the* Praise *of his great Name, the Joy of his dear Children, and their* Encouragement *to put their Trust under the Shadow of his Wings: I* have *the blessed* End *I* wish'd, *and the great* Reward, *which, of the* GOD *of Grace, I* sought.—*I commit the* Whole, *to the* LORD's Blessing: *And be intreated to ask it,* Dear Reader, *on thy Perusal of every* Part, *of the Gracious Dealings of* GOD, *with*

Thy Sincere Friend,
And
Servant in CHRIST,

A. D.

A Brief

ACCOUNT

OF THE

GRACIOUS DEALINGS

OF

G O D,

WITH A

Poor, Sinful, Unworthy CREATURE,

Relating to
The WORK of Divine Grace on the Heart, in a saving
Conversion to CHRIST, and to some Establishment in
HIM.

PART I.

By A. D.

*Come all ye that fear GOD, and I will declare what He
hath done for my Soul,* Psa. lxvi. 6.

L O N D O N:
Printed by J. HART, in *Poppings-Court, Fleet-street*: And
Sold by J. LEWIS, in *Bartholomew-Close*, near *West-
Smithfield*; and F. GARDNER, at *Milton's-Head*, in
Gracechurch-Street MDCCXLIII. [1743]

THE
PREFACE.

Christian Reader,

*M*Y Design in the following Sheets, was to bear a Testimony, as one of
God's Witnesses, to the exceeding Riches of his Grace, in the Salvation of
my Soul. But yet, when I first began to think about it, (having been
requested to engage in this Work) I could not, for some Time, find my Heart
inclined hereto: As being under a prevailing Sense of my own Weakness, to
say any Thing that might tend to the Advancement of God's Free-Grace,
and the Edification of his People. So that thou hadst never had the
following Narrative, if the Lord himself had not encourag'd me to attempt
this Work. And he sweetly drew my Heart, as being one of his Witnesses, to
bear this Testimony for Him, and his Way of saving poor Sinners, of whom
I am Chief. I saw a great Glory in those Words, Rev. xiv. 1. And I looked,
and lo, a Lamb stood on the Mount Sion, and with him an hundred forty and
four Thousand, having his Father's Name written in their Foreheads. And
as one of the Lamb's Company, I was made willing to bear my weak
Testimony to the All-sufficiency of God's Free-Grace, and the Insufficiency
of every Thing else for the Salvation of a poor Sinner. And thus to look forth
into the World, as having the Father's Name written on my Forehead: i.e.
As a living Witness of that infinite Mercy, and Grace of Jehovah, which he
declar'd to Moses, in that glorious Proclamation of his Name, Exod. xxxiv.
6. Altho', as I then thought, my weak Voice, in itself, could do but little to
advance the Glory of Free-Grace; yet, as in Consort with the Lamb's
Company, that sing the new Song, it might be of some Use: As the weakest
Voice in a united Company conspires to raise the Sound. Having this Hope,
I set about the Work, leaning on Divine Assistance, and thro' the good
Hand of God upon me, I have been comfortably carry'd thro' it.

    And now, That God's Free Grace, which hath saved me, may further
extend its Riches, in owning this weak Attempt; that the God of all Grace
may be glorify'd, and his People reap some Advantage; is the earnest
Desire of,

The Least of CHRIST's,

A. D.

A Brief
A C C O U N T
O F   T H E
GRACIOUS DEALINGS
O F
G   O   D, &c.

M Y Design in this little Tract, being to give a brief Account of the Lord's Loving-kindness to my Soul; I shall in Order hereto, give some Hints,

First, Of my Manner of Life from my Childhood.
Secondly, Of the Work of Divine Grace on my Heart, in a saving Conversion to CHRIST.
Thirdly, Of my being brought to some Establishment in HIM. And,
Fourthly, Something by Way of Reflection.

First then, As to my Manner of Life from my Childhood. It pleas'd the Lord to order it so, that I had the Advantage of a Religious Education; my Parents being both Gracious By Means of whose Care and Diligence, I was train'd up in the Ways of God: Being early instructed into the Doctrines and Worship of the Gospel, so far as my tender Years were capable of. I attended with my Parents upon the Ministry of the late Mr. *Hunt*, who was then Pastor of a Church of Christ at *Northampton*; which was the Place of my *first*, and also of my *second* Birth. I kept up private Prayer frequently, but not constantly. From a Child I was acquainted with the Holy Scriptures, and took Pleasure in reading them, with other good Books; especially Hymn-Books, which I greatly delighted to learn, and commit to Memory. My natural Affections at Times, were much rais'd in reading some Parts of the Bible, and other Books; so that I have preferr'd religious Exercises to the childish Vanity of Play with my Fellows. Which some judg'd to be the *Buddings of Grace* in my Soul. But, however, from a Child I was under *Convictions* at Times; and my Conscience was kept so tender, that I was easily touch'd with the Guilt of Sin, when I thought I had done any Thing amiss. And when I was under *Guilt*, it would hinder me from *Prayer*, 'till it was a little worn off. But then I thought to be *better*; and to Prayer I went again. And if I could pray with any Enlargement, my Conscience was eas'd, and I was quite whole, and went on with religious Exercises as before.

But notwithstanding my *Attendance* upon publick and private Worship, my *Notions* of Divine Mysteries, my *Memory* to retain the best Things, and my raised *Affections* in religious Exercises; I was, tho' I had little Reason for it, a *proud, self-righteous* Creature: And an awful *Stranger* and *Enemy* to God, and the Way of Salvation, as it is alone by the Person, Blood and Righteousness of Christ. For tho' I had Notions of these Things, yet, alas! the inbred Enmity of my Heart appear'd, in my attempting to join something of my own with Christ: *Seeking Life as it were by the Works of the Law.* Which is the *Way that seemeth right to a Man, but the End thereof is Death.* Proud Worm that I was, I valued myself upon my suppos'd Attainments, and thought my eternal Happiness secur'd thereby. I have been ready at Times to bless myself thus: (when I have seen other Children at Play) "Well, others are employed about Vanity; but I know better Things; I have been at Prayer, while others are at Play: Doubtless I am safe for Heaven." But if any one had ask'd a Reason of my Confidence; it must have been, if I had spoke my Heart, *Because I am better than others.* So wicked and vain was I, notwithstanding all my religious Seriousness; that I went about to *establish my own filthy Righteousness*; and was far from *submitting to the Righteousness of God.* And thus, in Unbelief, rejecting the SAVIOUR, I might have been left to go on, depending upon my own Righteousness, and to perish with Thousands in this splendid Way to Hell.

And here I would further observe, That, tho' I mostly had a false Peace from my supposed *Goodness*, yet at Times it was broken by my *Badness*. My Conscience would accuse me for my Vanities and Evils, as not being all of a Piece, as not acting consistently with that Shew which I made in Religion. And oft have I strove to stifle Convictions, and against the Force of them, when my Honour'd Father talk'd closely to me for the Good of my Soul. And lo, a little Time before the Lord wrought savingly on my Heart, I began to be more *airy* and *proud*, and to please myself with *Creature-Vanities*. And thus, being estranged from God, and an Enemy of Him, with my Back upon God, and my Face towards Destruction, I went on in Sin, towards eternal Death. And was so far from having any *Fitness* in me for Conversion to God, or any *Goodness* to move his Favour; that I had a *Fulness of Rebellion*, a *Fulness of Sin* in me to provoke his Wrath: And was fit Fewel for *everlasting Burnings.* And justly might I have been made an Example of God's Vengeance, of his fiery Indignation, in the Torments of Hell for ever.

But, Behold! to commend the Love of God towards me, he took me at my worst! For GOD, *who is rich in Mercy, for his great Love wherewith he loved me, even when I was dead in Sins, did quicken me together with Christ*, influentially, upon the Bottom of his having done it mystically. I was *cast out in the open Field, to the Lothing of my Person*. But the God of all Grace *pass'd by me, and saw me polluted in mine own Blood*; cover'd all over with Nature's Defilement: And lo! He said unto me, when I was in my Blood, *live*: Yea, he said unto me when I was in my Blood, *live*. For *my Time was the Time of Love*, Ezek. xvi. 5, *&c.* of Love's Manifestation, not of Love's Beginning. And this brings me to give some Hints,

Secondly, Of the Work of Divine Grace upon my Heart, in a saving Conversion to CHRIST. And thro' rich Grace, I had the Honour and Happiness of an early Acquaintance with God. It pleas'd the Lord to work savingly upon my Heart, when I was about thirteen Years of Age; tho' I can't fix the precise Time of its Beginning. Which I judge was the less discernible to me, by Reason of my being so frequently under Concern of Soul before. But, however, this I can say, that my Concern at this Time, was much *greater*, and more *lasting* than ever before: Nor could I find *Peace* where I was wont to find it.

There was a mighty Impression made upon my Heart, of the Reality and Consequence of a *future State*, either of Misery or Glory, of unspeakable Happiness, or inconceivable Torment; together with the *Nearness* of its Approach. Oh, *Eternity! Eternity* was ever before mine Eyes! And the *Worth* of my own Soul, as an immortal Spirit, capable of the highest Glory in the eternal Enjoyment of God, or of the utmost Misery in an everlasting Separation from him; was strongly impress'd upon my Mind. Again, the *Misery* of my natural State was set before me, as a Transgressor of the *Holy Law*: I thought all the Curses in God's Book belong'd to *me*. And further, the Law of God, was now open'd to me in its *Spirituality*; as extending to Thoughts, the most inward Motions of my Soul, as well as to my Words and Actions. And I was as particularly laid under its condemning Sentence in these Respects, as when *Nathan* said to *David, Thou art the Man*. Before, I cou'd hear the Minister speak of the Misery of *lost Sinners*, and not think *myself* concern'd therein; and still turn it over to *others*, which my Thoughts suggested to be the Persons he describ'd. But now I needed none to tell me, that *I was the Person* that was undone by Sin: And that, if I died in a State of Unbeleif, and Alienation from God, I must be damned for ever.

This rais'd a *Cry* in my Soul, (tho' I kept it as close as I cou'd from others) *What must I do to be saved?* Now I set about Religion in good Earnest; I pray'd, read, heard in a very different Manner than I had ever done before. But my Wound was too *deep* to be heal'd with my *own Doings* now. My Soul was remov'd far off from Peace, a dreadful Sound was in my Ears. The Law of God pursu'd me with its *Curses*, notwithstanding all my *religious Duties*; Yea, even for the *Sins* that attended them: Which 'till now, I was an utter Stranger to. Before, I was a beautiful Creature in my own Eyes, as wraps round with my fine Doings. But now I saw myself to be a most deformed Object, a loathsome Spectacle in the Eyes of GOD, and was so in my own Sight. My best of *Righteousness*, now appear'd to be but *filthy Rags*; which were so far from justifying me before God, that they really increas'd my Guilt, and Condemnation, by Reason of the Sin that clave to them. I saw *Sin* now in another *Light* than before. I saw the exceeding Sinfulness, and Hatefulness thereof, in its *Contrariety to God*, the Chief Good. The Guilt which before attended my Conscience, on Account of Sin, respected only the outward *Actions* thereof in my Life: But now I saw myself guilty, by Reason of *Heart-Sins*. Yea, mine Eyes were now opened, to see the filthy Fountain, whence all the defiled Streams, both in Heart and Life, did proceed. I saw that *I was shapen in Iniquity, and* that *in Sin my Mother did conceive me.* Yea, I saw myself a Sinner in *Adam*, my publick Head: Guilty and Filthy in his first Sin. Oh *here* I view'd my *mortal Wound!* And that it was from *hence*, that I was brought into the World a *Sinner*; with a guilty, filthy Nature, all over defiled from Head to Foot, as a Descendant from *fallen Adam*. Here I saw, that it wou'd have been a righteous Thing with God, to have cut me off in his Wrath, from the first Moment of my Birth, and sent me down into eternal Perdition. Again, I was convinc'd, that I had been doing nothing else but *sinning against God*, ever since I had a Being. And I wonder'd at *infinite Patience*, that had born with me, and suffer'd me to live so long out of Hell. I now, no longer thought myself to be *better* than others; but one of the *vilest* Creatures the Earth bore. Yea, I thought myself to be the very *Chief* of Sinners. For tho' restraining Grace had kept me from outward Enormities; yet I cou'd look upon those of the most flagitious Lives, and think myself a worse Sinner than they. *The Plague of my Heart* was now open'd; and oh, what a Complication of Sins, what Filth, and Abominations did I there see! These made me loath myself in my own Sight: So that from the very Inward of my

Soul, I have bemoaned myself in these Lines of one of Mr. *Shepherd's* Hymns:

> Sure I'm more *Vile* than any one
> Of wretched *Adam*'s Race!

Again, I was convinc'd of my own *Weakness*, and real Inability to do any Thing that was spiritually good; or in the least wise to help myself out of that miserable, distressed Condition I was in. I saw myself to be *Carnal, sold under Sin*. And that I was so far from being able to help myself out of that horrible Pit I was plung'd into; that the more I struggl'd to get out, the deeper I sunk into it. And this Inability to help myself respected, not only the *Guilt* and *Filth*, but also the *Power* of Sin. I saw, that I was held as in Chains under the Dominion of Sin. And the Power of Being, as well as the Guilt and Filth of Sin, was now a *great Burden* to my Soul. I saw, that nothing less than an omnipotent Arm could pluck me out of those amazing Deeps! And now I was *undone* indeed! Just ready to *perish* in my Apprehension; being fill'd at Times with terrible Fears of approaching Wrath. So that I have been in Dread in the Evening, when I went to Bed, lest I should lift up my Eyes in Hell before Morning.

Again, it pleas'd the Lord to convince me, that *Salvation* was alone by God's *Free-Grace*, thro' what Christ had *done*, as the Redeemer of Sinners. And that it was impossible for me to be sav'd, without *Faith in Christ*, of the special Operation of God. Further, I was fully convinc'd of the *Sufficiency* of Christ to save even the *worst* of Sinners. And that there was Salvation in *Him*, which the Chosen of God should assuredly obtain. Again, There was a Soul-ravishing, Heart-attracting Revelation of *Christ* made to me , in his infinite *Suitableness* as a Saviour, to my present Case as an undone Sinner: And also, of his infinite *Ability* to save *me* to the uttermost, from the Depths of Misery, to the Heights of Glory.

And tho' what I heard of Salvation as yet, was but, as it were, in *general Propositions*: As that Christ dy'd for the Chief of Sinners: And, He that believeth shall be saved, &c. From whence a Possibility of Salvation for *me*, was hinted: Yet so powerful an *Influence* had it on my Soul, that it kept me from Despair; and held my Heart at the Throne of Grace. And indeed, some Glimmerings of *Salvation by Christ*, together with a Possibility of its being for *me*, were so intermingled with my forementioned *Convictions*, that kept me from sinking into *Desparation*.

About this Time I was put upon some Doubt about Election, whether there was any such Thing. And received full Satisfaction from *Rom.* xi. 5. *There is a Remnant according to the Election of Grace.* But then, to know whether *I was elected*, this was my chief Concern. For the Notions I before had of the Doctrines of the Gospel, were not sufficient to comfort me now. I could no longer rest satisfy'd with knowing, that God had chosen a *Remnant* in his Son unto eternal Life; unless I knew my *own Interest* in electing Grace. Nor, that Christ had died for *Sinners*; without knowing that he loved *me*, and gave himself for me, *&c.* I saw it avail'd nothing as to Salvation, to know for *others*, unless I knew these Things for my *own Soul.* God's Election-Grace stood forth before mine Eyes in an amazing Glory. But oh, to know whether *I was one* of God's chosen! I saw the inexpressible Blessedness of those who were interested in Christ's Person, Love, Life, Death and Glory. But oh, the tormenting Fears, which at Times wrack'd my Heart, lest *I should stand excluded* from all this Grace! I was once, I remember, reading the seventeenth Chapter of St. *John*: And when I came to those Words, *I pray not for the World, but for them which thou hast given me, for they are thine*: My Heart was as if struck thro' with a Dart; fearing that I was none of the *Lord's*, but of the *World*: and as such stood *excluded* from Christ's Prayer. And those Words also was with Weight upon my Mind, *Psa.* lxxiii. 1, 2. *Truly God is good to Israel, even to such as are of a clean Heart. But as for me!* (for I went no further) from the first Verse I saw how infinitely Good God was to his *own People*, and how unspeakably Blessed *they* were, as interested in all his Goodness. So that from those clear and demonstrative Views I had of it; I could, with my whole Soul, join with the *Psalmist*, and say, *Truly God is Good to Israel, even to such as are of a clean Heart!* But then, from the first Clause of the second Verse, *But as for me!* I took in a vast Sight of my *own Misery*; and was fill'd with Fears, that *my State* was just the Reverse to that of those happy Souls, which were interested in God, and in all his Goodness. Yea, I sometimes found despairing Thoughts forcing themselves upon me; as if I was *irrecoverably lost*, when under a prevailing Fear, that I should be damned. And, at Times, I was fit to bewail my Misery, in a Verse of Mr. *Mason's* Poem upon *Dives* and *Lazarus*: viz.

"God's gone, He's gone, and what an Hell is this
To be depriv'd of everlasting Bliss!"

But thro' rich Grace, everlasting Arms being underneath me, I was not left to sink into *Despair*; nor was I long without *Hopes* that I should find Mercy. The Greatness and Sovereignty of *Jehovah's Mercy and Grace*; the Fulness and Freeness of Christ's *Salvation*; together with the indefinite *Promises* of the Gospel, were as so many Cords which powerfully drew my Soul, to venture into the Presence of God, and prostrate myself at the Throne of Grace, as a lost, undone Sinner, as it were with a *Rope about my Neck*: Or, as under a full *Conviction*, and an open *Confession*, of my having deserved to die the Death. I was, as it were, brought before the Bar of God, and ask'd if I had any Thing to say, why I might not be sent down to the Pit? And lo! I stood *guilty*: My *Mouth was stopp'd before the Lord*: And I *wondred* that he had spar'd me so long. I saw that I had *destroy'd myself*; And if I was the next Moment sent down to *Hell*, I could *justify* the Righteousness and Holiness of God therein. That Word was much to me upon this Account: *The LORD is righteous in all his Ways, and holy in all his Works*, Psa. cxlv. 17. Aye, thought I, he will be so, in *my Condemnation*, "if I am *punish'd with everlasting Destruction from the Presence of the Lord, and from the Glory of his Power*: His Righteousness and Holiness will shine forth herein." So that I had nothing to plead upon the Foot of *Justice*. But yet my Soul was mightily engaged, with the greatest Intenseness, to seek Life upon the Bottom of *Free Mercy*, and *Rich Grace* display'd in a crucify'd JESUS. Out of the *Depths* of Misery, I cry'd unto the *Depths* of Mercy: as the poor *Publican, God be merciful to me a Sinner!* And God's Design to exalt his Mercy, and glorify his Grace in saving lost Souls, did furnish me with Arguments to plead with him for the Display of these Riches in my Salvation, as the very Chief of Sinners. I thought if *I was sav'd*, there would be "ne're another such an Instance of "Grace in Heaven." And thus I have pleaded with God, That he would display the Riches of his Glory in saving *me*, to shew what a *God of Grace* he was; and what *Wonders* the exceeding Riches of Sovereign Grace, and Free Mercy could work for the most miserable.

Thus, as a poor, perishing Sinner, I waited at the Throne of Grace, with earnest *Longings*, and some *Hopes*, that Mercy wou'd bid me *live*. I saw that there was Grace enough in God to save me; and oft the Language of my Soul was like the Centurion's to Christ, concerning his Servant, *Say in a Word, and my Servant shall be healed*, Luke vii. 7. So have I said, speak but the *Word*, Lord, and my Soul shall be *saved*: Bid me *live*, and I shall *live* in thy Sight. I had Faith in Christ's *Ability* to save me. But oh, my Unbelief!

I question'd his *Willingness*. I was surrounded with a Crowd of Discouragements; which *forbid* my Soul crying after him. But so powerfully did the Father *draw me to Christ*, by revealing his infinite Fulness, and Freeness to save, together with his exceeding Suitableness to my Case, and that there was yet Hope for *me*; that, tho' attended with Fears, I press'd thro' all Difficulties, and cast myself at the Foot of Free Grace in Christ; resolving, that if I did *perish*, it should be at *Mercy's Feet*.

But, before I proceed further, I wou'd just sum up the *Effects of this Work* of the Holy Ghost upon my Soul. And by *this*, he took me off from old *Adam's* Bottom, of Self-Dependence, and doing for Life. By *this*, he laid all my Hopes of eternal Happiness, upon a new Foundation; even the Free Grace of God in Christ. By *this*, he made me low, and loathsome in my own Eyes; and Christ exceeding high, and precious in my Esteem. By *this*, he made me long for, and seek after Holiness as much as Happiness; yea, to esteem it an essential Part thereof. And, in a Word, by *this*, he made God in Christ, ALL to me; and every Thing else, *nothing*, in Comparison of Him. So that I could say, with the *Psalmist*, (in Respect of Desire, tho' not of Appropriation) *Whom have I in Heaven but Thee? and there is none upon Earth that I desire besides Thee*, Psa. lxxiii. 25.

In the next Place, I wou'd hint something of the *Means*, which the Lord was pleas'd to make Use of, in this Work upon my Heart. And the *Ministry of his Word*, was blest for increasing my Concern, and enlarging my Desires: tho' I found not that Soul-satisfying Consolation in it, which I thirsted after. I waited at Wisdom's Gate, with earnest Longings to find Christ. And every Lord's Day the Breathings of my Soul were wont to be, Oh, that this might be the Time wherein I might find JESUS! And the Manifestation of his Love to my poor Soul! And tho' I *found not him whom my Soul loved*, to the Satisfaction of my Desire; yet I did not give over *Seeking*, and my *Longings* were increas'd hereby.

Again, the *reading of God's Word*, was another Means which was greatly bless'd to my Soul, both for the Discovery of my Misery, and Revelation of the Remedy. The *Psalms of David*, and St. *Paul's Epistles* were very precious to me. I saw such a ravishing Beauty, and transcendent Excellency in CHRIST, that my Soul was ready to faint away with Desires after him, and I impatiently long'd for the Knowledge of Interest in him. Might I have had the whole *World* given me, Aye, *Thousands* of 'em, had there been so many, they wou'd all have been to *me* but empty, unsatisfying Trifles. I so long'd for *Christ*, that nothing but *himself* could satisfy me.

And if I had but HIM, I thought, I cou'd freely bear all the Miseries and Distresses which *his* can possibly be expos'd to in this present Time. Esteeming it a far happier State to *suffer Affliction with the People of God, than to enjoy the Pleasures of Sin for a Season*; or to be the greatest Monarch in the World that was Christless. The Spirit of the LORD did so *blow* upon all created Excellency, that made it *wither as the Grass*, or a *fading Flower* in my Sight; while the Glory of Christ was presented in its super-excellent Beauty, and Permanency; Which made HIM to *me the Chiefest of ten Thousand!* I saw such an inexpressible Glory in his *Person*, as well as in his *Salvation*, that HE was to *me, all Desires!* And the Thoughts of an everlasting Separation from HIM, as the Sum of all Perfection, and Fountain of Blessedness, wounded me to the Quick. Oh that Word, *Depart from me ye cursed*, &c. *Matt*. xxv. 41. How did it pierce my Heart! Oh what Abundance did I see, in that little Word, *Me, depart from ME!* Oh, thought I, if the Lord wou'd bid me depart from every Thing else, I cou'd *bear it*: But how shall I *endure it*, if I am bid to depart from HIM! I saw so much in CHRIST, that I judg'd none *happy*, but such who were *interested* in him; and none *miserable* but those *separated* from him. Yea, I saw, that an *Interest in him*, the Fountain of Blessedness, was enough to make *his* unspeakably blessed in the most afflicted Condition that could possibly befal them. This shone forth gloriously to me in those Words, *Psal.* cxliv. 15. *Happy is that People that is in such a Case: Yea, Happy is that People whose God is the LORD*. With *Heb*. xi. 37, 38. *They were stoned, they were sawn asunder, were tempted, were slain with the Sword: They wandred about in Sheep-skins, and in Goat-skins, being destitute, afflicted, tormented: Of whom the World was not worthy*, &c. The cxixth *Psalm* was also very precious to me. Oh how has my Soul breath'd out its Desires to God for Life and Holiness, in that *Psalm!* I saw such a Hatefulness in Sin, that made me loath it: And such an Excellency in Holiness, that made it exceeding desirable to me. Insomuch, that I once thought, "Well, if I must go to *Hell*: at last; I desire I may be *holy* here!" This, tho' I can hardly account for, I well remember. A Sense of the wonderful Goodness and Forbearance of God did at that Time mightily overpower my Heart. Which, together with the Suitableness of Holiness, to the new Nature wrought in my Soul, I judge to be the Reason thereof, And I can't but think, that there must be some *Hopes* that I should find Mercy at the Bottom of it also; which wound up my Heart to that Pitch of Love to God and Holiness: Altho' I was so far from *Assurance* of it, tho' I put it as a Question: As, suppose I should *not*, or if I should *not* find Mercy at last? desire I may be holy here!

And I may just mention a Temptation with which I was assaulted. When the Lord had shewn me the Plague of my own Heart, the Filthiness of all my best Performances, and wrought up my Soul into Hatred of Sin, and Love of Holiness: Satan set upon me thus, You would not sin against God for a World: Your "Prayers are Sin; therefore you should not pray." And he back'd his Temptation with this Word, the *Sacrifice* (or Prayer) *of the Wicked is an Abomination to the LORD, Prov.* xv. 8. By which I was struck down as with a Thunder-bolt, and fill'd with deep Distress. I had but this *one Way* of venting the Bitterness of my Soul: And if *this* was shut up, I knew not what to do: But it pleased the Lord to deliver me from the Power of this Temptation in a little Time, by shewing me, that it was my Duty to *pray*, and a great *Sin* to neglect it; and that tho' I could not pray *without Sin*, yet it was a *greater Sin* not to pray.

As for *Converse with Christian Friends*, I had not that Advantage: By Reason of a Temptation, which I mostly lay under, "That I should prove but a Hypocrite, that my Concern wou'd wear off, as my former Convictions had done, and that I should return again to Folly; and therefore it was better to say nothing." I accordingly endeavour'd to conceal my Trouble; but it was too *great* to be hid from my dear Parents. I could never *read* in the Family, but my *deep Concern* was very visible, altho' I strove to refrain Tears. And I remember, that one Time in particular, my dear Father, observing the same, took Occasion to speak to me about my Soul, and wou'd fain have known how it was with me. And tho' I long'd to tell him of my Misery, and bewail my undone Estate, yet lying under the above-mention'd Temptaion, I could say nothing, but only broke out into a Passion of Tears.

The Concern of my Soul, now, was exceeding *great*, to what I had ever before been acquainted with; and was attended with this *Difference*: In all my former Convictions, I was *glad* to get my Trouble off, and Ease of Conscience as soon as possible. But now I *dreaded* nothing more than that my Concern should wear off, without a saving Conversion to Christ, and the Lord himself, speaking Life and Comfort to my Soul. I knew, that if I was left in a State of Unbelief, to find Ease and Rest any where else, than in the Bosom of Christ, I must perish for ever; and therefore had a great *Dread* of carnal Security. I was desirous to be wounded to the Quick, to be search'd to the Bottom, and to endure the Pain of my Wounds, 'till Christ's own

Hand should heal me. And the Knowledge I had, that it was God's usual Way, first to *kill*, and then to make *alive*; was of great Use to me, and afforded me some Hopes, that the present Death and Distress I was under, might be but in Order to my joy and Life for evermore. And therefore I fear'd the least Interval of Distress, if not upon a right Foundation. That Word was very terrible to me at such Seasons, *My Spirit shall not always strive with Man, Gen.* vi. 3. Oh! thought I, now I am a going to be given up to a hard Heart, and left to perish in a State of Alienation from Christ! Not that I thought the holy Spirit would ever farsake that Soul, where he had begun his *saving Work*: But I fear'd that what I felt should rise no higher than his *common Operations*: Which, how great soever, do always leave the Soul short of Saving Faith in Christ: And it was his *special Operations* herein which I long'd for. There was, I remember, an Expression dropp'd in Company, where I was, that did very much affect me: It was this, "the least Dram of *Saving Grace* will land a Soul safe in Glory, when they which have Abundance of *common Grace* may go to Hell with it.' And, oh, how I long'd for one Dram of this *Saving Grace!*

Another Means, the Lord was pleas'd to make Use of, was a Book that was cast into my Hands, which treated of the Happiness and Glory of the Saints in Heaven; as it consists in a perfect Enjoyment of God, and Conformity to him: (its Author I know not, the Title-Page being rent out) This Book was greatly blest to my Soul, to give me to see more of, and long more earnestly for the transcendent Happiness of God's People.

Mr. *Shepherd's Penitential Cries* were also of great Use to me. Oh, how has my Soul breath'd out its Desires to God, in some of those Hymns! And particularly that for Communion with God! And tho' I could not say, my God, and my Christ: Yet I saw such a ravishing Glory in him, that made me thirst after the Knowledge of Interest. And oh, how blessed did I see those to be, who cou'd use that appropriating Word, *my* CHRIST! That my impatient Longings for Christ may be discern'd, I shall transcribe the Hymn: And my Soul was in it.

I.

ALas, my God, that we should be
    Such Strangers to each other!
O that as Friends we might agree,
    And walk, and talk together!
Thou know'st my Soul does dearly love
    The Place of thine Abode:

No Musick drops so sweet a Sound,
　　As these two Words *My God*.

II.

I long not for the Fruit that grows
　　Within these Gardens here;
I find no Sweetness in their Rose
　　When Jesus is not near:
Thy gracious Presence, O my Christ,
　　Can make a Paradise;
Ah what are all the goodly Pearls
　　Unto this Pearl of Price!

III.

May I taste that Communion, Lord,
　　Thy People have with Thee?
Thy Spirit daily talks with them,
　　O let him talk with me!
Like *Enoch*, let me walk with God,
　　And thus walk out my Day,
Attended with the Heavenly *Guards,*
　　Upon the King's High-way.

IV.

When wilt thou come unto me, Lord?
　　O come, my Lord most dear;
Come near, come nearer, nearer still,
　　I'm well when thou art near.
When wilt thou come unto me, Lord?
　　I languish for thy Sight;
Ten Thousand Suns, if thou art strange,
　　Are Shades instead of Light.

V.

When wilt thou come unto me, Lord?
　　For till thou dost appear,
I count each Moment for a Day,
　　Each Minute for a Year:

Come, Lord, and never from me go,
  This World's a darksome Place:
I find no Pleasure here below,
  When thou dost vail thy Face.

VI.

There's no such Thing as Pleasure here,
  My Jesus is my All;
As thou dost shine, or disappear,
  My Pleasures rise or fall:
Come spread thy Savour on my Frame,
  No Sweetness is so sweet;
Till I get up to sing thy Name,
  Where all thy Singers meet.

These Verses, also, spoke my very Heart.

Those falsly call'd the Sweets of Sin,
  Are bitter unto me:
I loath the State that I am in,
  And long to come to Thee:
But oh! Wilt thou receive him now,
  That's coming to thy Door?
For I can bring no Dowry, Lord,
  I come extremely poor.

And indeed, most of those *Hymns*, the Lord made of Use to me. Thus I went on, one while in *Hopes*, another while in *Fears*, for about four Months: And no Satisfaction could I get of my Interest in the Lord Jesus.

At length, it pleased the Lord to visit me with a very dangerous Illness; the Fever, with Convulsions in the Nerves to a violent Degree: So that my Life was despair'd of. All Means us'd for my Recovery proving ineffectual, I was given up of Physicians, and judg'd by all that saw me to be very near Death. My *Body* was fill'd with exquisite Pain; but the Agonies of my *Soul*, were a much greater Distress. *Death* stared me in the Face. I thought myself just ready to lanch into a *vast Eternity*: and knew not *what* would become of my poor Soul. And now my Distress rose high indeed! The Waves and Billows of God's apprehended Wrath passed over me: *I sunk in deep Waters, where there was no standing.* Necessity was upon me, I must venture on Christ, or perish; Believe, or Die: And the Conflict of my Soul, between Faith and Unbelief, was exceeding great. Like a Man a Drowning, I catch'd at every Twig; I labour'd to take hold of the Promises, to keep me from sinking. But if I got a little Support one Moment, my innumerable Transgressions, as so many Weights, came pressing in upon me, and sunk me the Next. Oh here lay the Difficulty, to *believe for myself*, in the Face of so much *Sin and Guilt!* The Avenger of Blood was at my *Heels*; Christ Jesus, the Hope of Sinners, was in my *View*: My Soul was fleeing for *Refuge*, to lay hold thereon: But oh the Weights which hung about me, did much hinder my *Motion*, the *Speediness* of my Flight! My Friends labour'd to comfort me: But I have oft thought this Verse very expressive of my Case, at that Time:

> Kind was the Pity of my Friends,
>   But could not ease my Smart:
> Their Words indeed did reach my Case,
>   But could not reach my Heart.

Nature conflicted with the Disease some Days, until being quite spent, I was brought, in all Appearance, unto the Point of Death. My Parents being put out of the Room, that they might not see me depart: I could not speak, but had my Senses perfectly.

And now, Behold, the Time of my *Extremity*, was GOD's *Opportunity!* HE *made the Storm a Calm, and brought me to my desir'd Haven!* I had Faith given me in that Word, *John* vi. 37. *Him that cometh unto me, I will in no Wise cast out.* And oh, the infinite Grace, and Faithfulness, I saw in it! Now I could believe for *muself* in the Face of ten Thousand Discouragements! I came to Christ, just as I was, a guilty, filthy, undone Sinner: Christ receiv'd me: I trusted my Soul with him, believing, that in infinite Grace and Faithfulness, he would in no Wise cast *me* out! Thus I was enabled to take God at his Word; and set to my Seal that he is true.

This was a wonderful Effect of omnipotent Power, and irresistible Grace; which the Power of Unbelief was not able to withstand! Nothing less than the *exceeding Greatness of God's Power*, could have rais'd up my Soul, from those Depths of unbelieving *Fears*, to *Faith in Jesus!* 'Twas nothing less than an *Almighty Voice*, that with one Word of Free-Grace, could create *Peace* in my troubled Soul, and cause both Winds and Waves to be *still!*

Now the Day began to dawn, glorious Light, even the Light of Life sprang in: And Death and Darkness fled before it! Now I could look upon the near Approach of my Dissolution with *Comfort*, and take *Pleasure* in the Views of Eternity. Oh, thought I, before another Hour, I shall be safe landed in Glory! And had I died then, I am well satisfied, that my Soul had been exceeding safe in the Arms of Christ.

But lo! My Wonder-working God, not only wrought Wonders for my *Soul*, but for my *Body* also. An unthought of Means was propos'd to my Parents, who had given me up, and design'd to use no more. But however, being press'd to make another Experiment, they yielded. My Case was desperate, the Remedy was so: A very skilful, tho' a very prophane Person order'd it: I receiv'd the Potion; and it put Nature into a mighty Struggle for a Time: But the Lord bless'd it, and order'd its Operations for Life. My convuls'd Motions ceas'd, and I strangely reviv'd, and cou'd speak in a little Time.

But oh, the *Difference* in my Language! I before had made my *Complaint* in the Bitterness of my Soul. But now my Mouth was fill'd with *Praises*. Every Corner of my Soul being overflow'd with Love, Life and Peace! Oh the *Joy* of God's Salvation, which I now felt! It was indeed *Unspeakable, and full of Glory!* My Soul was got where it long desir'd to be; even into the *Bosom of Christ!* I was rais'd from the Gates of *Hell* to the Borders of *Heaven*. And the Depths I was rais'd from, made the Heights I was rais'd to, the more Amazing! I felt the *Rock* beneath me: And my Feet being securely fix'd upon *Christ*, I look'd with amazing Wonder, both upward and downward. Downward, to that *horrible Pit* I was deliver'd from; and Upward, to those *Heights of Glory*, I should be rais'd to. And oh, how I admir'd, and ador'd *distinguishing Grace!* Now I could bless the Lord, that ever I had a *Being*. And in the Joy of my Heart, break out thus: Oh *Why me! Why me*, when *Thousands* perish! How is it that I should be a *Vessel of Mercy*, that have deserv'd to have been a *Vessel of Wrath* for ever! That I should be sav'd by *Free Grace! What Manner of Love* is This, that has pluck'd *me* as a Brand out of the Burning; while *others* are pass'd by, and left to perish, as the due Desert of Sin! *Bless the* LORD, *O my Soul, and all that is within me, bless his Holy Name!* I saw, not only, that Christ would not *cast me out*: But that he *receiv'd me to the Glory of God*. And that the Joy of God's Favour, which now fill'd my Heart, was an *Earnest of*, and would *issue in* that Fulness of Joy, and those Rivers of Pleasures,

which are at his Right Hand for evermore. The following Verses of one of
Mr. *Mason's* Hymn's, were exceeding precious to my Soul at that Time.

> O, was I born first from Beneath!
>   And then born from Above!
> Am I a Child of Man or God?
>   O rich, and endless Love!
> Earth is my Mother, Earth my Nurse,
>   And Earth must be my Tomb:
> But God, the God of Heaven and Earth,
>   My Father is become.
> Hell entred me, and into Hell
>   I quickly should have run:
> But O! kind Heaven laid hold on me,
>   Heaven is in me begun.
> This Spark will rise into a Flame,
>   This Seed into a Tree;
> My Songs shall rise, my Praise shall
>   Loud Hallelujah's be.

And as I call'd upon my own Soul to bless the Lord, so upon all round
about me, with the *Psalmist, O bless the LORD with me, and let us exalt his
Name together!* Thus I began the Work of Praise, which I believ'd would
be my eternal Employment in Heaven. The Lord having *brought me up out
of an horrible Pit, and set my Feet upon a Rock, he put a new Song into my
Mouth*: And *many saw it*, and were *glad*. A few Days after this, I was so
well recover'd, as to be left alone in my Bed, (it being Market-Day): But,
surely, I may say, I was never less alone than at that Time.

The Blessed Spirit did, as it were, take me by the Hand, and led me to
take a *Survey* of CHRIST, in all the Steps of his Humiliation, from his Birth
to his Death, as the Man of Sorrows, and acquainted with Grief for *me!* He
led me to take a View of Christ on the Cross, in the Agonies of his Soul,
and Torments of his Body, as bearing *my* Sin, enduring *my* Hell, giving up
himself a Sacrifice in *my* Room and Stead: To redeem *me* from endless
Misery, to eternal Glory! I view'd all my Sins, meeting upon JESUS! And
saw him *wounded for my Transgressions, and bruised for mine Iniquities!*
And oh, the Infinity of Grace which I saw, both in the Father's, and Christ's
Heart, in this wonderful Contrivance of infinite Wisdom, to save me by a

crucify'd JESUS! In the finish'd Work of Redemption, I view'd my Salvation wrought out. And a Perfection of Peace, Pardon, Life and Glory, come flowing down to *me*, in the freest Grace, thro' the Blood of Christ!

And oh the *Power* of the Cross! The Display of boundless Grace herein, set my Soul a Burning! I *look'd*, and *lov'd!* yea, I *look'd*, and *mourn'd!* The Fire of divine Love, melted my Soul down, and made mine Eyes a Fountain of Tears! Now I *look'd on him whom I had pierced, and mourn'd indeed*: With the sweetest, and yet the bitterest Mourning that ever my Soul felt! The exceeding Riches of Grace, in the free, full, and eternal *Pardon* of all my Sins, thro' a Bleeding JESUS, fill'd my Soul with *unspeakable Joy and Sweetness!* And yet at the same Time, as I view'd my Sins against CHRIST, meeting upon *him*, piercing, and wounding of *him*, I was in such *Bitterness* for him, that I never before found! Oh, thought I, were *my Sins* the Whips and Nails! Did these cause his Agonies, wound his Soul, fill his bitter Cup; which, in infinite Love, he drank off for *me!* Oh *vile Worm* that I am! Oh *hateful Sin!* Thou art the most loathsome, abominable Thing in my Sight! It was *me* the dear Lord Jesus *lov'd!* And yet it was *I that pierc'd him!* And oh how this *pierc'd my Soul!* Thus I was in *Bitterness for* HIM. Which yet was very consistent with those *unspeakable Joys* of redeeming Love, which at the same Time fill'd my Heart. This was one of the sweetest Days I have enjoy'd in this World. And in a Word, the Manifestations of God's Love to my Soul, in this Affliction, were so *great*, that I have thought, I could freely endure the *same Agonies* again, if I might have the *same Comforts*. It was the Time of my Espousals, and the Day of the Gladness of my Heart. But to go on.

The Lord rais'd me up from a *Sick-Bed*, From *Death to Life*, both in Soul and Body. I was as it were brought forth into a *new* World: All Things appear'd *new* to me. I convers'd with *new Objects*; or rather, in a *new Manner*, with the same glorious Objects, I had some Glimmerings of before. I felt *new* Affections, Desires, Delights, &c. I found my self deliver'd from *Mount Sinai*; and brought to *Mount Sion: The City of the living God, the heavenly Jerusalem, and to an innumerable Company of Angels, to the general Assembly and Church of the First-born which are written in Heaven, and to God the Judge of all. And to Jesus the Mediator of the New Covenant, and to the Blood of sprinkling, that speaketh better Things than the Blood of Abel*, Heb. xii. 22, &c. *Religions Duties*, were now very *precious* to me: Such as Hearing, Reading, Praying, Meditation, and Converse with Christians: And much of *God* I enjoy'd in them. The *Saints* were now my *own* Company: I esteem'd them, the Excellent of the Earth, in whom was all my Delight. *Lord's Days*, were the *Joy* of my Heart, *Sabbaths* indeed to me. And the Soul-rest by Faith, which I enjoy'd thereon, receiv'd an additional Sweetness, as I view'd it an *Earnest* of my etenal Rest in the Bosom of Christ. In short, my *Conversation was in Heaven*; and the World, Sin, and Satan *under my Feet*. And I was ready to think I should *always* live so: The Sin of my Nature, being at this Time, so mightily borne down, by those full Tides of Love and Life which overflow'd my Heart. But alas! I soon found that I was not got out of the *Reach* of my spiritual Enemies.

As I was engag'd in Meditation, on my dear Lord Jesus, a vile Thought darted into my Mind; which struck me with a strange Surprize. And I was straightway assaulted with a violent Temptation, "That all the Experience I had had of the Lord's loving Kindness, was but mere Delusion." Those Words came thundering in upon me, with amazing Terror, *2 Thess.* ii. 11, 12. *God shall send them strong Delussion, that they should believe a Lie: That they all might be damned.* And thus Satan apply'd them: "That I had even weary'd God with my incessant Prayers; and that therefore he had given me up to this strong Delusion, to believe my Safety in Christ, which was indeed but a Lie: That so I might be damned, and go to Hell quietly." And the vile Thought above-mention'd, he call'd in as a Witness of my being still in a State of Sin, But oh, the Soul-Distress I was then in! I had been rejoicing in CHRIST, *as mine*. But oh, a Thought of being *deceived!* and that my very Comfort was but a *Delusion*, sent on Purpose that I might go to *Hell securely!* what Agony and Torment did it put my Soul into! I was as it were snatch'd from the Bosom of Christ, and plung'd into the Belly of Hell. And alas, I knew not what to say to Satan, nor how to defend myself. This Thought that pass'd thro' my Heart, was unexpected to me; and I knew not how to reconcile it with my being in a State of Grace.

But in my Distress, I ran to God, and shewed before him all my Trouble. I pour'd out my Complaint into his Bosom: And he was graciously pleas'd to sent me an Answer of Peace immediately. Before I got off my Knees, the 7th Chapter to the *Romans*, from the 15th Verse, was brought to my Mind with great Light and Glory. Oh then it was, that the Lord the Spirit, did first open to *me*, the Mystery of *Sin* and *Grace*, the *New* and *Old Nature*, both dwelling together in my poor Soul. And that I must expect a *Conflict*, and had no Reason to question his *Work* upon my Heart, because I found such *Contrarieties* thereto working in me. The Experience of the great Apostle, did also give me a mighty Lift: Where he says, *That which I do I allow not; for what I would, that do I not; but what I hate, that do I. Now if I do what I would not, it is no more I that do it, but Sin that dwelleth in me*, &c. And having, with him, groan'd out my own Wretchedness, by Reason of an indwelling Body of Sin and Death: I was made, in believing Views of Deliverance, to give *Thanks to God, thro' Christ Jesus my Lord.* And to conclude, as he doth, *So then with the Mind I myself serve the Law of God, but with the Flesh the Law of Sin.* Thus the Lord gave me the Victory at this Time: And the Instructions I then receiv'd, have been of Use to my Soul ever since.

Quickly after this, I was assaulted with blasphemous Thoughts; attended with a strong Impulse to utter them: Which put my Soul to Pain. But blessed be my God, this lasted but a little while: He rebuk'd the Devourer, enabled me to run into Christ my Refuge; and there I found Peace and Safety. I was also tempted to question the Being of GOD; which was very distressing while it lasted. But thro' Grace I was soon deliver'd. And many were the Combats I had with Satan and Unbelief, about my Interest in the Lord Jesus. And when I knew not what to think, whether I was a Believer, or not: I have many Times been help'd to come to Christ, as a poor Sinner, just as I came at first. Being sweetly drawn by the indefinite Promises of the Gospel, to venture on Christ afresh, to cast myself into his Arms, to come to him with all my Weights and Burdens: And in his Bosom, I always found Rest.

I remember, once, as I was attempting to come to Christ, weary and heavy laden, that Word was again brought to my Mind with great Power and Sweetness, *Him that cometh unto me, I will in no wise cast out*, John vi. 37. So that I was fill'd with exceeding Gladness in the Views of my Safety in Christ's Arms. But presently Satan came in with a Temptation, thus: "You come to Christ as a *poor Sinner*, and think he'll receive you as *such*: But he receives none but such that are *given him* of his Father: And if you are not one of *those*, your coming to Christ will signify *nothing*; you'll be *cast out* notwithstanding: It's those whom his Father has *given him*, that he'll in *no wise cast out*." But oh, the Pain and Distress this cast my Soul into! Now I knew not what to do!

But however, I ran immediately to God, and told him how I had been robb'd and spoil'd of my Comfort: And pray'd him to give me some other Word of Promise, or else to bring the same again, with such mighty Power, that nothing might be able to take away my Joy of Faith in it. And his Ear being open to my Cry, he presently gave me an Answer to my Request. The same Word was brought again, with such Power, Light, and Glory, that made Satan and Unbelief, fly before it. *All that the Father giveth me, shall come to me*: Here I saw, that the Father's *Gift* of any Soul to Christ, was antecedent to its *coming* to him: And also, that it did *secure* its coming: That all the given Ones *shall come*, under the Father's Drawings; and that none but they, *could come*: And then, from the latter Part of the Words, I saw, that *so coming*, I should *in no wise be cast out*. But oh, the glorious Light that now filled my Heart! I saw, with amazing Wonder, that eternal Security I had, both in the Father's and Christ's Hands! I view'd my Standing in the Father's Grace, as a given One to Christ: And that it was nothing less than the almighty Power of his own Arm, that drew my Soul to Jesus! And that being thus brought by the Father to Christ, he would keep me safe for ever! Thus the Lord brought me out of Darkness, and the Shadow of Death, and brake my Bands in sunder.

But what shall I say? Many were the Temptations, and Soul-plunges, which at Times I met with: But out of them all the Lord deliver'd me. And for the most Part, I walk'd comfortably on, in the Light of God's Countenance.

As a *New-born Babe*, I earnestly *desir'd the sincere Milk of the Word*; and was often laid to the Promise-Breast. My dear Lord Jesus, was very familiar to me then: And I could not bear to live without sensible Communion with him daily. The least Degree of Absence was very grievous to me. And I was never at Rest till he open'd his Heart, and let me into his Boson again. I remember I was once so pained for the Discoveries of Christ's Love, that I thought, if he did not speedily manifest himself to me, I could not live. And being ready to faint and die under Absence, (tho' it was but for a little Space neither) I breath'd out my Desires in the following Lines of Mr. *Mason*'s Paraphrase on Song viii. 6.

Love me, my Lord, or else I die!
　　Thee, Lord, my Love doth crave!
If thou shouldst but my Love deny,
　　My Love would be my Grave.
None but a Christ, none but my Lord,
　　No Bribes can take with me;
A proffer'd World would be abhorr'd;
　　A Christ, and none but he!

And it was but a little while ere the Lord brake in with glorious Light, in that Word, *John* xiv. 1. *I will come again, and receive you to myself, that where I am, there ye may be also.* I had been just before thinking of the unspeakable Happiness of the Saints at Home with Christ, in that they were ever present with the Lord. And oh how suitable was this Word to me, while Mourning under Absence! My dear Lord open'd his Heart to me herein, and told me, that 'twould be but a little while ere he would receive me to himself, that where he was, I might be also: And that then I should be everlastingly fill'd, with the Enjoyment of him whom my Soul loved. But oh, how I rejoyc'd in my happy Lot, *To be for ever with him!* Thus my Communion with Christ began. And that Evening, I had such Discoveries of his Love to my Soul; and of that eternal Glory he had prepar'd for me; which fill'd me with Joy unspeakable: And I thought, *Eternity* little enough to praise him for that Visit. Oh the realizing Views, and sweet Fore-Tastes, I then had of the good Land!

But alas, all this while, *Babe-like*, I rather liv'd upon *Promises* given in, than upon CHRIST in them. I knew not how to *believe* without *Sight*. So long as *God's Love* flow'd into my Soul, and *my Love* flow'd out to him again, under the Attraction of his first Love: Just so long I could *believe*. But when the sweet *Sensation* abated, my *Faith* began to sink with it. But my kind Lord, always brought me some Cordial or other, to support me in my fainting Fits. After this Manner I was carried on for a Year, or little more (as near as I can remember) before the Lord brought me to some *Stability*, and *Strength of Faith* in the Dark.

Thus I have given a brief, tho' a broken Account, of the Work of divine Grace upon my Heart, in a saving Conversion to Christ. The Glory of it is much marr'd by the Shortness of my Memory. But however, I may sum up what I have said, in the Words of the Psalmist, *Psal.* xl. 1. *I waited patiently for the LORD, and he inclined unto me, and heard my Cry. He brought me up also out of an horrible Pit, out of the miry Clay, and set my Feet upon a Rock.* He likewise, after this, was graciously pleas'd to *establish my Goings.* Which brings me to give a few Hints,

Thirdly, of my being brought to some Establishment in CHRIST. And by the Word of the Gospel was I nourish'd up in Faith, and my new-born Soul strengthened. It pleased the Lord, in the Fifteenth Year of my Age, to incline my Heart to join with a Church of Christ, in *N---n*, over which the late Mr. *H---t* was Pastor. Under his Ministry, I was often laid to the Breasts of Consolation, and being fed with the Milk of the Word, which was suited to my present State, I grew thereby. In this House of the Lord, I oft sought for, and found my Beloved, both in his more general, and special Ordinances. So that, from precious Experience of the Lord's Loving Kindness in *Sion*, I could say with the *Psalmist, A Day in thy Courts, is better than a Thousand: I had rather be a Door-keeper in the House of my God, than to dwell in the Tents of Wickedness*, Psa. lxxxiv. 10. The Sight of God's Power and Glory in the Sanctuary, was precious to my Soul, and Fellowship with the Saints sweet. But yet, as I hinted before, I too much liv'd upon *Enjoyments*, and took up *God's Love to me*, as to the steady Persuasion of it, in the Light of my own *Sanctification*. I delighted to have my Interest in Christ *try'd*, by all the Marks and Signs of a Believer, which were continually laid down in the Ministry. When I could *find 'em*, my Heart was fill'd with Joy; but if there were any I did not *clearly discern*, I sunk in Sorrow. I was willing to have my Faith in the Promise *try'd* by the Fruits and Effects of it in my Heart and Life. And so childish was I, that I look'd for the *Effects of Faith*, when *Faith was not in Exercise*. Which is just as if a Person should look for the Beauty of the Spring in the Autumn-Season: Or seek to know what o'Clock 'tis by the Dial, when the Sun don't shine on't. And while I went this Way to work, I never attain'd *settled Assurance*. No, the Soul that enters into this Rest, by Faith, must have somewhat more stable than fleeting Frames to lean on. To go on then:

Such was the wonderful Kindness of my God, that *after I believed, I was sealed with the Holy Spirit of Promise*. It pleas'd the Lord to take me by the Arms, and teach me to go in the Way of Faith, when I had not spiritual Sense. I had been once, I remember, at a Meeting of *Prayer*, but not meeting with *God* in it, I return'd very sad. And as I was lamenting my Case, that Word was brought to my Mind, *Phil.* iv. 4. *Rejoice in the Lord always: And again I say rejoyce.* But my Heart straightway reply'd, "I have not enjoy'd God to Night, and how can I rejoyce?" Then the Word brake in again upon my Heart, with such a Ray of glorious Light, that directed my Soul to the true and proper Object of its Joy, even the Lord himself. I was pointed hereto, as with a Finger: In the *Lord*, not in your *Frames. In* the Lord, not in what you enjoy *from* him, but in what you are *in* him. And the Lord seal'd my Instruction, and fill'd my Heart brim-full of Joy, in the Faith of my eternal Interest, and unchangeable Standing in *him*; and of *his* being an infinite Fountain of Blessedness, for me to rejoice in alway; even when the Streams of sensible Enjoyments fail'd. Thus the Blessed Spirit took me by the Arms, and taught me to go. And from this Time I began to venture to foot it by *Faith*, when I had not the Prop of Spiritual *Sense* to lean on.

But yet I was attended with much Weakness, and oft ready to stagger thro' *Unbelief*. And at such Seasons I was for putting forth my Hand to lay hold on *past Experiences*. The Remembrance of which at Times has been precious to my Soul. But when I sought for my Satisfactions from *hence*, instead of deriving all my Life and Comfort from *Christ*, by fresh Acts of Faith; the Lord, in great Mercy, was pleas'd to draw a *Vail* over his Work upon my Soul; and direct me to stay myself upon *my God*, even when I *walk'd in the Dark* as to present Enjoyments, and had not the *Light* of past Experience. And this was to make me die unto a Life of Sense, in order to raise me up to an higher Life of Faith upon the Son of God.

And to this End, the Lord the Spirit went on to reveal CHRIST more and more to me, as the great Foundation of my Faith and Joy. He shew'd me my everlasting Standing in his Person, Grace and Righteousness: And gave me to see my Security in his Unchangeableness, under all the Changes which pass'd over me. And then I began to rejoice in my dear Lord Jesus, as always the *same*, even when my Frames *alter'd*. And further, my Heart was directed into the everlasting Love of the Father, and the Immutability of his eternal Counsels and Covenant about my Salvation, as the Ground of my strong Consolation, under all the Mutations I felt in my own Soul. That Word was very precious to me, *Heb*. vi. 17, 18. *Wherein God willing more abundantly to shew unto the Heirs of Promise the Immutability of his Counsel, confirm'd it by an Oath: That by two immutable Things, in which it was impossible for God to lie, we might have a strong Consolation*, &c. Oh the Grace and Faithfulness of God, which I saw in it! The Holy Ghost took the Word in Pieces, and led me into every Part of it, and likewise confirm'd it by other Scriptures. Thus the Lord began to establish me, and settle my Faith upon its solid Basis. And when I have been shaken by the Winds of Temptation, so that I was almost ready to be driven away; that Word was brought with great Power, *Gal*. v. 1. *Stand fast therefore in the Liberty wherewith Christ hath made you free*. By which the Lord strengthened me to keep my standing, by *Faith*, where *Free-Grace* had set me. About this Time also, the Lord was pleased mightily to impress upon my Heart, the great Duty of *taking God at his Word*, in the Declarations of his Grace in his Son; and likewise of *crediting* the Holy Ghost's Testimony of my Soul in the Word of Promise: By Means of which, I was enabled to resist the Temptations I met with to cast away my Confidence.

I have likewise experienced, when assaulted by Satan and Unbelief, that by an *immediate Flight to Christ*, I have got the *Victory* many a Time. I found it a vain Thing to stand disputing with these Enemies about my past Experience. And being, in some good Measure inured to a Life of Faith, I hasted away to Christ upon the first Assault. And have often found, that a *direct Act of Faith*, or a fresh Venture on Christ, has been attended with a *reflex Act*, or a full Persuasion of my eternal Safety in him, as having fled for Refuge to lay hold on this Hope set before me. For I saw it my Duty, not only to *obey the Command of God*, in believing on the Name of his Son Jesus Christ, but also to *take him at his Word*, as to my having eternal Life in him as such. As instance or two of my Experience in this Kind I may just mention.

I was once rejoycing in the Lord, and in the wondrous Blessings which surrounded me in him; and Satan came boldly in upon me, and told me, "That I was rejoycing in that which was none of mine: And urg'd it, that I was not a Believer." Upon which I stood not to *dispute* with him, about my past Acts of Faith, as I had too often done, but answer'd him thus: "Well, if I never have believ'd yet, it's Time for me to do it now." And immediately I attempted a fresh Act of Faith. I queried with myself thus: How is it with me now at this very Moment? Do I see myself, in myself, to be a lost perishing Sinner? Do I see Christ to be a full, free, mighty Saviour? And is it the Command of God, that I should believe on him whom he hath sent? Then let me venture on him for myself. And that Word came in, *John* vi. 47. *Verily verily I say unto you, he that believeth on me hath everlasting Life.* I saw that believing, was venturing, casting, trusting my Soul in the Hands of Jesus. And while I attempted to commit myself to him, I felt Power enabling me to cast myself, as an undone Sinner, in myself, for all Salvation, into the Arms of Christ, as the Mighty Saviour of God's providing. And upon this *direct Act of Faith*, I attempted a *reflex Act*, or a Believing that I then had everlasting Life in him, taking up my Persuasion hereof upon the infinite Truth and Faithfulness of Christ's Word. And strong was my Consolation, while I believed Christ's *Verily verily*, &c. The Words were thus open'd to me: *Verily verily*; a double Asseveration, giving the highest Assurance of the Thing to which it is annexed. *I say unto you*: I, that know both mine and my Father's Heart, Counsels, and Designs about the Salvation of Sinners; I that am Truth itself, and cannot lie or be unfaithful; *I say unto you, he that believeth on me hath everlasting Life*. He *hath it*, in the *Right* of it, as mine and my Father's Grant. He hath it *really*, let Sin and Satan say what they will to contradict it. He hath it *irreversibly, unalterably*; and none of the Powers of Darkness can hinder it. But oh, the Triumph of Faith I then broke forth into! *My Soul did tread down Strength.* Yea, the Enemies were forc'd to flee, they could not stand before the Grace and Faithfulness of Christ in his Word, held up by Faith.

Again, another Soul-plunge I was in; in which I sought to stay myself upon Christ, in some Promise or other, tho' most of them were then veil'd. But in a little Time that Word was brought to my Mind, *Isa.* xlv. 22. *Look unto me, and be ye saved, all the Ends of the Earth.* I saw the Words contain'd, first, a divine Command, *Look unto me*; and that this extended itself to *all the Ends of the Earth*; to Sinners at the greatest Distance. In Obedience to which, my Soul attempted a *direct Act of Faith*, or an immediate Look to Christ, as the only Saviour of the Chief of Sinners. And upon this direct Act, I straightway attempted a *reflex Act*, or a taking of Christ at his Word, as to my Salvation in Looking. I saw, that as the first Clause of the Words, *Look unto me*; contain'd a divine Command of *Faith*, so the next, *be ye saved*; a glorious Grant of *Salvation* to every Believer. And that it was as much my Duty to *believe* the Grace and Faithfulness of Christ in the one, as to *obey* him in the other. And being enabled so to do, I durst no more question my *Salvation*, than the *Faithfulness* of him that promis'd it. That Word also was brought to my Mind, *Isa.* xlix. 6. *That thou mayst be my Salvation unto the End of the Earth.* From whence I saw, that as Christ was lifted up as the *Father's Salvation* for poor lost Sinners, even to the End of the Earth; it was as impossible for *me to perish*, looking to him as such, as for *God himself to be Unfaithful.* Thus *believing*, I enter'd into *Rest*. And oft have found, that by the Light which sprang into my Soul, thro' *fresh Acts of Faith*, I could see to read my *past Experiences* with Comfort.

This I was willing to mention, that the dear Saints might be encourag'd hereby, if the Lord please, to go forward by fresh Acts of Faith, walking on in Christ as they have received him. And I dare say, that any Child of God may sooner arrive to Satisfaction of his Interest in Christ, by a fresh Act of Faith, than by looking back upon his past Experience in the Dark. It's the Appointment of God, that *the Just should live by his Faith*, Hab ii. 4. And one direct Act of Faith on Christ, or a fresh Look to Jesus, will bring more Light and Comfort to a distressed Soul, than a thousand Looks into itself, when the Spirit of God don't shine upon his own Work. Especially, if the Soul makes Conscience of taking God at his Word, as to its having eternal

Life, in believing on his Son. And it's a dreadful Thing to *make God a Liar*. We are all of us too much unacquainted with the abominable Nature of *Unbelief*, as it gives the *Lie* to infinite Faithfulness. Oh this easily-besetting Sin, under what specious Pretences doth it hide itself! Many of God's dear Children, dare not for their Lives, look any where else than to Christ alone, for *Salvation*; and yet are afraid that they shall not be *saved*. What's the Matter? Why, they do not *credit* the faithful God for themselves, in this Declaration of his Grace, that *whosoever believeth on Christ, shall not perish, but have everlasting Life*, John iii. 16.

But perhaps some poor Soul may say, I don't question the Salvation of *Believers*; but I am afraid that *I do not believe*. Why, *believing*, is the Soul's *looking* to Christ for Life, as the only Saviour of God's providing, lifted up in the Gospel. This was typ'd out by the Israelites *looking* to the Serpent of Brass in the Wilderness. And canst thou *look to Christ*, Soul? thou'lt *live. It came to pass when a Serpent had bitten any Man, that when he looked to the Serpent of Brass, he lived*, Numb. xxi. 9. And it's *the Father's Will, that hath sent Christ, that whosoever seeth the Son, and believeth on him, should have everlasting Life*, John vi. 40. Christ says, *look unto me*: He bids thee *look*, poor Soul, to HIM for Life, as a perishing Sinner. In Obedience then to his Command, cast up an Eye to JESUS, as the great Ordinance of God for Salvation. And immediately hereupon, take Christ at his Word; he says, *be ye saved*. Canst thou *believe it*, Soul? Thou must either believe that thou *shalt be saved*, in looking to Christ, or give him the *Lie*. Oh then, learn to *believe thy Salvation* upon Christ's *naked Word*: And stay not to see the *Effects* of Faith in thy Heart and Life, before thou wilt *credit* the Word of Christ, and the Testimony of his Spirit therein. For tho' *saving Faith*, is always attended with its *Fruits*; yet it's not the *Fruit* of thy Faith, but the *Faithfulness* of Christ in the Word, that ought to be the *first*, and *principal* Ground of thy Persuasion of Life and Safety in him. And if thou art help'd to believe thy Salvation, in looking to Christ, merely because HE hath said it, thou wilt soon find the blessed Effects thereof in thy Soul. Let but *Faith* look to Christ, and Salvation in him, and *Love* will straightway be upon the Flow; and *every Grace of the Spirit*, will be answerably exercised. Which in the Holy Ghost's Light, will become a *subordinate* Evidence, and serve to *corroborate* thy Faith: But put not that *first*, which ought to be *second*. The Grace and Faithfulness of Christ in his Word, is a *firm Basis* for thy Faith to rest on, amidst the greatest *Shakings*. *Hath* HE *said, and shall he not do it? Or hath* HE *spoken, and shall he not make it good?* Numb. xxiii.

19. Infinite Faithfulness must *fail*, before thou that look'st to Christ for Life, and tak'st him at his Word, canst *perish*. The Rock of Ages must *sink* beneath thee, before thou that art built thereon canst be *lost*. Go on therefore to honour Christ, by *looking* to him daily, and *believing* thy Salvation steadfastly in the Face of ten thousand Difficulties, and seeming Contradictions. 'Tis the *Excellency* of Faith, to *believe without Sight*, John xx. 29. *Abraham consider'd not his own Body now Dead, nor yet the Deadness of Sarah's Womb, He stagger'd not at the Promise of God thro' Unbeleif, but was strong in Faith, giving Glory to God: Being fully persuaded that what he had promis'd, he was able also to perform*, Rom. iv. 19, 20, 21. And *Abraham's* Children are call'd to exercise Faith in the same Way; *believing in Hope, even against Hope*, or in the Face of the greatest Improbabilities. Therefore let us *not cast away our Confidence, which hath great Recompence of Reward*. But to return from this Digression.

The Lord having brought me to some Stability and Rest of *Faith*, upon the Rock of Immutability, when I had not Frames to lean on, he was graciously pleas'd to make my Joy full, by casting in a rich Overplus of spiritual *Sense*. And tho' I now did not take up my Faith of Interest, principally from *Frames*; yet I had abundant *Experience* of the rich Overflowings of God's Love upon my Soul, and of the blessed Fruits of it in my Heart and Life. The Holy Ghost open'd to me such glorious Views of all that vast *Grace* wherein I stood, gave me to see my everlasting *Standing* in it, and to have frequent *Access* into it. I was indeed led into *green Pastures*, and made to *lie down*. The Doctrines of the everlasting Gospel were daily opened to me in their amazing Glory; every of which was a pleasant Pasture for me to feed in. And oh, how *my Heart burn'd within me*, while my dear Lord *opened to me the Scriptures*, in their Glory and Consistency! Now one was open'd to me, then another, and oft-times many, to explain one. Delightfully I view'd over the Wonders of infinite Grace display'd therein, and feasted upon all, as my own, as having an entire, and eternal Interest in the God of all Grace, and in all the glorious Provisions of his Grace, for the Salvation of Sinners thro' Jesus Christ. Thus kindly the Lord dealt with me, when *he stablished me in Christ, anointed me with the Oil of Gladness, seal'd me with the Holy Spirit of Promise, and gave him into my Heart, as an Earnest of the Inheritance of the Saints in Light!*

And in vain do the Enemies of the Grace of God, malign it with their old odious Calumny, *That it leads to Licentiousness*. For so long as God has a *People* in the World, he will have *Witnesses* to stand on the Side of *Free-*

Grace, as it constrains to *Holiness*. And among them, I'll cast in my Mite, and bear my Witness for *God*: That the more his glorious *Grace*, in my *Salvation*, did *appear* to my Soul, the more was I efficaciously taught to *deny Ungodliness and worldly Lusts, and to live soberly, righteously, and godly in this present World; looking for that blessed Hope, and the glorious Appearing of the great GOD, and our* SAVIOUR *Jesus Christ: Who gave himself for us, that he might redeem us from all Iniquity, and purify unto himself a peculiar People, zealous of good Works*, Tit. ii. 11, &c.

Thus, as enabled, have I given some Account of the Lord's loving Kindness to my Soul: In a few brief Hints, of my Manner of Life from my Childhood: Of the Work of Divine Grace upon my Heart, in a saving Conversion to CHRIST, and of my being brought to some Establishment in HIM. And now I come to the last Thing propos'd, which was,

Fourthly, Somewhat by Way of Reflection. And,

1*st*, To the People of God, under two Ranks.

1. To such of the Saints, who have a comfortable *Knowledge* of the Work of Grace in their Souls, I would say with the Psalmist, *O magnify the Lord with me, and let us exalt his Name together. I sought the Lord, and he heard me, and delivered me from all my Fears*, Psalm xxxiv. 3, 4. You have heard something of the Lord's loving Kindness to my Soul: *Glorify God in me*, Gal. i. 24.

2. To such of God's People, that have not, as yet, a full *Persuasion* of a special Work of Grace in their Hearts. You also have heard what the Lord has done for *me*; and I know you are apt to listen how it has been with *others*, which you judge are *Believers*; and to compare *your Experience* with *theirs*; in order to form a *Judgment*, whether the *Work of God* upon your own Souls be indeed *saving*. But, dear Hearts, be not too *critical* herein; for the Experience of the Saints, in many Particulars may *vary*, tho' in the general it *agrees*. Don't say then, upon reading this Narrative, "I have not been in all Respects thus: And therefore I fear I am not right." Hast thou (whoever thou art, that hast these Thoughts) been convinced of the Misery of thy natural State, that thou wast in a perishing Condition without Christ? And hast thou had a Discovery of Christ's Beauty, Excellency, and Suitableness to thee, in all thy Wants: So as to draw out thy Soul into earnest Desires after an Interest in this precious JESUS? And under a deep Sense of thy perishing Condition, hast thou been encouraged by God's Free Grace in Christ, to cast thyself at his Feet, to find Mercy: To commit thyself into the Arms of his Grace and Power, for all Life, and Salvation: with an

holy Venture, saying, as *Esther*, "*I will go in unto the King; and if I perish, I perish*. I see there is no other Way of Salvation: Here therefore I'll wait as an undone Sinner; it may be Free-Grace will *save me*; but if *not*, I can but *die*: And if I perish, it shall be at the *Feet of God's Free Mercy in Christ*." Hast thou, I say, at any Time experienc'd such Resolutions wrought in thy Soul? Thou art then exceeding *safe*, and thy *State* eternally secure: Tho' thou mayst not have so much *Comfort* in it, or *Satisfaction* about it, as some of God's Children enjoy. Hast thou been brought to CHRIST? What Matter *how?* Whether exactly in all Respects in the same *Way* that another was brought, or not? Is CHRIST thy Foundation, doth thy Soul rest upon HIM? Thou'rt founded upon a *Rock* that will never *fail* thee, or sink under thee. CHRIST will be thy *supporting Rock*, to preserve thee from sinking into the Deluge of eternal Misery, notwithstanding all the Weights of Sin, Guilt, and Fear that are upon thee: Thy *defending Rock*, from the Danger, and real Hurt of all the Storms and Tempests which may pass over thee: And thy *advancing Rock* too, from the Depths of Misery, to the Heights of Glory, And what tho' thy Father may not have indulg'd thee with such *Love-Feasts*, such sensible *Mirth and Rejoycing*, that some of thy Brethren, poor *Prodigals*, have met with at their Return: Yet, *thou art ever with him, and all that* HE *hath is thine!* Thou hast CHRIST, and thou hast ALL! All Life, Light, and Glory in the *Right* of it now; and thou shalt have the *Enjoyment* of it ere-long. Be content then that infinite Wisdom should carve out thy Time-Portion of Comfort. What tho' some of the Saints are favour'd to walk in the *Light*, Yet *trust in the LORD, and stay thyself upon thy God*, Isa. l. 10. Believe that he leads thee in a *right Way*, that's best for thee now: Thou shalt *see* it to be so erelong. It's but a little while ere the Sun will rise upon thee, and no more go down: Ere thou, that as yet hast had, but as it were, the *Day-Star* arising in thy Heart, shalt behold the *Sun*, in its Meridian Brightness. For Night and Darkness shall be swollow'd up in eternal DAY, *Isa.* lx. 20. Mean-while, labour to live by *Faith*: To go on trusting thy Soul in the Hands of Christ, taking him at his Word, as to thy eternal Salvation, as counting him faithful that hath promis'd: Thus glorifying of him in the *Dark*, until taken up to be glorified with him, in the Enjoyment of thy *Inheritance in Light*.

2*dly*, I would say somewhat to poor Sinners: And that of three Sorts.

1. To such that are openly *prophane*: If any such may read these Lines. Ah poor Souls, your Condition is exceeding *miserable*; and so much the more, because you *know it not*. I have declared somewhat of that *Concern*

I was under about my eternal State: What think you of *yours?* I had not run such Lengths in Sin, as, perhaps, you have done: And yet I saw I must perish for ever, if the exceeding Riches of God's free Grace and Mercy in Christ were not extended to my poor Soul. What think you then of your *own Condition*, that have openly prophaned the Name of God, and run on in a Course of Ungodliness; committing Iniquity with Greediness? How do you think to escape the Wrath to come? Remember, the End of these Things is Death Ah poor Souls, how dreadful is your Case! You are awfully estranged from God, without him in the World; you desire not the Knowledge of his Ways: But count it your Happiness to fulfil the Desires of the Flesh and of the Mind; yielding yourselves as willing Servants to Sin and Satan: And the *Wages of Sin is Death*, Rom. vi. 23. Every Sin, even the Sin of a Thought deserves no less than eternal Death: How *great a Death* then doth all *thy Sins* deserve, that art running on in a Course of Wickedness! And as Death is the *Desert* of Sin, so, if thou continue herein, and abide an Unbeliever, *Death* will speedily, and inevitably seize upon thee. First, *natural Death*: Thou shalt die in thy Sins, and under the Curse of God. And then follows the *second Death*, which consists in an everlasting Banishment from God, to suffer the Vengeance of eternal Fire, with the Devil and his Angels. Thou art therefore in a very dreadful Condition.

But it may be, thou wilt say, "I know that Hell will be my Portion, if I live and die in my present Case: But after I have had a little more Pleasure in Sin, I purpose to leave my sinful Course, to amend my Ways, and make my Peace with God."

But, poor Soul, what if Death should overtake thee suddenly, and Hell swallow thee up in a Moment? Therefore *boast not thyself of To-morrow; thou knowest not what a Day may bring forth*, Prov. xxvii. 1.

But if, through the infinite Forbearance of God, thou shouldest be spared a while longer; yet, if thou hast no Mind to leave Sins *now*, thou wilt have less then. For every Sin thou committest, *strengthens* the Chains of Darkness in which thou art held. Poor Soul, thou art under *the Dominion of Sin*; thy Lusts are so many Lords over thee. Yea, thou art in *Bondage unto Satan*: The Devil, the Prince of Darkness, possesseth thy Heart as his Throne; and holds thee fast under his Government by the Cords of thy own Sins: And thou art so far from *groaning* under thy Bondage, that thou *likest* it, and *yieldest thyself* a willing Slave to the Drudgery of Hell. So that it is a great *Mistake* to think thou hast *Power* to leave thy Sins when thou *wilt*. Alas, poor Soul, there is such a *Power* in the Kingdom of Darkness, in which thou art held; that no *Power* in thy self, nor in any other Creature, can rescue thee from it. So that thy Case is exceeding *miserable*: And so much the more, as thou art *insensible* of it. *Thou hast destroy'd thyself* by thine Iniquity, and if thy *Help* is not in the LORD, in that GOD thou resolvest to sin against, thou art *undone for ever*. Thou art sunk too *low* for any *created Arm* to reach thee: And if the omnipotent Arms of Divine Grace and Mercy don't *snatch thee* from the Power of Darkness, as *a Brand out of the Burning*, thou wilt perish for ever in thy own Deceivings.

But suppose thou *couldst reform*, and amend thy Ways: Yet *by the Deeds of the Law, shall no Flesh be justified in the Sight of God*, Rom. iii. 20. The *best Righteousness* of the holiest Saint on Earth, is insufficient to be his *justifying Robe*; yea, it is but as *filthy Rags*, Isa. lxiv. 6. What abominable Stuff then, must all *thy Doings* be, that hast no Faith in JESUS? For *without Faith it is impossible to please GOD*, Heb. xi. 6.

But suppose thou couldst from this Time, even to thy dying Moments *walk exactly*, as the holy Law of God requireth; (which is indeed an utter Impossibility for any fallen Creature to do: But) suppose it, I say, yet what wilt thou do with thy *past Sins?* Thou art deep in Debt, thou owest ten thousand Talents to Divine Justice, and hast nothing to pay. All thy future Obedience, couldst thou obey perfectly, is but thy *Duty*; and can't pay a Mite towards thy *old Debt*. In vain then dost thou think to bring thy external Reformation, and legal Repentance to stand before God, and make thy Peace with him. God out of Christ is *a consuming Fire*; and all thy best Doings are but as *Briars and Thorns*: And *who would set the Briars and Thorns against him in Battle? He will go thro' them, and burn them up together*. Such is the flaming Holiness, and Justice of his Nature, as well as of his Law, that he can't endure the least *Sin*, but will break forth like devouring *Fire* upon every Soul where it is found. Hadst thou, in thy whole Life-Time, been guilty but of *one Sin*, even the Sin of a *Thought*; such is the Purity of God's *holy Law*, that it would call thee a *Transgressor*, and lay thee under the *Curse*, as a wicked Person: And *there is no Peace to the wicked, saith my God*, Isa. lvii. 21. No, the Work of making Peace with a Sin-revenging God, was too *great* for all the Creatures, either in Heaven or Earth, to perform. So that thy Condition, in and from thy self, and from any other Creature, is both helpless and hopeless.

But yet, poor Soul, *don't despair of Salvation*. Tho' thou art under the Dominion of Sin and Satan, and can'st by no Means deliver thyself from this hellish Slavery; tho' thou hast no Righteousness to stand in before an holy God; and tho' thou canst not by all thy best Performances in the least wise appease offended Justice for any of thy Sins: Yet there is still Hope for such as thee in GOD.

There is a full, free, and an everlasting *Salvation*, already wrought by Jesus Christ, for poor Sinners, that every Way suits the Case of the very Chief of them all, *1 Tim*. i. 15. Christ has fulfill'd the Law perfectly: And thereby wrought out a complete Righteousness for Law-breakers, in which they may stand blameless before a God of infinite Purity, with the highest Acceptance: Peace is already made by the Blood of his Cross, an everlasting Peace between God, and poor Sinners. And Victory, a most complete Victory over Sin and Satan, is already obtained by Christ, the Captain of Salvation, for poor Bond-Slaves in this Thraldom, which could by no means deliver themselves.

And this complete Salvation is proclaimed in the glorious Gospel, as *free*, for the Chief of Sinners: And this Gospel of a crucified Jesus, is *the Power of God unto Salvation*, Rom. i. 16. That JESUS that once died for poor Sinners on the Cross, now lives to intercede for them on the Throne: And as a Fruit hereof, the holy Spirit of God is given to attend the Ministry of the Gospel, and make this glad Tidings efficacious for the Salvation of Multitudes of as great Sinners as *thou* art.

Be encouraged therefore to *wait at Wisdom's Gate*, to attend the *Ministry of the Gospel*, (that Ministry, which exalts the free Grace of God alone, as the Foundation of a Sinner's Salvation, the Righteousness of Christ alone, as the Matter of his Justification, the Blood of Christ alone, for the Satisfaction of Divine Justice, and cleansing the Sinner from all Sin, and the Spirit of Christ alone, as the Applier of this great Salvation) for who knows but *this Gospel* may be *the Power of God unto thy Salvation?* Wait therefore under the Ordinances of Divine Appointment, for the efficacious Workings of the Holy Ghost: as *the impotent Folk at the Pool of Bethesda, for the Moving of the Waters*, John v. 3. I know thou canst not *quicken* thy own Heart: But there is an *Almighty Energy* attends the Gospel: The All-creating Power of *God* goes forth in *the Words of this Life*, to quicken *dead Sinners*, tho' like *the Bones in the Valley, very dry*, and to make them *stand up upon their Feet, an exceeding great Army for God*, John v. 25. Ezek. xxxvii. 2, &c. And *Now is the accepted Time, now is the Day of Salvation*: God is now about this Work of saving Sinners by the Gospel of his Son: Therefore be encouraged to *wait* where *God works*; thou art not sunk too *low* for an Almighty Arm to reach thee. All Things are *possible with GOD*:

There is nothing *too hard for* JEHOVAH. He *can* save thee, he is infinitely all-sufficient to do it; and he *delights* to be gracious: Wait therefore where he works, for who can tell but he may be *gracious unto thee?* Waiting is thy *Duty*, as well as thy *Privilege*, this thou *mayst* do, this thou *canst* do: And know, that if thou dost it *not*, and herein *neglectest this great Salvation*, if thou perish at last, it will increase thy Guilt, and aggravate thy Condemnation. It will be *dreadful perishing* for such that have been *Despisers of the Gospel* in a Land of Light; that have *preferred Trifles* before the Words of this Life: Doubtless it will be a *Sting* that will *eternally wound the Conscience.* Be perswaded therefore to improve thy present Opportunities of Praying, Reading, and Hearing the Word: For God may take the Gospel from *Thee*, or Thee from the *Gospel*, before thou art aware. And if this Gospel, which thou despiseth, doth not reach thine *Ears*, and the Power of it reach thy *Heart*; thou wilt die in thy Sins, and be cast, as a Vessel of Wrath, into the vast Abyss of unutterable, and eternal Misery.

2. A Word or two to you, poor Sinners, who are *Self-Righteous*. I have told you somewhat of my Experience: That I had religious Education, and was kept back from those gross Evils, which many run into: I attended Divine Worship in Publick, and oft-times in Private, and had some notional Knowledge of the Truths of the Gospel. I found also, at Times some Stirrings of my natural Affections in reading God's Word, and other good Books, and in Learning of Hymns, and I had a Sort of Pleasure when I could pray with Enlargement. And upon these Accounts, I thought myself to be fair for Heaven, and better than others: And if infinite Mercy had not prevented, I had gone down to Hell with this Lie in my Right Hand. But God, having from the *Beginning chosen me to Salvation*, he did not leave me to rest upon this *sandy Foundation*, but set my Feet upon *Christ, the Rock of Ages*. And when God came to shew me the infinite Purity of his Nature, and the Spirituality of his Law; that it required perfect Obedience in Heart as well as Life, and that for the least Failure, even so small, as a wandring Thought in Duty, the Law accursed me: I soon found all my *own Righteousness* to be as *filthy Rags*. The Spirit of the Lord blow'd upon all my Performances, and those which look'd green and beautiful before, soon wither'd as the Grass. *My Comeliness was turned in me into Corruption*: And a Sight of God's infinite Holiness made me to cry out, *Wo is me, I am undone*, because of my Uncleanness. And how dost *thou*, poor self-righteous Creature, think to *stand before this holy* LORD *God?* Whatever are thy *Performances*, esteem'd by thee, either as Moral, or Evangelical; yet,

if thou *trustest to these*, as the *Matter of thy Righteousness before God*; thou wilt one Day find it *insufficient*: either here, in Mercy, or hereafter, to thy eternal Misery. *For the Bed is shorter than that a Man can stretch himself on it: And the Covering narrower than that he can wrap himself in it.* The approaching Storm of God's Wrath will *sweep away this Refuge of Lies, the Waters of his Indignation will overflow this Hiding-Place*: Isa. xxviii. 17, 20. *Thou mayst lean upon this House*, thy own Doings, which thou hast rais'd, in thy Imagination, as a Shelter from the Storm, *but it shall not stand, and hold it fast, but it shall not endure.* All thy Hope of Safety from any of thy own Performances, shall be cut off, and thy Trust herein shall be as the Spider's Web; soon swept away, as poisonous Dust, by the Bosom of Destruction, *Job* viii. 14, 15. Never think then to stand before God in the filthy Rags of thy *own Righteousness*; for if thou dost, thou wilt surely be found *naked*: All thy *Sins* will be charged upon thee, and *this*, as an additional Weight, will increase thy *Condemnation*, that thou hast *rejected* the Righteousness of Christ, hast not *submitted* to this glorious Appointment of God, for the Justification of a Sinner; but hast went about to *establish thy own Righteousness.* And thy *House*, thy *Hope* of Life, built upon this sandy Foundation, shall *fall*; thro' the amazing *Storms* of Divine Vengeance that shall beat upon it in the awful *Day of Judgment*, and *great shall be the Fall thereof*, Mat. vii. 27. Ah! poor Soul, there's nothing will stand thee in stead in *that Day*, but the *compleat Righteousness of Christ*; his active and passive Obedience; if thou art not found under the *Redeemer's* Blood and Righteousness, if HE is not thy Covert from the Storm, thy Hiding-place from the Wind; the Whirlwind of God's Wrath will drive thee away like Chaff into everlasting Burnings; and the Storm of his Indignation, as an overflowing Scourge will sweep thee into the Gulph of eternal Misery. *They that are incensed against Christ shall then be ashamed, they shall go to Confusion together that are Makers of Idols*: That have set up the Idol of their own Righteousness, instead of submitting to the Righteousness of God: but *Blessed* are all those that put their *Trust in him*. For in HIM *shall all the Seed of Israel be justified, and shall glory.* They shall be *saved in the* LORD (THE LORD OUR RIGHTEOUSNESS) *with an everlasting Salvation, they shall not be ashamed, nor confounded World without End*, Isa. xlv. 16, 17, 24, 25.

3. A few Words to such poor sinners, that are in some Measure *sensible* of the Misery of their natural State; and have had some Discoveries of Jesus Christ, the glorious Remedy, as infinitely able to save lost Sinners: And yet

are afraid that he will not save *them* in particular. Dear Souls, I have told you that this was once *my Case*. I saw myself to be a chief Sinner; and in my perishing Condition I came to the Throne of Grace, to find Mercy, allur'd by some *Hopes* that I might, attended with innumerable *Fears* that I should not; and yet *I obtained Mercy*: I found Jesus Christ to be as infinitely *willing* to save me, as he was able. Be encourag'd therefore to come unto the Throne of Grace, unto God in Christ, where *Thousands* have found Mercy: Yea, where never *any Soul* was deny'd its Suit. Whoever thou art therefore, that seest thyself to be *undone* by Reason of Sin, and utterly unable to *help* thyself out of this dreadful Condition, and hast a longing Desire after Jesus Christ, and his Salvation: Thou mayst come and receive Christ, and all Grace and Life in him, as the Father's free Gift to the Chief of Sinners. I say, thou *mayst come*, as it is a *Grant* from the Throne, the Royal Proclamation of Heaven, *Unto whoever will*, Rev. xxii. 17. But I know thy Weakness, thy Fears, and the Weights that hang upon thee, greatly hinder the Swiftness of thy Motion unto Jesus Christ, and to God in Him. But as Christ, and all his Grace, was prepar'd on Purpose for *such* as thee, yea, on Purpose for *Thee*: So, in the Lord's own Time, he will *strengthen* thy weak Faith, *encourage* thy Hope, and *take off* thy Burdens; and give thee Access, with Freedom to *Christ*, and thro' him by one *Spirit* to the *Father*. And mean while, come as thou *canst*: Tho' with a trembling Heart, attended with ten Thousand Fears, under the Guilt of innumerable Transgressions; and from the Knowledge of CHRIST the great SAVIOUR, as the Gift of GOD to perishing Sinners, ask him for thy own Salvation; and HE will give thee living Water to thy present Satisfaction, and everlasting Consolation, to thy Joy and Peace here, and to thine eternal Life and Glory hereafter.

There's an infinite *Ability* in the Redeemer to save: He can command thy Deliverance from Sin, Death, and Hell, in the Virtue of his own Death; and bid thee *live*, both by a creative and authoritative Voice. Yea, by one Word of his Mouth, he can speak full Salvation to thee in an Instant: Enough to take up an Eternity of Time for thy Enjoyment of it. Come then, with all thy Wants, and prostrate thyself at his Feet; there's *enough* in Christ to supply them all. Yea, there's infinitely *more* than enough! Were thy Wants ten Thousand Times greater than they are, it's all one when thou comest to this infinite Ocean. It's in a Manner all one for the natural Sea to fill the largest Vessel as the smallest Cockle-Shell; because of that *vast Body of Waters* which meet in it. But the Fulness of Christ is properly an *immense, inexhaustible Ocean*; that can never be drawn dry, or in the least wasted, by all the innumerable Multitudes of needy Sinners, that have been supply'd thence, are now, and shall be to an endless Eternity. The SAVIOUR is GOD: And as such he calls poor Sinners to look to HIM for Salvation. HE is the eternal SON of the eternal FATHER, that has all the essential Glories of the GODHEAD in Him; and therefore HE is an *Overmatch* for all our spiritual Enemies. And HE is EMANUEL, GOD *with Us*, GOD in our Nature; and as such HE is a *fit* SAVIOUR, the *anointed* SAVIOUR, and *able to save to the Uttermost*, even all *them that come unto GOD by HIM*. There is an infinite Merit in his *Blood, to cleanse thee from all Sin*, 1 John i. 7. A *Merit* that far surpasseth all the *Demerit* of thy Sin: The Blood of Christ hath a louder Cry in the Ears of Justice for Peace and Pardon, than all thy Sins have for Condemnation and Wrath; *Where sin hath abounded, Free Grace*, thro' this Blood, *doth much more abound*, Heb. xii. 24. Rom. v. 20. There's an infinite Fulness in his *Righteousness* for Justification. A *Fulness* that's large enough to cover all thy Nakedness, and to present thee Faultless, with the highest Acceptance, before a God glorious in Holiness. A *Fulness* that every Way answers the infinite Purity of Jehovah's Nature, and the Perfection of his holy Law. A *Fulness* that will make thee Out-shine, not only perfect *Adam* in his innocent State, but even the glorious *Angels* in Heaven. For poor Sinners are made, no less than, *the Righteousness of God in him*, 2 Cor. v. 21. There is also an infinite Fulness of *Grace and Holiness* in the Person of Christ, to present thee Unblameable before the Presence of Jehovah's Glory, notwithstanding all the Filth and Impurity of thy Nature: For this holy Jesus is made unto us *Sanctification*, 1 Cor. i. 30. And in him, likewise, there's an infinite Fulness of all *Grace and Glory*, to be communicated to thee thro' Time, and to Eternity: To make thee holy and happy here, and perfectly glorious for ever! But oh, who can conceive, much less express, the *unsearchable Riches* of Christ's Ability to save Sinners! To know it *fully*, is beyond the *Reach* of created Understanding.

And as Christ is *able to save to the Uttermost all them that come unto God by him*, Heb. vii. 25. So, he is as *wiling* as he is able. The infinite Willingness of his Heart is as *large* as the Almighty Power of his Arm. The *High-Priest's Breast-Plate and Ephod*, under the Law, was to be *fastened together by a Lace of Blue*, Exod. xxviii. 28. To shew, that the Heart and Arm, the Grace and Power of Christ, are inseperably *join'd* in a Sinner's Salvation. What Encouragement then hast thou to come to Christ, who has promis'd to give thee *Rest?* To cast thyself into his Arms, and stay upon his Grace, Power, and Faithfulness, who has declar'd, that he *will in no wise cast out* any poor Sinner, that *comes unto him*, the great Saviour? *Matt*. xi. 28. *John* vi. 37. He has given thee his *great Word*, that he is *willing* to save thee. Canst thou *believe it?* Or darest thou, thro' Unbelief, give him the *Lie?* Ah poor Soul, Christ has been *before-hand* with thee in Willingness. If he had not been *first* willing to *save thee*, thou hadst never been made willing to be *sav'd by him. His Love* has been a Love *preventing thee*: He did not stay for *thy Willingness*; but began *thy Salvation*, in giving thee a *new Nature*, before thou began'st to breath after it: That so thou might desire Life, and come to him for it. How *welcome* then shalt thou be to his gracious Heart and open Arms! Thou canst not please him *better*, than to come to him just as thou art, a miserable, helpless, undone Sinner; for all the Mercy, Grace, and Salvation thou wantest. He will not sent thee away *empty*. He has said, *Open thy Mouth wide, and I will fill it*, Psal. lxxxi. 10. Thou canst not ask more Grace than he *has* to bestow, and is *willing* to give. He *delights* to fill such needy, empty Souls, as thou art. This was the great *End* of his Death: His Heart was so willing to *save thee*, that he *died for thee*, that he might accomplish it. Yea, so intense was his Desire to *save thee*, that *thy Salvation* was Part of the *Joy* set before him, for which he *endured the Cross*. He took Pleasure in the Thoughts of it, so long since: And the Joy of it fore-view'd, carried him thro' the Agonies of Death. And now the bitter Work is over, and He's advanc'd to the Right Hand of God, having all Power in Heaven and Earth given him, that he might give eternal Life to Sinners: Dost thou think his Heart is *chang'd?* No, as he dy'd for thee on the Cross, so he lives for thee on the Throne: He is *Jesus Christ the Same*, in his boundless Love, Grace, and Mercy, *Yesterday, To-day, and forever*, Heb. xiii. 8. He is not now to *die* for thee: Tho' such is his unchangeable Grace, that if it was yet to do, he would go thro' *Death to save thee*: But, blessed be God, that Work is done, for ever done, and full Salvation, eternal Redemption obtain'd: And having entred into Heaven with his own Blood, on Purpose to save thee by the Almighty Power of his Arm: Dost thou think he will now *deny thy Request*; when to do it, would be to *deny himself*; not only in the Grace of his *Heart*, but in the very End of his *Death?* And canst thou think that his *Love* that is strong enough to die for thee yet, was there need; will not give thee *Life*, when he can save thee now, with a *Word of his Mouth!* Oh, Believe it, *the Willingness* of Christ's Heart to save thee, doth infinitely *surpass* the largest Desire of thy Soul, after his Salvation. What should *hinder* thee then, from an immediate running into Christ's Bosom, since there is such Room for thee in his Heart? I dare say, nothing but thy *Unbelief*: And, blessed be God, that shall not hinder thee, *always*, neither. Would it be an unspeakable *Joy* to thee, to get into Christ's Arms: let me say, it would be *much more* so to him. *The Day of his Espousals* with a poor Sinner, is the *Day of the Gladness of his Heart*, Song iii. 11. But if thou still doubt his *Willingness* to embrace thee: I'll only say, as *Philip* to *Nathanael, Come and see*: Come and *try* his boundless Grace; and *see* if it be not every Way as *large* as the omnipotent Power of his Arm! *John* i. 46. Oh come and cast thyself at the SAVIOUR'S Feet, and say, as that poor Man did, who was full of Leprosy, *Lord if thou wilt, thou canst make me clean*. And JESUS, in the Infinity of his Grace, will answer thee, as he did him, and say, *I will, be thou clean*, Luke v. 13.

F I N I S.

A Brief

ACCOUNT

OF THE

Gracious DEALINGS

OF

G O D,

WITH A

Poor, Sinful, Unworthy Creature,

Relating to
A Train of special PROVIDENCES attending Life, by which
the Work of Faith was carried on with Power.

Part II.

By A. D.

*Come and hear all ye that fear GOD, and I will declare
what he hath done for my Soul*, Psa. lxvi. 16.
*One Generation shall praise thy Works to another, and
shall declare thy mighty Acts.*
*I will speak of the glorious Honour of thy Majesty, and of
thy wondrous Works.*
*And Men shall speak of the Might of thy terrible Acts: and
I will declare thy Greatness.*
*They shall abundantly utter the Memory of thy great
Goodness, and shall sing of thy Righteousness*, Psa.
cxlv. 4, 5, 6, 7.

LONDON:

Printed by J. HART, in *Poppings Court, Fleet-street*: And
sold by J. LEWIS, in *Bartholomew-Close*, near *West-
Smithfield*; and E. GARDNER, at *Milton's Head*, in
Gracechurch-Street, 1743.
[Price One Shilling.]

A Brief

A C C O U N T

OF THE

Gracious DEALINGS

OF

G O D, &c.

HAving in a former little Tract, given a brief Account of GOD's Loving-Kindness to my Soul, relating to his Work of Grace upon my Heart in a saving Conversion to CHRIST, and to my being brought to some Establishment in JESUS; I shall now in *this* give some further Account of the LORD's gracious Dealings with me, relating to a Train of special Providences, attending my Life, by which the Work of Faith was carried on with Power. And as enabled I shall give some Hints,

First, Of these special Providences of GOD towards me. And,

Secondly, Make some Improvement. I begin,

First, With Providences. The Providences I chiefly intend to take notice of, are such that relate to my being *planted in the House of the* LORD, in order to my *Flourishing in the Courts of our* GOD. And,

I. The Providence I shall first mention, and take a little Notice of, relates to my Removal from that Church of Christ in *N—n*, where I first join'd, to another Church in the same Town, of which the late Mr. *M---re*, was Pastor. Some Hints of which, take as follow.

Mr. *H---t*, my first Pastor, was removed, and another Minister succeeded him. The Ministry of this Servant of Christ was of Use to me in some Respect; tho' I did not fall in with his Judgment in several Points. But he not insisting much upon them at first, I was willing to content myself, and pass by what I did not like.---But some Time after this, not finding myself edify'd under his Ministry, and my Dissatisfaction increasing, I thought it my Duty to acquaint him with it; and accordingly did it, after having sought the LORD about it. I thought I should meet with Opposition if I attempted it; and much indeed came on. But I saw such an Excellency and Preciousness in the Truths I contended for, that I thought at that Time, I could not only bear the Reproaches I might meet with on this Account, but even lay down my Life in the Defence of them, if the Lord had call'd me to it.---Many were the Trials, and great the Support I met with at this Time. A mighty Spirit of Prayer was upon me, the Liberty of GOD's Bosom was afforded me in the Day of my Distress, frequent were the Answers I receiv'd from him, and great the Familiarity I had with Him. So that I could say with the Apostle, *As the Sufferings of Christ abound in us, so our Consolation also aboundeth by Christ*, 2 Cor. i. 5.---In a Word, I soon found the Truth of what the Prophet asserts by Way of Interrogation, *Amos* iii. 3. *Can two walk together except they be agreed?*—Upon which I intreated the Lord to tell me what was my Duty in the present Case. And having receiv'd full Satisfaction, That it was his Mind I should remove my Communion from that Church to which I then related, to that over which Mr. *M---re* was Pastor; I accordingly did it.

This Providence of GOD, in removing me from one Church to another, I have great Reason to bless his Name for; as He made it an Introduction to all that great Glory, which I have since beheld in *Sion*. Upon my being new planted, the Lord water'd me; I cast forth my Roots as *Lebanon*, and my Branches did spread. The Lord Jesus, my chief Shepherd, led me, by the Ministry of his Servant, Mr. *M—re*, into fat, green Pastures. The Doctrines of the Gospel were clearly stated, and much insisted on in his Ministry. The Sanctuary-Streams ran clearly; and the Sun shone gloriously. I was *abundantly satisfied with the Fatness of God's House; made to drink of the River of his Pleasures, and in his Light, I saw Light*, Psa. xxxvi. 8, 9.

But notwithstanding my bright Days, I had some Nights. Several were the Temptations, and Times of Distress my Soul met with: tho' I did not question my Interest in Christ now, but other Temptations beset me. *Out of the Deeps I cried unto the LORD. And He sent from above, he took me, he drew me out of many Waters*, Psa. xviii. 16. The Light of the Glory of God, brightly shining into my Heart, discover'd my own Darkness, Dust and Soil; and made the Corruptions of my Nature hateful, and odious in my Eyes, in every of their Out-breakings, whether in Heart, Lip or Life. Oh how exceeding *sinful* did Sin appear to me now, while I viewed it in the Light of *pardoning* Love, and *justifying* Blood! Oh this *Body of Death*, with all its Members, how *lothsome* was it to my Soul! I was call'd to *wrestle against Principalities, and Powers, against spiritual Wickedness in high Places*. But the Lord cover'd my Head in the Day of Battle, taught my Hands to war and my Fingers to fight; and gave the Victory on my Side, either actively or passively. While in the *Strength of Christ*, I either trampled down mine Enemies, or when foil'd, again *overcame by the Blood of the Lamb*. Oh this precious *Fountain, set open to the House of David, for*

Sin, and for Uncleanness! How did it cleanse my Soul both from Guilt and Filth! And the Guilt of Sin being taken off my Conscience, I exceedingly longed to be freed, both from its Power, and Being. My Soul press'd forward, and reach'd forth after perfect Conformity to Christ. And my present Unlikeness was a great Affliction to me. But the blessed Spirit went on to open Christ to my Soul, in his infinite Suitableness to all my Wants.

I was once groaning under the Weight of Sin, and lamenting my *Unholiness* before the Lord. And on a sudden, a pleasant Thought pass'd through *my* Mind, concerning the Blessedness of the Angels, as they are perfectly *Holy*, without the least Taint of Sin. Oh! thought I, "They can serve God perfectly, while I'm prevented, and held down by a Body of Sin and Death." And immediately that Word came in, *Rom.* xi. 16. *If the Root be holy, so are the Branches.* In which I was pointed to *Christ*, the Fountain of Holiness: And mine Eye taken off from the Holy Angels, and fixt upon the Holy JESUS. But oh, what an Heart-raising, Soul-amazing Discovery, I then had of the Holiness of Christ, as my Head and Root! *If the Root be holy!* From the next Words, *So are the Branches*, in Connection with the former, I was taught two Things: 1. That as Christ, my *Root* was holy, so I, as a *Branch* in Him, was then presented to the Father, as perfectly *holy* in the shining Glories of my holy Head and Root. I saw, that tho' my *inherent* Holiness was imperfect, yet that I had a *perfect* Sanctification in *Christ*, a *compleat* Holiness in *Him*, as made of God unto me *Sanctification*; in which I was presented before the Throne, without the least Stain. 2. I saw a Fulness of Holiness in Christ my *Root*, not only for *Representation*, but also, for *Communication*. *If the Root be holy, so are the Branches*: So by *Representation*: And so by *Derivation*. Oh, here I view'd my personal Holiness, *secured*; even in Christ's *communicable* Fulness of Holiness, as my Root of Influence! I saw Holiness enough in Christ my *Root*, to continue, increase, and perfect my personal Holiness, as a *Branch* in Him. And oh how my Soul rejoiced in that *Security* I had, by virtue of my *inseperable* Union to Christ, of *perfect* Conformity to him!---Thus the Lord set me at Liberty at this Time, and again I went on rejoicing in Christ Jesus, as I was *then* compleat in him, and should *erelong* be made perfectly like him.

About this Time also, I was again assaulted with blasphemous Thoughts: And the Affliction lasted a great while, tho' I had some Respite at Times. But oh the cursed Noise of Hell, that was heard in my poor Soul! How grievous was it to me! I was at a Loss, sometimes, whether those horrid Thoughts were merely the Suggestions of Satan, or the Product of my own vile Heart: But in the main, I judged both concerned therein. I look'd upon these vile Thoughts to be originally cast in by Satan, altho' there was enough in my wicked Heart to catch the Fire of his Temptations. But however, this was the Improvement the Enemy would have made hereof, to have driven me into Despair. And as he was once urging it, that because such Thoughts had pass'd thro' my Heart, I had sinned the *unpardonable Sin*; the blessed Spirit, as my Comforter, did open to me, the free and full Forgiveness of all *my Sins*, thro' the Blood of Christ; in that Word, *Mat.* xii. 31. *Wherefore I say unto you, All manner of Sin and Blasphemy shall be forgiven unto Men.* By which I was melted into Love to God, Self-lothing, and Gospel-Repentance: And Sin and Satan fled at the Display of pardoning Grace, thro' the Blood of Jesus. And, indeed, I always found the *Blood of Christ*, to be the most effectual *Means* to quench the fiery Darts of Satan, the Flame of Sin, and to cleanse my Soul from all that Defilement it contracted during an Engagement.

By these Temptations, the Lord gave me to see more what *need* I had to be kept continually by his mighty Power, and to live by Faith on Christ daily, dealing with his Blood and Righteousness. And oh what a precious *Hiding-Place*, did I find CHRIST to be *from the Wind!* what a *Covert from the Storm!* Yea, my JESUS, was to *me, as Rivers of Water in a dry Place!* By these Temptations also, the Lord *humbled* me, while he gave me to see more of that Abyss of Sin that was in my Nature; that filthy Fountain which continually sent forth its Streams to the defiling of my Soul. And oh how precious was the Blood of Christ, as a Fountain set open for me to wash in! By these Temptations likewise, the Lord gave me to *admire* his distinguishing Grace the more, in *my* Salvation. While I saw my self, as in my self, to be no *better* than those that perish, and fit Fewel for *everlasting Burnings*. Oh the horrid Nature of *Sin*, which I then beheld, as it is *Enmity, irreconcileable* Enmity against God! And how intensely did I *hate Sin*, as *against a God of boundless Grace!* That Word has many a time been a Stay to me, when surprized by the out-breakings of the Enmity of my Nature, *Rom,* viii. 7. *The carnal Mind is Enmity against God: it is not subject to the Law of God, neither indeed can be.* I have thought thus: "These are dreadful Clamours that my Soul hears: But what will not an *Enemy* say? I am by Nature an *Enemy* to God; yea, such is the Corruption of my Nature, that it is even *Enmity* itself: it is *not* subject to the Law of God, neither indeed *can* be." And that Word has many times been sweet to me, when on one

Occasion or another, I have been in the Views of my own Vileness: *Was not Esau Jacob's Brother? saith the* LORD: *Yet I loved Jacob, and I hated Esau,* Mal. i. 2, 3. And that Word also, *Hos.* iii. 1. *Then said the LORD unto me, go yet, love a Woman (beloved of her Friend, yet an Adulteress) according to the Love of the LORD to the Children of Israel, who look to other Gods, and love Flagons of Wine.* I have been made to rejoice, that none of my Vileness could alter God's Love to me. He *knew, that I should deal very treacherously, and was call'd a Transgressor from the Womb.* And yet from the mere good Pleasure of his Will, he resolved to be Gracious, everlastingly Gracious to me. And when my Soul has been melted down under a Sense of God's everlasting Love to me, I have said to him, "Lord, since none of all my Vileness can make any Alteration *in thy Love*; let thy unchangeable Grace make an Alteration *in me!* Since *my Sin* cannot take away thy Love, let *thy Love* take away my Sin; let it change *me* into its *own* Image, that so I may *love Thee perfectly*, the Ocean of Love and Goodness!" And oh how glad have I been, that *none could pluck me out of Christ's Hands*, John x. 28. None of my Enemies, neither Sin, Satan, nor the World! *I give unto them eternal Life, and they shall never perish*: Oh how sweetly has the Holy Ghost open'd the Grace of Christ in these Words, in his free, absolute, irreversible *Gift* of eternal Life to *me!* And that everlasting *Security* I had in him from all Enemies and Dangers! And in a Word, The Establishment of my *Faith* in the great Doctrines of the Gospel, under the Spirit's Witness of my own particular *Interest* in all the wonderful Grace couched therein? I found to be of unspeakable Advantage to *stay* my Soul, and keep me from being *driven away*, when Tempests beat violently upon me. But to go on,

Mr. *M---re*, was a great doctrinal Preacher: And the special Advantage I receiv'd under his Ministry, was the Establishment of my *Judgment* in the Doctrines of the Gospel. My Communion with this Church was pleasant. But after I had comfortably walk'd with it for some Years, Things began to work for a Removal of my Place of Abode. And therefore,

II. The next Providence I shall give some Hints of, relates to the Lord's removing my Habitation from *N---n*, to *L---n*: Which was occasion'd by my entring into a Marriage-State, when I was 22 Years of Age.

The Privileges I enjoy'd in *Sion*, were very valuable in my Esteem. And when the Lord was about my Removal, I was afraid it might be attended with some Loss; and that my small Improvement of the Favours I enjoy'd, might have provok'd the Lord to take them away from me. But that Word was set home with great Power upon my Heart, concerning this Providence, Rom. xi. 22. *Towards Thee, Goodness*. From which I was fully perswaded, that the Lord's Design in removing me, was, the more abundant Display of his great Goodness, notwithstanding all my Unworthiness. And upon my Fixation at *L---n*, under the Ministry of the late Mr. *Sk---p*, I soon found the Truth of this Declaration of Grace. For the Waters of the Sanctuary were indeed, *risen Waters*; which fill'd my Soul with Wonder and Joy. I found the same Doctrines of the Gospel, *maintain'd*, and *vindicated* in the Ministry of Mr. *Sk---p*, as I was wont to hear under Mr. *M---re*'s, tho' not altogether in that *stated* Way, but with abundance of Glory, Life and Power.

These two great Servants of Christ, had different Gifts by the same Spirit; And the Ministry of both were greatly blest for my Edification in the Knowledge of Christ. Mr. *M---re*, was a Man of great Understanding in the Mysteries of the Gospel: And under his Ministry, as I hinted before, my *Judgment* was establish'd. Mr. *Sk---p*, was also a Man of deep Judgment; and superadded to this, he had *Quickness* of Thought, *Aptness* of Expression, *suitable* Affection, and a most *agreeable* Delivery, every way suited to engage the Attention of an Auditory: And the Corronis of all was, that wonderful *Power* which attended his Ministry, both for the Quickning of the Saints, and the Conversion of Sinners. He had a peculiar Gift of *opening the Scriptures*, one Text by another; which cast a great Light upon the sacred Oracles. He also delighted to set forth *heavenly* Things by *earthly*; his Ministry abounded with *Similies*; Which, when aptly apply'd, do much illustrate the Truth, and help our dark Minds to take it in. Under *his* Ministry, I was as it were put to School, to learn again those Truths, in a *greater* Light and Glory, which I had some *blessed* Knowledge of before: And the special Blessing I received under it, was, the more abundant *Life and Power* of the Truths known. I found the Gospel, under *his* Preaching, to be indeed, *The Ministration of the Spirit, and Life*: And the Word of God, to be as a *Fire*, melting my Soul down. Oh the Light and Glory I *saw*, the Life and Heat I *felt* in the Doctrines of the Gospel, under the irradiating, enkindling Influences of the Holy Ghost, in *his* Ministry!

Upon my Removal to *L---n*, I had *transient* Communion with the Church of Christ under the pastoral Care of Mr. *Sk---p*. But after I had walked with 'em thus for some Time, it was thought proper, my Abode being *fixed*, that my Communion should be so too. Whereupon I requested my Dismission from that Church of Christ at *N---n*, to which I then related, to that with which I then walked. Which being granted, I was received into full Communion with this Church of Christ at *L---n.* My Fellowship herewith was sweet: The Lord dwelt in this *Sion,* for *me, abundantly blest her Provision,* and my *poor Soul was satisfied with Bread: He clothed her Priest,* her Minister *with Salvation, and* I, with *her Saints,* did *shout for Joy.* Oh the Glory of God, that I saw in this House of his! This Dispensation was indeed, *towards Me Goodness!* For in this, as well as my other Remove, from one part of the House of God to another, I passed on *from Glory to Glory:* And with the rising Display, was proportionably *changed into the same Image by the Spirit of the Lord.* In this Garden of God, *I sat down under the Shadow of my Beloved with great Delight, and his Fruit was sweet to my Taste.* And the Sweetness of Christ's Grace-Fulness, his Fruit as the *Apple-Tree,* suited to my present Necessity, and Capacity, did quicken my Appetite, and set my Soul a longing for that happy Day, when I should feast upon his glory-Fulness, as *the Tree of Life in the midst of the Paradise of God.*

But tho' my Enjoyments were *great,* yet still I found myself attended with a Variety of Trials. I had my Times of Heaviness. But *the Father of Mercies, and the God of all Comfort,* was graciously pleased to *comfort me in all my Tribulations.* His infinite *Love* under all, and in all, was so abundantly *shed abroad in my Heart by the Holy Ghost,* that made me *patient,* and *joyful* in all my Distresses. Yea, I was not contented, barely, to be *patient,* and *submissive* to the Will of God under Trials, unless I *gloried in Tribulation.* I saw so much of my Father's *Heart-Love* in every Twig of his Rod, that carried on my Soul to *bless him* for every Stroke. Yea I thought, "That his very *Denial* of the Mercies and Favours I requested, and Sense thought I wanted, was to me, a *double* Portion of Kindness": My Heart was so *overflow'd* with his Love. *As having nothing, I possess'd all Things.* And oh, how well pleased was I with my Portion in *God!* One GOD in CHRIST, was my Soul-satisfying ALL! That Word was exceeding precious to me, *To be a God unto Thee,* Gen. xvii. 7. Oh here I saw, that whatever God had [*sic,* r. was] in *himself,* that he was to *me* in Christ: I saw, that all his infinite Perfections were engaged in Covenant for *my good.* And that Word also, I found, and did eat it, and it was unto me the Rejoicing of my Heart, *Deut.* xxxiii. 23. *O Naphtali, satisfied with Favour, and full with the Blessing of the LORD: possess thou the West and the South.* I saw myself so *encompassed* with Favour, and *surrounded* with the Blessing of *Jehovah,* that my Soul was therewith *abundantly satisfied,* and so *full* that I could *desire no more,* either for Temporals, Spirituals, or Eternals, than what was settled upon me in God's everlasting Covenant with his Son. I saw, that I need not ask to be *new blest*, but only for the *Communication* of those Blessings thro' Christ, with which I was *anciently blest* in Him; and so leave it with infinite Wisdom to distribute those Riches, which infinite Grace bestow'd. And in the Faith of my being so abundantly, and irreversibly blest, I went forth to *possess* all those vast Stores I had in GOD! The Faith of God's *Love* has many a time made me, with unspeakable Pleasure, to submit to his *Will*, when he crost *mine*: I have delightfully lost my Will in *God*'s, and *there* also I have found it. I *lost* it, as corrupt, while the Holy Ghost subdued the Rebellion of my Nature; and I *found it*, as sanctified, while he drew me into a sweet Acquiescence with God's good Pleasure. Under the sanctifying Operations of the blessed Spirit, I have liked what my *Father* liked; and have well approved of the most trying Dispensation, because it was *his Will*. And his Will, in this respect, I took to be, not a mere Act of *Sovereignty*, but an Act of his *good Pleasure*, flowing from, and founded *upon* his boundless Love, and infinite Wisdom, in his eternal Counsels about the Glory of his Grace, in my Happiness and Salvation. I saw that his boundless Grace towards *me* in Christ, was so *great*, that it set his infinite Wisdom a-work to contrive the Channels in which it should flow. And that in *the exceeding Riches of his Grace, he had abounded towards me in all Wisdom and Prudence*, in the Settlement of all Things relating to my present and eternal Happiness, by an Act of his Will, as the Result of his eternal Counsels; according to which, all Things in his Providence were wrought. As *Eph.* i. 11. *Who worketh all Things after the Counsel of his own Will.* He worketh all Things, not merely after his *Will*, but after the *Counsel of his Will*. From hence I saw, that there was no Part of his *Will*, but what his *Counsel* was concern'd in; and no Part of his *Counsel*, or what his infinite Wisdom saw best, but what his *Will* resolved upon. And the Lord made this of great Use to reconcile me to the *Will of his Providence*, as I saw it founded upon the *Will of his Counsel*, or the eternal Counsel of his Will. And in a Word, in *all* my Trials, *everlasting Arms* were underneath to support, and round about to imbrace me.

In the next Place, I shall take a little Notice of my being remov'd to *W---k*. After I had been some Time at *L---n*, the Providence of God so order'd it, that there was a far greater Prospect of Advantage, with respect to my Husband's Business at *W---k*: Upon which he thought it best for us to go down thither for that Season. This was not a total Remove from *L—n*; we went only as Sojourners for a while. But tho' there was an Appearance of greater *outward* Advantage; yet I was afraid it would be attended with much Loss, as to those great Privileges I then enjoy'd in *Sion*; which made it a *Trial* to me. And when it first appear'd, I was afraid I had provok'd the Lord to bring it upon me as a Rebuke for my Unprofitableness. But that Word was brought, with great Power, *Jer.* xxxi. 20. *Is Ephraim my dear Son? is he a pleasant Child? I will surely have Mercy upon him.* By which the Lord satisfied me, That *that* Dispensation was not brought upon me as a Rebuke, but in a way of Mercy, and pure Loving-kindness. And oh the Heart-melting Discovery I then had of my Father's Love and Grace, in calling me his *dear Child*, and, especially, his *pleasant Child!* Oh! thought I, "*What manner of Grace is this*, that my Father should call me a *pleasant Child*, notwithstanding all my Ingratitude! He might have call'd me his *dear Child*, as I stand in the Dearness of *adopting Love*, and yet have dealt with me in a way of Rebuke for all my Unkindness as an *unpleasant Child!* But how is it that he should say I am a *pleasant Child*, notwithstanding all my Baseness! Oh surely it is as he views me *in Christ*, where HE *beholds no Iniquity in Jacob, nor Perverseness in Israel!*" Thus kindly the Lord dealt with me. Quickly after this, I saw more of the Vileness of my own Heart; and again I began to think, How justly the Lord might bring this Dispensation upon me as a *Rebuke*. But, while I was cast down, the Lord brought this Word to comfort me, *Hos.* xi. 9. *I will not execute the Fierceness of mine Anger, I will not return to destroy Ephraim; for I am God, and not Man, the Holy One in the midst of thee, and I will not enter into the City.* From which I was sweetly taught, the great Reason of that wonderful Forbearance the Lord exercised towards me; as it lay in his great BEING, as he was GOD, and not Man. And that tho' I was a provoking Creature, yet because of his infinite Grace, Mercy and Faithfulness, he would not return to destroy me, or *alter* the Thing that was gone out of his Mouth concerning me. And in the Faith of this Grace, I went down to *W---k*.

But quickly after I was there, began to be in great Heaviness. And, with *David*, I said, *Why art thou cast down, O my Soul? and why art tho disquieted within me!* And I found the great Reason to be, because I was *seperated* [*sic*] from my sweet Enjoyments in the House of God, and from the Company of the dear Saints. Upon which, I began to argue with my self thus, "Why, if I was in a *Den*, or *Cave* of the Earth; if the *Lord* was with me, *his Presence* would make it *a Palace*." And by this Thought I was turn'd home to my Father's Bosom. And from this Time I sought for my Satisfaction in GOD himself, when I had not those outward Means of enjoying him my Soul wished for. And I was wonderfully favour'd with intimate Communion with God, in that Place, by which my Joy was full. But when, from the Sweetness of *private* Fellowship with *my Beloved*, I came hungering and thirsting for the Enjoyment of him in *publick* Ordinances, I found him not *there*, as I was wont. And I was at times, *sick of Love*, and ready to faint away for want of him. At other Times, indeed, I was favour'd with his Presence, and he fed me in an *uncommon* Way, even by means of *Contraries*; or the contrary to what I heard. While I was at *L---n*, I was as *a Hind let loose. I went in and out and found Pasture*. Mr. *Sk---p*, was fill'd with *the Spirit of Adoption*; and in *full Assurance of Faith*, he had Freedom of Access unto God in Christ. And *my Soul*, together with *his*, did most delightfully breathe out it self into the Bosom of God, both in Prayer and Praise. *His Preaching* also, brought me *glad Tidings of great Joy*. But when I came to *W---k*, I found a strange Alteration: I was got into another *Climate*, much further off the Sun. I thought, when I came first, "Surely, this People worship *without* the Blood of Jesus." They stood at such a Distance from God in Prayer; and as for Preaching, I thought it little more than Form. But something of the Lord's gracious Dealings with me, in this Place, being expressed in a Letter, that I wrote to Mr. *Sk---p* from thence, I think it may not be amiss to insert it.

Very dear and honour'd Brother,

MAY the boundless Love of the Father, in its eternal Flow thro' the Mediator, abundantly grant the Desire of your Heart, by daily anointing you with fresh Oyl; as it descends from the Fulness of our glorious Head, for the Supply of each Member of his Body, in their several Places and Order! Oh! 'tis a living Communion with your glorious anointed *Head*, in all the Fulness of the Spirit, which it hath pleased the Father should dwell in him, that alone can make you an *able Minister* of the New Testament, a *skilful Workman* rightly to divide the Word of Truth. Oh what Cause have *you* to be thankful for a Supply of the Spirit of Jesus! That *you* should not be left, with many, to make a Composition of Matter, merely out of other Mens Judgments, and then commit it to a few dead Notes to read to the People! Oh how glorious a Thing it is, to know the Mind of Christ, under the Holy Ghost's Revelation! and to preach the Gospel, under a special Unction from the Holy One!

Dear Sir, I can't but take it exceeding kindly that you wrote to us; for which I return you many Thanks. My Father was pleased to give me a good Meal by Means of some Things you wrote. I am glad to hear of your Prosperity: The Lord continue and increase it! I should be glad if it please my Father to cast my Lot among you again. My Soul was warm'd by those three Things, you wrote, that go to the Completion of Love. I bless my God, I know by Experience, what it is to be made *perfect in Love*, both as to its Nature, and Settlement, under the Spirit's Witness of personal Interest. But oh how little do I know, and how greatly do I long after a *Perfection in Love* to a compleat Assimilation! Oh! well might you say, that the "*Third* and *last Thing was greatest.*" For verily it is exceeding great and comprehensive; full of Majesty and Glory. Well might the Apostle say, *There is no Fear in Love*, 1 John iv. 18. For were we but once come to that Perfection in Love; how powerfully should we be constrain'd to Obedience to all the Laws and Commands of *Sion's* King, our glorious Head and Husband, and how Evangelick would it be? How free from servile Fear, as such that are no more Servants?

As to our spiritual Entertainment, We have something of the Gospel; but with Abundance of Mixture, that greatly eclipseth the Glory of it. Yet I can't but say, That *My Lord feeds me*; al-tho' I am *like a Lamb in a large Place*. My Soul doth *eat the Fat, and drink the Sweet, and the Joy of the Lord is my Strength*: Which *makes my Feet like the Feet of Hinds*. He feeds me with royal Dainties, Meat from the King's Table; even such upon which Himself feeds. *Psa*. xxxvi. 8. I think my Soul's Liberty and Joy, in near Approaches to the Throne, has oft-times grew by the Opposites I mostly see and hear in this Place. Oh how has Grace abounded towards vile, unworthy *me!* Not only to distinguish me from the *World*, but also from this Company of *Professors*; (and it may be some of 'em *Believers*) that while *they* stand at a Distance, as so many Strangers; unworthy I should be brought nigh, as one that is spotless thro' Blood, and splendidly glorious in the Marriage-Robe! Oh! to walk in the comfortable *Knowledge* of my Interest, when most walk at *Uncertainties*; and at best, seem but to work and strive to *get* that, which I know is freely, fully, and irreversibly *given me* in Christ Jesus: Even all that is comprehended in that *eternal Life*, which by an eternal Act of Settlement, was made sure to *Christ* and *His!* Oh here it is my Soul gathers Strength and Life, notwithstanding all that Sin and Death that works in me; even while I view my Father's *Love*, as the Source and Origin of all my Happiness and Glory, to be infinitely *unchangeable!* Here I behold the

Project of Eternity, (for the exuberant shining forth of the Glory of the divine BEING, in the Advancement of the Mediator, and his Seed, into Union and Communion with *Jehovah*) laid in such infinite *Depths of Wisdom*, that not all that Inundation of Sin, which came in by my first Father *Adam*, no, nor all my personal Transgressions, could ever be able to raise [*sic*, r. rase, i.e., raze] it, to alter this glorious Design! No; *The Counsel of the LORD shall stand, and he will do all his Pleasure.* I must confess, that *my Neck is an Iron Sinew, and my Brow Brass*: That *I am bent to Backsliding*, and have *done as evil as I could.* I, in myself, am an abominable, vile, and hatful Creature. But *what then?* Can *this* alter my Father's Heart? Oh! *No*; It is *unchangeable!* And as it can't alter his *Heart*, so neither the *Thing* that is gone out of his *Mouth*, Psa. lxxxix. 34. Because I am a *disingenuous Child*, will He *disinherit me?* Oh! No. He'll *cleanse me*, but not *destroy me.* He *knew I would deal very Treacherously.* And yet Grace breaks up, in free Forgiveness, thro' Blood, with a go [*yet*] *love a Woman beloved of her Friend, yet an Adulteress*, Hos. iii. 1. Oh how this *Love breaks my Heart!* I am *loved* into Self-loathing! I am *loved* into Hatred of Sin! I am *loved* into godly Sorrow! Oh how the *Fire* of this *Love* melts my Soul into Gospel Repentance! Oh! that I should be so *unkind* to my *kind* Father, that has not only loved me immanently and eternally in himself, but has loved me manifestatively; yea, loved into the Knowledge of Christ; yea, loves me frequently in the Displays of his Unchangeable Heart, notwithstanding my many, repeated Provocations! Oh! what shall I say? Surely, *Grace reigns!* Oh help me to *praise HIM!* I have nothing else to bring but a Tribute of Praise. I must for ever lie in the Dust at his Feet, as an undeserving, Hell-deserving Creature; while I behold *that Love*, that was eternally fixt on me *in Christ*, so freely flowing forth thro' this *smitten Rock*, even to a *mighty Deluge*, like the Waters of the Flood, over all the highest Mountains of *my Sins*; triumphantly carrying on *my Happiness*, in a begun Deliverance from Sin and Satan, working me up into an initial Conformity to God's *First-born*; (the eldest Glory-Son, the supreme Pattern above) and will undoubtedly carry on this Work, till in a Visibility of Glory, as a Jewel made up, I shall shine forth as the Sun, completely bearing his Glory-Likeness: *The Image of the Heavenly!* The eternal *Flow* of this Love, will waft me into Love's *Ocean*; there for ever, with my Lord, as a Vessel of Mercy, to be filled with Glory; in being swallow'd up in GOD, the Ultimate of Enjoyment! Of which we can but little conceive.

Indeed you have rightly judged, "That hitherto it has been rather, Christ loving and embracing *me*, that I *Him*, in the Trial of Faith in the Dark." For I am even filled with Amazment, while I see, that none of all *my* Vileness, is able to stop the Current of *his* Love!

Oh! it was well you said, "The best Wine is reserv'd till last; and that what we enjoy here, can't lessen our Enjoyment at last." For what is it we enjoy here, but GOD? And GOD can't be *lessened*. The Sun communicates of his Influences, in which we are warmed, and enlightened; and yet there's never the less Light or Heat in the Sun for all that it communicates. And if it may be so said of the *Creature-Sun*, how much more of our GOD! And as there will be never the less to be *enjoy'd* at last, for what we enjoy *here*; so neither do I conceive, that the *Sweetness* we have tasted *here*, will in the least *cloy* the New-Man's *Appetite*, or render the Marriage-Supper *less sweet. The Lamb shall lead us to living Fountains*; (not a standing Pool) and the *living Virtue* of these *living Waters*, will constantly maintain in us a *living Appetite*; which will fit us for a delightful Participation, with our Lord, of *that Glory*, which will be *new, new* to Eternity! --- I humbly conceive, That it will be something *higher*, than barely, *Salvation*, that will fill our Souls with *new Pleasures to Eternity*. I conceive, there is *more* in that *Oneness* our Lord has pray'd for, *John* xvii. 21, 22. *That they may be one in us, as thou Father and I am one.* Some Rays having shined into my Soul, That my *highest* Glory will consist, in a *sharing* with my Lord, in *that* Glory of Oneness: even the *highest* Union and Communion with the infinitely Boundless DEITY! And Oh! is not here Room enough, in the *highest* Glory-Communion, that ever *Creatures* can enjoy, with the boundless DEITY, dwelling in our *own Nature*; for the *largest* Soul to expiate, and without the *least* Cloy, with *new* Wonder, delectably to take *in* an inconceivable Variety of Glory to Eternity! What is there in that *Covenant-grant* given out to *Abraham*, Gen. xvii. 7. *I am thy God, and the God of thy Seed!* But oh! how glorious is it, if we trace it to the *grand Original*, even the *eternal Deed of Settlement*, on Christ and his Seed! Of which *that* was but a *Copy*. Surely here's *his*, and *my* Charter, even in the Volume of the everlasting Rolls! And if our *Lord*, in the Joy of his Heart, says, *The Lines are fallen unto me in pleasant Places*; and that he hath a *goodly Heritage*, in having of *us* for his Portion; Oh how much more may *we* say so! What manner of Love is *this*, that *our* Inheritance by Lot, should be no less, than to have the LORD Himself for *our Portion!*

Well might our Lord say, I *will not leave you Orphans*, John xiv. 18. And as we are not left Fatherless, so neither are we left Comfortless, or destitute of a Habitation. For what saith the *Psalmist?* LORD, THOU *hast been our Dwelling-place in all Generations*, Psa. xc. 1. And with what a Glory doth this break up in the New-Testament, to be no less than *dwelling in* GOD, as HE is LOVE. 1 John iv. 16. They that have no Dwelling-houses, are exposed to Heat and Cold, and all manner of Storms. But oh how safe are *we*. Let the Weather be how it will *without*, we are safe *within*; our Dwelling-place is in the *Rock of Ages!* And, Oh! were we blest into an *abiding in Love*, a constant Dwelling at home in our Father's Heart, no Storms whatsoever, neither moral, nor providential, could hurt us. The Thunder and Lightning of *Mount Sinai*, can neither hurt, nor affright the Soul, that securely dwells in the *Man Christ Jesus*, as an Hiding-place from the Wind, and Covert from the Storm. And as *these* can't hurt us, so neither can all the Mutations and Changes we see in the *World*. There is such a Thing as entring into *Rest by Believing*, That the *Government* is laid upon *Christ's Shoulder*; and that all the *cross Lines of Providence*, are drawn exactly *correspondent* to the *Counsel of Jehovah's Will*; all working together, and unanimously carrying on the vast Design of his *Glory*, and the *Good* of his Chosen, in a glorious *Order* of infinite Wisdom.--- But I must break off, desiring a Share in your Prayers, that I may be under fresh Oil, and greatly skill'd in Dealing with a *full Christ*, under all my *felt Emptiness.*

And now, May *the great Shepherd of the Sheep, brought again from the Dead, by the Blood of the everlasting Covenant*, make you perfect in Love, keep you faithful, and make you useful; preserving you Blameless till the Day of his appearing! concerning which he hath said, *Surely I come quickly. Amen. Even so come Lord Jesus.* In HIM I rest,

Your unworthy Sister,

A. C.

Thus kindly the Lord dealt with me during my Stay at *W---k*; and in a little Time he gave me the Desire of my Heart, in fixing my Abode again at *L---n*. Free Grace, and wise Love, to display its Glory, carried me down to the Place, was with me there, and brought me up thence with Gladness.

Upon my return to *L---n*, I was again laid to *Sion's Breasts*, and *milk'd out, and was delighted with the Abundance of her Glory*. In *private* also, my Enjoyments were very great. The everlasting Love of God, Father, Son and Spirit, was gloriously open'd to me; and so let out upon my Heart, as to fill me with Joy unspeakable and full of Glory. Oh the rich Fore-Tastes I had of the Glory of Heaven, at some particular Times of Communion with God! Two of which I'll just mention.

It pleased the Lord, on a certain Day, to break in upon me with Heart-melting, Soul-amazing Discoveries of his Love. And I was particularly led into the *Father's*, and the *Son's* Grace, as displaying its Glory, and laying out its Riches in my eternal Salvation thro' a crucified Jesus. Upon which, as my Soul was engaged in blessing the Father for *his* Love, and the Son for *his* Grace; I attempted to give Thanks for the *Spirit's* Love. But when I came to *this*, I thought I did not so clearly discern the Love of the *Spirit*, as I did the *Father's* and the *Son's*. Whereupon my Soul immediately breath'd out its Desires to *him* that *searcheth the Depths of God*, That HE would open to *me* his *own* everlasting Kindness! And as soon as I had done Prayer, that Word broke in upon my Heart with great Glory, *Rom.* xv. 30. *And for the Love of the Spirit*. In which I saw, that *Love* was ascribed to the *Spirit*. And straightway it was follow'd with this Word, *1 John* v. 7. *And these Three are One*. One in *Essence*, One in *Will*, and so One in *Love*. From hence the blessed Spirit, was graciously pleased to lead me into *his* infinite, eternal, and unchangeable Grace; and told me, "That it was from *his* everlasting Love, (having loved me as the *Father* and the *Son* loved me) that he came down at the appointed Time, to quicken me when dead in Sins. And that in infinite Grace, HE *passed by me, and saw me polluted in my own Blood*; but none of my Pollutions could alter *his* Grace, that *my Time was the Time of Love*, of *his* Love, as well as of the *Father's* and the *Son's* Love. And that from hence *he* said unto me, *Live*; possess'd my Soul for Christ, and new created me in him. And this, tho' HE *foreknew* all my Rebellion and unkind Carriage towards him." And further, HE told me, "That from *his* unchangeable Love, he still *abode* with me, as the *Comforter*, notwithstanding all the Contrarieties of my *Nature*, to his Holy Person and Work; and that from *his* invincible Grace, He would abide with me for *ever*, and *perfect* what concern'd me." But Oh, what Soul-ravishing Pleasures I then felt in Communion with *God* in *Love!* My Soul was as it were sensibly *clasp'd* in the sweet Embraces of Father, Son and Spirit! And while with *open Face I beheld as in a Glass the Glory of the LORD, I was changed into the same Image, from Glory to Glory, as by the Spirit of the Lord*: And had a Taste of *Canaan's Grapes* in the *Wilderness*.

Another Time I was under Illness of Body, and other Trials: And having a tender Mother, such Thought sprang up in my Mind, "If I was with *her* she would pity me." Which had no sooner passed, but that Word was brought with great Power, *Isa.* xlix. 15. *Can a Woman forget her sucking Child, that she should not have Compassion on the Son of her Womb? Yea, they may forget, yet will not I forget thee.* In which, under the *Attraction of infinite Love*, I was brought, in a Moment, into the *Bosom of GOD.* "Oh! thought I, What Folly is it in *me* to hanker after the Bowels of a *Creature*, that have all the Bowels of GOD, in the *Mediator* to go to!" And from that Time, most Part of the Night, the Lord opened his Heart to me, in a wonderful Manner. My Soul was fill'd with the Joys of God's Favour; and particularly led to admire it in one of its Fruits, *i.e.* as Clothing me with a justifying Righteousness: in that Word, *Isa.* lxi. 10. *I will greatly rejoice in the LORD, my Soul shall be joyful in my God, for he hath clothed me with the Garments of Salvation, he hath covered me with the Robe of Righteousness.* Oh! here I saw myself *well dress'd, compleat*, without a *Spot* in the *Righteousness of Christ*; an Object of God's *Well-pleasedness*: Notwithstanding all the Imperfections of my Heart and Life! And Oh, what Life, Light, and Glory, my Soul drank in, from that River of Pleasures, which I found in the Bosom of GOD! I needed none of the *Creatures* to comfort me; GOD was my ALL, and infinitely *enough!* Now, thought I, my Body being weak, "*I'll go to sleep in the Bosom of* CHRIST." But I was more highly favour'd: From that Time, for about an Hour, I was as it were cast into a SEA of GLORY! The Spirit of God went on to open to me amazing Prospects of the Glory of Christ's Righteousness: from *Rev.* xii. 1. *And there appeared a great Wonder in Heaven, a Woman cloth'd with the Sun.* Here I saw myself cloth'd with CHRIST. But Oh the *Glories* I then beheld in the *Person*, and *Obedience* of the *Son of God!* I saw myself wrap'd round with the *Righteousness of* GOD; and splendidly glorious, in the Eyes of *flaming Purity*, as I stood in this *shining Dress!* And from the transcendent Heights of this *Glory-sun*, I look'd down upon the perfect Righteousness of *Adam* in Innocence, and of the holy *Angels* in Heaven, and saw *no* Glory in these, in comparison with the super-excelling *Glory* of *Christ's* Righteousness. *Theirs*, thought I, in its highest Elevation, is but a *Creature-Righteousness*; but the royal Robe with which I am arrayed, is the Righteousness of GOD, *i.e.* of *God-Man*, the *Mediator*, where the *divine* Perfections shine gloriously! Oh, here I saw, That no other Garment, but this *God like* Robe, could honourably fit my *High* Relation, as *The Bride the Lamb's Wife!* This *alone*, I saw, could *fit me* to stand for ever in the Glory-presence of JEHOVAH, with the highest Complacence. And my Soul was brim-full of Joy and Wonder, at this amazing Provision of infinite Wisdom and Grace: This

Robe of Righteousness, that gloriously arrayed me in *Time*, and would be my *everlasting Dress* beyond it! And, as *cloth'd* with this *Righteousness*, I was led to view myself *encompass'd round* with *Covenant-Mercy*: from that Word, *Psal.* xxxii. 10. *Mercy shall compass him about.* I beheld the Mercy of *Jehovah*, as a boundless Ocean, and myself in the *midst* of it; so that nothing could come *at me* but what came thro' a *Sea of Mercy.* No Afflictions, Temptations, or Trials, of what Kind soever, could *touch me*, but must come *thro'* this infinite everlasting Mercy, and *by it* be turn'd into Mercies to me. I was indeed, cast into *Mercy's Ocean*, and delightfully *div'd* into its *infinite* Depths. And upon every new Discovery, I cry'd out, with the Apostle, *Rom.* xi. 33. *Oh the Depths!* And in a Word, By this *Hour's* Communion with GOD, I thought I knew something what *Heaven* would be.: In the Morning, I said, with *Jacob, This is none other but the House of God, and this is the Gate of Heaven*, Gen. xxviii. 17. Thus *familiarly* did the Lord deal with *Me*, a vile sinful Worm!

And further, It pleased the Lord to exercise me with a Variety of Trials. *But when I passed thro' the Waters, and thro' the Fires, HE was with me, and the Rivers did not overflow me, nor the Flames kindle upon me.* My Crosses were so mixt with Comforts, that I have rejoyced in my Tribulations. In a Verse of Mr. *Bunyan*'s, thus;

> If Gall and Wormwood they give me,
>   Then God doth Sweetness cast,
> So much thereto, that they can't think
>   How bravely it doth taste!

Not but I had my Times of Heaviness; but when I was cast down, the Lord raised me up again, and *comforted me on every Side.* I had Trials from within and from without: But tho' *cast down, I was not forsaken.* I'll instance in one; *i.e.* The Body of Sin and Death.

I was once exceedingly *burden'd* with the Corruptions of my Nature, my Soul *groaned* under the Weight of indwelling Sin: I did not question my *Relation* to Christ, but, Oh! my present *Unlikeness* grieved me. And while I was *bemoaning* myself, that Word was brought, *Song* iv. 7. *Thou art all fair, my Love, there is no Spot in thee.* Which gave me *some* Relief; as I view'd my Compleatness in Christ. But my *great Burden* being my own present *Unholiness*, I still wanted the Lord to say something to comfort me particularly under *That*. And immediately this Word was brought, *1 Cor.* xv. 49. *And as we have born the Image of the Earthly, we shall also bear the Image of the Heavenly.* Oh! *This* suited my Case; a Word in *Season*, how *good* is it! *We* shall *also bear the Image of the Heavenly.* From hence, the blessed Spirit gave me a glorious Prospect of the *Security* of my perfect personal Holiness. From the Word, *As*, As *we have born the Image of the Earthly, we shall also bear the Image of the Heavenly*: I was led to see, *how* my Holiness was secured, *i.e.* in *Union*. That, *as* I had born the *Image of the Earthy*, both the natural and corrupt Image of the *first Adam*; by virtue of *Union* to him as a *common* Head and Root; *so* I should also bear the *Image of the Heavenly*, by virtue of my *Union to Christ the second Adam*. And further, I had a delightful View of the glorious Perfection of that Holiness which was secured for me. That, *as* I had born the corrupt Image of the *first Man, extensively*, so that there was no Part or Power of Soul or Body, but what was wholly defiled; *so* I should also bear the *Image of the Heavenly*: That all the Perfections of the *Man Christ*, Soul and Body, as HE came under the Fulness of anointing, should spread themselves thro' my *whole Nature*, to the making me perfectly *like him*. And Oh the *Glory* I then saw, in that perfect *Conformity to Christ*; in his Grace, and Glory-Image, which was *secured* for me in my *Union* to him, as my Head and Root! I saw a Fulness of the Holy Spirit in Christ, to be *communicated*, to make me perfectly Holy. And that this blessed Spirit, notwithstanding all Opposition, would carry on his begun Work in me, until *Grace* was perfected in *Glory*. And with Joy I committed it to *his* Care, and trusted it in *his* Almighty Hand. And, Oh the Joy of Faith, that then filled my Heart! I began to sing, tho' a *Captive* in myself, in full Assurance of that *Liberty* I then had *in* Christ, and should erelong have *through* him. Thus my bowed down Soul was raised up at this Time. And whatever were my Distresses, the LORD saved me out of them. But to go on.

During my Abode at *L---n*, I was highly favoured with the Enjoyment of God, both in publick and private. But after I had been there near five Years, it pleased the Lord to take away my Yokefellow by Death. And some Circumstances attended, which made it very trying. But my kind Lord comforted me. He was graciously pleased, in infinite Condescension, to reason with my troubled Heart, in order to reconcile it to his Stroke; in that Word, *Isa.* xxvii. 7. *Hath he smitten him as he smote those that smote him?* q. d. [*quaaque die*, every day] I have *smitten thee* indeed, but *how* have I done it? Think upon my *Grace* herein: I have not smitten *thee* as I smite mine *Enemies*; I have not brought this Stroke upon thee in *Wrath*, as a *Curse*, but in *great Mercy.'* And by this I was in some measure quieted under the Hand of God, ashamed of my peevish Carriage under the Rod, and thought well of what HE had done, altho' the Dispensation was very dark. But,

III. This brings me to follow divine Providence in another of its Tracks. Upon the Death of my Husband, the Lord removed me to *N---n*, and again fix'd my Abode there.

When I left *L---n*, Things looked dark to me. But yet, in Faith, I was help'd to adore infinite Wisdom, that order'd the most minute Circumstances of my Trial. And with Pleasure I thought, "It will be but a little while ere the Mysteries of Providence shall be fully open'd to me, as having been all subservient, under the Management of infinite Wisdom, to the Glory of God, and my highest Advantage."

As I was on my Journey to *N---n*, I was full of Heaviness. But my dear LORD JESUS, sweetly called me to his Bosom, to take up my Delights in HIM, as the ever-living Fountain of my Joys, in that Word, *Rev*. i. 18. *I am He that liveth, and was dead; and behold, I am alive for evermore.* But oh! the Glory I then saw in my *living* JESUS, that was *once dead*; while he open'd Himself to me, *thus*: "I was *dead*, I once bare *thine* Iniquities, dyed in *thy* Room, *finished* Transgression and made an *End* of Sin. Look to *me* therefore as *once dead*; here's *Rest* for thee under the *Burden* of all thine Iniquities, thou could'st have no Joy in *me* if I had not been *once dead*; look to *me* therefore as once upon the Cross, and in the Tomb. But let not thy Faith stay *here*, I am *risen* and *ascended*; look to *me* therefore upon the *Throne*. I am *He that liveth*: that liveth for *thee*, as the Fountain of all thy Joys. *I live*, tho' the *Creatures die.* Come to my Bosom then, take up thy Delights in *me*, converse with *me* as thy *living Husband* at God's right Hand: For, *behold, I am alive for evemore!*" Thus, with loving Kindness, my sweet Lord Jesus, drew me to Himself, as my everlasting ALL! I was returning to my Father's House; but my Lord bid me look upon all Creature-Enjoyments as *dying* Things, and ever take up my Rest in HIM, the *Life* of all my Joys. And Oh! the transcendent Glory of *my Beloved*, which I saw from *Heb*. i. 11, 12. They *shall perish*, (i.e. the Creatures, even the Heavens, the most durable of them) *but* THOU *Remainest: And* they *all shall wax old as doth a Garment; and as a Vesture shalt thou fold them up, and they shall be changed: but THOU art the same, and* thy *Years shall not fail.*

Oh the Superlative Fairness of *my Beloved!* HE was to *me, The Chiefest of ten Thousand!*

Thus Free Grace brought me to *N---n.* But presently my Mind was again fill'd with Distress. And that Word, the Lord made a great Stay to me, I Cor. vii. 29, 30. *Brethren, the Time is short. It remaineth, that they that have Wives, be as tho' they had none; and they that weep, as tho' they wept not.* The Views of the near Approach of Eternity, when all Tears should be wiped from my Eyes, quieted my Heart under its present Trouble. Another Time, the Lord spake comfortably to me in that Promise, *Heb.* xiii. 5. *I will never leave thee, nor forsake thee.* q. d. [*quaque die,* every day] "*Creatures* may *leave* thee, even *all* of 'em; but *I'll never leave thee*: Thou hast me with thee in all the Changes which pass over thee: *I'll never leave, nor forsake thee* thro' Time, nor to Eternity." That Word also, was exceeding precious to me, *Isa.* liv. 10. *For the Mountains shall depart, and the Hills be removed; but my Kindness shall not depart from thee, nor the Covenant of my Peace be removed, saith the LORD, that hath Mercy on thee.* I was led to view the Mountains and Hills, as the most *lasting* Parts of this lower Creation. But "*These*, saith the LORD, as *durable* as they are, shall *depart*; but *my Kindness* shall *not* depart from *thee*; it shall *outlive* all thy Trials, yea *Time* it self. It's *my* Kindness, that shall not depart from *thee*; which is, sympathizing, succouring, pardoning, delivering, and in all, *everlasting Kindness*; that shall not *depart from thee*." But Oh how this wonderful Grace *Fill'd me!* I had *enough*; I needed no more than I had in this *infinite, eternal Kindness!* And further, my kind Father, acquainted me with the gracious Design of his Heart, in *this*, as well as my other Trials, from that Word, *Deut.* viii. 15, 16. *Who led thee thro' that great and terrible Wilderness,* &c. *that he might humble thee, and prove thee, to do thee good at thy latter End.* Thus was I carry'd thro' this Trial, by the kind Supports, and sweet Embraces of the *everlasting Arms.*

In the next Place, after I had been at *N---n* some Time, I was again married; And the Lord gave me that Word, concerning it, *Gen,* xxii. 17. *In Blessing, I will bless thee.* Which infinite Faithfulness has since made good. Upon this Change, I had a Mind to return to *L---n*; for my Heart was *there*, because I enjoy'd so much of GOD, under the Ministry of Mr. *Sk---p.* But the all-wise Providence of God, so over-ruled Things, as to fix our Abode at *N---n.*

Here I was surrounded with Mercies; had many Comforts, and many Trials. But the Lord was very familiar with me in them, gave me suitable

Promises under them, exercised my Graces, and did me much good by 'em, and at length delivered me out of them. Oh how sweetly have I been resign'd into the Will of God, under trying Circumstances! So that I could not wish to be disposed of any other Way, than just as I was. I liked the *Generation-Work* infinite Wisdom allotted me, and desired to *serve the Will of God herein, before I fell asleep*. And that Word the Lord gave, to comfort me under my Trials, *Isa.* xli. 10. *Fear not, for I am with thee.* In which he thus spoke to me, "Be not *afraid*, wherever *I lead thee*, for I am *with thee*, to sympathize with thee in thy Sorrows, to sustain thee under thy Burdens, and bear the heaviest End of them; to sanctify all thy Trials, to pardon all thy Imperfection under them, and at last to deliver thee from them." And then I *trusted myself* with my *dear Lord Jesus*, my sweet Companion, and went on *rejoycing in Tribulation*. And I must say, That I could not have been without *any* of my Afflictions, but with *manifest* Loss. Oh the infinite Mercy, Grace, Power and Faithfulness, I have seen display'd, in supporting me under them, exercising me by them, and delivering me out of them!

After I had been married a little Time, Mr. *Sk—p* died, which was a great Grief to me. For I long'd for the Water of Life thro' *that* Channel; but when the Pipe was broke, and no Hope left of my hearing him any more, I was full of Heaviness. Under this Trial of *his Death*, I was sweetly reliev'd by *Christ's Life*, as the Head of the Church, having all the Fulness of the Spirit in him, to give Gifts unto Men, for the Work of the Ministry, for the Edification of his Body. Tho', at Times, I was afraid that my Ears would be no more so bless'd, under the Ministry of the Word, as they had been under *his*. But the Lord, in wonderful Grace, in his own Time, raised me up another in his Stead. And therefore,

IV. The next Providence I shall take Notice of, relates to the Lord's removing me from *N---n*, to *W---h*.

This, as I look'd upon it to be a wonderful Appearance of God for me, in his infinite Grace and Faithfulness, in fulfilling the Promises he gave me, notwithstanding many Deaths which pass'd over 'em, I wrote a particular Account of some Years ago; according as I had purposed to do, if I saw the Promises fulfilled. My End in writing it, was, to bear a Testimony for GOD, in his infinite Grace and Faithfulness to his Promises; and also to encourage the dear Saints to trust in him for promis'd Mercies, in the Face of the greatest Improbabilities. When I first wrote it, I did not design to make it thus publick. And perhaps, some may blame me for giving such a particular

Account, of what pass'd between God and my Soul, in any one single Providence, in this Place. But as it was on my Heart to write it so particularly, and not knowing but the Lord may make it of Use to some of his Children in like Circumstances, and that *they* may be glad to hear how it fared with *me*; for *their Sakes* I shall give the Account as I then took it; and beg the Excuse of *others*, who may think me guilty of Breach of Order.

Some Hints of what passed between God and my Soul, concerning my Removal from *N---n*, to *W---h*.

The Lord having been pleased to remove me from *L---n,* where I enjoy'd much of his Presence under the Ministry of Mr. *Sk---p*, he fix'd my Station at *N---n*. While I was in *L---n*, I longed for the Word of the Lord, dispensed on his own Days, more than for my necessary Food. Oh with what great Delight did I sit down under the Shadow of my Beloved, in the Ordinances of his House! I found his Fruit sweet unto my Taste; while the Lord made good that precious Promise, *Isa*. xlix. 9. *They shall feed in the Ways, and their Pastures shall be in all high Places*. But when I was again fix'd at *N---n*, I soon found a sad Alteration: For instead of breaking forth into Singing, from that Fulness of Joy I had wont to have in God's Presence, my Soul sat solitary, and mourn'd in secret; like the Dove that has lost her Mate, because *my Beloved* had withdrawn himself. The joyful Spring I once had, caused by the near Approach of the Sun of Righteousness, was now over; and I found a sad Autumn succeeding, when his sovereign Influences were withdrawn.

During my Bridegroom's *Absence*, my Soul went *mourning*, as without the Sun: Tho', I bless his Name, that at Times when he saw me *faint* for the Vision of his Face, he was graciously pleas'd to give me a *Glimpse* of his Glory; which reviv'd my drooping Spirit, and recover'd me from my Swooning-Fits. For I found his *Cheeks to be as a Bed of Spices*; or a *Side-look of Christ's Face*, (as one well observes) when we hadn't the full *Vision* of his Glory, to be exceeding delightful. But tho' it was thus with me at Times, yet for the most Part I sat *sorrowful*. I remember'd the former Loving-Kindness of the LORD, when I walk'd in the Light of his Countenance, when the powerful Breath of his Spirit, made the joyful Sound reach my Ears, yea, my very Heart; and I greatly fear'd, that I should no more drink, as I had done, *of the River of* God's *Pleasures*, till I got home to my Father's House, in whose *Presence is Fulness of Joy*, and at whose *right Hand are Pleasures for evermore*. I found Grief, Love, Desire, Humility and holy Resignation, variously working in me.

I remember'd the *Advantages* I had by my Lord's sweet *Presence*; and I mourn'd for his *Absence*; as saith the *Psalmist*, Psa. xxx. 7. *Thou didst hide thy Face, and I was troubled.*

I thought on the Excellencies of *my Beloved*, and the heavenly Sweets my Soul found when infolded in his Arms; and then I was *sick of Love for him*: As saith the *Spouse*, when she sought her absent Lord, charging *the Daughters of Jerusalem*, that if they saw him, they should tell him, *she was sick of Love*, Song v. 8.

And oh the vehement *Desires* I had after his Return! My Soul was like *David's*, when he said, *As the Hart panteth after the Water-Brooks, so panteth my Soul after thee, O God. My Soul thirsteth for God, for the living God: When shall I come and appear before God?* Psa. xlii. 1, 2. Oh how I long'd to *see* his *Power* and his *Glory*, as I had seen HIM *in the Sanctuary!*

I thought on my own *Unworthiness* of his former Favours; and my Soul was *humbled* within me; and drawn out to desire that he would give me Grace to live to him in Holiness and Righteousness all my Days, as judging it but my reasonable Service; if I might not be dandled on the Knee and laid in the Bosom as I was wont to be.

I remember'd his *sovereign Right* to unveil his Glory, or hide his Face as he pleaseth, and I was in some Measure bow'd to his divine Sovereignty. Yet so, as that an earnest Desire was mostly kept up in my Soul, that if it might be consistent with the Glory of his Grace, he would turn again, cause his Face to shine, and save me out of my Distresses.

Sometimes, indeed, I was too *careless*. But the Lord did not leave me long in that Frame; but was wont to favour me again with fresh Discoveries of that suitable Fulness that was laid up in Christ for me. I saw that there was not only a Fulness of Life in him, suited to quicken me at *first*, when I was dead in Sin; but a Fulness also, that was sufficient to revive me *under*, and recover me *from* all my Backslidings. The Views of which gave Wing to my Desires, and made 'em swift in their Motion after the long'd-for Blessing. And oh the infinite Grace of my God! He look'd down upon me with an Eye of ender Compassion, and heard me bemoaning myself, as he did *Ephraim*, Jer. xxxi. 18. and he was pleased to deal with me according to that gracious Promise, *Isa.* xli. 17. *When the Poor and Needy seek Water, and there is none, and their Tongue faileth for thirst, I the LORD will hear them, I the GOD of Israel will not forsake them.* He shew'd a special Regard to the Breathings his own Spirit had wrought in my Soul. And having design'd to give the Mercy, he was graciously pleased to honour me with a Variety of Exercise about it; that so it might be brought forth in a more triumphant Glory. The Lord was not willing (if I may so say) to give the Mercy *alone*, but would cause me to possess the *double*; by finding Work for every Grace of his own Spirit.

And he began to lay a Foundation for my *Faith*, by giving me that sweet Direction and gracious Promise, *Psa.* xxxvii. 5. *Commit thy Way unto the LORD: Trust also in him, and he shall bring it to pass.* This was the *original Promise*, on the Grace and Faithfulness of which I was made to *rest* near two Years before my Removal. From hence I was help'd to *commit my Way*, in my projecting Thoughts, *unto the LORD*, and had some Expectation rais'd in my Soul, that I should have the Desire of my Heart, even in this World, tho' I knew not from what Quarter it should come. At Times, indeed, I was *afraid* of the contrary; but even then I was comforted, that if I should not again see God's Power and his Glory, as I had seen him in his Sanctuary *below*, yet that my Soul should be absolutely satisfied when I was brought home to his House *above*. But this precious Promise being cast into my Heart, became a living Seed, and taking Root there, it sprang up into Desires, Expectations, and earnest Prayers to the Lord, for the long'd-for Mercy.

Some Time after this, that Word was set home upon my Mind, *Hos.* ii. 15. *And I will give her her Vineyards from thence, and the Valley of Achor for a Door of Hope, and she shall sing there, as in the Days of her Youth, and as in the Day when she came up out of the Land of Egypt.* From hence I was made to *see*, in some Measure, the Riches of the Glory of God's Grace, which shines forth in his Promise towards his *backsliding Children*: And had some Persuasions wrought in my Soul, that he would thus deal with *me*: And those Words founded very sweetly, *she shall sing there, as in the Days of her Youth.* I call'd to mind the joyful Days of my *Youth*, and the sweet *Songs* I sung while the Glory of the Lord fill'd the Temple where I dwelt; and some secret Persuasions that it should be so with me again, did afresh animate my Soul to seek the Lord for the Fulfillment of this Promise to *me*.

And here, by the Way, I may take Notice, that tho' my Soul earnestly desired Deliverance, yet I was very loth to leave the Place where I dwelt; my Business being so suitable and advantageous, and my Habitation so commodious, that I oft thought, *I would never leave the Town.* But, Oh the Glory of that *Power* which is able to *conquer* the stoutest Heart! The Lord having design'd some better Thing for me, than to stay there, he sweetly drew my Heart after himself, by giving me such a quick Remembrance of the *Sweetness* of his own Presence, which made his Absence so exceeding *bitter*, that I could take no Pleasure in the insnaring Things of Sense. The former *experienc'd* Sweetness of Communion with God, together with the *new-presented* Glory of a Possibility of enjoying him again in this World, did so radiantly shine upon my Soul, that I soon found all *worldly Glory* to die about me. An advantageous Business, and a pleasant Habitation, were now in little Esteem with *me*, who wanted the Advantage of *God's Presence*, and the ravishing Prospect of *his Glory* in his House. Any Business, or any Place would now have satisfied me, could I but have found my satisfying Rest in GOD.

I sought him in his Ordinances, in one Place and another; but alas! I found him not. So that my Soul was pained with Love-Desires, for *Want* of a wish'd Enjoyment of my *sweet Lord*. And once, in particular, I remember that my Soul was ready to *faint*, as if I could not *live* without him: And I groaned out my Desires thus: "Oh that the Lord would give me but HIMSELF, whatever he does with me in this World! If he would give me but Food to eat, and Raiment to put on, so that I had *his* Presence, I should be contented." And such a Thought came into my Mind, "if I was *Moses*, I would *ask him*." I thought, if I was such an *intimate Favourite* that I could almost get *any Thing of him, this* should be my Request. But, thought I again, "I dare not tell him, I would be contented with mean Circumstances, so I might but get a Place in some House of his, where his Glory shines; my *Heart is so deceitful and desperately wicked*, that I dare not tell him any such Thing." But tho' I durst not *Word* it with him, yet HE saw the strong *Workings* of my Heart, and heart the Groanings of his Prisoner; and was well acquainted with those vehement *Desires* which his own Spirit had wrought in me, on Purpose that he might shew the more Grace, in *satisfying the longing Soul, and filling the Hungry with good Things*. For I was now like *David*, when he cry'd out, *O God, thou art my God, early will I seek thee: My Soul thirsteth for thee, my Flesh longeth for thee in a dry and thirsty Land where no Water is: To see thy Power and thy Glory, so as I have seen thee in the Sanctuary*, Psa. lxiii. 1, 2. And *I esteemed the Law of his Mouth more than Thousands of Gold and Silver*, Psa. cxix. 72.

But my *kind Lord*, did not long leave me in this languishing *Love-sickness* for himself. So *great* was his *Grace*, that notwithstanding my great Sinfulness, Unworthiness, and Misimprovement of his former Favours, HE came *leaping o'er these Mountains, skipping o'er these Hills*: He *flew* for my Relief, and did as it were *ride upon the Wings of the Wind!* His providential Wheels were *swift* in their Motion to bring me a Sight of my *Well-beloved*; and tho' at *first Look*, he seem'd to appear in *Disguise*, yet he soon took the *Veil off his Face*, and enlighten'd me with his *Glory*.

And here I may again take Notice of one of the Things, that thro' the Weakness of my Flesh, was insnaring to me, *i.e.* the House I liv'd in: Which made me loth to leave the Town. But the Lord having design'd to remove me; behold, the Way he took to rapp my Fingers off from that I was ready to catch at! The House was presently sold over our Heads, and we must turn out. When I first suspected this, the Thoughts of it were very displeasing to me. But my kind Lord, quickly began to explicate this Providence, by the Promise I first had for my Deliverance: And I thought thus: "Who can tell? it may be the Lord is going to fulfil that Promise, of giving me the Desire of my Heart, by this Providence." This pleasing Thought quieted me, and blunted the Edge of my Sorrow, which I should have had in parting with a pleasant House, if the Lord had not loosen'd my Heart, by giving me to long so for the Pleasures of his House, that I thought if I might but see the Glory of *his House*, I should be contented if *mine* was ever so mean a Cottage. Various were the Exercises of my Mind under this Providence; and I was inclin'd to enquire of the Lord, whither [*sic*, r. whether] he was about to remove me?

But here I may take Notice, that before this, Mr. *G---t*, of *W---h*, had preach'd several Times at *N---n*, and I had heard him with Pleasure. And once, in particular, he was so filled with the Spirit, in Prayer, that I saw a very great Glory of the divine Presence in him. And my poor Soul was brought *nigh*, to worship with him in the Fellowship of the same Spirit. Oh, what a mixing of Spirits did I then feel, while in the Language of Faith, he breath'd out these Words: "The World is a troublesome Ocean; but we rejoyce in our skilful Pilot: Our dear Lord Jesus, we are exceeding safe in thine Arms: Let's sail on in the Ocean of thy Love!" And oh, how sweetly did we then sail together, while one and the same Wind, wafted us both into the Bosom of Christ! Oh then it was, that *my Soul* was knit to *his*, while I catch'd the heavenly *Fire*, that set *his* Heart a *Burning*. And as the Saints Fellowship in Worship, is *always* exceeding pleasant and glorious, when they have Access thro' Christ, by one Spirit to the Father; so it receives an additional Glory and Sweetness, when the Souls enjoying it have been almost *famish'd* for Want thereof: And thus it was with *me*. Light is *always* sweet, and a pleasant Thing it is for the Eyes to behold the Sun. But let

Light, glorious Light, break forth immediately out of Darkness; it must needs have a *Transcendency* of Glory in the Eye of the Beholder, and the Sensation be *exceeding* quick: While the precedent Darkness serves as a Foil, to set off the Glory of its Lustre.

And here, by the Way, if the Saints Fellowship in the Spirit of Grace, which yet is *increasing*, by that which every Joint supplieth, has such a ravishing Sweetness, and spiritual Glory in it: What will be their Fellowship in *Heaven*, when the whole mystical Body shall be *compleat*, and the Spirit of *Glory*, from Christ the Head, shall fill every Member of the Body! Tongue can't utter, no, nor Heart conceive, the Joys of that eternal *Rapture*, the Saints shall be swallow'd up in, when they shall have Glory-Communion with Christ, and each other! Every Member of the Body, being then marshall'd into Order, shall eternally be fill'd with *Glory*; while Glory from Christ the *Head*, runs as it were thro' each *Member*, into *other*: As the Spirits from the Head, run thro' the natural Body, for the Supply of all the Members, in their several Places, according to their proper Functions. Oh, who can tell what the *Communion of Saints* will be, when they shall come to the *Glory* of that *Oneness*, our Lord has pray'd for! *John* xvii. 21. What the *Love-Delights* of Christ, and the Saints will be, in their mutual *Glory-Communion* with each other, is beyond our present Capacity to take in. This *new Wine* will [*sic*; r. would] burst our *old Bottles*; and therefore the wise Master of the Feast, has reserv'd it till *last*; even till we sit down at the *Marriage-Supper of the Lamb*: And then he'll set the *best Wine* abroach, when we are able to bear it. Oh *then*, we shall for ever admire the unfathomable *Depths* of God's *wise Grace*, which form'd the Head and Members *together*, in its vast Womb! Then we shall see ourselves *One*, both with *Christ*, and *one another*, to the eternal *Endearment* of or Souls to each other. Then we shall *see* that we could not have been *without one another* in the Lord: For as the whole mystical Body, is said to be *the Fulness of Christ* the Head; so answerably, every Member of that Body, may be said to be the Fulness of each other. For if one Member was *wanting*, the Body would be *incompleat*; and so *lose* of its Happiness and Glory. But, to return from this Digression.

The Lord having, as was said, under the afore-named Providence, drawn out my Heart to enquire, Whether he was about to remove me? And also, Whether I might go to *W---h?* (For thither I was most bent, in Case of a Removal) he did not give me an immediate Answer: But drew out my Soul into earnest Longings, and Pleadings with himself, that I might know his Mind concerning this Thing. And quickly after, that Word was brought to my Mind, with great Power and Sweetness, *Gen.* xviii. 17. *Shall I hide from Abraham that Thing which I do?* In which I heard an encouraging Sound of familiar Grace. But straitway [*sic*; r. straightway] I thought, "*Abraham* was *the Friend of God*, a peculiar Favourite: And he would not *hide* from *him* his Secrets: But will he *tell me?*" Then that Word was brought, *Gal.* iii. 9. *They which be of Faith, are blessed with faithful Abraham.* Upon which, I was farther carried on, under fresh Encouragement of Faith, to plead with the Lord, that he would *tell me*, whether he would have me *go* or *not*. And while the Answer was delay'd, my Soul breath'd out itself, into the Bosom of Christ, in a Verse of a Hymn, thus:

We're Bone now of thy Bone,
    To thee we're made so nigh:
Thou hid'st thyself, now from thyself:
    Oh therefore, tell us why?

Soon after this, I heard the *Voice of my Beloved*, who said unto me, *If thou know not, oh thou fairest among Women, go thy Way forth by the Footsteps of the Flock, and feed thy Kids beside the Shepherds Tents*, Song i. 8. From these Words, *Go thy Way forth by the Footsteps of the Flock*: I received a gracious *Grant*, and special *Command* to follow the *Flock*, or *that* Flock my Heart was most upon; as hearing that the great Shepherd led them into green Pastures. From the following Words, I reciev'd a double Instruction: As, 1. I understood 'em to be a divine *Command*; binding me to Duty and Obedience. And so, *Feed thy Kids beside the Shepherds Tents*, was as much as if the Lord had said, "*Go*, place thyself *beside the Shepherds Tents*, or *that* Shepherd's Tent, thy Soul desires to be near, and *wait* there in a Way of Duty." And 2. I took these Words as a gracious *Promise*. And so, *Feed thy Kids*, &c. was as much as if the Lord had said, "thou *shalt feed* beside the *Shepherds Tents*, or in *that Place* where thy Soul desires to be." And this was back'd with that precious Promise, *Psa.* xxxvii. 3. *And verily thou shalt be fed.*

This kind Answer of my dearest JESUS, did make my Soul exceeding glad and thankful. And as he now had bid me *go forth*; he was further pleas'd to acquaint me, that HE would be *with me*: By bringing that gracious Word home to my Heart, *John* x. 4. *When he putteth forth his own Sheep, he goeth before them.* And as I apprehended the Way to be difficult, and at present shut up; HE was graciously pleas'd to give me a View of the Greatness and Glory of his own *mediatory Power*, as exalted at God's right Hand: from *Rev.* iii. 7. *I am* HE *that openeth, and no Man shutteth; and shutteth, and no Man openeth.* And what he did for his Servant *Paul*, was also encouraging to me, when he sent him to preach the Gospel: As *I Cor.* xvi. 9. where he says, *A great Door and effectual is open'd unto me.*

But no sooner almost, under some Encouragement of Faith, did I begin to think of a *March*; but the Enemies began to *oppose*. Carnal *Self-Love*, that always prefers the Interest of the Flesh, before the spiritual Enjoyment and Service of the Lord; began to set forth the Worth and Greatness of those worldly Advantages, I was at present in the Enjoyment of: Together with the Folly of leaving real Enjoyments, for but hop'd for, and imaginary Supplies. Unbelief also, distrusting the Lord's appearing for me in a new Place; began to represent a great many Straits and Difficulties I was like to meet with, if I should remove. And both agreed to tell me, "it was such a Piece of Folly, that hardly any Body would be guilty of."

But oh, the Kindness of the Captain of my Salvation! He did not leave me to defeat these Enemies in my own Wisdom and Strength: But gave me fresh Instructions about what his Servant *Abraham* once did, when called *to go out*: And what was *my Duty* to do in the present Case: And likewise strengthened my Soul to follow him; by bringing that Word to my Mind, *Heb.* xi. 8. *By Faith Abraham, when he was called to go out into a Place which he should after receive for an Inheritance, obeyed; and he went out, not knowing whither he went.* This Word, the Lord was pleas'd to manage by his own Power, upon my Heart, while I thus understood it: *Abraham* was *called of God* to leave his Kindred, and his Country, and go unto a Place that the Lord would shew him; having a Promise of the divine Presence and Blessing. And he *went out*, in the Obedience of Faith, *not knowing whither he went*: Or not knowing the Situation, Goodness, or Extension of the *Place* that the Lord had promis'd him. And thus, in like Manner, I saw it my Duty to do. Having received a divine Command to *go forth*: And also a gracious Encouragement that the Lord would *go before me*, and open a Door for me: I resolv'd, in divine Strength, to go forth, as soon as the Lord in his Providence should *open a Door* for my outward Supply; altho' *I knew not* how great or lasting it should be; yet, in *Obedience* to his *Command*, I resolv'd to cast myself on his Care and Providence.

After this, my Faith was led more particularly to view the *Power* of Christ, as he has all Power in Heaven and Earth given unto him of the

Father; and that in Subserviency to the Salvation of the Elect: from John xvii. 2. *As thou hast given him Power over all Flesh, that he should give eternal Life to as many as thou hast given him.* That is, in all the *Beginnings* and *First-fruits* of it, by the glorious *Gospel* here; as well as the *Completion* of it, in ultimate *Glory* hereafter. So that, seeing the Kingdom of Providence, subservient to the Kingdom of Grace; I was led in Faith, to ask the Lord Jesus, "That he would magnify his own Power, in granting me a Supply for my natural Life, in *that Place* where he had already promised me a spiritual Supply for my Soul." And many were the gracious Promises I receiv'd as an Answer to this Request. As, *I will open Rivers in high Places, and Fountains in the midst of the Valleys*, Isa. xli. 18. *Bread shall be given thee, and thy Water shall be sure*, Chap. xxxiii. 16. *And verily thou shalt be fed*; Psa. xxxvii. 3. *The Dragons and the Owls shall honour me: because I give Waters in the Wilderness, and Rivers in the Desert, to give Drink to my People, my Chosen*, Isa. xliii. 20. *I will give Men for thee, and People for thy Life*, Ver. 4. *Blessed shall be thy Basket and thy Store. Blessed shalt thou be when thou comest in, and blessed shalt thou be when thou goest out. And in all that thou settest thy Hand unto*, Deut. xxviii. 5, 6, 8.

Upon this, my Soul being filled with joyful *Expectations* of the Lord's Appearing for me, we made some *Enquiry* at *W---h*, whether there was any likelihood of our outward Supply. For I would fain have had the Mercy *just then*. The House being sold, where we liv'd, and we to remove, I was loth to go into another at *N---n*. Whereupon, I intreated the Lord that he would not suffer me. And some Hopes I had, that I should have my Request. But the Lord was pleased to disappoint me in this: and to exercise me further, by bringing a great *Death* upon the *Promise*, for about a Year.

Well, when this Death first appear'd, I was ready to be discouraged, as tho' my Prayers and Faith were in vain. But what I once heard Mr. *G---t* speak in Preaching, was brought to my Mind to stay me. It was this: "That when the Lord does not give his Children an immediate Answer of their Requests, in the very Things they ask: "Yet, if he does but speak to them, and tell 'em the Reason of his present Dispensation; it might be esteem'd as an Answer of Prayer. As when *Joshua*, in Prayer, was arguing before the Lord, about Israel's being smitten before their Enemies: the Lord tells him the Reason of it: *Get thee up*, (says he) *Israel hath sinned*, Josh. vii. 10,11."

And tho' the Lord did not answer *me*, in the very *Thing* that I requested; yet he was pleased to give me a Hint of two or three Things that might be the *Reason* of it. As thus: I thought, "It may be the Time of the Fulfilment of the Promise, is not yet come." Or, "It may be to fulfil some other Promise; and some of my own Prayers too: and one Request in particular that I had put up to the LORD: *viz.* That he would work Things about so in his Providence, as to hide me from the Strife of Tongues, in removing me." For I was afraid of some of my Relations, lest they should reflect upon me, for leaving that profitable Business I was then employ'd in.

Having these Hints then; (all which prov'd true in the Event) I took 'em as one kind of Answer of prayer: and so my Mind was stay'd. And as I was thinking, That tho' Things were delayed; yet surely, *That* must be the *Place* where the *Promises* were to be fulfill'd: This Word dropt upon my Mind: *Thither cause thy mighty Ones to come down*, O LORD, Joel iii. 11. Which I understood as a Direction for me to pray to the Lord, that he would cause his *mighty Angels*, as the Ministers of his Providence, to *come down*, and work Things about by *their Ministry*, so as to fulfil *his Designs*, in bringing me to *that Place*. Another Word also, I had for my Instruction and Comfort: *At the beginning of thy Supplication, the Commandment came forth. But the Prince of the Kingdom of Persia, withstood me one and twenty Days*, Dan. ix. 23, and x. 13. From which I was again comforted; and look'd upon the Thing as *granted*; and that I should certainly be brought *thither*: Tho' there was somewhat at present that did stand in the Way, and might hinder it for some space of Time. This Word, likewise, was brought to me, *Behold I send an Angel before thee, to bring thee into the Place prepared*, Exod. xxiii. 20. Thus, being satisfied about the *Sureness* of the promis'd Mercy: I was resign'd into *God's Will*, as to the *Time* of it; believing that he would bring it forth in its proper Season, in which it should appear most beautiful.

And by this Time I was made willing to go into another House; which I did, in Obedience to divine Providence. And I dwelt in it, much like a Stranger, or Pilgrim in a Tent, or Tabernacle that was shortly to be taken down. I look'd upon *W---h* to be my *own Place*: and my self, in my present Habitation, to be like a *Stranger* that shortly expects to be sent for Home. And that Word was much to me, *At the Commandment of the* LORD, the Children of Israel *journeyed, and at the Commandment of the* LORD, *they pitched*, Numb. ix. 18. Thus at the Commandment of the Lord, I did as it were pitch my Tent in that House: And I rested in it, like the Children of Israel in their Tents, waited till the Cloud should be taken off the Tabernacle, the Glory of the LORD go before me, and the Trumpet found a March: By the Lord's saying to me by his Spirit, and by his Providence, *Arise, my Love, my fair one, and come away*, Song ii. 13.

But while the Mercy was delay'd, the Lord suffer'd the Enemies, Satan and my own unbelieving Heart, at Times, to bring me evil Tidings: like the unfaithful Spies, who told the People, That the *Land* was not so *good* as the Lord had promis'd; and that it was impossible for 'em to *possess it*, because of the *Giants* that dwelt in it, *Num.* xiii. 31, 32. But the Lord did not leave me long under Discouragements, but was wont by some *Promise* or other, to raise my *Faith* in his own Grace and Faithfulness. And then the Language of Faith, like that of the good Spies, was this: *The Land which the* LORD *our God giveth us, is an exceeding good Land: and we are well able to possess it.*

Once I was saying, in my Thoughts, "That the Lord did not appear for me; nor regard my Prayers." And he spoke to my Heart, and sweetly overcame my Unbelief by that Word, Isa. xl. 27. *Why saist thou, O Jacob, and speakest, O Israel, My Way is hid from the LORD, and my Judgment is passed over from my God?* And that Word also, did often strengthen my Faith, *Num.* xxiii. 19. *Hath* HE *said, and shall He not do it? or hath* HE *spoken, and shall He not make it good?* And that Word likewise, *Isa.* lv. 12. *For ye shall go out with Joy, and be led forth with Peace: the Mountains and the Hills shall break forth before you into singing, and all the Trees of the Field shall clap their Hands.* And yet for all *this*, I was up and down in Faith, with respect to my *Expectations.*

One Time, I remember, I was much cast down by this Suggestion: "That if I was where I desired to be, I might not meet with the Comfort that I expected: Yea, that it was very unlikely I should." For thus the Case was represented to me: "That I had been used to hear great Men in the Gospel: *Fathers* in Christ, that had attain'd to great Knowledge in the Doctrines thereof: which was the Food of my Soul: And how then could I expect to hear such Things from such a *young Man* that I had my Eye upon?"

By this Representation, I was cast down for a little while. But the Lord was pleas'd to raise up my Faith, by somewhat I heard Mr. *G---t* speak, a little Time before, which was to this Effect: That God could do great Things by weak Means: "If God will use *Rams-horns*; (said he) they shall throw down *Jericho's Walls.*" So I thought, If God will use this Instrument to *feed my Soul*, nothing shall *Hinder it.* And my kind Lord went on to confirm my Faith in this, that he would feed me by Him, according to his Promise, by bringing several Scriptures with Power to my Heart.

I think one, or both of these, was first brought: *The Weak shall be as David, and David as the Angel of the LORD*, Zech. xii. 8. *A little one shall become a Thousand, and a small one a strong Nation*; Isa. lx. 22. And this also, *I will make Darkness Light, and crooked Things straight*, Chap. xlii. 16. From whence I gather'd, that Mr. *G---t* should grow and increase in ministerial Gifts and Graces. And further, The Lord was pleas'd to tell me, That HE would put a *Word into his Mouth* for me, *Deut.* xviii. 18. And that HE would *give me a Pastor after his own Heart, that should feed me with Knowledge and Understanding*, Jer. iii. 15. By this I saw, that I should be fed by Him, with Knowledge and Understanding in the great Doctrines of the Gospel. And it was confirm'd, by *Isa.* xlix. 11. *I will make all my Mountains a Way, and my High-ways shall be exalted.* This Scripture was thus opened to me: I will make all my *Mountains*, or the high Acts of my Grace, which are firm as Mountains, a *Way*, in which I will visit and feed thy Soul: While the *High-ways* of my Love and Grace are exalted in his Ministry. *Exalted* they shall be: but that's not all, for I will make them a *Way*, an *efficacious* Way, in which I will *commune with thee*. Thus I saw, That the Lord would enable him to preach these great Things, that so I might be fed.

But still I wanted to know, whether *his Soul* should be led into 'em, so as to feed delightfully upon them Himself: that so we might feed together. And then these Words were brought: *They shall see Eye to Eye, with the Voice together they shall sing*, Isa. lii. 8. *And He shall stand and feed in the Majesty of the* LORD, *Micah* v. 4. And, *I will satiate the Soul of the Priests with Fatness, and my People shall be satisfied with my Goodness*, Jer. xxxi. 14. And, *There the glorious LORD will be unto us a Place of broad Rivers and Streams*, Isa. xxxiii. 21. And, *Chap.* lxvi. 11. *Ye shall milk out and be delighted with the abundance of her Glory.* And, *Upon all the Glory there shall be a Defence*, Chap. iv. 5.

And when the Lord gave *Being* unto all this *Glory*, in the *Promise*; my Soul made haste, bow'd down, and worship'd: Adoring the Riches of his Grace, in that he not only promis'd to *feed me*, but so richly and abundantly to *satisfy me!* And from this Time, I was rais'd to expect, That the Lord would do great Things for me, by that *very Instrument* I had my Eye upon. So that I rejoyc'd in him, and blest God for him, as given me already in the Promise.

But instead of my being brought to possess the great Things in the *Promise*; a *great Death* presently seem'd to be upon it. Mr. *G---t* falls bad of a *Quinsy*, and his Life seem'd to be in very great Danger.

But oh, the Distress that seized my Soul with the News of it! The Lord, who but a little while before, had made me so exceeding glad, by giving me amazing Prospects of the *promis'd Glory*; now seem'd, in his Providence to *stay the very Child of Promise*, in whom all the Promises were! But surely, it is almost impossible to tell what a Trial this was to me.

Let but any of the Children of God consider, What a desolate sorrowful Case I was in, upon the *Loss* of Mr. *Sk---p*, and view how strongly the Lord wrought up my Soul into vehement Desires and earnest Supplications, that HE would raise up *another* to feed me in his Stead. And then let them see all these vast Desires satisfy'd, in the forenam'd *Promises*; and think upon that unspeakable *Joy* which fill'd my Soul, when there was another rais'd up in the Promise! which I look'd upon to be so *faithful*, that Heaven and Earth should pass, sooner than it should go unfulfill'd: Yea, let 'em add to this, The *Earnest* and sweet *Fore-tastes* I had had of the *promis'd Glory*, in sweet Communion with God, under hearing him preach now and then. Let 'em, I say, lay these Things together: and then let 'em view the Lord, appearing as if he was about to *stay all* my new-born Hopes, earnest Expectations, and blooming Joys, together with his own Promises *at once!* And perhaps they may give a little Guess at the Pain my Soul felt, while my Father's Hand was lifted up, as if he would strike the Blow.

However, the Stroke not being yet given, I was encourag'd to run into my Father's Arms, and pray him that he would not strike. The Case was thus represented to me: "That it may be I might get his Life as an Answer of Prayer." And that Scripture was brought to my Mind concerning *Hezekiah*, where the Lord, as an Answer to Prayer, promis'd to add to his Days fifteen Years, 2 *Kin.* xx. 6. And that also, where *Paul*, speaking of *Epaphroditus*, says, *For indeed he was sick nigh unto Death: but God had Mercy on him; and not on him only, but on me also, lest I should have Sorrow upon Sorrow*, Phil. ii. 27. From these I was encourag'd to flee unto the Mercy of the Lord, with a *who can tell* but he will deal thus with *me?* And those Words sounded sweetly, *Upon me also, lest I should have Sorrow upon Sorrow.* From whence I gather'd some Hopes that the Lord would not strike the Blow: and that in *Mercy to me*; lest I should have *Sorrow upon Sorrow.* I had one *Sorrow* in parting with Mr. *Sk---p*, and if the Lord had taken Mr. *G---t*, it would indeed have been *Sorrow upon Sorrow*: but *lest* it should be so, I was in Hope that the Lord would *spare him.* But this Encouragement, tho' strong enough to carry me in with an immediate Address to the Throne; was not yet so powerful as to cast out all

Fears of Success: And *Fear* in this regard, had Torment: so that I quickly fell into great Distress.

This Dispensation shock'd my *Faith*: I thought, "If the Lord *did* take him away, I knew not how to reconcile it with his *Faithfulness*." And when I consider'd, that *the just* LORD *would do no Iniquity*, if he did remove him: then I thought, "Surely I must have been *mistaken* as to the Person in whom the Promises are to be fulfill'd." And again I thought, "Surely I was *not* mistaken; it must be *Him*." And thus was I much like the Disciples, when their Lord was crucify'd, their Faith was *non-plust. We trusted* (say they) that *it had been He that should have redeemed Israel*, Luke xxiv. 21. But now they seem to *doubt it*: They knew not how to reconcile the present Circumstances, with their former Faith about the Lord Jesus.

And as it try'd my Faith, so my *Love* also; whether I could give him up to the Stroke. And tho' I was not wholly unreconcil'd to the Will of God, yet it went very near me. And I found Love, Grief, Fear, and vehement Desire strongly working in me: So that while his Life hung in Suspense, I was in pain to know the Issue. And that Word was some Stay to me, *John* xi. 40. *If thou wouldst believe, thou shouldst see the Glory of God*. But quickly my Fears prevail'd again.

At length, I desired that the Lord would give me some Intimation of what he would do in this Matter. And these Words were brought with Power and Sweetness, *For the* Oppression of *the poor, for the Sighing of the needy, now will I arise, saith the* LORD, Psa. xii. 5. *That* they *be not as Sheep which have no Shepherd*, Num. xxvii. 17. *Rejoice with Joy for Jerusalem, and be glad with her all ye that love her*, Isa. lxvi. 10. *For the Lord hath visited and redeemed his People. And hath raised up an Horn of Salvation for us*, Luke i. 68, 69. *Thou hast redeemed my Life from Destruction*, Psa. ciii. 4. *And brought back my* Soul from the Pit of Corruption, *Isa*. xxxviii. 17. From these Words my Mind was stay'd, as being sweetly persuaded that the Lord, in Mercy to his People, would spare his Life. But yet when the Power of 'em was off my Mind, I fell into Fears again. And then that Word, *John* xi. 40. was brought again, as a Reproof of my Unbelief: *Said I not unto thee, that if thou wouldst believe, thou shouldst see the Glory of God?* Upon which, asham'd of my Unbelief, I was in some measure helpt to trust the Lord again.

Thus I went on, between Faith and Fear, until I received the welcome News of his Recovery. And then, with joyful Wonder at divine Kindness, being fully persuaded that his Life was granted as an Answer of Prayer, I look'd upon him to be given me anew, as it were from the *Dead*; from thence I received him, as *Abraham* did his *Isaac*, in a Figure, *Heb.* xi. 19. And I rejoyc'd afresh in him as my Father's Gift, and lov'd him dearly. Yea, I was afraid, that I should exceed, in making too much Account of the Creature; and thereby hew out a *broken Cistern that could hold no Water*.

But notwithstanding the great Joy I had in God, when his Life was spar'd, I soon found myself attended with Fears lest he should yet be taken from me. And I thought that I had never been thoroughly reconciled to it. But presently the Lord put this Question to my Heart: "Whether I could be wiling to give him up, if *God might be glorified thereby?*" And together herewith, there was such a Ray of *divine Glory*, broke in upon me, that did as it were at once, draw away my *whole Soul* after it. I was as if I lov'd *nothing* but *God's Glory*, or at least, nothing in *Comparison* therewith. I was now strongly, and yet sweetly drawn to offer him up as a *Sacrifice* to God's Glory. Oh, how freely, and fully did I then give him up into the Hand of the Lord, to glorify himself concerning him, just as HE pleas'd! Oh how delightful [*sic*; r. delightfully] did my Heart give up its *dearest Interest* to *God's Glory*; esteeming it my *highest Happiness* to glorify him! My Soul was made to give up its long'd-for, and expected Enjoyment of God's Favour *here*; which was dearer than my Life; and to wait for Satisfaction till I came to *Heaven*: If HE might be *glorify'd* hereby, in his Greatness and Sovereignty, as having a supreme Right to give, or take from me as he pleas'd. And not only in his Sovereignty, but in his Wisdom too: For tho' I was at a Loss to know how the Promises should be made good, if Things were not as I expected; yet I was made to give up my *own* Wisdom, as Folly, and as it were to lose it in *his* infinite Understanding: Believing all his Ways to be *right*; tho' by me *unsearchable*, and *past finding out*.

And further, upon my being thus resign'd into God's Dispose, I found such full Satisfaction in his good Pleasure, whatsoever it was concerning me in this Respect; that I even look'd upon this very Thing to be one Kind of *Fulfilment* of the Promise. For the End of the Promise, being to satisfy the Desires of the longing Soul; and my Soul being so abundantly satisfy'd, and at Rest in God's Will; I thought the Promises were in one Sort *fulfill'd*: And knew not then, whether they would be fulfill'd any other *Way* or *not*, or whether the Lord intended any *other*, than to glorify himself, by making me submit to his Will, in drawing out my Desires to the utmost, and then crossing them. And I thought, if it was so, I should be very well pleas'd, if I might glorify him *that* Way.

But yet, seeing the Lord has various Ways, and several Times of fulfilling the Promises to his People; my Heart was hereby held at the Throne of Grace, and still kept waiting to see what the Lord would do; as not knowing but that he might still have a Reserve of Kindness for me, and that so *great*, as to give me all *again*, that I had been enabled to resign. And a little of the Frame of my Soul at this Time, may be seen in a Letter which I then wrote, with Design to send it to a Christian Friend: Which is as follows.

Beloved Brother,

I Am willing to let you know, that the Lord has brought me to his Foot. I trust, as an Answer to our Prayers. He has loosen'd me from the Creature, and made me cleave closer to himself, as the Eternal Fountain, and Well-Spring of all my Consolation. He has made me willing to be *deny'd*, what I earnestly *sought for*: If by *this* HE might be the more *glorified*. I am made willing to be deny'd that *one Thing* my Soul sought after; which was, the Delights of the divine Presence in Ordinances, and to wait for that Solace, till my Father takes me into the full Enjoyment of himself; if by this HE will gain any *Glory*. So that I can now say, *Here I am, let him do with me as seemeth good unto him.* The Blessed Spirit has presented the *Glory of God* as such a *lovely Thing*; that in this Case, he has drew away my *Soul* after it: And not only made me to *submit*, but even to *love* that HE should be glorified, and *rejoyce* in it: Esteeming it far better that GOD should be *glorified*, in his Greatness, Sovereignty, Power, and Wisdom, than that I should barely be *satisfied*. And yet, satisfied *I am*: For if I never *have* what I *hoped* for; yet, if GOD will get any *Glory to himself*, by drawing out my Desire, and then crossing them, I esteem it *well worth the Exercise*. And now my Soul is even as a *weaned Child*, that is weaned from the Milk, and drawn from the Breasts: And I am willing that the Lord should glorify himself, which Way HE pleases.

The Lord has sometimes made me willing to *want* a Mercy; and then has *bestowed it*: Willing to *bear* Affliction; and then has *wrought Deliverance*. And if my Beloved should yet say, by his Spirit, and in his Providence, *Arise, my Love, my fair one, and come away*: I should *leap at his Voice*, and confess that it is every Way like the GOD *of all Grace*, and as such, desire HE might have the *Glory*. But I *bow* to his royal Pleasure. Believing my Interest in my Father's *Heart*, I am at his *Dispose*: Rejoycing in that HE will be glorified, however he deals with *me*. I desired [*sic*; r. desire] you may glorify him on my Behalf.

And now, dear Brother, that you and yours may be enriched with the Blessings of the upper and the nether Springs, made to shine in Holiness here, and in Glory at Christ's Appearing: Is the earnest Desire of,
Yours in Him,
A. D.

Thus my Soul, having had a ravishing Prospect of the Glory of GOD, in his Wisdom, Greatness, and Sovereignty, was as it were at once drawn after him by the powerful Loadstone of his *Love*. For it was the Views of HIM, as my own gracious God and Father, that made me submit to *his* Wisdom, if he should cross *mine*. 'Twas *this* humbled me in the Dust, and made me lie down in my own Creature-Littleness, that so HE might glorify himself upon me, in his infinite Greatness, and sovereign Dominion over me; as having a supreme Right to deal with me as *he* pleas'd.

And from hence, finding such a mighty and sudden Alteration in me, my *whole Soul*, being as it were turn'd upside down in a *Moment*, I was instructed into the Glory of divine Power; and how *easy* it was with God, to take all Sin out of my Nature, when the appointed Time came.

And further, upon the Review of what had pass'd, my Heart being still kept, in some Measure, in the same Frame, I was made to look upon it as bearing some Analogy with *Abraham's offering up Isaac. Abraham* had obtain'd the Promise of *Isaac* by Prayer, when he said, *Lord GOD, what wilt thou give me, seeing I go Childless, and the Steward of my House is this Eliezer of Damascus? Behold, unto me thou hast given no Seed: And lo, one born in my House is mine Heir,* Gen. xv. 2, 3. And the LORD said unto him, *This shall not be thine Heir, but he that shall come forth out of thine own Bowels shall be thine Heir,* Ver. 4. Nor was *Isaac* promis'd *alone*: But all the Promises concerning the *Messiah*, and his eternal Salvation in *him*, were comprehended in this Promise of *Isaac*; from whose Loins He was to spring. As it follows: *And he brought him forth abroad, and said, Look now toward Heaven, and tell the Stars, if thou be able to number them: And he said unto him, so shall thy Seed be. And he believed in the LORD, and he counted it to him for Righteousness,* Ver. 5, 6. And when *Abraham* had his *Isaac*, he view'd all the *Promises in him*, and his Soul *clave unto him*: And yet the Lord bid him *offer him up.*

Thus, in some Measure, it was with *me*. I had sought the Lord; and obtain'd a Promise that HE would give me the *Desires of my Heart*, and feed me by *that* Shepherd, whose Tent I desired to be near. And all the other Promises of what the Lord would do for me by *him*, seem'd to be comprehended *in him*. So that my Soul *clave to him* as my Father's Gift: And yet he bid me *resign him up*. And what the Lord said unto *Abraham*, when he call'd him to offer up *Isaac*, was much unto me, *Gen.* xxii. 2. *Take now thy Son, thine only Son Isaac, whom thou lovest, and offer him for a Burnt-Offering.* The Lord is here very particular in his Requirement: Take now thy *Son*; (says God) which is a Term, that as it bespeaks *Relation*, so *Affection* also; it carries *Endearment* in it, even the Endearment of a Father's *Heart* to his Son. And yet the Lord stops not here: It is as if he should say, it is not *any* Son that I require of thee; but thine *only Son Isaac*: Thine only Son by *Promise*. And, as if this was not enough: It's *he* whom thou *lovest*: Thine *Isaac* (whose Name signifies Laughter, or Joy) whom thy Soul is *knit to*: Take *him* now (says God) and *offer for a Burnt-Offering*. And *my Soul* was in some Measure like *Abraham's*, when he *stretch'd forth his Hand to slay the Lad*. And because it was done in his *Heart*, the Lord speaks of it as if it was done by his *Hand, Heb.* xi. 17. *And he that had received the Promises, offer'd up his only begotten Son.* So that I look'd upon the *promis'd Mercy* as *offer'd up*.

And yet, from the Lord's dealing with *Abraham*, in giving him his *Isaac again*; I was encouraged to wait upon God in Hope, that as he had glorified himself as a *sovereign Lord*, in making me willing to give up the Mercy into his Hand; so that now he would glorify himself as the *God of all Grace*, in giving it to me *again*; which I earnestly desired, with Submission to his Will. And soon after this, that Word was brought, *I know the Thoughts that I think towards you, saith the LORD, Thoughts of Peace, and not of Evil, to give you an expected End, Jer.* xxix. 11. From whence I was persuaded, that that very *Thing* which I had *expected* in the Promise, should be given me. And from this Time I was, in the main, kept waiting at the Throne of Grace, in Expectation of the Mercy: Tho' I had my Fits of Unbelief, and my Heart was not always alike engag'd in wrestling with the Lord about it. Sometimes there was a *Faintness* in my Desires and Supplications: And then the Lord would bring some Promise or other, by which he reviv'd my Faith, and gave Wing to my Desires afresh; so that with renewed Strength, my *Soul follow'd hard after him*. But 'twas *his* Hand that held *my* Heart; or else my Heart would soon have let go its hold of *Him*. But because it was his Design to give me the *Mercy*: He therefore kept my Soul hungering and thirsting *after it*, on purpose that he might shew the more *Grace*, in *satisfying the longing Soul, and filling the Hungry with good Things*. And that Word was a precious Encouragement to my Faith, and a strong Plea for me at the Throne of Grace, where the Lord says, *If thou draw out thy Soul to the hungry, and satisfy the afflicted Soul, then shall thy Light arise in Obscurity, and thy Darkness be as the Noon Day*, Isa. lviii. 10. I thought, "If it was so pleasing to the Lord, that his People should shew Mercy and Kindness to the Necessitous; that he makes such gracious Promises upon their being found in the Performance of this Duty: much more would HE Himself delight to shew Mercy and Kindness." The reasoning of my Soul from hence, was much like that, *He that made the Eye, shall not HE see?* &c. So, thought I, "He that has said, *If thou draw out thy Soul to the Hungry*, &c. I will do thus and thus: shall not HE much more do so, from that pure Delight he has in exercising Loving-Kindness?" And oh, how earnestly did I plead with him, that HE would *draw out his Soul*, or all the Perfections of his *Nature*, to the satisfying of *me*, a poor hungry, thirsty Creature! Much like the *Psalmist*, when he said, *O continue thy Loving-kindness!* Or, O *draw out* thy Loving-kindness! as some render the Word.

But to proceed, the Lord having, as was said, given Mr. *G---t's* Life, as an Answer of Prayer; I took it as an *Earnest* of my being fed under his Ministry. And having has some further Encouragement from the Lord in this Respect, we did again enquire, whether there was any *Door* open'd yet for our outward Supply in that Place. And there was *none*; nor any *likelihood* of it in that Way which my Thoughts were most upon. By reason of which I was much discouraged, as if the Promise *fail'd*. But as I was looking upon the Trees in the Garden, it being Winter-Season, The Lord was pleas'd to instruct me from thence. That as it was *Winter* with the *Garden*; so now it was the *Winter-season* with respect to the *Promise*. And that it was as unreasonable for me to conclude, that there would never be a *Spring-time of the Promise*, because I saw no Appearance of it: as it would be to think, That there should never be a *natural Spring*, because the Trees in Winter look so much like dead ones. And as I was thinking about the distinct Fulfilment of particular Promises, what is spoken about the Seed-corn, in order to set forth the Resurrection of the Dead, was brought to my Mind, and apply'd by way of Analogy to the Promises: *1 Cor.* xv. 36, 37, 38. *That which thou sowest is not quickned, except it die. And that which thou sowest, thou sowest not that Body that shall be, but bare Grain, it may chance of Wheat, or of some other grain. But God giveth it a Body as it hath pleased him, and to every Seed its own Body.* From hence I saw, That the *casting* of the Promises into the Heart, was like the *casting* the Seed-corn into the Ground. And as the Corn first *dies*, before it is quickned; so, usually, there are *Deaths* pass over the Promises, before they spring forth in the Glory of the [*sic*; r. their] Fulfilment. And further, I was made to see, That every particular Promise, was like a distinct *Seed*, that was assuredly to bring forth an answerable Crop. And that, As God giveth to every Seed its own *Body*; so to every Promise its distinct *Accomplishment*. And as GOD giveth to every Seed its own Body, as *pleaseth* him; so to every Promise its own particular Fulfilment, both as to Manner, and Degree, as HE pleaseth.

Having this Instruction, my Faith was again strengthened in the Expectation of the Fulfilment of every particular Promise I had receiv'd, according to the full Intent of the Mind of GOD therein; notwithstanding the present Death that was upon them.

Quickly after this, The Lord in his Providence order'd it so, that usually I went one Lord's Day in a Month to hear Mr. *G---t*: Which I look'd upon as a *partial* Fulfilment of the Promises, and also an *Earnest* of their compleat Accomplishment. Before I went, I sought the Lord, that HE would go with me, and delight my Soul with Communion with *Himself.* And that Word was very precious to me on this Account, *Song* ii. 1. *I am the Rose of Sharon.* Christ's Voice in it to my Soul was this: "*I am the Rose of Sharon,* or, I will be unto thee the *Rose* of Sharon in *that Place*: I'll give thee Communion with *myself,* by which thy spiritual Senses shall be delighted, in beholding my transcendent Beauty, in smelling of my transcendent Fragraucy, and I'll make thee blessed, by a Communication of my Blessedness: as I am *the Rose of Sharon,* for thee to have *Communion with.*" And those Words also were very sweet to me, *Ver.* 13. *Arise, my Love, my fair One, and come away.*

And what the Lord had *said*, he did indeed make *good.* For my Beloved did very familiarly open Himself to my Soul, and display his Glory under Mr. *G---t's* Ministry; So that *I sat down under his Shadow with great Delight, and his Fruit was sweet unto my Taste.* And the Lord put Words into his Mouth for me: which He was pleas'd to bless for the Strengthening of my Faith, about the *compleat* Fulfilment of the Promise, in my being brought to dwell there constantly.

A poor weak Creature I was in Believing; for when the Lord try'd me, I was ready to faint. But when I heard Mr. *G---t* preach from *Isa.* xlii. 3. *A bruised Reed shall he not break: and the smoking Flax shall he not quench: he shall bring forth Judgment unto Truth*; I was much Strengthned, the Words being opened exactly agreeable to my Case. And such a Fountain of Grace was opened in that Sermon, that was almost ready to overcome my weak Nature. But yet still, I was up and down in Faith, even after *this*.

One Month's Day, I was prevented going: and the next, when I went, Mr. *G—t* was not at home: by reason of which I was much discouraged; as thinking, that the Lord did speak against me in it. And the Enemies broke forth upon me, with a *"Where is now your God?* What's become of your *Prayers?* "You see He don't *regard you*." By this my Heart was so burden'd, and harden'd, that I knew not what to do. But after a while, I got a little Liberty to *breathe* after the Lord: and I thought, "Oh! That I could have such *Freedom* with him as I have had: then I would *tell him* my Case." For my Temptations were strong, That the LORD had *forgotten me*, and had not *Compassion on me*. But with glorious Power, He broke in upon my Soul with that Word, *Jer.* xxxi. 20. *Since I spake against him, I do earnestly remember him still: therefore my Bowels are troubled for him, I will surely have Mercy upon him, saith the* LORD. GOD's Voice herein to me, was *this*: "I have indeed been speaking *against thee*, in my Dispensations: but I have not *forgotten thee*, in Relation to my Promise. I have not *forgot* what I *told thee*, I *remember* thee still: yea, I *earnestly* remember thee; my whole *Soul* is engag'd in the *Remembrance of thee*. And tho' thou hast been *try'd* since I spake against thee, and hid my self: Yet my *Bowels* are *troubled* for thee all this while: I have a Fellow-feeling with thee in all thy Distresses: and I will surely have *Mercy* upon thee, and be *faithful* to my Promise." Upon this I went Home joyfully, being afresh confirm'd in my Expectations of the Promis'd Mercy.

And quickly after, another Method for our outward Supply came into our Minds. And having sought the Lord, and receiv'd some Encouragement that it should succeed: we desired a Friend to enquire, and use his Interest with one that we had our Eye upon to be assistant to us in it. But the Lord's *Time* being not yet fully come, there was a *Death* upon this our new Project. Which, when I was acquainted with it, was very *trying*. But yet I was comfortably borne up under it, by this Scripture: *I form the Light, and create Darkness*, Isa. xlv. 7. Oh! The Thoughts of God's wonderful Ways, in bringing Light *out* of Darkness: Yea, in *making* the precedent Darkness;

on purpose that the Light might shine the more gloriously; did mightily bear up my Soul. The Dispensation indeed was *dark*; yet I was not *discouraged*: I thought, "The Lord was on his Way, to glorify *himself*, and save *me*: And therefore he had created this *Darkness*, that so his own Glory, in forming *Light* out of it, might shine the brighter." And this Word also, was a mighty Support to me: *Wherefore when I came, was there no Man? when I called, was there none to answer? Is my Hand shortned at all, that it cannot redeem ? Or have I no Power to deliver?* Isa. l. 2. I thought the Lord had been speaking, and calling in his Providence, upon that Person our Eye was upon. But there was *no Man* would help us; there was *no Answer*, but what was quite contrary. Well, said the LORD, *Is my Arm shortned at all, that it cannot save for all this?* Oh! how sweetly did these Words sound in my Soul, *Is my Hand shortned at all?* q. d. [*quaque die*, every day] "Have I ever a *Whit* the less Power to effect what I design; because the Creatures will contribute *nothing* towards it?" Oh! how sweetly did the LORD open his *own Power* to me, in its glorious *Self-sufficiency*, to fulfil his Promises, as it stands *alone*, without the *Help* of Creatures; and as it can *turn* all Hearts to subserve its Designs. Whereupon, I spread my Case before the Lord: and told him, *That there was no Man would help me*: and pray'd him, that his *own Arm might be made bare*. And then, in the Joy of Faith, trusting the LORD in the dark, I compos'd the following Lines, as expressive of my Case.

> The LORD makes *Darkness*; and it's *Night*,
> And HE doth make the Darkness *Light*.
> Blest are the Men that *trust him so*;
> *His* Power, and Goodness, they shall know.

> *His Glory*, and *their Life* secure;
> Bound up in's *Covenant* most sure:
> HE'll slay their Foes, and HE their Friend,
> Will give them *an expected End*.

Thus I was at this Time: but at other Seasons, while the Mercy was *delay'd*, and nothing but *Deaths* upon it, I was often set upon by Satan, and my own unbelieving Heart, with their usual Insult, *Where is now your God?* q. d. [*quaque die*, every day] "You made your Boast, that the Lord would *appear* for you: and that he was a *God hearing Prayer*, that he was *nigh* to you in all that you call'd upon him for. But you *see*, there's no such Thing: Where's any Appearance of it *now?*"

And one Time in particular, these Enemies *urg'd it* upon me, *That it was in vain to seek the Lord*: and a great deal they spoke very *reproachfully* against the most *High*:

So that my Soul was *burden'd*, because they lift up their Voice against GOD: and my Spirit was mightily wrought up into an holy *Indignation* against them. Upon which, I took up the Bible to read: and opened (accidentally to me, tho' designedly by the Lord) upon the 74th *Psalm*: Which was so peculiarly expressive of *my Case*, as if it had been made on purpose for *me*: so that I could not but wonder at the *Exactness* of it: Especially from the 18th Verse to the End. *Remember this, that the Enemy hath reproached, O* LORD, *and that the foolish People have blasphemed thy Name. O deliver not the Soul of thy Turtle-dove unto the Multitude of the Wicked, forget not the Congregation of thy poor for ever. Have Respect unto the Covenant: for the dark Places of the Earth are full of the Habitations of Cruelty. O let not the Oppressed return ashamed: let the Poor and Needy praise thy Name. Arise, O God, plead thine own Cause: remember how the foolish Man reproacheth thee daily. Forget not the Voice of thine Enemies: the Tulmult of those that rise up against thee, increaseth continually.* This *Psalm* was expressive of my Case in a five-fold Respect: As,

1. With respect to that Sense I had of the Enemies *Blasphemy*, and *Reproach*, being against God: They have blasphemed *thy Name*, says the *Psalmist*, ver. 18. And they rise up against *Thee*, ver. 23.

2. With respect to that *Burden* which I had upon my Spirit by reason thereof: Upon which Account the *Psalmist* styles Himself, and the People of God, *oppressed*, ver. 21.

3. With Respect to that Sense I had of my own *Inability* to help myself; together with that Expectation I had of the Lord's appearing for me: Which is exprest by his styling Himself with God's People, *poor and needy*, and by his praying that they might not return *ashamed*, ver. 21. Which is as much as to say, We have *hoped* in thy Mercy: O let us not *miss* of our Expectation.

4. With respect to that holy *Indignation*, and mighty *Zeal* for God's Glory, which was wrought in my *Soul*, as also in the *Psalmist*, when he said, *Arise, O God, plead thine own Cause*, ver. 23. q. d. [*quaque die*, every

day] "*I can't bear it*, Lord, that thine *Honour* should be thus laid in the *Dust*, by the *Tumult* of them that rise up against *thee*." And then

5. All this was answerably turn'd into a *Representative Prayer* before the Lord: *Remember this*, O LORD,--- As ver. 18, &c. which consisted of three Parts, 1. A Representation of the *Case*, both with respect to the Ene-mies Rage, and Slanders *against God*, and Oppression of *my Soul*. 2. An humble Imploring the Lord's *Appearance* to vindicate his *own Honour*. And 3. An earnest Supplication, that the Lord would not give up *my Soul*, his *Turtle-dove*, into the Hands of the Wicked: nor suffer *me*, his *oppressed, poor* and *needy* one, to *return ashamed*: but so appear for *my Help*, and for the *Confounding* of mine Enemies; that I might *praise his Name with joyful Lips*.

And some sweet *Freedom* I had with the Lord in Prayer to tell him, that he had *never left me* in any Strait or Difficulty whatsoever. And the Remembrance of his *former* Loving-Kindnesses, strengthened my Faith to plead for his *present* Appearance. And the Lord was pleas'd to give me an immediate Answer of Peace, in Tidings of Deliverance, by bringing that Promise to my Mind, with Power and Sweetness, *Their Redeemer is strong, he shall throughly plead their Cause*. Here I saw, the Almighty Strength of *my Redeemer* engag'd to *plead my Cause*: Yea, that he would *throughly* plead it. The Lord had made many *Promises* of *great Things* that He would do for me: and my Soul had made her *Boast of God*: and while he *hid Himself*, the Enemies began to *triumph* over me, as if I had no such Privilege in having such *Promises*; or such a *God* to go to, as I had thought of. But when God arose, and shone forth in this Promise; his Enemies were *scatter'd*, and they that hated him *fled before him*. Oh! the *Glory* of God's Power, Faithfulness, Love and Grace that broke forth in this Promise, drove all *the Beasts of Prey to their Dens!* And that I might see more fully how the Promise was brought in, I look'd it: and found it, *Jer.* l. 34. The Verse before, when I came to read it, was made of great Use to me: *Thus saith the* LORD *of Hosts, the Children of Israel, and the Children of Judah were oppressed together, and all that took them Captives, held them fast, they refused to let them go*. This *Verse* answer'd *my Case*: I was took *Captive* by Satan, and Unbelief, misrepresenting the LORD, and his Dealings with me: and they would have *held me fast, refusing to let me go* forth in the Triumph of Faith in the Dark; rejoicing in the God of my Salvation, when the Fig-tree did not blossom, &c. Yea, and as to the outward Face of Things, there was a *holding me fast* in the Place where I was; and a *refusing to let me go* unto the Place the Lord had spoken to me of. But the Promise comes in, notwithstanding all Opposition, with a *Thus saith the* LORD: *Their Redeemer is strong, the* LORD *of Hosts is his Name.* Which Words set forth the omnipotent *Power*, unchangeable *Grace*, Covenant *Faithfulness*, and glorious *All-sufficiency* of the LORD, in his Resolution to *redeem*: Who has all the Powers, both in Heaven and Earth at his Command: *Jehovah of Hosts is his Name.* And then follows, *He will throughly plead their Cause.* I saw from hence, That there was not any *Circumstance* of my expected *Happiness*, relating unto any of his *Promises*; which was the *Cause* now in debate, but he would *throughly plead it.* And then comes the glorious End: *That he may give Rest to the Land, and disquiet the Inhabitants of Babylon.* That is, give his People *Release* from all their Enemies, and the peaceful *Possession* of all promis'd Favours: to the *Vexation and Confusion* of their Enemies. The 45th Verse also was very precious to me. *Therefore hear ye the Counsel of the* LORD, *which he hath taken against Babylon: and the Purposes that he hath purposed against the Land of the Chaldeans: surely the least of the Flock shall draw them out.* From whence I was made to *believe*, that it was the Lord's Design to *confound* the Enemies, by such a *weak one as I*, that was as the *Least of the Flock.* And as I read on, in the 51 Chapter, the Lord comes, in the 5th Verse, to give the *Reason* of all this Grace: *For Israel hath not been forsaken, nor Judah of his God, of the* LORD *of Hosts; though their Land was filled with Sin, against the Holy One of Israel.* This also was very sweet to me: I was perswaded, that, tho' my Soul was fill'd with *Sin* against the *Holy One of Israel*, yet, I had not been *forsaken*; no, nor ever *should be*: because *Jehovah* was *my God.*

By this Consolation, the Lord was pleas'd to give me, he not only strengthned my Faith at *present*, and made me triumph over my Enemies; but also laid a further Foundation for it, in *aftertimes* of Trial.

Upon this Victory, having been made to *run into the Name of the* LORD, *as my strong Tower*; and from thence having had a Sight of the Sureness of, both my own Deliverance, and the Destruction of my Enemies: I began, as an *Inhabitant of the Rock, to sing*: And with a holy Scorn, as being far above the Reach of any Enemy, in the Triumph of Faith, I compos'd and sung the following Lines.

> JEHOVAH's *Name*, a *Tower* is:
>   Thither the *Righteous* fly:
> In *Safety* dwell, find perfect Bliss,
>   Which sets them up on high.

Out of the *Reach* of Enemies,
   In *Triumph* there they sing:
No *Evil* can God's Saints surprize,
   That *trust* under his Wing.

JEHOVAH screens them from all Harm;
   Their Enemies rage in *vain*:
HE'll save them by his mighty Arm;
   And put their Foes to pain.

Then let the *Saints* for ever sing
   In this their *Hiding-Place,*
High Praises to their conquering KING,
   For his amazing Grace!

In this Triumph of Faith, I was carried on at Times, notwithstanding Things look'd dark.

About this Time, the Lord was pleas'd to answer a Request I had put up to him in the Beginning-part of my Exercise: Which was this: That he would so dispose of Things in his Providence, as to *hide me from the Strife of Tongues* in removing me. (For I fear'd some Reflections might be cast upon me if I *left* my Business) And in Answer to this, the Lord *took my Business away* some Time before he remov'd me: Which was very effecting [*sic*; r. affecting] to my Soul. I saw, that the Lord was on his Way to fulfil his Promises: and that his shutting up my Way in *that* Place, was in order to open it in *another*. Which was like *Life from the Dead to* me.

And here I may take Notice, that the Lord was pleas'd to exercise me with one particular Providence, that to me look'd exceeding *dark*; and seem'd utterly to *forbid* my Removal: it seem'd as if it would make against the *Glory of God* if I went. Upon which, I sunk so *low* in my Faith and Expectations, as to think, that I must *never* remove: nay, even to resolve so. I thought, "Surely the Lord will 'fulfil his Promises some other Way than what I have look'd for." But after some time, the Lord gave me to see, that it was my Duty to *trust him* with what concern'd his Glory, as well as what concern'd my own Happiness; and he enabled me so to do: and made me willing to *go*, and *trust* under the Shadow of *Jehovah's Wings* for all the Happiness I desired, and to screen me from all the Evil I fear'd. And those

Words were very sweet to me, *Ruth* ii. 11, 12. *Thou hast left thy Father and thy Mother and the Land of thy Nativity, and art come unto a People which thou knewest not heretofore. The LORD recompense thy Work, and a full Reward be given thee of the LORD God of Israel, under whose Wings thou art come to trust.* I was from hence taught to trust the LORD; and sweetly encouraged to believe that whatever I parted with for *his Sake*, and the *Gospel's* he would restore it, even to an *hundred-fold in this Life*: Which was attended with a humbling Sense of my own Unworthiness, while I admire the Riches of divine Favour to such a worthless one as I, who came to *trust* under the Shadow of *Jehovah's Wings*.

The Dispensation that seem'd dark, did indeed look as if it would *hinder* my Removal; or at least *eclipse* the Glory of it. And that Word was often upon my Mind, *2 Thes.* ii. 7. *That which letteth, will let, until it be taken out of the Way.* But so wonderfully did the Lord work, that he made the breaking out of that *very Thing*, which seem'd to forbid my Removal, to be the *Means* of its being taken out of the Way, in order to my removing comfortably. *Lo, these are Parts of his Ways, but how little a Portion is heard of him?* Job xxvi. 14.

At some times, when I kept my Eye upon the Grace, Power, and Faithfulness of the Promiser, I went on in believing Expectations of the Fulfilment of the Promise: At other times, when Things look'd dark, I was often ready to be discouraged. But it pleased the Lord, (I think, for about a Quarter of a Year before he removed me) to work up my Heart into a full Perswasion, which most commonly prevail'd, "That I should not see Death, until I had seen that Salvation of God, which I had been expecting." And that Word was much to me, *Luke* ii. 26. *And it was revealed unto him by the Holy Ghost, that he should not see Death, before he had seen the Lord's Christ.* So, I was perswaded, that I should not *see Death*, before I had seen *God's Salvation* in the *Fulfilment* of the Promises. And that Word also, was a great Confirmation to me, *Mic.* vii. 20. *Thou wilt perform the Truth to Jacob, the Mercy promised from the Days of old.* And that Word also, strengthned me greatly, *Isa.* lxvi. 9. *Shall I bring to the Birth, and not cause to bring forth? saith the LORD: shall I cause to bring forth, and shut the Womb? saith thy God.* Things seem'd, by this Time, to be brought to the Birth: In that I was removed out of my pleasant House, my Business taken from me: and our Hearts quite wean'd from the Town. And this Scripture was of mighty Force to strengthen my Faith, that the Lord would surely *perfect* what he had *begun*; and remove me, notwithstanding whatever lay

in the Way. *Shall I bring to the Birth, and not bring forth? saith the LORD*:
I thought, that *all* that was in *Jehovah*, was engag'd to do it. And the next
Words, did as greatly strengthen my Faith in the Expectation of future
Favours, both of the upper, and of the nether Springs, after my Removal.
Shall I bring forth, and shut the Womb? saith thy God. From whence I saw,
that as *sure* as the LORD was *my God*, so *surely* he would *follow me with his
Goodness.* I was indeed a poor fainting Creature, and not without my
Temptations, "That I should not meet with what I expected, either for Soul,
or Body, after my Removal." But this Word of the Lord strengthned me.
And that Word also I had, with respect to *Soul-Comfort*, Isa. li. 12. *I, even
I am he that comforteth you.*

And one Time, when I had some Fears about *outward Things*, the Lord
broke in upon my Heart with his majestick Love and Grace, by that Word,
Jer. ii. 31. *Have I been a Wilderness unto Israel? a Land of Darkness?*
"What art thou afraid to *trust me?*" said the Lord. Have I ever *fail'd thee?*
Remember how much Kindness I have shewn to *thee*, all along, in a
distinguishing Way from *others*. Thou hast seen my Wonders, time after
time. And what, afraid to trust me *now?* Dost think I will not appear for thee
in *another Place? I shall be with thee there*, as the Fountain of thy Supply:
and do but think, what it is to have ME? and what I have been to thee
already? and trust me for the *future.*'

But oh! how this kind Reproof broke my Heart at once, for my
Unbelief, and ungrateful Carriage to my gracious Father! I thought, I was
the *vilest* of any of his Children: because he had shewn such distinguishing
Kindness to *me*. I thought, I dealt with the true and faithful GOD, who
cannot deny himself; as we are wont, in a common Proverb, to say we
would do with the vilest of Men, even to *trust 'em* no further than we can
see them. Oh the *Baseness* of Unbelief!

And further, the Lord having thus sweetly hinted my *Unkindness*, he
was graciously pleased to tell me, of the Riches of *his Mercy*, in pardoning
me: in that Word, *Isa.* lv. 7. *Let the Wicked forsake his Way, and the
unrighteous Man his Thoughts: and let him return unto the LORD, and he
will have Mercy upon him, and to our God, for he will abundantly pardon.*
I saw, that tho' I was not in a wicked, unrighteous *State*; yet I had a wicked,
unrighteous *Nature* still dwelling in me: which put forth itself in answerable
Thoughts, and *Ways*; which I was called to *forsake*. I saw, that it was an
unrighteous Thought, to think, "That the faithful, gracious GOD, would be
worse than his *Word*, or cease to act like HIMSELF." And these unrighteous,

unbelieving, hard *Thoughts* of mine, he call'd me to *forsake*: telling me, that he would have *Mercy* upon me, and abundantly *pardon* me. Oh! *this* melted my Heart: I thought, "if ever any of his Children needed *abundant Pardon*, it was *Me*, who was so *abundantly sinful.*" And the Truth is, so *base* was my unbelieving, ungrateful Carriage, and so oft *repeated* towards my dear Father, during the Space between his *giving*, and *fulfilling* the Promises; that if He had not been *Jehovah*, the *God of my Mercy*; I should never have been put into the *Possession* of promis'd Favours. But this Word of the *Psalmist*, was of great Use to me, on this account, *I will come into thy House in the Multitude of thy Mercy, Psa.* v. 7. Oh, the Multitude of *God's Mercy*, swallow'd up the Multitude of *my Sin!* and gave me Freedom of Access to him, and Boldness of Expectation from him, notwithstanding *all* my Vileness!

Sometimes indeed, I was ready to *sink* in Faith, when I saw how *evilly* I requited the Lord for his Kindness; and how *unbecoming* my Carriage was to my *great* Expectations. I saw, the Lord might justly rebuke me; and that if he dealt with me after my Carriage, I must never have what I expected. But, Oh! his *tender Mercies*, in *fatherly Forgiveness*, were constantly flowing out towards me. That Word was precious to me, *Zech* iii. 4. *Take away his filthy Garments from him. And I will cloath thee with Change of Raiment.* I saw it a precious Privilege, to have an Intercessor at the Father's right Hand. That Word also, was sweet unto me, *1 John* i. 7. *If we walk in the Light, as he is in the Light, we have fellowship one with another, and the Blood of Jesus Christ his Son, cleanseth us from all Sin.* Oh, it comforted my Heart to see, that I should have *Fellowship* with GOD, in making my Requests to him, and He with *Me*, in hearing and answering the same; while the *Blood of JESUS cleansed me from all Sin!*

And one Time in particular, I had a very *great* Sense of my own Vileness, and Ingratitude, in misimproving divine Kindness; together with an *overcoming* Sight of the Riches of God's Grace, in pardoning me: Which made me *shrink down* as it were into *nothing*, before the Majesty of it. I think that Word first broke in upon my Heart, *Isa.* xlviii. 8. *I knew that thou wouldst deal very treacherously, and wast called a Transgressor from the Womb.* And then, *Isa.* xliii. 25. *I, even I am he that blotteth out thy Transgressions for my own sake, and will not remember thy Sins.* But oh, how I *loath'd* myself for all my Abominations! I saw myself so loathsomly *unlike* my near Relation to God, while he let out his Heart-love upon me, that having Freedom of Access into his Bosom, I ask'd him, "Whether he *knew me* in this my wretched Case, and polluted Condition?" Not that I question'd my *Relation*, or his *knowing* of me as his *own*: But I wanted him to *tell me*, what his Heart, and Thoughts were *just then*, when I was so *loathsome* in my own Eyes. And he gave me an Answer like HIMSELF, in that Word, *Exod.* xxxiii. 12. I knew [*sic*; know] thee *by Name, and* thou *hast found Grace in my Sight*. But oh! how this *melted* my Heart! Then I said, "But is thy Grace *enough* for me, Lord, I have such an *Ocean* of Vileness in me?" And he said, *My Grace is sufficient for* thee, *2 Cor.* xii. 9. Thus Grace *superabounded* over all the *Aboundings* of my Sin; and the *Lord's Work* went on notwithstanding.

And further, another Method of Employ came into our Minds; which we attempted to make some Trial of: But lo, it *fail'd*. The *first* Way our Thoughts were upon, did not *succeed*: The *second* was under a present *Death*: (Tho' that was it, the Lord design'd to make use of) The *third* came to *nothing*. But that Word bore up my Faith, *Hos.* vi. 2. *After two Days will he revive us, in the third Day he will raise us up, and we shall live in his Sight*. I thought, what our Eye was *first* upon, and also this *last*, were the *two Days* of Death and Disappointment we had pass'd already: after which he would revive us, and the *third* we should live in his Sight: Or, that the *second* Method, which we had some Encouragement from the Lord about, tho' it was under a present Death, should again be *revived*, and *succeed*. Which accordingly fell out. And the Lord wrought Wonders to complete the Call of Providence for our Removal.

And a short Time before I remov'd, Things being seemingly, *come to the Birth*, I thought it my Duty to set some Time apart to seek the Lord, for the *bringing them forth*: for still I saw, That it was *his Arm* alone, that must bring Salvation. And accordingly, as one destitute of Help from any *other*, I made my Supplication to the *Lord*. And that Word was an Encouragement to me, *Psa.* cii. 17. *He will regard the Prayer of the* Destitute, *and not despise their Prayer*. And that Word also was a great Stay to me, *Isa.* lvii. 13. *But he that putteth his Trust in* ME, *shall possess the Land, and shall inherit my holy Mountain*. And having been helpt to pour out my Soul before the Lord; I waited for some gracious Intimation what he would do for me. And he was pleas'd to say, with great Power, *See, I have hearkned to thy Voice, and accepted thy Person*, 1 Sam. xxv. 35. Oh! this abundant Grace, *melted* my Heart into Thankfulness. I thought, "That if the Lord had only said, *I have granted thy Request*: It would have been an Answer brimful of Grace: But that he should add this, *of accepting my Person*; was very amazing!" I thought, "The Answer he gave me, not only included my present Deliverance, but additional Favours also: even no less than, taking me into his *Bosom*, and delighting to hold *Communion* with me: So *great* was his *Grace!*"

But one Thing more, I would just take Notice of: A little before my Deliverance came, I met with a very great *Trial*. My Husband being gone [on] a Journey on Account of some Business, sent me Word when to expect him Home: And he, being prevented, stay'd three Days longer than he design'd. This prov'd *such* a Trial to me, that I can't well express. I was terrify'd with Thoughts that he was Dead: and Satan and my own Unbelief set on me, and said, "*See*, this is the Fruit of your Prayers: You thought you should have been *deliver'd*; but see what comes of *praying so much* about any Thing." And I thought, one Part of his Journey might have been spar'd, and the Business done by Letters; which I had some Encouragement from the Lord about: But because there seem'd some Difficulty in doing it *this* Way, I *yielded* to let him go to effect it. Wherefore I was *afraid* that the Lord would rebuke me, for not trusting of him. So that, what between my own Fears, and the aforesaid Taunts, I was *sorely Distrest*. And such Thoughts were apt to rise: *As if I could serve the Lord no longer.*

Thus my *Dross* came up, when I was in the *Furnace*. And the Lord was pleas'd to give me a humbling Sight of that base *Hypocrisy* that still lurk'd in my Heart; which exactly agreed with what is said of the *Hypocrite*, Job xxvii. 10. *Will he delight himself in the Almighty? Will he always call upon God?* Which Interrogations, are strong Affirmations, that he will *not* delight himself in the Almighty, *nor* always call upon God. Thus, while I thought the Lord would *grant my Requests*, and shew *Kindness* to me; I could *call upon God*; but when he seem'd to *shut out my Prayers*, and *rebuke* me, then I was ready to *fail*. And the Sin of my Nature boiled up thus, just before I was deliver'd, I thought it was much like what is said of the *Israelites*, Psa. cvi. 7. *They provok'd him, at the Sea, even at the Red Sea.* But blessed be God, tho' such *great* Wickedness appear'd in my Heart, yet there was still *another* Principle also, that did delight in the LORD: Which he was pleas'd to exercise by this Trial. And then I thought, that I *would* always call upon GOD, whether I had sensible *Answers* of Prayer, or *not*: Esteeming it my *reasonable Service*, to glorify GOD, in his *Sovereign Dominion* over me, (which I saw to be the Foundation of Worship) and in his being *a God hearing Prayer*, by waiting at his Throne continually, with *all* my Desires, *referring* them to his sovereign Pleasure, either to *grant*, or *refuse* as HE saw meet. Yea, my Heart chose, and delighted in his Service, *merely* that I might *glorify him*; whether ever I had that *Advantage* by it, I desir'd or *not*. I thought, "It was no Wonder if the Lord should not give *me* such sensible Answers of Prayer, as he did to *others* of his Children, since I was the most *unworthy* of them all." Yet still, with *Joshua*, I resolv'd to *serve him*, that so I might *glorify him* as the God of all Grace, believing him to be indeed a God hearing Prayer; altho' he should deny *me* particular Requests. Thus my Soul, under the Influence of divine Grace, was made to *desire* that God might be glorify'd in his Greatness, and Sovereignty, in doing with *me* as HE pleas'd; yea, to *delight* in the Thoughts hereof: and also to lie down in my *own Shame*, under a Sense of my Nothingness and Unworthiness. And so the Lord did me *good* by this Trial. By suffering Sin to break out in my Heart, he shew'd me the *Hypocrisy* of my old Nature, by exercising the Graces of his own Spirit, he prov'd the *Sincerity* of the new Creature.

And further, He did not leave me *comfortless* in disconsolate Circumstances, but was graciously pleas'd to revive my sinking Spirits, by giving me fresh divine Cordials; I mean, the fresh Application of the Life-giving Words of his Mouth: One of which was, *Psa.* xxxi. 19. *O how great is the Goodness which thou hast laid up for them that fear thee; which thou hast wrought for them that trust in thee; before the Sons of Men!* From this I was made to believe, that *his* Goodness, *that* Goodness I had been *expecting*, was still a Goodness *laid up* for me, very secure; and should erelong, be a Goodness *wrought out* too, which when it was accomplish'd, would be so admirable, that as one astonish'd in the Review, I should cry out, *Oh how great is thy Goodness!* These Words also reviv'd me: *Light is sown for the Righteous, and Gladness for the Upright in Heart,* Psa. xcvii. 11. *Weeping may endure for a Night, but Joy cometh in the Morning,* Psa. xxx. 5. I thought, "It was now *Night-Season* with me, but there was a *Morning* to come; and that this might be the *last Trial* I should meet with, before *Deliverance* sprang in; and that it might be thus *darkest*, just before *Day-break*." And these Words of an Hymn, were very precious to me:

And when this dismal Night is spent,
Twill be a glorious Morn.

I thought a *Morning without Clouds*, was just at Hand; that would appear very glorious; like *clear Shining after Rain*. I was made to look upon myself, being set on work to draw the *Chariots* of God's Promise and

Providences, relating to this Removal, to be like a *Company of Horses*: as Christ compares his Spouse, *Song* i. 9. And answerably hereto, I thought, "It was no Wonder if I met with now and then a *Slough* that requir'd the Extension of *all* my Strength; the Exercise of *all* my Graces, to *get thro'*." And I thought, The *present Trial* I was under, was the *last Pull* I should have; that when once I got up *this* Hill of Difficulty, my Way would be *all* smooth and pleasant; that, as one having *obtain'd* the Victory, I should *run away* with the Conquest.' And as I thought, so it was. Another Word also that strengthned me while the Trial lasted, was, *1Sam.* xi. 13. *There shall not a Man be put to Death this Day: for to Day the LORD hath wrought Salvation in Israel.* And likewise what *David* said, 2 *Sam.* xix. 22. *Shall there a Man be put to Death this Day in Israel? for do not I know, that I am this Day King over Israel?* Now, as both these Kings, would not suffer a Man to be put to Death, in that Day the Lord had wrought Salvation for 'em, lest they should obscure the Glory of it: So I thought, "The Lord would not suffer my Husband to *die*; which was the *Thing* I was afraid of, because it was the *Day of God's Salvation*, which I had so long expected; that so the Glory of it might not be *eclipsed*, nor my Rejoicing in it *hindred*." Thus, sometimes I went on in *Faith*, at other Times I was prest down with *Fears*; which beset me every Night, when I look'd for his Coming, and was still disappointed. But usually, Faith got the *Victory* over Fears, and laid me to *rest* in divine Faithfulness.

But, a little while before he came, I was ready to *sink* with Fear that he was *drowned*; the Waters being out. And so *weak* I was, that I went to fetch a *News-paper* with a Design to read it, to see if it gave Account of any Person that was drowned that Week. And when I had got it, I sought the Lord, before I attempted to read it: "That if I should meet with any such Thing in it, I might be enabled to bear it to his Glory." And this Word dropt upon my Mind, I think, before I took it up to read it, *He that believeth, shall not make haste*, Isa. xxviii. 16. And the Lord shew'd me, That it was my Duty to wait on *still* to see *his* Salvation; and that I was departing from *Him* in attempting to read this *Paper*, to see if there was any Person drowned, when he had told me, That he should not *die*. By this the Lord *humbled* me for my Unbelief, and *revived* my Faith again in his Promises. Which made me very *thankful* to him. And I laid aside the Paper without Reading of it, being transcendently better satisfy'd, by looking over divine Mercy and Faithfulness, than I could have been by any Thing I should have met with there. And then again I began to *rejoice greatly in the LORD, and to joy in the God of my Salvation, altho' the Fig-tree did not blossom, nor Fruit was found in the Vine*: there being nothing to feed Sense.

And lo, while I was *thus* exercis'd, my *Husband* came Home. But when I saw him, surely I was like the *Disciples*, when they saw the *Lord, They believed not for Joy, and wondred*, Luke xxiv. 41. I could scarce believe my Eyes, for *Joy* and *Wonder*. Surely I may say, as *Jacob* concerning *Esau*, that I saw his *Face, as the Face of God*, Gen. xxxiii. 10. Oh, what an *overcoming Sight*, was that divine Mercy and Faithfulness, that attended the several Circumstances of his Journey, and his safe Return! Now the Day-spring began to *visit me*, the glorious Morn *brake*, and the Light of my expected Deliverance, *advanc'd swiftly*. Every Thing that *hindred*, was removed *out of the Way*, and the Call of Providence *compleated*: The House we liv'd in *dispos'd of* without any Loss, and *another* provided immediately. And I saw the LORD in all this: according to that Promise I had receiv'd some time before, to encourage me in waiting on for his Appearance, *Hos*. vi. 3. *Then shall we know, if we follow on to know the* LORD. Another Time also, I was earnestly desirous, not only for Deliverance, but to see the LORD in it: and that Promise was given me for Answer, *Matt*. v. 8. Blessed are the pure in Heart: for they shall see GOD. And now I *saw* him *indeed!* In the Glory of his Mercy, Love, Grace, Power and Faithfulness!

With Joy I left the Town: according to that Promise, *Isa*. lv. 12. *Ye shall go out with Joy, and be led forth with Peace: the Mountains and the Hills shall break forth before you into singing*. And as we was journeying, we met with a little Difficulty: but that Word carried me thro' triumphantly, and made me believe that we should be safely preserv'd thro' all the Difficulties of the Way, *Num*. xxiii. 21. *The* LORD *his God is with him, and the Shout of a King is among them*. And some sweet Communion I had with the Lord, by the Way: I heard the Voice of *my Beloved*, saying unto me, *rise up, my Love, my fair One, and come away. For lo, the Winter is past, the Rain is over and gone. The Flowers appear on the Earth, the Time of the singing of Birds is come, and the Voice of the Turtle is heard on our Land*, Song ii. 10, 11, 12. And the Lord said, *Ask what I shall give thee*, 2 Chron. i. 7. And my Soul answer'd, "LORD, *Thy Great* SELF! Communion with THEE, is what my Soul desires." And the Answer I receiv'd, was, *If any Man serve me, him will my Father honour. And he that loveth me, shall be loved of my Father, and I will love him, and will manifest myself to him. And we will come unto him, and make our Abode with him*, John xii. 26. and xiv. 21, 23.

At length I was safely brought to my Journeys End. But oh, how I *wondred* at divine Kindness, when my Beloved brought me *Home!* Is it *so!* thought I, What has HE *lov'd me hither!* I can't *express* the heavenly Pleasures, and amazing Joys, which fill'd my Heart in the *Review* of this Appearance on the Lord for me.

And when *the King brought me into his Banqueting house, his Banner over me was Love.* He entertain'd me with his rich Kindness. The first Lord's Day I heard Mr. *G---t,* he preach'd in the Morning, from *Song* i. 4. *Draw me, we will run after thee: the King hath brought me into his Chambers: we will be glad and rejoice in thee, we will remember thy Love more than Wine: the upright love thee.* From these Words, he shwe'd, The peculiar Kindness of Christ, the royal Bridegroom of the Church, in bringing her into *his Chambers.* By which he apprehended, The bringing her into intimate *Communion* and *Familiarity* with himself, opening to her the *Secrets* of his *Heart:* which fills the Spouse with unspeakable Joy and Gladness. This he look'd upon to be much the same with what is promis'd *Psa,* xlv. 14, 15. *She shall be brought unto the King in Raiment of Needle-work: the Virgins her Companions that follow her, shall be brought unto thee: With Gladness and Rejoicing shall they be brought: they shall enter into the King's Palace.* And while he was opening the Glory hereof, the Lord brought this Word, with Power to my Heart, *Luke* iv. 21. *This Day is this Scripture fulfil'd in your Ears!* Oh! I saw, that this very *Day*, or the present *Dispensation* of Favour I was under, in bringing me into that Palace of the King; was the very same with what he was speaking of, concerning the Spouse, the Queen, being brought into the *Chambers*, the *Palace* of the King, *with Gladness and Rejoicing*: Which now my Soul was *full of!* And *then was I in his Eyes as one that found Favour*, Song viii. 10.

Being now got into *Canaan,* I may give a Hint of the *Goodness* of the Land. And like literal *Canaan,* it was, *An exceeding good Land. A pleasant Land. A Land flowing with Milk and Honey. A Land of Hills, and Valleys that drinketh Water of the Rain of Heaven: A Land that Jehovah careth for, and his Eyes are upon it, from the Beginning of the Year to the End thereof. A Land of Brooks of Water, of Fountains, and Depths that spring out of Valleys and Hills. A Land wherein Bread is eaten without Scarceness,* &c. *Num.* xiv. 7. *Psa.* cvi. 24. *Exod.* iii. 8. *Deut.* xi. 11, 12, and viii. 7, &c. And as all this was literally true of *literal Canaan,* so did I find it eminently true, in a spiritual Sense, concerning this *Land of Promise,* I was now in Possession of. Which filled my Soul with joyful Wonder, that *the Lines should fall unto me in such pleasant Places*, and that it should be my Lot to have such *a goodly Heritage*, Psa. xvi. 6. Here I feasted upon the rich Provisions of *Free-Grace*, and delightfully drank of that *River, the Streams whereof made glad the City of God*, Psa. xxxvi. 8. and xlvi. 4. *The Glory of* GOD, *and of the* LAMB, *did lighten* the City where I dwelt, *Rev.* xxi. 23. And *a pleasant Thing it was for* my spiritual *Eyes to behold the Sun*, Eccles. xi. 7. Or, the *Glory* of GOD, as the God of *all Grace*, shining in the Face of JESUS CHRIST, *2 Cor.* iv. 6. *Glad* I was, as a poor *freezing* Creature, in my *Nature-Coldness*, and *Hardness*, to get thus *near the Sun of Righteousness*; whose penetrating Rays, *warm'd* my cold Soul, and *melted* my hard Heart. A *weak, fainting, wounded* Creature I was; and therefore *glad* to sit down under the *strengthening, reviving* Influences of *his healing Wings*. A *black* Creature I was, and therefore *glad* to get within the *Shine of that Sun*, which *transforms* all it looks upon, into the *same Image*, and makes 'em shine forth in its *own Glory*. My royal Bridegroom made a *Feast* for me; a *Love-Communion-Feast* it was: That was *glorious* in its Provisions, *glorious* in its Distributions, and *glorious* in its Society: The *Father, Son*, and *Holy Ghost*, holding *Communion* with *sinful Worms! Rejoycing over 'em to do them good*, causing them to *drink of royal Wine in Abundance*; that so they might *forget their Poverty, and remember their Misery no more!* But what shall I say? *Words fail* to set forth *spiritual Glory*; it being *unspeakable!* It's only *that* Eye that has *seen it*, that can take in the *true Idea* of it: *That* Palate alone that has *tasted it*, knows *its Sweetness*. Let them then that are *spiritual*, judge of the *Goodness* of *Immanuel's Land*, from what themselves have tasted of its *Milk and Honey*; by which their *Eyes have been enlighten'd* in this Matter, *1 Sam.* xiv. 29.

And not only was I favour'd with *spiritual Privileges*, but with *outward Enjoyments too*: The Lord took Care of me as to this Life, according to his faithful Word.--*Blessed be the LORD God, the God of Israel, who only doth wondrous Things. And blessed be his glorious Name for ever, and let the whole Earth be filled with his Glory* Amen, *and* Amen. *Psa.* lxxii. 18, 19.

And now, having given some Account of my obtaining this great *Mercy*, I would take a short Review of the several *Graces* of the Spirit, which were *exercis'd* herein: Which bear some Analogy unto what our Lord compares his Spouse, Song i. 9. even to *a Company of Horses. I have compared thee, O my Love, to a Company of Horses, in Pharoah's Chariots.*

This Scripture was open'd, and apply'd to me, by the Spirit, as near as I can remember, a little while before this Exercise *began* about my Removal: And was of *great* Use, both for my Instruction and Consolation, at Times, all the while my Exercise *lasted*. From these Words I was taught,

First, That our Lord compares the whole *Church*, collectively, in Regard to its several *Members*, unto *a Company of Horses*.

Secondly, That every particular *Believer* is so compar'd, in respect of the several *Graces* of his Spirit wrought in them.

Thirdly, That both *all* the Saints, and *all* their Graces, have their proper Work assign'd them. Which, according to the Comparison here, is to *draw*, like *Chariot-Horses*.

Fourthly, That the Saints should draw *together*, and that the several Graces of each Saint should be *jointly* exercised; and run *together*, as *Chariot-Horses* go by *Pairs*, drawing together the same Chariot.

Fifthly, The high *Value* of the Saints, and the *Worth* of all their Graces; in that they are compar'd unto *Horses in the Chariots of Pharoah*, or unto King's Chariot-Horses; as being the *best* of that Kind they are compar'd to.

Sixthly, That they are so compar'd, 1. For Beauty, and Excellency. 2. For Order, and Usefulness. And, 3. For Strength, and Courage. All which are to be seen in *King's Chariot-Horses*: But especially in the Charior-Horses of KING JESUS. And,

Seventhly, That the *Chariots* of King *Jesus*, which his *Horses draw*, are his *Promises*, and *Providences*; in which HE rides forth, for his Honour, to take his Pleasure, and to do his Work.

And being taught thus far, the next Thing I wanted, was to take a particular *View* of those several *Graces*, the Holy Spirit had wrought in me, upon which Account I was compared to *a Company of Horses*, &c. For it was the particular Application of it to *me*, that most affected me: I have compar'd *thee*, &c. And the several *Graces* I was instructed into, which, like so many *Pair of Horses*, should *run together*, or be *jointly exercis'd*, in drawing the *Chariots* of God's gracious *Promises*, and special *Providences*, were *these*:

Faith,		Love.
Hope,		Joy.
Humility,	and	Patience.
Self-Denial,		Godly Fear.
Zeal for God's Glory,		Gospel Repentance.

I did not at once, see all these Graces to be of Use to draw the Chariots: Tho' for Order's Sake, I place them together. The Lord knew what Exercise he had appointed for me, and therefore was pleas'd to instruct me before-hand, what was my Duty, and his Design. And when he set me on Work to *draw* those *Promises* and *Providences*, relating to my Removal, this *Scripture*, thus open'd, was of great Use to me.

The Lord has *not said to the Seed of Jacob, seek ye me in vain*: Nor shall the Exercise of any Grace be *fruitless*. They who, in this Respect, *sow to the Spirit*, shall undoubtedly *reap* an answerable Crop. Not that there is any *Worth* in the Exercise of these Graces, which *deserve* the Mercies they obtain. For when we have *done all, we are but unprofitable Servants*. We can *deserve* nothing for our Service, because we *owe all* that we are capable of doing; and it's but *our Duty*. But yet our gracious God, will not suffer our *Labour to be in vain*: Nor will he be *unrighteous* to his own Promise, in *forgetting* his People's *Work of Faith, and Labour of Love*. Now then, as to the *Exercises* of these Graces.

I found *Faith*, and *Love*, run together in *obtaining these Promises*. Faith in the Fulness of Christ's Grace, Wisdom, Power, and Faithfulness; as every Way fit to save me out of all my Distresses, and to the Utmost of all my Desires. And Love also, in vehement Longing after my absent Bridegroom, Nor did they draw the *Promises* only, but the *providential* Fulfilment of them too: Until which happy Day, Faith *saw 'em afar off*, and in its renewed Exercise, *was persuaded of 'em*; and Love *embrac'd them*.

Again, *Hope*, or earnest Expectation of the Fulfilment of the Promise, with its Concomitant, *Joy*, sweetly *drew together*.

Further, *Humility*, under a deep Sense of my great Unworthiness of such high Favours, together with *Patience*, or quiet waiting the Lord's Time of appearing for me, was another *Pair* of Graces put to *Exercise*.

Again, I found *Self-Denial*, crossing the Interests of the Flesh, and *godly Fear*, or reverential Obedience, *running together* with it.

Once more, *Zeal for God's Glory*, in seeking the Fulfilment of his faithful Promises, and in bearing a Testimony of God, in the Face of all the Enemies which oppos'd, together with *Gospel-Repentance*, or mourning for, Hatred of, and turning from Sin, under a Manifestation of free Pardon, *kindly wrought* in me.

And as *Horses*, that run in the *Winter-Season*, may sometimes meet with such *difficult* Way, that requires the Extension of *all* their Strength to *keep on* the Road; so it was with all these *Graces*. Sometimes *one* was try'd, sometimes *another*. And I could easily discern, how *Faith*, and *Love, Hope*, and *Joy, Self-Denial*, and *Godly Fear*, were *Chariot-Horses*. But when I was come into the *Deep* of my own *Unworthiness*, and saw that *Contrariety* that was in me to every Grace, and the Lord stay'd *longer* than I thought of; and I was told, *that I had made my Boast of him in vain*: Then my Strength began to *fail* me; and I thought,. *"Where are the Horses now?* How am I like *a Company of Horses?* Surely I can't *draw the Chariots now."* But then I was helped to cry to HIM that *gives the Horse his Strength*, that he would *renew my Strength*, for the *Work* he call'd me to. Which he was graciously pleas'd to do: And e're I was aware, *Humility*, and *Patience, Zeal for God's Glory*, and *Gospel-Repentance*, were set on *Work*: And the Lord shew'd me, that *these* were *Horses*, and of Use to *draw the Chariots*, as well as the *other*.

Thus I have given a large Account of my being brought to *W---h*. But after I had been there some Time, Things seem'd to work as if the Lord was about to remove me from *thence*: Which prov'd a *great Trial* to me. And some brief Hints of the Exercise of my Mind under it, I shall next give.

This *great Mercy*, of my being brought to *W---h*, and put into the *Possession* of those promis'd Favours, which I so *long pray'd for*; became *exceeding dear* to me. And the Frame of my Soul, tho' in a spiritual, and higher Way, may be compar'd to that of a fond, affectionate Mother: Who hugs her dear Babe in her Arms, being exceeding loth to part with it; not only from those living Pleasures she has, and hopes from her living Child; but also from her Heart's being more endeared to it, by the Remembrance of all that Pain and Sorrow, Labour and Travail she was at to bring it forth. So that now having the Child in her *Arms*, bound to her Heart by various *Ties*, if but a Thought of *losing it* makes an Approach, at once it seems to bring a double Death on her Joys.

I can think of nothing in *Nature*, that can so aptly represent the Frame of *my Mind*, with respect to *this Mercy*, as this Similitude doth. So that having the Babe in my *Arms*, the Enjoyment of which afforded me living Pleasures, together with the Remembrance of its being the Fruit of the Travail of *my Soul*, in Tears and strong Cries; yea, the Fruit of the Travail of *Christ's Soul*: (For not only the *Elect* themselves, but all those *Mercies* and *Favours* which are the *Fruits* of the Father's Grace, was the *comprehensive Birth*, his travelling Soul brought forth) I look'd upon this *Child of Promise*, and my Heart was *knit* to it. I view'd the *beautiful Birth*, as the Off-spring of the *Father's* Grace, the Fruit of the *Son's* Death, and glorious

Intercession for me above: And also as the Fruit of my *own Prayers*, that went up to the Father, in the Beloved's Name. And oh, how my Soul *clave to it!*

Whereupon, my Father, seeing the *Child* so *dear* to me, was graciously pleas'd to *try me*, whether I would be willing to *part with it*; by appearing in his Providence, as if he was about to *take it from me*.

But oh, the *Yerning of Bowels* my Soul felt! I run to my Father's Bosom, and pray'd him to have *Compassion* on me. I told my Lord Jesus, that he knew what it was to have *his* Heart *endear'd* to the Fruit of the Travail of *his* Soul; to a full Resolution, that none should pluck them out of *his Hands*, nor rob 'em of a Mercy he *dy'd for*. And I intreated him, by all that *Dearness*, the Mercy I ask'd for, stood in, both to *him* and *me*, that he would *continue his Loving-Kindness*. Humbled under a Sense of my *own* Vileness, acknowledging *his* Justice, if he should *smite the Child dead*, and yet *pleading* his free Promises, his unchangeable Grace, and infinite Patience: my Soul *intreated* the Mercy might be spar'd. Under a Sense of the Difficulties which seem'd to occur, I fled to his infinite Wisdom, to find out Ways to glorify *himself*, and save *me*. Sometimes I put my Cause into his Hand, as my Friend in the Court above; and could for a while, *rest* in his Management; while I view'd all his mediatory Works, as *honourable and glorious*, Psal. cxi. 3. At other Times, so vehement were my Desires for the Continuation of the Mercy, that I could scarce bear a Thought of *parting with it*. I can't express the Frames my Soul was in, thro' the Greatness of oppressing Fear. I liken'd myself to a Man *condemn'd*, whose Heart was *harden'd*, and shut up under the Terrors of his Sentence; who, yet, upon a Pardon being granted, would presently be *melted* into Tears. So I thought, that tho' my Heart was *shut up* at Times, that I could not pray for the Mercy, under the Greatness of oppressing Fear, lest it should *not* be granted; yet, that if the Lord should give it me *again*, and bring me News of a Pardon for all my Unkindness, in being unwilling to part with what HE call'd for; it would soon *melt* my Heart, and make my Soul asham'd of my ungrateful Carriage (which doubtless was very sinful) for which I was many Times *grieved*. And some Hopes that I should obtain my Desire, made me long to glorify God in the mean Season. Oh! I have thought, "That I could not be contented with having the Mercy granted *anew*, unless I was help'd to glorify God, while it seem'd to hang in Suspense, by being willing to *part* with it, if HE pleased." For I saw Abundance of *base* Ingratitude, and *vile* Unbelief, in being *loth* to give up the Mercy into my Father's Hand, for

Fear he should take it from me: Which reflected the greatest Dishonour upon his gracious Heart. At Times, indeed, I was help'd to *commit it to him*, and *trust it in his Hand*: Believing that HE was infinitely more concern'd for me, than I could be for *myself*. But, alas, at other Times, I was ready to *pluck it back*, and be *afraid* to trust the Lord: Which *griev'd* my Soul, that I should carry it so *unkindly* to my dearest Friend. Oh how apt are we to make *Idols of our fair Jewels, of* our Lord's *Silver, and his Gold!*

Whereupon, my Heart was drawn out to ask two Requests of the Lord. The *first* was, "that HE would enable me to *glorify him*, by giving up the Mercy into his Hands." The *second*, "that he would *glorify himself*, in giving it again, if *he* pleas'd." The which I attempted, with a Soul full of *Burden*, but was soon set at *Liberty* to speak my Heart to him. And before I had done my Requests, I receiv'd, in Part, a gracious Answer to the first. For while I was bewailing *my* Ingratitude, in the Remembrance of *his* Kindness, that particular Instance of it, in his *giving his only Son for me*, was brought to my Mind; and my Heart, in some Measure, chang'd into the Image of *that Love*: Even to *give up this Mercy*, which was as an *only Child*, the *dearest* and *nearest* of outward Favours, I ever enjoy'd. Soon after this, *the Glory of God*, as the End of my Being, was brought to my Mind: And this Thought drew on my Heart to Resignation: "That now I had an Opportunity to *glorify God*, in giving up a *Mercy* that was the *dearest* I ever had, or might have in this World." And my Heart, out of *Love* to God's Glory, not so much in the Views of his Graciousness, in giving me a Mercy back again, as sometimes I have experienced, but in pure Love to his *Glory*, was drawn out to desire to make a *Surrender* of it to him. And tho' I found some Backwardness, yet I was drawn on to do it thus:

"Lord, *take the Mercy*; do with it just as thou pleaseth: *Slay it*, if thy *Glory* lies here: I now *resign it up*, into the Bosom of infinite Grace, Wisdom, Power, and Faithfulness: Now, *Father, Glorify thyself*, which Way thou pleasest."

And a great *Value* for God's Glory was rais'd in my Soul. I thought, "What is *my Being*, or all *my Enjoyments*, in Comparison of *God's Glory!* Surely, they are but as *nameless Nothings!*"

And as my Heart was drawn out to give up its *dearest Interest* to God's *Glory*, with some Delight and Pleasure; so my Soul was griev'd, that my Love and Zeal did burn with no more vehement a Flame. But I was help'd to make this Act of Resignation in the *Name of Christ*; and to look for all its Acceptance, as it went up to the *Father*, in the Perfections of my *resigning Head*: Who, in the greatest Act of Resignation that ever was, brake forth, with a *not my Will, but thine be done*. Oh how *vehement* was the Flame of *Christ's Love*, to his *Father's Glory*, when HE thus resign'd himself up to his *flaming Wrath! Christ's Surrender*, was made in the *Fulness* of the Holy Ghost's *Fire: Mine*, was but an *ascending Spark*, in Christ's *vehement Flame!* And blessed be God, for this Way of Acceptance.

My Soul being thus *resign'd* to God's Glory, I found a pleasurable *Satisfaction* in the Review: And judg'd it far *better* to glorify God, than *merely* to enjoy him; under the *bare* Notion of my Happiness consisting in *that* Enjoyment. And surely, if we were *ingenuous*, we should cast the Drop of *our Happiness*, into the infinite Ocean of *God's Glory*: Accounting *his* Glory, *our* highest Happiness, whatever he doth with us.

And further, in this Worship of my Lord, my Heart was wrought up in some Measure, into an holy *Forgetfulness*, of what I had resign'd; with respect to any *Peremptoriness* in my Requests for the Re-obtaining of it. My Soul earnestly desired, that I might call nothing *my own*, but *God's great SELF!* And that I might always *cleave to HIM*, as the eternal *Fountain* and *Well-Spring*, of all my Pleasures. And yet all this *consistent* with the *vastest* Desires of the Mercy, if it might not *thwart* his Glory.

Quickly after I had resign'd the Mercy, that Word was brought with great Power to my Heart, *Gen.* xxii. 16, 17. *By my* SELF *have I sworn, saith the* LORD, *That in Blessing, I will bless thee, and in multiplying, I will multiply thee.* It was spiritual Blessings, and Faithfulness [*sic*; r. Fruitfulness], my Faith apprehended in the Promise. And Oh what a Security of these did I see, while the Lord open'd unto me his Covenant-Engagements, as having sworn by his own Great SELF! *By my* SELF *have I sworn*, &c. q. d. [*quaque die*, every day] "By all that is *in* ME, by all the Perfections of *my Nature*: As, Love, Grace, Mercy, Wisdom, Power, Faithfulness, &c. *That in Blessing, I will bless thee*." Oh! here I saw, that ALL that was in GOD, was engaged to do me Good; that HE took all his Motives from within HIMSELF to bless me, and that all Covenant-Blessings were absolutely, and eternally secured to me in the Unchangeableness of JEHOVAH, in all the infinite Glories of his Great BEING! And this notwithstanding all my Unworthiness, Vileness, &c. For if ALL that was in GOD, was sufficient to make me *blessed*, I should not *want* Blessedness. But, oh! the Heart-melting, Soul-raising, Heart-attracting Nature of this Discovery! What wonderful Glory did I then *see!* What Power did my Soul *feel!* What Joys then *fill'd* my Heart! I put it among the *best* Times I have enjoy'd in this World.

But tho' I was sweetly resign'd into the Will of God at this Season, yet at other Times I was greatly distrest. Still Things seem'd to work for my Removal. And that which most tried me, was, the Promises I had of the *Continuation* of the Mercy, when yet Providence seem'd to *thwart them*. I thought they must have been immediately fulfilled, by preventing my going away at all, from that Place. But the Design of the Lord in them, was, (as I have seen since) To assure me, that the Mercy should not be taken away (or in the least touched as to the *Right* of it; nor altogether as to the *Enjoyment* of it: But that, in great Grace, I should still *possess it*, notwithstanding all my Unworthiness, and Provocations. These Promises answer'd the End for which they were brought, *viz*, To comfort my Soul while the Mercy seem'd to hang in Suspense: And also to assure me of my *future* Enjoyments [*sic*; r. Enjoyment] of it: Altho' my *present* Enjoyment was to be *interrupted* for a Season. Which being for wise Ends, concealed from me then, did afterwards very much *try me*. And therefore,

V. The next Step of Providence, I shall take some Notice of, is, The Lord's Removing me from *W---h*, to *W---*.

When this first appear'd, I was very *unwilling* to it: I used *my* Interest at the Throne, and pray'd Christ to use *his*, to *prevent* it: (which was not in vain in the *End*, but brought the Mercy to me in a greater Glory) but at present, all seem'd be in *vain*. The Promises I had from the Lord, that the Mercy should not be taken away from me, (by reason of my limiting Him, as to the exact Time, and Manner of their Fulfilment) did also *heighten* my Trial. For these seem'd to be in *vain* too. And tho' I had been enabled to resign the Mercy up to the Lord; yet I was not without Hopes that he would still *continue it*, but *now* it seem'd to be quite taken away from me. I *looked for Light, but behold Darkness!* Things work'd so *contrary* to my Expectation, that I knew not *what* to make of them. But my Mind was somewhat stay'd, by the Lord's saying unto me, *I am thy God*, Isa. xli. 10. "I am *thy God* still: Thou may'st be sure of *that*, tho' thou knowest not *what* I am doing with thee in the Depths of my Providence." And when I was afraid that the Lord would take the Mercy from me, on account of my Sin, that Word was brought to my Heart with Power, unto much Sweetness, Peace, and Soul-melting, *Isa*, xliii. 25. *I, even I am HE that blotteth out* thy *Transgressions for mine own Sake, and will not remember* thy *Sins*. That

Word also was some Stay to me, *Jer.* xxxi. 17. *There is Hope in thine End, saith the* LORD. But for the most Part I was fill'd with Distress.

And down I went to *W---*, before I had been at *W---h* a full Year. Thus short-lived was my sweet Enjoyments, and my Mind was in great Heaviness. But I was somewhat refresh'd in the Views of that Glory reserved in Heaven for me. Oh! thought I, "How much Glory has my Soul *drank up* in this World! And yet is as *thirsty* as ever. But there's Glory *enough* laid up for me, to satisfy my vast Desires to an endless Eternity. And when once I get *Home*, I shall never *lose* my Enjoyments, or be *turn'd out of Doors* more!" But for the present, my *Misimprovement* of the great Favours I lately enjoy'd, made me fear that the Lord (as Mr. *Rutherford's* Phrase is) had "Cast me over the Dike of the Vineyard, as a dry Tree." But oh the Temptations which beset me, while the Enemies, Satan, and Unbelief *triumph'd* over me, with a *Where is now thy God? What's* become of thy "Faith and Hope *now? Where are* the Promises thou thought'st would have prevented thy coming *hither?* And as thou hast *misapprehended* them concerning this Dispensation, thou may'st as well have been *mistaken* in all those thou hast had about thy eternal State." Thus the Enemies would fain have improved my present Distresses, to have driven me into far greater. But the Lord strengthened me to resist Satan, steadfast in the Faith. And that Word was very precious to me, *Col.* i. 5. *For the Hope which is laid up for you in Heaven.* From which I had a fresh View of that glorious Inheritance, the *Object of my Hope*, as securely *laid up* for me in Heaven, whatever Trials I might pass thro' in this World. And this helpt me patiently to endure my present Afflictions. But tho' *this* Temptation to question my eternal State, was, thro' divine Kindness, soon vanquish'd: Yet there was *another* with which I was terribly assaulted: and it lasted, for a great while, at times: *viz.* "That I was an *outcast*, in respect of God's Manifestative Favour, that the Lord had *forgotten* me, as to that loving Kindness which, in a wonderful Manner, had wont to be extended towards me, in all my times of Distress." But something of the kind Succours I received from the Lord under *this* Temptation, may be seen in a Letter that I wrote to Mr. *G---t*, when I had been at *W---*, near two months: Which was a follows,

Dear and honour'd Brother,

I Received your Letter with Gladness, and thankfully own your Kindness therein. I bless the Lord, I was refreshed by what you wrote. And am made to rejoice, with Wonder, that the Careful, Gracious *Eyes of the* LORD, are constantly *fixt* upon me, always *waiting* to be Gracious to me in all Cases and Places, and therefore in *this*: so that I need not *fear* any Enemy that may beset me, nor any Want that may attend me. And if it had not been so, where had I been long e're this? surely *among the Congregation of the Dead!*

I rejoice with you, for all the great Goodness you are made a Partaker of, in that our gracious Father is still drawing out his loving Kindness towards you, giving you Assurance of his everlasting Favour; by which you are changed into the same Image, from Glory to Glory. And also in that he is still keeping your Feet from falling, covering your Head in the Day of Battle, putting a new Song into your Mouth, and bringing you up out of the *Wilderness, leaning upon your Beloved.* Leaning upon his omnipotent Arm, which is strong enough to bear you up under all your Weakness; and leaning upon his Bosom also, where your benumbed Limbs get fresh Warmth and Nourishment, by which they are made nimble in their spiritual Motion. And this Happiness of *yours*, as a Fellow-Member of Christ's Body, makes *mine* more full.

As to the Exercise of my Mind, since I came here, I can say but little of it in this Paper; but in order to shew the Lord's gracious Dealings, I would say something. I have been, at times, covered with *thick Darkness*, and the *Beasts of Prey* came out and raged violently against me. But the *Lion of the Tribe of Judah*, has deliver'd my Soul from those Lions which would have *smitten my Life down to the Ground.* And while the Clouds were so terrible Dark, I was refresh'd with the Thoughts of God's *turning them round by his Counsels, and causing it to come whether for Correction, for his Land, or for Mercy*, Job xxxvii. 12, 13. And as I met with this Darkness, in my own Mind, so also I felt *Coldness*, by which the Limbs of the New-Creature were so *benumbed*, that they were unfit for Motion in divine Service. Yea, my Heart was almost *frozen*, and so *contracted*, that it could not run *into* my Father's; nor pour out my Supplications *into* his Bosom. But instead thereof, I was ready to run *from* Him, and have *hard* Thoughts of my tender Father; as if HE *had forgotten to be gracious*, and would *be favourable no more*; or, at least, that *I was forgotten* and *forsaken*. And my Guiltiness sometimes made me fear, that HE had *made a Way for his Anger.* Tho' the Remembrance of what HE said to me, somewhat stay'd me, as to this. But being tempted to think false Things of Him, and of his Dealings with me, I was ready to run away *from* him, and so to *swoon* and *die* for want of

Food. Sometimes I thought, *I could not serve him.* Yea, I think I have found something of *strange Rebellion*, and too much *Unthankfulness* for present Mercies.

Thus while my Father *hid* Himself, *I went on forwardly in the Ways of my own Heart.* A Wonder of Grace it is, I was not suffer'd to *run* whither my Enemies would have *driven* me! The careful, gracious Eyes of the Lord being fixt upon me, HE *saw my Ways,* and resolved to *heal me*; and he did it by *restoring Comforts to me.* His Bowels broke forth, with an *Oh! thou Afflicted, tossed with Tempest, and not comforted!* Isa. liv. 11. He caused me to hear Joy and Gladness, in that Word of his Grace, verse 7, 8. *For a small Moment have I forsaken thee, but with great Mercies will I gather thee. In a little Wrath I hid my Face from thee, for a Moment, but with ever-lasting Kindness will I have Mercy on thee.* And with this loving Kindness he *drew me* into the fresh Exercise of *Faith* in his everlasting Favour, and the Truth of all the Promises of his Grace; which I, by reason of Darkness, knew not how to *reconcile* with his present Providences. And by this Love-look HE *humbled* me under a Sense of all my Vileness, in pretending, with the Line of my *own* Wisdom, which is but Folly, to fathom the unsearchable Depths of *his* wise Providence. And then I cry'd out, with *Job, I have heard of thee by the hearing of the Ear, but now mine Eye seeth thee. Wherefore I abhor myself and repent in Dust and Ashes.* And, *once have I spoken, yea, twice, but I'll proceed no further.*---Thus Grace answer'd my Cavils at this Time. And when the Sun was *up,* the evil Beasts *hasted* to their Dens; and I saw *whereabout I was,* even in that *same Grace,* where I viewed my Standing before the Night came on. Then I said, "I'll complain no more of my Father's Dealings." — But, did I *keep my Word!* Ah! *no.*

The Sun *withdrew,* to *mourning* I went again; the Enemies that were put to Flight, gathering up their scatter'd Forces, *Rendezvous'd afresh*; the Night *came on,* and I, growing *dark and cold,* could make but a *faint* Resistance. At length, thro' the Enemies *within,* the Enemies *without* enter'd; and an Army of *black Doubters* was presently muster'd. And if the LORD had not been on *my Side,* when they rose up against me, they had *swallow'd me up quick.* But the Captain of the LORD's Host, lift up *Salvation* for an Ensign; and then I *sought* under a *Banner of Love* display'd. What shall I say? *infinite* Patience has been extended towards me, and *Bowels* of Compassion have yerned upon me!

My Heart has often been for *making Tabernacles,* where I saw *Christ's Glory.* And HE observing how *loth* I was to come down from the pleasant

Mount, for fear I should *lose* his sweet Company; was graciously pleas'd to call me, to *come with* HIM *from Lebanon*. And knowing how hard we are to believe his Presence with us, when we *leave* Lebanon, he doubles it: *With* ME *from Lebanon, my Spouse*, Song iv. 8. By *Lebanon*, as applicable to my Case, I apprehended, The *pleasurable Place* where I saw the *Majestick Glory*, of the GOD *of all Grace*, while *I sat down under the Shadow of my Beloved*, and found *his Fruit sweet unto my Taste*. The Invitation to come away, was thus: as if my Lord had said, "Don't stay in thy Desires at *Lebanon*, nor think *I'm* left behind; I am *with thee* still; I have something to do *here; Come with* ME, therefore from Lebanon. *Look from the Top of Amana, Shenir, and Hermon, from the Lions Dens, and the Mountains of the Leopards.*" By *Amana, Shenir*, and *Hermon*, I thought might be apprehended, Those *Dewy Mounts* where my thirsty Soul had wont to be *refreshed* under the sweet Distillations of Gospel Life, and Blessedness. For the *Psalmist* speaking of the *Dew of Hermon which descended on the Mountains of Zion*, says, *There the* LORD *commanded the Blessing, Life for evermore*, Psa. cxxxiii. 3. And as the Lord call'd me to come with him from Lebanon, so to *look* from these *dewy Mounts*, even the very *Top* of 'em. And thus he said, "Don't look *back* my Spouse, as if all thy Happiness lay *there*; but cast thine Eyes *forward* unto the transcendent Glories which are in ME: Thou hast ME to *look* to still; and there is more to be seen and enjoy'd in ME, than ever thou didst yet *behold*, even upon the very *Top* of those Mounts." And sweetly my LORD call'd me to take up my Solace in *Himself*, in this Verse:

> Let *my* fair Glories thee entice
>   To come along with *me*:
> *Forsake* thine earthly Paradise;
>   Thy Paradise *I'll be*.

Again, HE call'd me from all terrifying Objects; from the *Lions Dens*, and the *Mountains of the Leopards*. "Come away, said HE, my Spouse, from those *Beasts of Prey* that would devour thee; *look* from the *Lions Dens*, run into my Bosom, and dwell at *Peace*; I am thy Refuge, where thou may'st be safe from all that would harm thee." Thus my kind Lord *call'd me*, and his powerful Voice gave me Motion; (for I found what he said, to be *Amen.*) And so, *looking, I came.*---But did I *stay?* Ah! not *long.*

Again, I *wandred from my Place*, as the *Bird* from her *Nest*; and the *Birds of Prey* found me; and doubtless they had *devour'd me*, but that my gracious Lord was *swift* in his Motions for my Deliverance. *As Birds flying, defending he has defended; and passing over he has preserved me*, Isa. xxxi. 5. When *weary* and *heavy laden*, by taking the Burden upon my *own* Shoulders, my Lord has call'd me to HIM, and promis'd to give me *Rest*, Matt. xi. 28. When, by reason of *Darkness*, I knew not *what* to do; he has bid me *trust in the Name of the* LORD, *and stay upon my God*, Isa. l. 10. *Wounded* I have been, and that in my *Eyes*, so that I could not *see* the Glories of divine Love, thro' the Vail that was on its Face. But then *Eyesalve* has been bestowed, for the Recovering of my Sight. So that I have been made to believe, that, *whoso is wise, and will observe these Things, even they shall understand the Loving-Kindness of the* LORD. Aye, Loving-Kindness in commanding, and raising those *stormy Winds*, by which God's poor sea-faring Children are *tost to and fro*, and *reel like a drunken Man*; for when at their *Wits End*, these *see the Works of the* LORD, *and his Wonders in thee Deep*, Psa. cvii. 24, &c.

And once, when I was praising the Lord for his *former* Mercy, which a while ago ravish'd my Heart with its unvailed Glory; I look'd upon the *present* Scene, and seem'd to *lose* the Sight of Mercy's Face, thro' the intervening Cloud; and my Musick began to *flat*. But in order to raise my Notes of Praise high, Mercy's Eye *pierc'd* the Cloud, and *look'd* upon me with a Ray of its Glory, in those Words, Psa. cvii. 1, 2. *O give Thanks unto the* LORD, *for* HE *is good: for his Mercy endureth for ever. Let the Redeemed of the* LORD *say so.* Then said the Lord, "What, didst thou see the Glory of my Mercy the *other Day*, and canst *now* praise in the Remembrance of it, and yet are *stopt* in thy Notes about my *present Mercy?* Why? *my Mercy endureth for ever*: It's as *great* towards thee *now* as *ever.* What tho' a *Vail* is on its Face, it's the *same Mercy still*; and therefore *say so still.*" And then *high* Notes of Praise, for *everlasting* Mercy, together with *low* Notes of mournful Lamentation, for all my *unbelieving* Thoughts, and *hard* Speeches, sweetly *joyn'd* in Consort; while I heard this sweet *Whisper, I will be merciful to their Unrighteousnesses, and their Sins, and Iniquities, I will remember no more!* Oh! then I *mourn'd* that I should not *believe* in the *Dark.* "Oh! my *Unkindness*, thought I, that ever it should be *me!* If it had been some *other* of God's Children, that hadn't had such Testimonies of Love and Grace, it would not have been so *much*: but that it should be I, that have been *so favour'd!*" Thus I repented at this Time.

But yet, again, at another Season, my Heart began to *mutter* its former Language. And while I was thinking on the Views I had while with *you*, of the Greatness of divine Love, I began, and said, "Well, I thought Mercy would have *prevail'd* for me, and that Love had been *strong enough* to have given the Victory on my Side, and that Christ would have *used* his Interest for me at the Throne, for obtaining the Favours my Soul desired." And the Lord heard me speak *my Thoughts*, and was graciously pleas'd to tell me *his Thoughts*: In that Word, *Isa*. lv. 9. *For as the Heavens are higher than the Earth, so are my Ways higher than your Ways, and my Thoughts than your Thoughts.* And then opening his *Heart* to me, he thus said, "*Thou thought'st* that my Love to thee was great, infinite, unchangeable, invincible, so that nothing could *overcome* it, and that it was so strong that it would *conquer all Opposition*: And thou thought'st *right*. But *my Thoughts*: the Thoughts of *my Heart*, in my Grace towards *thee* were still *higher, Immeasurably* higher than *thy highest Thoughts*; even as *the Heavens are higher than the Earth!* And from *thy* high Thoughts of my Grace, *thou* contrivedst the highest Ways *thou couldst*, for my Love to display itself in; and verily *thought'st* it must come *that Way*. But the Plottings of *my Heart*, to shew my vast Grace towards *thee*, were still *higher* than *thine*: *My Ways*, as well as my Thoughts, are *immeasurably higher*; every way answerable to my *great* BEING, and the infinite Depths of *my Wisdom*."

And when the *Lord* the Holy Ghost, had thus *directed my Heart into the Love of God*, with *Moses, I made haste, bow'd down, and worshipp'd*: Adoring infinite *Love*, which so far *surpasseth Knowledge*: Aye, and infinite *Wisdom* too, that *contrives all the Ways* infinite Love walks in! And when a Ray of infinite Wisdom broke in upon my Heart, my own Wisdom fell down before it, as Folly. *Believing*, I began to *admire its Ways*, thus; "Lord, What was *smiting*, as *higher Way* of shewing thy Kindness towards me, than *embracing!* What, *turning me out of Doors*, an *higher Way* than to let me *dwell in thy House!* Oh how *unsearchable are thy Judgments, and thy Ways past finding out!*" Oh! then I *long'd* for Grace to *serve him*, and that if I might not, with *Mary*, stay to kiss and embrace his Feet, yet that, like *her*, I might be sent with some Messge to his Brethren!

I have reason to bless God for the Holy Spirit, as the *Spirit of Counsel*. For HE has counsel'd me to carry it *friendly to Christ*, esteeming it, my highest Honour and Happiness to do any *Service* for him, altho' it should be attended with some *Loss* as to the Enjoyment of him. And as HE has been the Spirit of Counsel to instruct me, so also the *Spirit of Might*, to assist me, and make his Counsel efficacious. By which I have been made to acquiesce with that Word, *Mark* x. 44. *He that will be chiefest among you, let him be Servant of all.* If it is but to be a Servant *of* a Servant of Christ, it is *an Honour*. Those Words of the Apostle, have been of great Use to me in this Sense, *Phil*. iii. 7, 8. *But what Things were Gain to me, Those I counted Loss for Christ. Yea doubtless, and I count all Things but Loss for the Excellency of the Knowledge of Christ Jesus my Lord.* My Heart was wrought up to think thus: "If I did certainly *know*, that Christ Jesus my Lord, would be glorified in my coming hither, I should straightway count all those Enjoyments, which before I esteemed a *Gain* more worth than *Worlds*, to be but *Loss* in comparison of the excellent Knowledge of *his Glory*." I thought if the Question had been put thus: "Wilt thou stay here, and *enjoy him*, or go away, and *glorify him?*" and so left for *me* to chuse, and cast the Lot which Way *I would*, my very Soul would have cast it for *his Glory*. And that Word was encouraging to me, *Prov*. xvi. 4. *The Lord has made all Things for himself.*

Thus I have cause to bless the Lord for *his Goodness*, and to lament that *mine* is, even still, but like the *Morning-Cloud*, and the *early Dew, that quickly passeth away*. It's *well* for us, that there is something more *stable* than our *own Frames* to rejoyce in; even that substantial, unchangeable, never-failing Goodness of JEHOVAH, which is secured for us in his ever-lasting Covenant; all the Blessings of which are *sure*, because they stand upon the absolute Grace of his *Heart*, and the immutable good Pleasure of his *Will*. And as the laying up of his great Goodness *for us*, was according to his *own Heart*, so also, the dispensing of it *to us*. For, *not by thy Covenant*, says he, when he bestows any special Favour upon his dear Children.

Let us mutually pray, and praise for *each other*, while at a *Distance* on this stormy Ocean. 'Twill be but a little while ere we shall *meet* in the quiet Haven of Christ's Bosom; and together with all God's dear Ones, take up our Rest for ever in the Embrace of HIM whom our Souls love: While the Vision of his Glory, satiates us with new Pleasures for evermore! And then Time and Place shall *part us no more*. All our Father's Children are exceeding *near* both to him and one another. And as we are all *one* in Relation, so we shall be all *one* in respect of Habitation. And when once we get Home to our Father's House, then, no more Sin, Sorrow, Changes or Death;

but, instead thereof, perfect Holiness, Joy, Life and Glory to an endless Eternity!

The Peace of God which passeth all Understanding,
keep your Heart and Mind thro' Christ Jesus.

With dear Love to your whole self, I rest
Your unworthy Sister in Christ,
A. D.

Thus the Lord was with me amidst Distresses: And something further of the Exercise of my Mind under 'em, may be seen in the following Letter, wrote to the same Person, from the same Place.

Very dear and honoured Brother,

I Received your welcome Letter, and am glad the Child is better, but sorry to hear of your and your Wife's Illness. A Mercy it is, that there's a *Life* in reserve for us, that's well worth the *Name* of it: A Life that will have no Kind, nor Degree of *Death* attending it. 'Twill be but a little while ere we shall have done with a Body of Sin, and a Body of Affliction too: When once we get to the *City* our God has prepar'd for us, we shall have no more Sickness, Sorrow, Pain nor Death attending us: For *the former Things will be passed away.*

I was thinking a while ago, about my being so *soon* remov'd from the Place which was to me like *Canaan, a Land of Promise*; and the Lord's dealing with *Abraham* was brought to my Mind, *Heb.* xi. 9. *He sojourn'd in the Land of Promise, as in a strange Country*: And *Acts* vii. 5. *He gave him none Inheritance in it, no not so much as to set his Foot on.* And that Word was then precious to me, *Heb.* xi. 16. *God is not ashamed to be called their God: For he hath prepared for them a City.* I saw, that neither *Abraham*, nor I, nor any of the *Heirs of Promise*, shall *miss*, of our Expectations of those *great Things* which we have apprehended in the Promise of our own great GOD: Tho' we may *mistake*, as to the particular Manner, Time, or Degree of their Accomplishment in *this World*; yet we shall not *miss* of our Expectations at *last. For* HE *hath prepar'd for us a City*: The Privileges of which are so glorious, and lasting, that GOD himself, as the glorious and eternal GOD, will not be ashamed of being call'd *our*

GOD, because he has made such *Provision* for us, that is every Way answerable to his own glorious *Greatness*; and the Nearness of his *Relation* to us.

I thank you for your Letter, I take it kindly, and look upon it as a Part of Christian Friendship, that you will hold this Kind of Communion, since Providence prevents us of any that is more immediate. I rejoyce that the Lord is still with you in your Work; and crowns your Labours with Success: Which is a Privilege not easily valued. Oh what is it to enjoy GOD in his House! Blessed are the People that *dwell* where his Glory shines!

As to your Complaints of Carnality, Hardness of Heart, and Ingratitude towards God, and his People; from sad Experience, I must join with you. For surely, in these Respects, I am *worse* than ever. At Times, I am so *burden'd*, as if my Heart would break; and sometimes so *harden'd*, that I can't pour out my Soul before the Lord, but run away from him, and, like the *Prodigal*, would *fill my Belly with Husks*. And such mighty Struggles are in my Soul, that I am at a Loss to judge of my own Experience: And with unutterable Groanings I breathe after Deliverance. I find a little Ease, when I can get to my Father, and pray him to see *what ails me*. I am glad that I shall not *ever* be *term'd, forsaken*; but that the Lord will *turn again, and have Compassion*. And sometimes I pray him to deliver me *again*, upon the Bottom of that same Grace which has *hitherto* sav'd me out of all my Distresses. Oh! I am griev'd that I can *love him no more*, when I have had *so much Love* manifested unto me! Surely I am one of the *basest*, and most *ungrateful* of any of his Children! I can't perfectly judge how it is with me: But I think the Strife is between *Love, vehement* Love, to the *Enjoyment* of him, as I was wont; and a *Desire* to love *him*, and *his* Glory, above *my own* Happiness, in that respect, and to submit to *his* Will when he crosseth *mine*.

For the first, it is *Love to Christ*, indeed; so *great*, that seems to overlook this *great World*, with all its Enjoyments, as *unsatisfying* Things; and fees *no* Glory, nor can find *any* Rest, *beneath* the Bosom of my glorious Bridegroom. And when *this* Works, if the Enjoyment of *him* was to be *purchas'd*, I would give him a *World* for it, if the World was *mine*. And when I have seen that I have *nothing* to give, and that HE *needs* nothing; in Vehemency of Soul, I have said, "then, Lord, *give me all freely!*" But tho' this *is* Love to Christ, yet 'tis *weak* Love, *childish* Love. The Babe *cries*, if taken from the *Breast*. I love *Communion* with my Bridegroom, because of the *heavenly Delights* that are in it. But I want to love *himself*, and his *Glory*, more than the *Enjoyment* of him. My Love is not yet *sublimated* enough, nor *heighten'd* out of *Self*, as I could wish. I find it a *hard Thing* to *deny* spiritual Self, in the Delights of spiritual Sense. And it grieves me that I am such a *tough, stubborn Piece*, so *unfit* for my Lord Jesus to make *any Thing of*. Mr. *Rutherford* says, "Let my Lord make any Thing of me, so he makes but his own Glory out of me; I have enough." And I have thought so too at Times; but now he comes to *prove me*, Oh how sadly do I *shrink* in the Trial! I think upon his Servant *Moses*, how he loved *God's Glory* more than his *own Happiness*; when the Lord told him, that if he would let him *alone*, to destroy his *People*, he would make of *him* a great Nation, *Exod.* xxxii. 10. But as if he took no Notice of that, God's Glory lying nearest his Heart, "What then, as if he should say, will become of thy great Name? *Wherefore should the Egyptians speak and say*, &c. Ver. 12." I think also, how it was with *Paul*, when, that God might be *glorified*, in the Conversion of his Kinsmen, he could even *Wish himself accursed from Christ*, Rom. ix. 3. And when I see how far short I am of this Perfection, my Soul is humbled within me.

But yet, when this Frame of Mind gets the Ascendant, to wit, a *Desire* to love God, and *his* Glory, above my *own* Happiness, and to submit to *his* Will when he crosseth *mine*: Then I find some Sparks of that heavenly Fire, which in them broke forth into such a vehement Flame. There are some Moments, wherein the Lord makes me willing that HE should be *glorified*, whatever becomes of *me*. Yea, when I have seen but, as it were, the *Dawn* of his Glory, I have been well pleased; and have thought, "that Love to his Glory would *hold me*, notwithstanding the *swift-wing'd Motions* of Love to the Enjoyment of him." But this is my Misery, I'm so *bent to Backsliding!* I am glad that the Lord can *bend me for himself*, Zech. ix. 13. And I see, that if *his* Hand, don't *hold* my Heart in *that* Bent, I straightway *fly back again*. I see, that I am like a *Bullock, unaccustom'd to the Yoke*: But yet there is something in me that is willing to *bear it*. And the Language of my Soul is, "Lord, *tame me, yoke me*; glorify thyself in, and by me, notwithstanding all the *Opposition* that is in me!" Thus, *What will ye see in the Shulamite.—As it were the Company of two Armies*. Oh pray for me, that the Lord would give me an *ingenuous* Temper, that so I might give him *leave* to do what he will with me: And that he would make *Luz*, a *Bethel*.

I was refreshed by your Letter, and see how the Lord carries on his Work in your Soul in the Midst of Darkness; and encouraged to hope that he would deal so with me. The Lord suffers the Enemies to *oppress us*, and then strengthens the New-Creature to *breathe* after Deliverance. And every of its *Groans*, speaks no less, than the fresh *Triumph* of its Life over Sin and Death. And every *breathing* after the Perfection of any Grace, directly tends to the immediate Increase of that Grace. Thus, our God, brings Life out of Death, Joy out of Sorrow, and Light out of Darkness. Oh how wonderful are his Works!

I rejoyce that you see a greater *Necessity* of Holiness than ever. I take it as an *Earnest* of your Increase in it. It's a special Mercy to see our *own Want*; and no small Part of the Spirit's Work, to convince us of *our Need*. He usually does so before he *supplies us*. He first, as the Spirit of *Conviction*, shews us our Wants, and then, as the Spirit of *Supplication*, he causeth us to seek to God for Relief; when, as the Spirit of *Consolation*, he designs to *supply all our Need out of his Riches in Glory by Christ Jesus.*

As to my *Knowledge* of divine Truths, I find it is very *small*: Especially if it be reduced to that which is *practical*; or to that Knowledge which influences the Soul into an answerable Practice. I am entirely of your Mind, "That our Refreshment in Truths, depends upon the Spirit's Breathing." Our Comfort depends not, barely, upon the *Newness* of their Discovery; but upon the *Degree* of the Spirit's Breathing. If the Spirit shines upon *old-known* Truths, we behold 'em in a *new Glory*: And if he breaths in 'em *afresh* upon our Souls, we're fill'd with *new Life* immediately. Wishing you may increase with all the Increases of God: I commit you to *Israel's* Keeper: And rest

Your Sister in Christ,
A. D.

Thus I have hinted something of my Soul-Conflicts when removed from *W---h*. I look'd upon my Enjoyments *there*, to resemble the *Land of Promise*, which the Lord gave to his People *Israel*, of old: And my Removal from *thence*, to bear some Analogy with their going into *Captivity*. And I was deeply humbled, under a Sense of my *own Vileness*, while I look'd upon this Dispensation, as a *Rebuke* for my Misimprovement of former Favours. But the Lord spake comfortably to me in those Words, *Lam.* iii. 31, 32. *The LORD will not cast off for ever. But tho' he cause Grief, yet will he have Compassion, according to the Multitude of his Mercies.* And in that also, *Jer.* xxxi. 10. *He that scatter'd Israel, will gather him, and keep him as a Shepherd doth his Flock.* And *Lev.* xxv. 23. *The Land shall not be sold for ever: For the Land is mine, for ye are Strangers and Sojourners with me.* From these, and other Scriptures, I was at Times, fully satisfied that the

Lord would yet shew Kindness, and bring me again to my *own Border*: Tho' there was no outward Appearance of it *then*, but quite the Reverse. For I saw myself surrounded with such Difficulties, that none but an Almighty Arm could deliver me from. And I was comforted from *Zech*. i. 8. to the End. From which Verses I was taught the following Truths: As, 1. That the Lord Jesus is *with* his People in their *low Estate*, Ver. 8. 2. The great *Care* the Lord takes of his Children, and that special *Inspection* he makes into their Case and Circumstances when in *Captivity*, Ver. 9, 10, 11. 3. That tho' the People of God should be destitute of any *Creature-Assistance*, yet *Christ* will *intercede* for their Deliverance, at the appointed *Moment*, Ver. 12. 4. That Christ's Intercession with the Father is always *prevalent* for the Deliverance of his People, in the most *desolate Circumstances*, Ver. 13. 5. That the *Opening* of God's Bowels to his Children in Distress, and the *fresh* Promises of Deliverance at such a Season, is the *Fruit* of Christ's prevailing for them in Heaven, Ver. 14, 15, 16, 17. And 6. That whatever *Force* has been used to *carry* God's People into *Captivity*, or may be employ'd to *hold 'em there*; yet God will raise up *Instruments*, and a Sufficiency of *Strength* on the *Side* of his People, to *counter-poize*, and *overcome* the Power of the Enemy, so that nothing shall *hinder* their full Salvation, when the appointed *Moment's* come: No Opposition shall *stand* before Almighty Strength, Ver. 18, &c. All which, being apply'd to my own Soul in particular, afforded me great Relief, under my then present Trials: And my Faith was strengthen'd to *expect* Deliverance. But while the Mercy was *delay'd*, I often had my *Fainting-Fits*; in which the Lord sweetly reviv'd me, by some Promise or other, and encourag'd my Soul to *wait on*. That Word was once very precious to me, *Isa*. li. 14. *The Captive Exile hasteneth, that he may be loosed, and that he should not die in the Pit, nor that his Bread should fail.* The Lord's dealing with *David*, also was very encouraging to me, *Psa*. xviii. 16. *He sent from above, he took me, he drew me out of many Waters.* Another Time, when I was much *tried* by Reason of the Promises which were given me, being *cloth'd* with contrary Providences; the Lord broke in upon my Heart, with great Glory, and told me what great Things he would do for me, in those Words, Song vi. 11, 12. *I went down into the Garden of Nuts, to see the Fruits of the Valley, and to see whether the Vine flourished, and the Pomegranate budded. Or ever I was aware, my Soul made me like the Chariots of Aminadib.* And at another Season, the Lord gave me to see my Deliverance secured in the Infinity of his Love, from Song viii. 6, 7. *Love is strong as Death, Jealousy is cruel as the Grave: The Coals thereof* *are Coals of Fire, which hath a most vehement Flame. Many Waters cannot quench Love, neither can the Floods drown it: If a Man would give the Substance of his House for Love, it would be utterly contemned.* From these Scriptures the Lord gave me to see such abundant Matter of Encouragement to wait for him, as those that watch for the Morning, that I was unwilling to *lose it.* And therefore that I might the better *retain* what the Lord had taught me, in order to direct my Soul in its Duty of waiting for him, I *wrote it down.* But what I then wrote for my own Use, being since design'd for publick Good, I have put, with small Additions, into two little Tracts:[*] And shall therefore say nothing of it here. But some further Account of the low Estate I was in at *W---,* and how the Lord help'd me to exercise Faith on Christ for Deliverance, may be seen in the following Letter, I wrote to Mr. *G---t* from thence.

    Much honoured and beloved Brother,

MAY *the Peace of God that passeth all Understanding, keep your Heart and Mind thro' Christ Jesus!* I bless the Lord, he was graciously pleas'd to make what you wrote to me sweet and savoury. I thought, "If the Grace of God is so *great,* that it will take up all the Ages of Time to tell the Story of it; how *vast* must be its Preparations for the Entertainment of all the Heirs of Grace beyond Time!" Again, I thought, "If there has been such a *Display of Grace,* in the Advancement of our Nature, in the Person of Christ, and of our Persons, in relation to HIM, into such a Nearness of Union with GOD, what *Favour* might we not expect from *so great Grace!*" I saw from hence, what great Encouragement I had to approach the Throne with the *greatest* of my Requests, seeing I was made *so nigh:* And that this Grace of *Union,* was but like laying the *Foundation,* upon which all the after Displays of Favour was to be *built.* I was also help'd to *prize* the Blessed Comforter, who *tells* the Story of Grace, with such Almighty Energy.

    I have great Reason to bless the Lord, for his continued Goodness towards me; my Soul is still held in *Life,* notwithstanding all that Death of Corruption, Temptation, and Desertion I pass under. I call the Lord's

---

[*]*Meditations and Observations upon the 11th and 12th Verses of the 6th Chapter of Solomon's Song.* And, *Brief Hints on God's Fatherly Chastisements, &c.*

present Dealings with me, *Desertion*: Because he is withdrawn, as to those frequent Manifestations of divine Favour, I was wont to be blest withal; the Fruit of which was, frequent Access into his Bosom. But blessed be his Name, I am not *wholly* deserted in this Respect. For now and then I hear sweet *Whispers* of his everlasting Kindness, and am *told* how full of Grace his Heart is towards me in my present Condition, and that he designs to deliver me. I am variously exercis'd: But I sometimes think, that the Lord is but preparing great Mercy for me; and that my being *afflicted, tossed with Tempest, and not comforted*, is but in order to *lay my Stones with fair Colours.*

I was a while ago, much cast down, under a Sense of my having *lost*, in a great Measure, that daily Savour of the Things of God; that had wont to be upon my Spirit; and that Word was with Weight upon my Mind, *Mat.* v. 13. *If the Salt have lost his Savour, it is thenceforth good for nothing, but to be cast out, and trodden under Foot of Men*, I saw, that I deserv'd nothing less than to be cast to the Dunghil, as a useless Creature. Upon this I thought, that I would go and tell my Lord Jesus, "That I had grievously departed from him, and that I was good for nothing but to be *cast unto the Dunghil*: And ask him, if he would deal so with me." Which I did; and soon after that Word was very affecting to me, *1 Sam.* ii. 8. *He raiseth up the Poor out of the Dust, and lifteth up the Beggar from the Dunghil, to set them among Princes.* And I thought, if he should lift me from the *Dust* of my present Lowness, and from my deserved *Dunghil-Condition*: Oh how shall I be beholden to *Free-Grace!* Oh! thought I, to be lifted from my present poor, low, useless Condition, this is a Dunghil indeed! And I pray'd him that he would tell me *again*, whether he would deliver me: Tho' I did not *deserve* that he should speak to me; because he had done it again and again, and I had been *unbelieving* quickly after I had heard his Voice; But I entreated him to speak *once more*. And quickly after, that Word broke in upon my Heart with great Power, *Acts* xvi. 31. *Believe on the Lord Jesus Christ, and thou shalt be saved.* 'Twas *Salvation* from present felt Deadness, to a Life of renew'd Quickenings, from apprehended Distance, to a Life of sensible Communion, from a barren, useless Condition, to a Life of Service, and Fruitfulness to God, that *I wanted*. And oh how sweet was the Tidings, that there was *yet* Salvation for me, in these Respects! Oh how sweetly did these Words sound, *thou shalt be saved!* Saved out of the *Deeps* thou art at present in! And that Word follow'd it, *John* xi. 25. *He that believeth in me, tho' he were dead, yet shall he live.* Oh how did those

Words reach my present Condition, *tho' he were dead, yet shall he live!* I'm dead *indeed*, thought I, but there is yet Life for me: Believing in the Lord Jesus, I shall *yet* live. And that Word also was brought, *Heb*. vii. 25. *Wherefore he is able also to save them to the Uttermost, that come unto God by him, seeing he ever liveth to make Intercession for them*, And oh how sweet was those Words, *to the Uttermost!* "Oh! thought I, I am not got beyond Christ's Power to save: Tho' the present Trial is the *deepest*, and the most *unlikely* to be deliver'd from: Yet he is *able to save to the Uttermost*, even to this very Time and Case." From these Words, I was instructed into my Duty of believing *afresh* on the Lord Jesus, as exalted at the Father's right Hand, on Purpose to save his People out of all their Distresses. And I had such a View of his being in *Office* to save me, from these Words, *because he ever liveth to make Intercession*, as I think I never had before. I saw it my Duty to *believe* on him afresh, in all the Fulness of his Grace, Wisdom, and Power, as in Office to save me. And the Encouragement I received hereto, was, the Certainty of the Event, *thou shalt be saved*. Then my Soul breathed thus: "Oh that I could steadily believe that he *would* save me!" And then those Words came, he is able to save all that come: That *come*, thought I, I'll come then with all my Wants, with all my Distresses, and cast *myself* as a poor, needy, helpless Creature, upon the Fulness of *his* Grace, Wisdom, and Power, as HE is in Office to save me out of all my Distresses, and to the Utmost of all my Desires.' And the Blessed Spirit who had given me this Encouragement, gave me also Soul-Motion: So that I *came*, and *cast my Burden upon the LORD*, and my weary Soul found *Rest*. For I quickly enter'd into the *Assurance-Rest* of Faith, that I *should* be saved; and that my believing on the Lord Jesus, for this *Time-Salvation*, would be as effectual to obtain its End, as my believing on him for the *eternal* Salvation of my Soul.

But oh! I am a poor unsteady Creature; I have been *sinking* in my Faith since then. And once, in particular, when I was in a *Fainting Fit*, these Thoughts were suggested to my Mind: "What, hast thou had *twenty Years* Experience of the Grace and Faithfulness of GOD, and afraid to trust him in this Case?" And herewith I had a glorious View of the Lord's *past* Appearances for me, and that he was the *same* in his Grace, Power, and Faithfulness, *now*, as he was *then*. Whereupon *I put it into his Hand*; desiring that he would give me what my Soul long'd for, if consistent with his Glory. However I *trusted him* with this Jewel, of my desired and expected Salvation, that he would keep it *for me*, and, in his own Time, give it out *to me*. Yea, I *commit it to him*, and was willing it should be disposed of, just as *his* Grace would cast it; whether for my enjoying it, or not. And such Thoughts were suggested to my Mind, "Do, *trust him, try him*, this once, and see how *gracious* he will be." And being help'd to cast my Care upon him, I was presently as light and chearful as if nothing ailed me. And further, I had such a distinct View of his being my tender, wise, strong, and faithful Friend, that I freely put it into his *Heart* and *Hand*. And these Scriptures were precious to me, *Isa*. xxvi. 4. *Trust ye in the LORD for ever: For in the LORD JEHOVAH is everlasting Strength: 1 Pet*. v. 7. *Casting all your Care upon HIM, for HE careth for you*: And *Prov*. xvi. 20. *Whoso trusteth in the LORD, happy is he*.

Sometimes HE helps me to *trust* him, sometimes to *wait* for him, and at other Times vehemently to *long* for him; even to a kind of *Fainting*, or *Love-sickness*: and sometimes I am quite the *Reverse* to all these. But yet the Lord gives me gracious Hints, *that he will come*. And when I hadn't that Assurance, yet he leads me into the Depths of my own Wants and Distresses; and makes the Declarations, and Promises of his Grace, together with his Dealings with his People in such Circumstances, to be very sweet to me; and I am help'd to *cast myself* upon the *Grace*, which shines forth in all these, to be dealt with accordingly.

I was a while ago, blessing the Lord, that I had yet any room to hope for so great Grace, as to be brought *out* of Captivity; and made to feed, and lie down safely: and that Word dropt upon my Heart, *Isa*. xlix. 8, 9. *To cause to inherit the desolate Heritages*, &c. I saw that Christ was given for this very End, to *say to the Prisoners, Go forth to them that are in Darkness*, or in Captivity, *Shew yourselves, to cause to inherit the desolate Heritages*. I thought, "That all the while the Lord's People was in *Captivity*, carried away from their *Lot* that fell to 'em in the *Land of Promise*, their Heritage was *desolate*." It is not said, the *People* was desolate, (tho' a captive State is so) but their *Heritages* were desolate. Oh! this Grace *melted* me: That whoever fills the *Place*, that fell to any of GOD's dear ones by Lot, they shall never take the *Right* of Inheritance from them: For GOD looks upon it to be but a *desolate Heritage*, till the right *Owner* is brought to *inherit it* again. It's the Father's Will, that Christ should cause his desolate Captives, to inherit their desolate Heritages. And when they're got Home, then follows the glorious Feast HE makes them, Ver. 10. which, at that Time, was very sweet to my Soul.

Since then, I was *fainting* in my Hopes, Desires and Expectations. But the Lord broke in with this Word, *Rev*. ii. 25. *That which thou hast already, hold fast till I come*. Oh the *Grace* of this Word also! I *took* the gracious Hint: and, amaz'd at his Kindness, said, "Lord, what wilt thou *come!* wilt thou *indeed* come! Let it then be according to thy Word. Come, *leaping on the Mountains, skipping on the Hills*; come, flying on the Wings of *Love*: Come, in all the Grace of thy *Heart*, in all the Grace of thy *Covenant*, in all the Grace of thy *Relations* to me!" Thus I fell a *praying*, while my Lord kept me *believing*. Again, I was affected, not only with the *Sureness* of my Deliverance, but with the *Manner* of it also: That it should be by my Lord's *coming himself* to fetch me. I thought, he might have said, I'll *send* for thee, but he said, I'll *come*. I saw that this was the Language of my *kind Bridegroom*: And like as if a tender Husband having his dear Bride at a Distance, should not be content with sending his *Servants* for her, but will come *himself* to fetch her Home. Such kind of Love may be seen in Creatures: And I saw that Christ was resolved that none of them all, should shew more Kindness than HE, in his *Bridegroom-Compassions*, according to his *Bridegroom-Relation*.

Bless the Lord with me: And help me by your Prayers: *Forget not the Afflictions of Joseph*. To the abundant Grace of our own God, I commit you: Wishing you a Life of joyful Communion with him here, and an abundant Entrance into Glory hereafter.

With endeared Love, I rest

Yours in Christ,

A. D.

Thus the Lord enabled me to exercise *Faith* for Deliverance, and was graciously pleased to *acquaint* me with it: And my longing Soul, with stretch'd out Neck, *expected it*.---But the Promises I had while at *W---h*, about the *Continuation* of the Mercy I enjoy'd there, which, I now saw, secur'd my *Right* to it, altho' my *Enjoyment* of it was interrupted for a Season; together with those Promises I receiv'd since my *Remove*, of my being again *restor'd* to my former Privileges; were all of 'em to pass under a *great Death*.---Instead of the Lord's Appearance to bring me again to *W---h*, which I expected, I was visited with an Ague and Fever, which being continued long upon me, threatned no less than my Death in *this Place*. And *until the Time that his Word came*, in the Fulfilment of it, *the Word of the*

LORD tried me, Psalm cv. 19. But, blessed be his Name, *his Grace was sufficient for me.*

When I first fell sick, the Lord drew *near* to my Spirit, and *comforted* my Heart with that sweet Promise, *Isa*, xliii. 2. *When thou passest thro' the Waters, I will be with thee; and thro' the Rivers, they shall not overflow thee: When thou walkest thro' the Fire, thou shalt not be burnt, neither shall the Flame kindle upon thee.* My Soul was affected with the *Bowels* of my heavenly Father: Oh! thought I, "If HE left me for a Season *alone* as it were, without his sensible Presence, while I was walking thro' a little dirty Way, yet now I'm come into deep Waters, he'll be *with me here.* Aye, not only *into* the Waters, but *thro'* them also; even to the End of the Affliction." And so it was; for I was much favour'd with his Presence throughout my long Affliction, which lasted for many Months. And tho', at Times, I was exceedingly *tried*, because all Things in Providence, seem'd to thwart the Promises; yet was I made to believe, and rejoyce in the Grace, and Faithfulness of my GOD, under all; and to think, that if I should not *know* what he was then doing with me, in this World, yet Glory would *untie the Knot*: That when I came to Heaven, I should see all the Mysteries of divine Providence *opened*, in a full *Conformity* to the faithful Promises of JEHOVAH. And that Word was very sweet to me under a Soul-conflict, when I seem'd near Eternity, *2 Sam.* xxiii. 5. *Altho' my House be not so with God; yet he hath made with me an everlasting Covenant, ordered in all Things and sure: For this is all my Salvation, and all my Desire, altho' he make it not to grow.* The Experience of *David* herein was very precious to me: And I was help'd to bring it down to my own Case, thus: Altho' I should not see the Promises *fulfilled* in that Way which I have *expected*, yet they are all *sure*; and I cannot *miss* of the Grace and Blessings the Lord intended in them: For he hath made with me an *everlasting Covenant*, in which is all my *Salvation*, and all my *Desire* too. I was likewise much favour'd with *Assurance* of my Interest in Christ, and Right to the heavenly Inheritance: And I could freely have gone Home to the Enjoyment of it, had my Father call'd me. But yet there was a *Desire* kept up in my Soul, if consistent with the Divine Will) that I might see the Grace and Faithfulness of God, in *fulfilling* the Promises as I had *expected*, and that in the *Triumph* thereof I might go home to Glory. But however the Lord dealt with me, I was *resign'd* into his Will, *believing* he would do that which was most for his Glory, and my Good. And, to comfort me under my Trials, I had a sweet View of my *fixed standing* in Christ, amidst the *shaking Storms* which pass'd over me, from *1 John* v. 20. *And we are* in *him that is true, even* in *his Son Jesus Christ.* I likewise had precious Views of the *Glory* I should have when at Home with Christ, from *Rev.* vii. 16, 17. *They shall Hunger no more, neither Thirst any more, neither shall the Sun light on them, nor any Heat. For the Lamb which is in the midst of the Throne shall feed them, and shall lead them unto living Fountains of Waters; and God shall wipe away all Tears from their Eyes.* Which Words I chose to be the Subject of my funeral Discourse, if I had died then.

But the Lord's Design was to *raise* me from a sick Bed, and give me to *see* his promised *Goodness*, in the *Land of the living*: And some Intimations hereof, he was graciously pleased to give me, from these Scriptures, *Hos.* ii. 19, &c. *And I will betroth thee unto me for ever, yea, I will betroth thee unto me in Righteousness, and in Judgment, and in loving Kindness, and in Mercies. I will even betroth thee unto me in Faithfulness, and thou shalt know the LORD. And it shall come to pass in that Day, I will hear, saith the LORD, I will hear the Heavens, and they shall hear the Earth, And the Earth shall hear the Corn, and the Wine, and the Oil, and they shall hear Jezreel. And I will sow her unto me in the Earth.* From these Words, I was fully persuaded, that I should *know the* LORD, in his Grace and Faithfulness, in my *full* and *compleat* Deliverance from all my present Distresses, into that Happiness and Glory I had long'd for and expected. Another Scripture the Lord made use of to this end, was, *Isa.* xxv. 6. *And in this Mountain shall the LORD of Hosts make unto all People a Feast of fat Things, a Feast of Wines on the Lees, of fat Things full of Marrow, of Wines on the Lees well refined.* By the Words, *in this Mountain*, I was particularly pointed to that Part of Mount *Zion*, where I *once* beheld, and *then* long'd to see the Glory of JEHOVAH. By the promis'd *Feast*, I understood that rich and glorious Fulness of Soul Provision, which should be made for me, in *that* Church, by the Lord, according to the State of the King, *as the* LORD *of Hosts*. The rich Dainties of this glorious Feast, suited my *longing Appetite*, and the *Freeness* of it, as for *all People*, my *great Unworthiness*. The Glory of my Deliverance, likewise shone forth, from *Isa.* xxxiii. 24. *The Inhabitant shall not say, I am sick: The People that dwell therein shall be forgiven their Iniquity.* From these, and other Scriptures, I was persuaded, that the Lord would *raise* me from a sick Bed, and *restore* me to my former Privileges; yea, cause me to *possess the double.* But still my Affliction *continued*, and my Faith was *tried.*

And once, in particular, there was a *Complication* of Distresses upon me: I saw myself surrounded with 'em on *every Side*; and that I was utterly incapable to help, or deliver myself form the *least* of them. Trials *press'd hard*, plunged I was into the *Deeps*: And out of the Depths of *Misery*, I cried to the Depths of *Mercy*. Oh! thought I, "Sure never any Child of God, needed his *Bowels* more than I!" And being left *alone*, I ran to my *Father*, poured out my *Heart* into his Bosom, shewed before him *all my Trouble*, and pray'd for the Extension of his *Bowels* according to the Depths of my Distresses. And presently that Word was brought, *Phil.* iv. 19. *My God shall supply all your Need*: And thus open'd, "If thou *needest* his *Bowels*, thou shalt *have them*." And these Words immediately followed, *Jer.* xxxi. 18, 19, 20. *I have surely heard Ephraim, bemoaning himself thus, thou hast chastised me, and I was chastised, as a Bullock unaccustomed to the Yoke,* &c. *Is Ephraim my dear Son? is he a pleasant Child? for since I spake against him, I do earnestly remember him still: therefore my* Bowels *are troubled for him: I will surely have* Mercy *upon him, saith the LORD*. That Word also brake in upon my Heart, *Isa.* lvii. 18. *I have seen his Ways, and will heal him.* But, oh! what a *Soul-amazing, Heart-melting* Discovery of *boundless* Love and Mercy I then *had*, every Way *suited* to my Weakness, Unworthiness, Sinfulness, and Miseries of all Kinds! What a *Sea of Grace* was I cast into! I saw ALL that was in GOD, engaged for *me*; and that my full Salvation by *Jehovah's Arm*, was secured in the infinite Grace of his *Heart*. His having Mercy upon me, in the *outward Dispensation*, in the inward Working, Yerning, or Troubling of his *Bowels*. And I had *enough*; as much as my Soul could *wish: Full Salvation*; and what was more, *Jehovah's Heart*: Which made the promis'd Deliverance flowing from it, *doubly* sweet to me. Oh how *abundantly* was my Soul satisfied as with Marrow and Fatness, and made to drink of the River of divine Pleasures, while I view'd the *Source* and *Origin* of all my Salvation in JEHOVAH's *Heart!* Oh the Heart-ravishing Prospect I then had of the *Glory of GOD!* Oh! thought I, "it's worth while to *die*, to *see GOD!*" And I could bless him for giving me my Being in *Nature*, in order to my seeing of HIM, as *the God of all Grace!* I think I *never* had such an *Opening* of the Bowels of God towards me, as at *that* Season.

By the *Bowels* of GOD, my Faith apprehended, the infinite Tenderness, and boundless Compassions of his *Nature*; as HE is, JEHOVAH, MERCIFUL, *Exod.* xxxiv. 6. And by the *troubling* of his Bowels, I apprehended, his actually taking into his *Thoughts*, the Miseries and Distresses of his

Children, in all the vast Grace, and infinite Tenderness of his *Heart*, at the appointed *Moment* of their Deliverance; whence his *whole SOUL* flows out towards 'em, in infinite *Resolutions* to do them good, according to his eternal Counsels. The *Fruit* of which is, the vehement *Out-breaking* of his *kindled Repentings*, in *changing* afflictive Dispensations, into prosperous Providences for his Children; or, his having *Mercy* upon them, *Psa*. xl. 17. *Exod*. iii. 7, 8. *Jer*. xxxii. 41. *Hos*. xi. 8, 9. I knew that there was no Change in God's *Heart* towards his People; but yet I saw that there was *more* contained in those Phrases, of *troubling of his Bowels, kindling of his Repentings*, &c. than, *barely*, the Change of the *Dispensation*. They seem'd to me to set forth, the *internal Workings* of his unchangeable Heart, in his eternal Grace, and infinite Compassions towards them, as *productive* of their Deliverance, at the appointed Moment. And my Joy in GOD, proportionably rose, with my Apprehensions of his *boundless Grace* herein!

And further, I was particularly favour'd with Communion with *Jesus Christ*: And my Soul set a *longing* for the greatest Familiarity with him in his House. That Word had been precious to me, *Isa*. lvi. 5. *Unto them will I give in mine House, and within my Walls, a Place and a Name better than of Sons and of Daughters: I will give them an everlasting Name that shall not be cut off.* But I wanted to be like the beloved *Disciple*, who *lean'd on Jesus Breast at Supper-time*: And I ask'd my dear Lord, *How he would deal with me?* Who gave me this gracious Answer, *Jer*. xxxi. 25. *I have satiated the weary Soul, and I have replenished every sorrowful Soul.* In which my kind Bridegroom, spake his *Heart*, and told me, "That he would *satiate* my *longing Soul* with his *Love*; that I should have his *Heart* in all the Provisions of his *House*; and that he would *replenish* me, with the Joys of his *Presence*, as I was a *sorrowful Soul*, on account of his *Absence*." Which was *all* I wanted. The Privileges of *Christ's House*, were very glorious in my View; but I thought, was it possible to separate my highest Enjoyments *there*, from *Christ's Heart* in them, they would all be to me, but empty, unsatisfying Things. I so *thirsted* for his Heart-Love; and with it he told me, HE would *satisfy me*: That I should have HIMSELF, as well as his *Benefits*. That Word, also, was very precious to me, *Isa*. xxxiii. 17. *Thine Eyes shall see the King in his Beauty.* At this Time I was extremely weak in Body, and the Lord was exceeding near to my Spirit. I lay as it were at the Mouth of the LORD, in the Bosom of GOD. And some Verses were dictated to my Mind, which were very precious to me. I did not compose them under divine Assistance, as many other, I have been enabled to do; but they were as if dictated to me by the LORD himself. But as I did not get 'em penn'd down presently, I lost all but the two first, and could not afterwards regain them. The two first were as follow:

Now I'll contend *no more*;
 In *Anger* I'll not *smite*:
Because of *Love* that was *before*,
 In which I do *delight*.

My Kindness on *thee fixt*,
 Like *rocky Hills* to ME:
And I can *ne'er forget*
 The LOVE I bear to *thee*.

The next Verse, as near as I can remember, call'd me forth to behold GOD's Ways of delivering me.

Thus the Lord, gave me Hints of the great Things he would do for me. And from this Time, the Day of my Deliverance began to *dawn*; and the increasing Light of it, like the Morning, altho' attended with some Clouds, hasted apace to its *noot-tide* Glory. The Lord *debated* with my Affliction, and *mitigated* the Violence thereof. He *remember'd* that I was but Dust; and *spared me*, that I might recover Strength. And this Affliction which seem'd to me to militate *against* the Promise, the Lord made the *Means* of their Fulfilment. For by Reason of its long Continuance, my Nature was so weakned, that it was *necessary* for me, for the Recovery of my Health, to return again into my own Air. It was *continued*, to bring me to this Necessity; and make way for my Removal: And it was *mitigated*, to enable me for my Journey. Thus my Deliverance came forth, *from the LORD of Hosts, who is wonderful in Counsel, and excellent in Working*. My dear Lord Jesus, had told me, that HE would *come*, and fetch me thence. And when I was just upon the Remove, I wanted him to tell me, whether it was HIM, in this Providence. And immediately that Word brake in upon my Heart, with great Power and Glory, *Psa*. xxxv. 3. *I am thy Salvation*. Q. D. [*quaque die*, every day] "It's I, I my SELF, am *thy Salvation*: I that have *promised it*, am now *performing it*: Behold me, therefore, in my vast Grace, Power, and Faithfulness, *coming* in this Providence to save thee."

VI. The next Wonder of special Providence, I come to give some Hints of, is, the Lord's bringing me back from *W---*, and fixing my Abode again at *W---h*. The Weakness of my Body, made it *doubtful* to some of my Friends whether it was my Duty to *attempt* such a Journey. But it being apparent that I was not like to recover, if I abode in *that* Place, I look'd upon it as a Call to remove. But while I was musing upon the Difficulties of the Journey by Reason of my Illness, I was ready to be *afraid*, and at a Loss to know whether I should attempt it at *present*. But I was comfortably *satisfied* by the Lord's bringing home that Word to my Heart, Song viii. 5. *Who is this that cometh up from the Wilderness, leaning upon her Beloved!* From whence I was persuaded, that it was my Duty to *come up*, even from that *Wilderness-Condition* I was then in, *leaning upon my Beloved*. In Dependence therefore upon his Almighty Power and Grace, I set forward. And that Word was very sweet to me by the Way, when I was ready to be discouraged, *Deut.* xxxiii. 27. *Underneath are the everlasting Arms.* By which I was comforted, and help'd to believe, that these mighty Arms would carry me safely thro' my present Difficulties. Nor did I trust the Lord in vain: For Almighty Power, and never-failing Mercy brought me safe to the Place, where I expected to see Abundance of promis'd Glory.

Thus being, to the Joy of my Heart, redeemed from my *Captive-State*, and brought again to my own Border, I went to attend upon God in his House, on a Day appointed by the Church for a solemn Church-meeting. At which Time Mr. *G---t* expounded those Words, *Isa.* xl. 9. *Say unto the Cities of Judah, behold your* GOD. And the Lord made it a Day of great Gladness to my Heart. Oh how *precious* was the Word to my Soul! *How suitable* to my Case! I thought it was on Purpose for *me*, and that the Lord by his Servant call'd me at that Time, in an especial Manner, to *behold my* GOD, and his wonderful Appearances for me, in that *amazing* Dispensation of Favour, I was *then* under.

But quickly after this, I was again *tried*. For tho' I was brought to the Place, where I expected to see the Glory of God in *Sion*, yet my bodily Weakness was such, that it seem'd as if it would *prevent* my Attendance upon Him in his House: And the next Lord's Day I was *hinder'd* from going to the Meeting. This proved a *great Trial* to me, under which I was ready to *faint*. But the Lord brought that Word with great Power to my Heart, *Mark* xvi. 7. There *shall ye see him, as he* said *unto you.* By which I was strengthened in Faith, and again help'd to *believe*, in the Face of all present *Contrarieties*, that I should yet *see* my Beloved, in that very *Place* where I had *expected* his Presence, according to what he had *said* unto me, in all those glorious Promises he had given me of that Mercy; which at this Time were again brought to my Mind, to the filling of my Heart with Faith and Joy. Those Words also were very sweet to me, *1 Cor.* iii. 21. 22. *All Things are* yours: *Whether Life or Death.* From whence I was persuaded, that *Life* was *mine,* natural, spiritual, and eternal: And in particular, that *natural Life,* and a fresh Increase of it in a comfortable Measure of Health, should be given me, in Subserviency to my Enjoyment of spiritual Life and Glory in *Sion.* For this therefore I sought the Lord, and HE graciously heard my Cry; so that I strangely revived in a little Time. And as my Body was strengthen'd to attend upon God in the Ordinances of his House, so my Soul was exceedingly favoured with the sweet Enjoyment of his Presence therein.

My Beloved *brought me to his Banquetting House, and his Banner over me was Love.* A glorious Feast HE made for me in *that Mountain,* or *Hill of Sion,* where he promised to satiate my longing Soul. And oh, how familiarly did my *Royal Bridegroom* deal with *me,* a vile Worm! How did I *lean on his Breast at Supper-time!* What *Openings* of his *Heart* was I favour'd with? So that my Soul was *abundantly satisfied,* as with *Marrow and Fatness,* and fill'd with joyful Wonder at his boundless Grace! The Lord made me to *possess the double,* according to his Promise. So that I oft thought, *I lost nothing* by going into *Capitivity,* because I had such a *double Portion* of Joy and Happiness upon my *Return. Then was I in his Eyes as one that found Favour!* And the *Royal Grace* of my Beloved, ravish'd my Soul with its *unveil'd Glory!* "Oh, thought I, what Manner of Grace is *this* towards vile *me,* that whoever goes without a Mess from the King's Table, in an Ordinance, *I shall not!*" For I seldom, if ever, attended divine Worship, but I enjoy'd more or less of the sensible Presence of GOD therein; I *felt* his Power, and *saw* his Glory: So *wonderfully* was I favour'd!

Thus the Lord restored me to the Enjoyment of all those Privileges which for a Time had been suspended. And I was made to *see* the Faithfulness of GOD, in the *Fulfilment* of all those *Promises* which, before my Removal, I had had of *this Glory.* And was filled with *Wonder* at that infinite Wisdom, and boundless Grace, which had brought forth the *promised Mercy,* in a triumphant Glory, from under all that Death and Darkness which passed over it, in *contrary Dispensations.* And now, again, my Soul was as *a Hind let loose. I fed on the Ways, and my Pastures were in all high Places.* And while the LORD *my Shepherd,* led me into *green*

Pastures, by the *still Waters*, Oh what delightful Solace did I find! Yea, in the Midst hereof HE caused me to *lie down* and rest, as being persuaded that I should not *again* be driven out from this my Inheritance.

And here I may take Notice, that before my going to *W---*, I had a Desire to join with the Church of Christ at *W---h*, over which Mr. *G---t* was Pastor. Upon which I sought the Lord to acquaint me with his Mind therein. And that Word was very sweet to me on this Account, *Gen.* xxiv. 31. *Come in thou blessed of the LORD, wherefore standest thou without?* But still I wanted the Lord to say something further to me, about his granting me Desire in this Respect. And that Word was brought with great Power, *Mat.* xv. 28. *Be it unto thee, even as thou wilt.* Upon this, I wrote for my Dismission from the Church at *L---n*, to which I belong'd, to the Church at *W---h*, aforesaid. But instead of my receiving the *expected Mercy*, a great *Death* passed upon it. The Gentleman who was to write, falling sick, I had no Letter till after my Removal, when, as to the outward Face of Things, it seem'd as if it would be of no Service to me. But yet I had some Hopes, notwithstanding, that the Lord would bring me back again to *W---h*, and that then, upon this recommendatory Letter, I should enjoy the desired Blessing of dwelling in that House of God. Which accordingly came to pass. For upon my being brought back again, and restored to all my former Privileges, as aforesaid, I had this additional one granted, of being *join'd to the Church*, and enjoying a full and most delightful Communion with that Company of favoured Saints.

But, Oh! the infinite Grace that I saw, in my being brought into this House of God, and privileged with beholding of his Glory there! I saw it to be *great Grace*, that bestowed all the *great Privileges* I enjoy'd; and a wonderful Extension of its *Riches*, in that this promis'd Glory was, *once* and *again*, given me as an Answer of Faith and Prayer. Oh, what an *additional* Brightness, was put upon this *great Glory*, while I saw, boundless Love, infinite Faithfulness, and Almighty Power bringing it to me, at *first*, thro' so many Deaths! And again, restoring it to me, with Advantage, after innumerable Trials, in a State of Captivity!

Again, The Glory of infinite, free, reigning Grace, in bringing this Mercy to me, once and again, notwithstanding my *great* Unworthiness, Disingenuity, and *evil* requiting the Lord for all his Kindness; did wonderfully ravish my Soul. Oh the Glory I *saw*, the Joy I *felt* in *abundant Pardon!* I thought, the Lord extended more Grace unto *me*, in giving me a Place in his House, than to any *other* of his Children, because I was more vile and undeserving. And when I have been near *him*, I have told him, "That if I had had to do with all the Grace of Creatures, united in One, it had been too little for *me*, I had long since exhausted it. No created Grace could have borne with my Provocations. But I was glad that *his* Grace, was the Grace of JEHOVAH, an infinite, inexhaustible Ocean, that I could never draw dry, nor lessen!" And while, adoring, I fell down before the Immensity of Grace, my Soul was *humbled*, my Heart *melted*; I *hated* Sin, and *lothed* myself for all my Abominations. And glad was I of that precious Word, *Psa.* xlviii. 3. *God is known in her Palaces for a Refuge.* For while the Lord, in boundless Grace, and infinite Forbearance, suffer'd me to dwell in that *Palace* of *Sion*, I saw, that I continually needed his *Name*, as a *strong Tower*, to run into for Safety: Even *that* Name, *Exod.* xxxiv. 6. The *LORD, the LORD God, Merciful and Gracious, Long-suffering, and abundant in Goodness and Truth.* Oh, this *glorious Name*, as display'd in Christ, how glad was my poor Soul, to *run into it* for a *Refuge!* And in it I *found* Sanctuary. For my own God went on with me, in Christ, *forgiving Iniquity, Transgression, and Sin.* Yea, so great was his Grace, that he dealt with me as if I had never offended him by my disingenuous Carriage! He not only let me *dwell* in his House, notwithstanding my Unworthiness and Vileness, but he *welcom'd* me to this blest Abode, was very *familiar* with me there, and *rejoiced over me to do me good, with his whole Heart, and with his whole Soul!* According to this Promise which he gave me when in Captivity.

Thus kindly the Lord dealt with me! And by his Loving Kindness he drew out my Heart into vast Desires to *serve him.* I *longed*, even to *Fainting*, to do something for his Glory, before I went home to the full Enjoyment of him. And that Word was very precious to me on this Account: (when under a deep Sense of my Unworthiness, Weakness, and Unfitness for his Service) *Isa.* xxx. 18. *Therefore will the LORD wait, that he may be gracious unto you.* Oh how *sweet* was this Declaration of Grace to my poor Soul! I was hence encouraged to hope in the Lord's Mercy; and was persuaded that he would take the Opportunity of my Unworthiness, Vileness, &c. to glorify the Riches of his Grace, in conferring this Honour upon me, to employ me about some Service of his Glory.

Quickly after this, it pleased the Lord to lay his afflicting Hand upon me, and bring me near to the Gates of Death. And in the Faith of God's everlasting Kindness, and that Glory he had prepar'd for me, I could freely have gone Home. But in the Review of my past Life, while I look'd back upon the Lord's wonderful Goodness towards me, and all the *great Things* he had done for me, I was much grieved that I had done so *little* for *Him*. I was wonderfully favoured with overcoming Discoveries of God's Love. And had sweet Peace with him in the Faith of his passing by all my Transgressions; but this pierced my Heart, that my dear Father had had so *little Glory* by me in an active Way. I knew that I should glorify him *perfectly*, when I came to Heaven; but then I thought, I should not have the Opportunity of glorifying him *before Men*, as I might have while in the Body. And my Heart being much drawn out in Desires to do something for GOD, before I was taken home to the full Enjoyment of him: I ask'd this Favour of the Lord, "That, if consistent with his eternal Purpose, he would spare my Life a little longer; and that the whole of my remaining Days, under the Influence of his own Spirit, might be cast as a *Drop of Service*, into the *Ocean of his Love*." And I had such Views of my *Nearness* to Him, and of the *Interest* I had in his Heart, that I was persuaded he would *grant* my Request, if it was *consistent* with his Glory, and for my Advantage. And quickly after, that Word was brought with great Power to my Heart, *Exod.* xv. 26. *I am the LORD that healeth thee*. And that also, *Jer.* xxxi. 4. *Again I will build thee, and thou shalt be built*. From whence I was persuaded, that the Lord would raise me up again. But my Faith was *tried* before I received the Mercy. The Affliction continued, and I grew weaker; so that I knew not what to think of it. And I was troubled at the Weakness of my Faith: "Oh! thought I, how little a while can I hold it with my dear Father, trusting his infinite Faithfulness in the Dark?" And those Words were brought to my Mind, with great Sweetness, *Isa.* lx. 1, 2. *Arise, shine, for thy Light is come, and the Glory of the LORD is risen upon thee. The LORD shall arise upon thee, and his Glory shall be seen upon thee*. By the first Clause, *Arise, shine, for thy Light is come*: I was ready to think the Lord intended a gracious *raising* me from a sick Bed, to serve and glorify him as my Soul desired. And these Words, *The Glory of the LORD is risen upon thee: The LORD shall arise upon thee, and his Glory shall be seen upon thee*: Were very precious to my Soul. Oh! with what Pleasure did I behold the LORD himself, my *Glory-Sun*, as the *Fountain* of all my Light! I saw myself like the *Moon*, to be a *dark Body*; but yet, thro' Grace, made a *receptive Body*, or a Body capable of receiving Light and Glory, by the LORD, the *Glory-Sun*, his arising upon me. *The LORD shall arise upon thee*. Oh! here I view'd all my present and future Brightness, both in Grace and Glory, secured. *And his Glory shall be seen upon thee*: From this I saw, that all *my* Lustre was but the Reflection of *his* Glory cast upon me: *My* shining, but the Brightness of *his* Rays. But, oh! how my Soul was *humbled* in the Dust under a Sense of my own Darkness, and raised up to *admire* Free-Grace, in this Provision of Light and Glory for me!

From the whole, my Heart was full of Joy, and my Soul encouraged to Hope, that the LORD would *raise* me up again from a sick Bed, *arise* upon me with his own Brightness, in order to *fit* me for Unsfulness, and cause his Glory to be seen upon me, in a Life of Service to his Honour. Altho', by Reason of the *Continuance* of the Affliction, I was ready to be at a Loss, whether my dear Lord intended hereby, my arising from a sick Bed, to shine under his Rays, in a Life of Usefulness here on *Earth*; or my arising into my Glory-Sphere in *Heaven*, to shine forth for ever in the Fulness of *his* Light. Both looked very *glorious* to me; and *my Will* was bow'd to the *divine Will*, and I waited for a further *Explication* of the Promise in Providence. Those Words also, were much to me, *James* v. 14, 15. *Is any sick among you? Let him call for the Elders of the Church, and let them pray over him. --- And the Prayer of Faith shall save the Sick, and the Lord shall raise him up; and if he have committed Sins, they shall be forgiven him.* Accordingly I did so; and I was persuaded, that if the Lord design'd to *spare me*, my Life should be given as an *Answer of Prayer*. And those Words sounded very sweetly, *The Lord shall raise him up.* And blessed be his Name He did so; tho' I was some Time ere I recovered Strength.

Under this Affliction, I was confined nine Lord's Days from publick Worship: And my Soul *longed* exceedingly, for the Privileges of God's House; even to *fainting* for the Courts of the LORD: Oh! what a *Glory* did I see in *Sion*, as GOD, the Father, Son, and Spirit dwelt there! And as it was the Dwelling-Place of Saints and Angels! Oh, thought I, that *my Feet* might again stand *within her Gates!* That I might again be privileged to *behold her Glory!* Sometimes, under humbling Views of my own Vileness, and Unworthiness to dwell in *Sion*, I thought, my dear Lord had *frown'd me away* from his Presence there: And said unto me, in this afflictive Providence, as unto *Peter*, Mat. xvi. 23. *Get thee behind me.* And I was *griev'd* for all my unkind, and disingenuous Carriage towards my dear Lord. And while I fear'd, the Affliction was a *Rebuke*, the fore-mention'd Word, was sweet to me, *If he have committed Sins, they shall be forgiven him.* And while I mournfully thought, I was cast *behind* Christ, that Word was very precious to me, *Luke* xxii. 61. *And the Lord turned, and looked upon Peter.* Oh! the Grace that I saw in this *Love-Look*, cast upon poor *Peter*, to *melt* his *Heart* into Gospel-Repentance! And I waited for a Manifestation of this infinite Favour: When Christ, as the LORD, *Jehovah*, that *changeth not*, would *look* upon me again, in a *Turn* of the Dispensation, with a *fresh Ray* of boundless Grace, and set me *before his Face*, as one of his dear Favourites, to enjoy his sweet Presence in his House as I was wont. And, blessed be his Name, HE did not stay long, ere he gave me the Desire of my Heart. And tho' I mourn'd while I was kept back from the Lord's House, yet was he very *gracious* to me, in that at *all Times*, when his Children met together to feast in *Sion*, I had a Portion, a Mess was sent *me* from the King's Table. In which I saw, that in infinite Bowels he earnestly remember'd me still.

During this Affliction, I was many Ways *tried*. But the Love of GOD was so shed abroad in my Heart, that made me have high and honourable Thoughts of HIM, and of all his Dealings with me. And once, in particular, when I was thinking the Affliction *long*, my Heart was sweetly wrought up into Submission to the divine Will, believing that the Time of it was well-order'd, both for God's Honour, and my Advantage. I was help'd to reason with my own Soul, thus: "Wouldst thou *now*, if God should grant thee thy Desire, be *releas'd* from thy Trials, or have and Degree of them *abated*, upon Condition that GOD should *lose* any Glory thereby?" And my very Heart answer'd, *no*. "Well then (as I was help'd to reason) be content to have Things just as they *are*, during GOD's Pleasure. They are so *well-order'd*, that nothing could be *better* than it is; and the Affliction shall last no *longer* than the Glory of God, and thy Good are *concern'd* in it." But oh, how sweetly did I, at this Time, both *lose* my Will in GOD's, and *find* it there too, with the greatest Complacency! Yea, I saw so much Grace, Wisdom and Faithfulness, in the bestowing, managing, and over-ruling all my Trials, that made me *love* the *Work* of my *Lord's Hands*, tho' it was in *Affliction-Chains*.

But, notwithstanding the many Trials which attended me, my *Consolations* were abundant. While the Lord kept me in the *Furnace of Affliction*, I had the Joy to see *himself* with me there. And oh! the infinite Grace, and sympathizing Bowels I saw in my dear Lord Jesus, from those Words, *Mat.* xxv. 36. *I was sick*, &c. I saw, that there was not any, the least Affliction that touched *me*, but what HE had the most inward *feeling* of, yea, counted it as *his own!* And oh, with what Pleasure did I rest my weary Head, in the Bosom of my Beloved, my sweet Companion in Tribulation!

And as I saw Love enough in Christ's Heart to satisfy me, and make the Affliction easy while it lasted; so also I was favour'd with precious

Prospects of the Glory reserv'd for me; from those Words, *1 Pet.* i. 4. *To an Inheritance incorruptible and undefiled, and that fadeth not away, reserved in Heaven for you.*

It was with great Delight, I beheld the Inheritance reserved for me in Heaven, set forth, in this Text, under three Metaphors; 1. That of *white Robes,* Rev. iii. 4, 5. As Tokens of Victory, Purity and Honour. And to shew the *Perfection* of its Glory, as set forth under *this* Similitude, it's said to be *undefiled!* I saw with Pleasure, that when once I had got on my white Robes of *Glory,* there would not be the least Spot of *Sin,* or *Sorrow,* to darken or sully them; or so much as a *Possibility* of Defilement. 2. I view'd the Glory prepar'd for me, under the Similitude of *a Feast.* As, *Luke* xii. 37. And to set forth the *transcendent* Excellency of it as such, it is said to be *incorruptible!* The richest Dainties of an *earthly Feast,* are subject to *Putrifaction,* and may become *nauseous.* But the Glories of the *heavenly Banquet* have no *Corruptibility* in them, nor shall they ever grow *Stale!* Our Feast in Heaven, will be *ever Beginning,* and *never* have an *End!* The *Glories* we shall feast upon, will be *new, new* to Eternity; and our *Appetites* as *new* and *constant* as the Feast! 3. I saw the Glory reserved for me, set forth under the Metaphor of the *Spring,* the Spring-Season of the Year. And to shew its *Permanency,* in this respect, it's said, that it *fadeth not away!* The natural *Spring* is a very pleasant, delightful Season, when the Earth, Trees, and Plants under the fresh Approach of the Sun, appear with new Life and Glory. But then, there's no Spring in *Nature,* but has an *Autumn* to succeed it. But the *Glories* of the heavenly State, will be ever *green* and *flourishing!* We shall then enjoy an *everlasting Spring* (both in Regard of the *ever-growing Displays* of infinite Glory, and also of its *eternal Influence* upon us) when we *eat of the Tree of Life, which is in the Midst of the Paradise of GOD!* Rev. ii. 7.

Again, as I was favour'd with precious Views of the Glory prepar'd for me, so also with the *Medium* of its Communication. From *John* xvii. 23. *I in them, and thou in me, that they may be made perfect in one.* Oh, with what Pleasure did I see, from hence, that all my Communion with GOD in Glory, would for ever be enjoy'd in his SON! O, the *beautiful Order* of all Glory-Communications to the Head and Members! Thou in ME, says CHRIST: There's the *first* and *immediate* Communication, the *upper* Glory of the *Head.* And I in *them*: There's the *derived* Glory of the *Members* in its highest Perfection.

Thus the *Glory* prepared for me, together with the *Medium* of its Communication, *viz.* the glorified *human Nature* of my *dear Lord Jesus*, were very *precious* to me, and I *long'd* for the Enjoyment of it. But, as the Lord had given me to see a great Glory in *serving him in this World*, drawn out my Desires after it, and also given me some Hopes and Expectations of it; I *waited* for this Honour to be conferred upon me. And the LORD's *waiting to be gracious* to me in this Respect, did much *encourage* my Soul when under *humbling Views* of my own Vileness, Unworthiness, and Unfitness to do any Thing for GOD. That Word also, was precious to me on this Account, *Rom.* v. 2. *By whom also we have Access by Faith into this Grace wherein we stand.* I saw, that if ever I did any *Service for GOD*, I must *stand in Grace*: 1. For the Honour of *Employment*, or a being *call'd* to this or that Service. 2. In Grace, for *Assistance*, if ever I did any Thing aright. 3. In Grace, for *Success*, or a gracious *owning* of my weak Attempts to serve the LORD. 4. In Grace, for *Pardon*, or free *Forgiveness* of the Iniquity of my best Duties. And 5. In Grace, for *Acceptance* of all my weak Performances. I was also instructed into my Duty of constant *abiding in Christ by Faith*, and being *strong in the Grace that is* in *him*. And likewise into my Privilege, of having *Access*, under the Manuduction of the Holy Spirit, into the *Grace wherein I stood*. And while my Soul was *drawn out* into vast Desires after Abundance of Grace to serve the Lord; he gave me sweet Encouragement that my Prayers should be *answer'd*, in this Respect, from *Rom.* viii. 27. *And he that searcheth the Heart, knoweth what is the Mind of the Spirit, because he maketh Intercession for the Saints, according to the Will of God.* I was hence persuaded, that tho' I could not *cloath* my vast Desires, with Words *fully* expressive thereof, yet that my Heart was under the *all-searching* Eye of *Jehovah*; he knew the *Mind* of the Spirit. And also, that as this Drawing out of my Soul, was from the Intercession-Work of the Holy Spirit in me, so I should be satisfied; because he maketh Intercession for the Saints, according to *the Will of GOD*. "Oh, thought I, it is because there are *vast Preparations* of Grace made for me, that such *vast Desires* are wrought in my Soul after it: And how *much* would my thirsty Soul *take in*, if it might have its Fill!" Then that Word came, *Ps.* lxxxi. 10. *Open thy Mouth wide, and I will fill it.* As if the Lord had said, "Take in as much Grace as thou *wilt*; stretch thy Desires as wide as thou *canst, I'll fill them*." That Word also was brought, *1 John* ii. 24. *Ye shall continue* in *the Son, and* in *the Father*. But, oh, what an *Ocean of Grace* did I see myself *enclosed in!* I saw myself, as standing in Union to *Christ*, and the *Father* in him, *Cast as it were into a Sea of Grace!* Where, like the Fish in the Water, it was but *opening my Mouth*, the Mouth of *Faith*, and *taking in* all the Grace I wanted, for all Kinds of Service, out of that *inexhaustible Fulness* with which I was surrounded!

Thus my kind Lord, made this Affliction a fair *Seeds-time*, from whence I expected a *joyful Harvest*. And when I had received all that Instruction, and Consolation, the Lord design'd me under it: he then raised me up, and restored me to the Enjoyment of all the Privileges of his House: Which I esteem'd a *Gain*, more worth than *Worlds! I fed in the Ways, and my Pastures were in all high Places*. Scarce any Opportunity I had of meeting with the Saints, for publick Worship, but I enjoy'd GOD in it. And as in *his*, so in my *own House*, I feasted upon his *loving Kindness*, which is *better than Life!* And my Fellowship with the Saints, after I was raised from this Affliction, was exceeding sweet. There was a double Glory upon it. So that I every Way delighted myself in the LORD's great Goodness! But while I was in the midst of all my Enjoyments, lo, another Scene began to open. Which brings me,

VII. To the last Step of Providence I shall take Notice of, *viz.* the Lord's removing my Habitation from *W---h*, to *Great Gransden*, in *Huntington-shire*, the Place of my present Abode. But before I speak any Thing particularly about my Removal, I must give some Hints concerning the Occasion of it.

It pleased the Lord, some considerable Time before, to call my Husband to the Work of the Ministry. From the Time that the Lord wrought upon his Heart, in a saving Conversion to Christ, which was about the seventeenth Year of his Age, he had a very strong Desire after the Ministry of the Gospel. And tho' he was then an Apprentice to a Clothier and Draper, yet this Desire after the Ministry prevail'd so far, that he requested his Father to buy out his Time, and bestow that Money which he design'd to set him up for a Tradesman, in giving him Learning for the Ministry, that so he might be more fully qualify'd for this great Work, which he so much desired. And after a Time, his Father consented to give him Learning. And to School, in several Places, he was put for some Years. And thus from a Desire after the Ministry, he went on in the Pursuit of his Studies. But after we were marry'd, for our present Subsistence, he did something at his Trade: As I hinted before, in the Account I gave of our being brought to *W---h*. And thro' several trying Things that fell out, it was some Time e'er the Desire of his Heart was given him, in his being stately employ'd in the

Work of the Ministry. But having been call'd to the Work, by a Church to which he join'd, he preach'd occasionally for a while at several Places. And thus he preach'd during great Part of the Time of our last Abode at *W---h*, which was about three Years, at several Places, some of which were pretty far distant. And he having heard of a poor People at *Great Gransden*, which wanted Supply, the Lord laid it upon his Heart to give them a Visit. Which accordingly he did, was kindly received, and invited to assist them as often as he could. Soon after my dear Yokefellow had preach'd at *Gransden*, he was invited likewise to preach at *Croyden*, four Miles distant. The People at both those Places made but one Church; and were used to keep up their Meetings (when they had a Pastor, or a stated Minister) at both Towns; one Lord's Day at *Gransden*, and another at *Croyden*, successively. And as the People wanted Supply for both these Places, and our Habitation was far distant, it was their Desire, that we should in a little Time remove the Place of our Abode to reside amongst them, in order to serve them wholly.

This Change of Providence when it first appear'd, prov'd a *great Trial* to me. Being led by my great Shepherd into those *green Pastures* which his own Love bestow'd, once and again, as an Answer of Faith and Prayer, I felt the most delightful Solace, was made to *lie down*, and very unwilling to remove. Like *Peter* in the Mount, I said, *It is good to be here*. My Heart was so knit to my present Enjoyments, that nothing but an Almighty Power could loosen it. As for my dear Husband, I thought he might leave these People at a Distance, and be as useful in other Places near at hand.

But once, when he was representing their Case to me, "As a little Handful of Saints that loved the pure Gospel, and had been wont to bear a Testimony for it; by reason whereof they had many Enemies that would be glad to see them scatter'd; and that now, being in low Circumstances, the Cause of Christ was like to sink amongst them, unless they had a suitable Supply": I found my Heart *moved* with Compassion towards them. And soon after, the Lord brought that Word to my Mind, *Acts* xvi. 9. *Come over into Macedonia, and help us*. From whence I was taught, that if I could be any Means of Helping the Cause of Christ, and the dear Saints in that Place where Providence seem'd to call me, by removing thither, it was my *Duty* to be willing to yield them the utmost Assistance I could. By this Word, while the Power of God therein was upon my Heart, I was changed into the Likeness of it, notwithstanding the former strong Propense of my Soul the other Way. Thus the Lord began to give me a Turn of Mind, as to my Abode at *W---h*.

But still there was *Unwillingness* in me, and many were the *Objections* I raised from it. But that Word came home to my Soul in the great Power of God, *John* xxi. 15. *Lovest thou me?—Feed my Lambs*. In the former Part of these Words, *Lovest thou ME?* My Lord open'd a Soul-overcoming View of all his *own Love* manifested to me, and particularly in the *Gift* of those precious Enjoyments which I was so *loth* to leave: And then HE putting the Question to my Heart, Lovest thou ME? I found my Soul, under the strong Attraction of *his Love*, mightily drawn out to *love HIM* again. I felt my *Bowels move*, and all the *Love of my Soul*, upon the *Flow*, like a *swift* Stream, *hasting apace* into the Ocean of *his Love*, from whence it sprang. And then, in the latter Part of the Words, *Feed my Lambs*; he put it upon *my Love* to HIM, just then set all on a *Flame*, by the enkindling *Fire* of *his first Love*. But oh, how sweetly and powerfully my dear Lord *drew me*, to give up all *my Enjoyments* into *his Glory*, and to take *that*, as my *Soul-satisfying* Enjoyment! HE *woo'd me, won me, overcame my Heart*, in those Moments of his *Love-Power*; and I as *freely* gave up all those precious Privileges, which his boundless Love bestow'd, as *ever* I received 'em from him! Oh, the *Glory* of my LORD! what a *ravishing* Preciousness, and *transcendent* Excellency did I see in it! Now I judged it *far better* to glorify him, when call'd to any Piece of Service, than *merely* to enjoy him. My Soul being on a Flame of Love to his Glory, I could, with unspeakable Pleasure, *deny* spiritual Self, in the *Delights* of spiritual Sense, (a Thing which before I had long'd, and pray'd for' but found it hard to come at) and take up my LORD, his *Glory*, *Honour*, and *Interest*, as my Soul-satisfying ALL!

And by the unspeakable Sweetness I felt in this holy Resignation wrought in my Soul, and complacent Acquiescence in the *Will of GOD*, I was led, afresh, into the Goodness, Excellency, and Glory of *God's Law*, which commandeth, *To love the Lord our God with all our Heart, Soul and Strength*, Mat. xxii. 37. Oh how *pleasant* did I find Obedience to *this* Command, while with my Mind, or new Nature, *I served the Law of God*, Rom. vii. 25. as being *under it to Christ*, the King of *Sion?*

Thus my Lord made me *willing* to serve HIM *in the Day of his Power*. And oh, how sweetly those Words sounded, *my Lambs!* my Soul was *endear'd* to Christ's Lambs, as *his*: So that I thought, if *they* might be *fed*, I could freely give up all *my Enjoyments*, the green fat Pastures I then lay down in. Yea, I so lov'd *Christ* and his *Lambs*, that I thought, I should make a *Feast* out of my *Lord's* Glory, in *their* Supply; however it might be with *me*. And as by this one Word of Christ's Mouth, he made me *willing*, if call'd, to remove with my dear Yokefellow, that his Lambs might be fed; so he put the People into *my Heart*: And I felt such an *endear'd Love* to them, and a kind of *natural Care* for 'em, that at Times I was fit to wonder at, seeing they were all of 'em personally *unknown* to me.

But soon after this Willingness was wrought in my Soul, I met with many Discouragements from my own Unworthiness, and Inability to do any Thing for God; and was ready to fear that my Removing would be but of little Service to the Cause of Christ. But amidst the Multitude of my Thoughts within me, the Lord broke in with the Comforts of his Holy Spirit, in those Words, *Isa*. lviii. 10, *&c. If thou draw out thy Soul to the Hungry, and satisfy the afflicted Soul, then shall thy Light arise in Obscurity,---Thou shalt raise up the Foundations of many Generations; and thou shalt be called, the Repairer of the Breach, the Restorer of Paths to dwell in.* From hence I was comfortably persuaded, that if I *drew out my Soul* to these Hungry, and *satisfy'd* these afflicted ones, my Labour should not be in vain in the Lord. And oh! how sweet these Words sounded, *Thou shalt be* called, *the Repairer of the Breach!* &c. How sweetly did the Lord hereby *allure me* into that Piece of Service which his Providence seem'd to *call me to*; and also *assure me* of Success if I ventur'd on't, and of his gracious Acceptance of my weak Endeavours to serve him therein! The Lord, as I hinted, had drawn out my Soul, a little Time before, into vast Desires to *serve him*, and the *same Desires* being kept up in my Heart, these Words were a precious Encouragement to me, that I *should* do something for GOD, in drawing out my Soul to the Hungry, notwithstanding the deep Sense I was under of my Weakness and Unworthiness: And oh, what a *yerning of Bowels* did I then feel towards them!

But presently this Objection started up in my Mind, "Their Church-State is not *broken*; and how can I then be called, *the Repairer of the Breach?*" In Answer to which, the Lord led me to see, that tho' their Church-State was not broken, yet they were reduced to low Circumstances; the Lord having withdrawn his wonted Favours from them, in regard of their comfortable Supply for the Administration of the Word and Ordinances: And that whenever the Lord withdrew from his People, there was always a Breach made upon *Sion's* Glory. Upon this, I saw, that there was Room for the promis'd Grace to be extended; and was persuaded, that if I did *draw out my Soul to the Hungry*, I should be called, *The Repairer of the Breach*, &c. And,

Further, at this Time also, the Lord gave me a Soul-ravishing Prospect of the Glory of the Work of building up *Sion*, from *Psa*. cii. 13. *Thou shalt arise, and have Mercy upon Zion: For the Time to favour her, yea, the set Time is come.* And Ver. 16. *When the Lord shall build up Zion, he shall appear in his Glory*. From these Words, I saw, that notwithstanding God's withdrawing from his People at Times, and their being reduced thereby to a low Estate; yet he had his *Time*, his *set* Time to *favour* 'em; in which HE would *arise, and have Mercy* on them. And that the *building up of Zion*, depended upon the LORD's *appearing in his Glory* there. But oh, this Work of *building Zion*, what a *Glory* did I see in it! In as much as GOD, the Father, Son, and Spirit, as the great Efficients; and all the Saints and Angels, as Instruments, had in all Ages been employ'd in it! And oh, thought I, what an Honour will it be to *me*, a sinful Worm, to have but the least Finger in this Work! In a Word, my Heart was so enflam'd with Love to *Zion*, that I took *Pleasure in her Stones*, and *favour'd her Dust*: Even while I view'd 'em but as *loose Stones*, as it were, lying here and there, and *scatter'd Dust*; yet being *Zion's* Stones and Dust, I took great Pleasure in them, felt great Yerning of Bowels towards 'em, and a wonderful Desire wrought in my Soul, after their Building, Beauty and Glory.

But, further, another Objection arose in my Mind from the Weakness of my *Sex*, which, together with my *personal* Weakness, did greatly tend to discourage my Hopes of doing any Service to the Cause of Christ. But in Answer unto this, the Lord brought that Word to my Mind, *Mic*. vi. 4. *I sent before thee Moses, Aaron, and Miriam*. In this I saw, that the Lord had honour'd some, even of the *weak* Sex, to be of Service to his People; and that he could do so again were it his Pleasure. From hence also, I was much encouraged to Hope, that the Lord had some Work for *me* to do; and that he would graciously *use* me for the Good of this People, which he had made me so willing to serve, if in his Providence he should call me to remove. That Word also, did much encourage my Hope, and quicken my Desires of serving the Lord and his People, *Rom*. xvi. 1. *I commend unto you, Phoebe our Sister, which is a Servant of the Church which is at Cenchrea.* "Oh, thought I, if such a weak Worm as I, might be a *Servant* to a Church of Christ, what a Mercy should I account it!" And as I saw a great Glory in being a Servant of the Church, so in the *meanest* Service that could be done for my Lord and his People. I thought I could not do *much*: The most I judg'd myself capable of, was a willing, chearful Attendance upon a Servant of Christ, my dear Yoke-fellow, in the great Work of the Ministry, if his Lord and Master should in an especial Manner call him to labour in that Part of his Vineyard where for some Time he had been employ'd. And that Word, the Lord was pleas'd to bring to my Mind with Power and Sweetness, as a gracious Direction about the particular Work in which I myself ought to be engag'd, *1 Tim.* iv. 12. *Be thou an Example of the Believers, in Word, in Conversation, in Charity, in Spirit, in Faith, in Purity.* By this also the Lord wrought up my Heart into earnest Desires of all Usefulness and Fruitfulness in my Place and Station, to the Glory of his Name and the Good of his People; and particularly those, which in a special Manner I was then concern'd for. That Word also, at the same Time, was very precious to me, *Rom.* i. 13. *That I might have some Fruit among you also, even as among other Gentiles.*

Thus have I given a brief Account, how Almighty Power sweetly won my Soul, and wrought it up into an hearty Willingness and earnest Desire of serving the Lord and his People, in removing from *W---h*, to *G---n*, if by divine Providence I should be further call'd thereto.

But quickly after, there was a sudden Turn, and the Face of Providence in this Affair alter'd. And then I thought, "it may be the Lord's Design in what has pass'd, was only to *try* my Faith and Love, whether I would be willing at his Call, to give up my Enjoyments, preferring his Glory above all; and not to take them away from me." However, I was exceeding glad that his own Hand made my Heart willing to *give* whatever HE *call'd for*. And I had a Persuasion of his Acceptance of my wiling Mind, from *1 Kings* viii. 18. *Then didst well that it was in thine Heart.*

But after a while, there was an Appearance of a fresh Call to *G---n*. My Husband having visited them according to their Desire and his Promise, he found their Hearts much knit to him; and upon their Request he went and preach'd to them once a Fortnight. And after a little Time, they were very desirous to have him come to settle among them, if we could take up with what they could do towards our Subsistence. And the Lord engag'd the Heart of my Yokefellow to trust him, and made him desirous to go, to serve this little Handful of his People. And as for myself, tho' I had for some Time laid aside Thoughts of removing; yet when the Lord renew'd the Call of Providence, and seem'd about to call me to an actual Resignation of what he had before made me willing to give up: I was, thro' his Hand holding my Heart, still of the same Mind; *willing* to resign whatever HE call'd for, and to go at his Bidding. And as for the People, the Lord having put 'em into my Heart, I found Bowels of Compassion afresh working in me towards 'em. A Desire to serve them, and a Kind of natural Care for their Good. Which made me *willing* to venture a Remove, with my dear Yoke-fellow, to dwell among them.

But notwithstanding my Willingness to serve the Lord and his People, I found my old Objections, arising from my own Weakness, Unworthiness, &c. afresh starting up in my Mind, together with this new Suggestion, "That I might be *mistaken*, as to the Hope I had, that my Removal might be of some Service to the Cause of Christ; and that I should *lose* what I was in Possession of, in *Hope* of that I might never attain." In answer to which, the Lord led me to look back upon those Scriptures, by which he at first, encouraged my Soul to venture on this Work, and go at his Bidding. As, *Acts* xvi. 9. *John* xxi. 15. *Isa.* lviii. 10, &c. And upon the Review hereof, I was directed, and enabled in some Measure, to *take God at his Word*; believing that if, at *his* Bidding, *I drew out my Soul to the Hungry, I should be called, the Repairer of the Breach*, &c. And those Words were of Use to me, *Exod.* xxv. 2, 3, 4, 5, 6, 7, 8. *Speak unto the Children of Israel, that they bring me an Offering*, &c. *And let them make me a Sanctuary, that I may dwell among them.* There was also an Expression dropp'd by Mr. G---t in a Sermon, which the Lord bless'd for strengthening and comforting my Soul, when under discouraging Views of my own Inability; which was this; "Thy poor Cries and Prayers help to build God a Sanctuary." "Oh, thought I, if I can do nothing else but *wish* well to *Sion*, and *pray* for its Prosperity, I shall be of *some* Use: And what Grace is it, that the Lord should accept the Desires of such a weak Worm as I!" And that Word follow'd it, *2 Cor.* viii. 12. *For if there be first a willing Mind, it is accepted, according to that a Man hath, and not according to that he hath not.* In which the Lord satisfy'd me of his gracious Acceptance of that *Willingness* of Soul to serve him, which his own Spirit had wrought in me; notwithstanding my Inability to *do* the Service I would. And the Discovery hereof, humbled my Soul, melted my Heart, and rais'd me up to bless the Lord, and admire his infinite Grace herein.

And further, as I was wont to be peculiarly favour'd with the Enjoyment of God in his House, so once, in particular, while I was feasting upon the heavenly Sweets provided there for me, my Lord put this Question to my Heart, *John* xxi. 18. *Lovest thou me more than these?* q. d. [*quaque die*, every day] "Dost thou Love my Glory, Honour and Interest more than *these*, thy Enjoyments? Canst thou now leave *all*, part with the *full Board* thou now sittest at, and willingly for *my* Sake, go serve my People;

preferring *my* Glory in *their* Supply, above *thy* present Happiness?" And my Soul, under the sweet Attraction of his *Love*, made Answer, with *Peter, Yea, Lord, thou knowest that I love thee.*

Another Time, it was much imprest upon my Mind, "That I had great Need to abide in that House of God, where I then felt his Power, and saw his Glory, that so my *Graces* might be *increas'd*; and that if I did not, I might be a great *Loser* thereby; and not have those *Opportunities* of Growth in Grace and Holiness; which I *then* had, and were so desirable to me." These discouraging Thoughts *try'd me*; but I was help'd to repel them thus: "If I should in some Respects be a *Loser* thereby; yet if the Glory of God may be the more *advanced* by my removing, I am well pleased to give up all *my* Interests into *his* Glory; which is dearer to *me*, than all personal Advantages." Upon which, those Words were brought to my Mind with great Power, *John* xiii. 31, 32. *Now is the Son of Man glorified, and God is glorified in him. If God be glorified in him, God shall also glorify him in himself, and shall straightway glorify him.* From which I was taught, 1. That when Christ the Head of the Church, was actually call'd to that great Piece of Obedience to his Father's Will, in Suffering for our Sakes, HE esteem'd it, a *glorifying* of him: *Now is the Son of Man glorified.* 2. That by his perfect Submission to his Father's Will, in giving himself a Sacrifice for the Sins of his People, in their Room and Stead, God the Father was *glorified: God is* glorified *in him.* And 3. That Christ lost *no Glory*, by emptying himself of *all*, to glorify his Father: But as God was glorified in Christ, so Christ was glorified in God: In that HE straightway took him from the Cross to the Throne, rais'd him from the Depths of his Humiliation, to the Height of his Exaltation; set him at his own Right Hand, and glorified him in HIMSELF: *If* GOD *be glorified in him, God shall also glorify* HIM *in himself, and shall straightway glorify him.* From hence also, I was persuaded, that as it far'd with the *Head*, so with the *Members*; and that I, in particular, should lose no *personal Glory*, by preferring GOD's *above all.*

Another Objection started up in my Mind, from my great *Weakness* of Body; occasion'd by that ill State of Health I was in. I thought it look'd *strange* to me, that I should undertake such a *distant* Remove, with an Eye to serve the Lord Jesus, that was so often in my own Apprehension, just upon my *last* Remove out of Time into Eternity. In answer to this, the Lord brought that Word, *Luke* xii. 43. *Blessed is that Servant, whom his Lord when he cometh, shall find so doing.* From this, and the preceding Verse, I was satisfied, that if I should not live long after my Remove to *G---n*, yet it would be a great Blessedness, to be found *serving* the Lord and his People, even then when he *came*, by Death, to take me Home to Glory.

Thus the Lord answer'd my Objections, and made me willing to serve him. And tho' I thought I could do but *little*, yet I saw a great Glory in doing *any Thing* for GOD. Those Words were much upon my Mind, *Mark* ix. 35. *If any Man desire to be first, the same shall be last of all, and Servant of all.* Oh, what a Glory did I see in being *Servant of all!* I thought, "That great Princes, when they went about any Business, had a Retinue to attend them, according to their State; their *upper* and *under* Servants. And if it was an Honour to be a Servant to an earthly King, tho' one of the most *inferior*: Oh how *much more* was it *so*, to be a Servant to the *King of Kings*, tho' the *least* and *last* of all!" In a Word, I thought my great Lord, had Work to do at *G---n*, that my dear Yokefellow was call'd to go as an *upper Servant*, and myself as an *under One* to attend him. And I saw such a Glory in my *Lord's Work*, that I esteem'd it an unspeakable Dignity and Privilege, to be employ'd in the *least* Part of it!

Upon the whole, the Lord having thus wrought upon my Spirit, I ran to him as the God of all Grace, for all the Supplies I *needed* for his Service. My Soul long'd to serve my dear Lord Jesus; but, Oh, my Unworthiness, Weakness, and Unfitness lay with Weight upon my Mind. And under the Spirit of Supplication, I poured out my Heart before him: And pray'd him to glorify his Grace, in taking me into his Service, notwithstanding my *great* Unworthiness; to glorify his Power, in my *great* Weakness; and his Wisdom, in using me, notwithstanding my great Unfitness. I thought, "If the LORD look'd over all his Children, he could find none among them so *unworthy, weak*, and *unfit* for his Service as *myself*." I saw, I *needed* the Riches of boundless Grace, almighty Power, and infinite Wisdom to be *extended*, if ever *I was us'd* to do any Thing for God. And therefore to the Throne of Grace I came, poor and needy, weak and sinful, with *all* my Wants; to find Mercy, and Grace to help in Time of Need. And, in Faith of his infinite Grace, I told my Lord Jesus, "There was none but HIM, would take such a poor Creature as I was into his Service!" I saw, if he took *me*, he must take me to do *all* for me: Not only to pass by, and pardon my *Unworthiness* and *Provocations*, but also to give me an *Heart* to serve him; and when that was done, he must give me an *Hand* too. Free Grace must *empty* me, *incline* me, and *assist* me, or I could do *nothing*. And that Word was brought to my Mind, with great Power and Sweetness, *John* xii. 26. *If any Man serve me, let him follow me.* Which I took, 1. As my Lord's gracious *Grant* of the Desires of my Soul to serve him, *q. d.* [*quaque die*, every day] "*If any Man*, (let him be ever so unworthy, *&c.*) *serve me*, (or have a *Desire* to serve me) *let him follow me*; (or *let* him serve me.) I'll not refuse to take any poor Soul into my Service, that longs to serve me." And, Oh, how glad was I of this Grace! 2. I took this Word as a gracious Direction of my Work; or, from hence I was taught, what my Employment should be, *viz.* to take *Christ*, as the great *Pattern* of all my *Obedience*, and labour to follow his Example: *If any Man serve me, let him follow me.*

Soon after, our Removal drawing on, I set apart a little Time to intreat the Lord, that HE would *go with us.* And I much desir'd that HE would again tell me, now we were just upon going, that this our Removal was according to *his* Will, and *well-pleasing* in his Sight: And not having an Answer so immediately as I could have wish'd, I began to *faint.* But presently that Word came, with abundant Light and Evidence, *Mat.* xiv. 27. *It is I, be not afraid.* Then, *glad* of my Saviour's Voice, I said, with *Peter, Lord, if it be* THOU, *bid me come unto thee on the Water*, Ver. 28. Oh, thought I, "Is it my LORD, that calls me to yonder Places? Is HE about to appear in his Glory, and build up *Sion* there? I'll venture to him on the *Water*; my Soul can freely venture, with my Lord, thro' all the *Trouble* I may expect to meet with in a World of Trials." And thus I came to *G---n*, where our dear Friends gladly receiv'd us.

And here, let the Saints observe, that tho' I was again remov'd from *W---h*, after three Years Abode there this last Time, yet this Remove was vastly different from my former, when I look'd upon myself to be sent into Captivity. I was not now, *driven out* from my Inheritance, and *oblig'd*, in a great Measure unwillingly, to *leave* the Glories I enjoy'd there. But I freely *went out* thence, or went out *free*, under an Advance of Glory, into my Lord's Service. When the LORD redeem'd me from my Captive-State, and brought me again to my own Border, I lay down safely, believing that I should not be driven out from thence. Nor was I disappointed. For tho' the Lord *remov'd me*, HE did not *drive me out.* No, HE *allur'd* me thence, and most joyfully I *follow'd* HIM, or rather, *went with* HIM, to another Place. CHRIST and I *changed*: I gave HIM my sweet Enjoyments, and HE gave *me* his glorious Service, something to *do* for him. And into my Work, HE put so much *Glory*, that made it, in the Scale of my *Faith*, more *weighty* than my great Enjoyments! And when the Lord call'd me thus to serve him, HE said unto me, *Come up hither*, Rev. xi. 12. And indeed in this Change of Providence, I pass'd on *from Glory to Glory*, from one Part of my

Inheritance to another, from the *Sweet* of enjoying CHRIST, to the *Honour* of serving HIM: Which the Lord made *ineffably* sweet to my Soul! And so there was no *Infringement* of the LORD's promis'd Goodness, but rather an *Extension* of it, with respect to some particular Promises which he gave me, about Fruitfulness and Service. As *that*, when in Captivity, *I will sow her unto ME in the Earth*, Hos. ii. 23. And *that*, when I was brought again to my own Border, *Arise, shine, for thy Light is come, and the Glory of the LORD is risen upon thee. --- The LORD shall arise upon thee, and his Glory shall be seen upon thee*, Isa. lx. 1, 2. And thus, in Hope of serving CHRIST, I joyfully came, as I said, to *G---n*.

And now I shall give a brief Account of what follow'd; in order to shew somewhat of the Lord's gracious Dealings with me in *this* Place. Quickly after our being fix'd at *G---n*, our Friends set apart a Day for solemn Fasting and Prayer, to seek the Lord for his Direction, Assistance, Blessing, and Presence, in all the Work they might engage in, relating to his House. And here I must just hint, that tho' the Lord had made me willing to leave all my *Enjoyments* in his House at *W---h*, and to come to live at *G--n*, to do all the little I could, to serve his Cause here; (as I declar'd before) yet when I came, I had no Thoughts of being separated from my *Church-Relation* at *W--h*. But to this Meeting I went, to seek the Lord with our Friends, and pour out before him the earnest Desires of my Soul for their Prosperity. And the Lord was greatly with us that Day, and alter'd my Mind before I came away, with respect to my *Church-Relation* at *W--h*. And which Way HE did it, will in some Measure appear, by inserting Part of a Letter I wrote to the Church, to request my Dismission from them, *viz.* that Part of it wherein I gave the Reason of my Request. Which was as follows:

"It remains now, that I give you some Account of the Reason of my Desire to join with them. And I can assure you, that it is not in the least, from any Diminution of my Love to you: Nor had I any Thoughts of being remov'd, as to Relation, when I was remov'd, as to Place. But, on the Day above-mention'd, I went to seek the Lord with them, desiring Prosperity to the Builders, not in the least designing to be laid in the Building. And while they were wrestling with the Lord, to undertake the Work HIMSELF, and strengthen their weak Hands, that Word was brought to me with Power, *Isa.* xxxv. 3. *Strengthen ye the weak Hands*. Wherein the Lord spake very particularly to *me*, to engage in the Work. And tho' I lov'd his CAUSE, as considering it to be but *one* in all Places, and the Interest of the same LORD; yet my Soul clave to *you*, so that I could not tell how to bear losing my

Relation to you. But the Power of God upon my Heart, I could not wholly resist; yet was for delaying, and making Excuses, as if my joining with them, could not much strengthen them. But the Lord spake to me again, as to his Spouse, *Song* ii. 14. *Let me see* thy *Face*. And tho' I felt an attracting Power in the Moments of drawing, yet still I found some *Unwillingness* remain. After this, that Word was brought, *Mat.* xii. 30. *He that is not with me, is against me*. From whence I was taught, that if it was the Mind of Christ, to build him an House, and to engage the Hearts of his Children here, in that Work; if I was not *with* him in it, yielding all the Assistance I could, I should really be found to be *against* him. This broke my Heart; for I could not bear to be against Christ; and my Spirit was laid under such *Awe*, that I could *gainsay* no longer. And further, from that Word, *Acts* ii. 1. *They were all with one Accord in one Place*: I was taught, that since the Lord had cast my Lot in this Place, with his People who desire to carry on his Cause, it was my Duty to be of *one Accord* with 'em. I was also further encouraged by that Word, *Mat.* xxv. 40. *In as much as ye have done it unto one of the least of these my Brethren, ye have done it unto me*. From whence, the Lord told me, "That if the least of his Brethren wanted any Assistance, and I did help them, he would take it as done to himself." And to shut it up in a Word, the Lord gave me to see such a *Glory* in his CAUSE, even when *weakest*, and under the *greatest* Disadvantages, *like a little Leaven hid in the Meal, and a Grain of Mustard-Seed cast into the Earth, the smallest of all Seeds*; that my Soul *lov'd it* exceedingly: In its Rags, as well as in its Robes; in its Beginnings and Buddings forth, as well as in its full-blown Glory! And tho' the Instruments that carried it on might be *weak*, yet I saw that the LORD, strong and mighty, was in it. And I thought, if I had a *thousand* Souls, I could give them *all*, to serve CHRIST and his CAUSE. Thus, tho' Love to *you*, wrought strongly in my Heart, yet Love to *Christ's Cause* here, in its weak Beginnings, out-wrought it.------"

This was the Account I gave the Church, as the Reason of desiring my Dismission from them. There was also another Word, that at the same Time did much attract my Soul to join in Church-Relation at *G---n*, Hag. i. 8. *Go up to the Mountain, and bring Wood, and build the House; and I will take Pleasure in it, and I will be glorified, saith the LORD. Go up to the Mountain*, &c. From hence I was taught my Duty, to do my Utmost to *build God's House*. And the gracious Declaration that follows, *I will be glorified, saith the LORD*: did sweetly draw my Heart to engage in the Work: It being so suitable to the earnest Desires of my Soul, after the Advancement of the

Lord's Name and Cause in this Place. It was as if the Lord should have said to me, 'Dost thou desire to have my *Name exlated?* Then go about the Work I bid thee; and I will be *glorified.*' Thus being sweetly *allur'd* to this Piece of Obedience, I wrote for my Dismission, as before hinted. — And this Church having desir'd my Husband to join with them, he requested his Dismission from the Church to which he related, and was received into *this*. And they being desirous to get into Order, gave him a Call to the Pastoral Office. Which he declaring his Willingness to accept, a Day was appointed to set him apart thereto. And *Oct.* 10, 1732. he was solemnly set apart to the Pastoral Office in this Church, in the Presence of Messengers from several Churches.---And I also, upon my Dismission from the Church I belong'd to, was received into this Church.

And blessed be God, *here* I have felt his Power, and seen his Glory. The Ministry of my dear Yoke-fellow being blest for my Edification and Comfort; and the Ordinances of Christ's House fill'd with his own Presence. Yea, I have in some good Measure, seen the Desire of my Soul, in the Lord's blessing his Ministry to the Edification of the Church. Christ's Sheep and Lambs have been *fed*: And *their* feeding in pleasant Pastures, has made *me* a Feast: *In their Joy, I have rejoyced.* And as the Lord was with us, to the *Comfort* of the Saints; so some poor Sinners have been brought out of *Darkness* into God's *marvellous Light*; and the Lord has *added* several to the *Church*, such, we doubt not, that shall be *saved in the Day of the Lord Jesus.*

Many have been the Appearances of God *with*, and *for* this little Church, which *our* Eyes have seen. And we hope our greatest Glory is still behind: That what we have already seen, is but like the Day-Star, to the Rising-Sun. *Poor and Needy* we are indeed; but we trust *the LORD thinketh upon us*: And will graciously dwell with, stand by, and own us, notwith-standing all our Unworthiness. And that whoever slights us, we shall always find Favour with the *GOD of Sion*, who doth not *despise the Day of small Things.*

Thus have I given a brief Account of the Providence of GOD, in bringing me to *G---n*. And as a Desire of the Glory of God, and the Good of Souls, *brought* me here; so, thro' Grace, the same Desire *keeps* me here: Waiting, and Longing to see the Advancement of CHRIST's Kingdom amongst us! And the rising Glory of this little Hill of *Sion*: That while *the Root of Jesse, stands for an Ensign of the People, unto HIM the Gentiles may seek, and his Rest be glorious!* And right glad shall we be, if our kind

Lord, will graciously please to own *us*, as Instruments in his Hand, for the Glory of his great Name, the Advancement of his Cause, and the Service of his Church, in our Day and Generation, before we fall asleep in JESUS, and are taken Home to our eternal Rest in his Bosom.

And as to myself, in particular, the LORD has greatly blest me with respect to personal Usefulness, since my Abode at *G--n*. I would humbly hope, yea, I know thro' Grace, that the Lord has made me of some Use to his People *here*, in Converse with them. And *here* has the Lord employ'd me to write many Letters to his dear Children in divers Parts; which thro' his Blessing upon them, have refresh'd their Souls. Yea, *here* has the Lord given me a Heart, and Opportunity, an outward Call, and inward Inclination, to write and publish many little Tracts: Which thro' his gracious Assistance, and kind Providence, have been brought out, and dispersed abroad in divers Places and Nations. And blessed be his Name, HE has given me to hear, that he has us'd most of them for the Good of his People. And I doubt not, HE will use them all, to some or other of his dear Children. *This is the LORD's Doing, and it is marvellous in* my *Eyes*, Psa. cxviii. 23.

These Things I mention, not by Way of *Boasting* of what I have done for *Christ*; but to give the Glory to my *Lord*, for what HE has done for *me*. My Soul is humbled within me, and I am asham'd to think, how little I have *done* for my dear Lord Jesus! And that I have *lov'd* HIM so little in what I have been enabled to do! And tho' what I have been helped to do in the Service of Christ, is very *little*, to the *great* Obligations I am under; yet is this *little*, exceeding *much*, with regard to my *great* Unworthiness, and the *great* Grace which my Lord displays, in every little Thing which HE honours me to do for HIM. I will therefore on the one Hand, lament my own Barrenness; and on the other, rejoyce in the Lord, and bless his Name, for every Kind and Degree of Fruitfulness, which he hath given me.

And truly, I am fill'd with Wonder, while I view, how my Lord *prepar'd* me for his Service: By working in my Heart, vast Desires after it; by giving me gracious Encouragements and Promises to allure me into it; by answering all my Objections, which arose from my great Weakness and Unworthiness; by shewing me where all my Strength lay; and by his enabling me to flee unto HIM, for all the Supplies of Grace which I needed, for all the Service that HE had design'd for me.--- And when the Lord had thus prepar'd me for his Work; Oh how wonderful is his infinite Love and Mercy, his Wisdom, Power and Faithfulness, that HE should *use* the Chief of Sinners, to do any, tho' but the least Service, for the great SAVIOUR!---

And often have I admired divine Kindness, in that *Freedom* from worldly Incumbrances, and *Liberty* for spiritual Service, which the Lord hath given me, since I came to *G---n*. And on these Accounts, sweet have those Words been to my Taste, *Psa.* lxxxi. 6. *I removed his Shoulder from the Burden: His Hands were deliver'd from the Pots.* And *Psa.* lxxviii. 70, 71. *HE chose David also his Servant, and took him from the Sheep-folds, from following the Ewes great with Young. He brought him to feed Jacob his People, and Israel his Inheritance.* And surely, with that Favour which the LORD bore unto his *Israel* of old, and unto *David* his Servant, hath HE remembred *me*, in my Measure, tho' the least and last of all! The Lord has remembred for *me*, his Mercy and his Truth, and has been gracious to me, according to his Promises. --- Yea, HE has done more, far more for *me*, than what I apprehended in the Promises, when he first apply'd them with Power to my Heart. GOD's Thoughts of Grace, in the precious Words of his Mouth, did far exceed my Faith. And particularly with Respect to those Promises, which HE gave me concerning my Usefulness to his People, before, and at my coming to *G---n*. Which I, in my narrow Conceptions, thought, must have been *restrain'd*, with my personal Acquaintance, to those *few* Saints for whom I was more immediately concern'd. But the Lord that call'd me to *feed his Lamb's* has *extended* my Usefulness to *many* at a great Distance, by Writing, and Printing, far beyond what I thought of! So that I may say concerning his *great Goodness* towards me, since I came to *G---n*, that the Lord hath *done* for me, *more exceeding abundantly than I could ask or think!* And *to* HIM, my wonder–working GOD, the God of all Grace in CHRIST, *be Glory and Dominion for ever and ever.* Amen!

Thus having finish'd as briefly as I could, the Account propos'd, of the LORD's gracious Dealings with me, relating to a Train of special Providences attending my Life, by which the Work of Faith has been carried on with Power: I shall,

Secondly, With a few Words to the People of GOD, by Way of Improvement, conclude the whole.

Dear Souls, I have told you somewhat of the LORD's gracious Dealings with me, even with *me*, who am *not worthy of the least of all the Mercies, and of all the Truth* which HE hath shewn unto me, in a Variety of special Providences, by which I have been conducted thro' the *Wilderness*, thus far on towards *Canaan's* Land. *O magnify the LORD with me, and let us exalt his Name together!* Psa. xxxiv. 3. And from what has been said, learn,

1. To *seek* the Lord in your Distresses. I *sought* HIM,   and he was found of me: And in many Steps of his Wonder-working Providence, HE appear'd to be a GOD *hearing Prayer*; that *hath not said to the Seed of Jacob*, even to *me*, the least of them all, *seek ye me in vain*.

2. Beware of *limiting* the holy One of *Israel*, as to the exact Time, or Manner of fulfilling the Promises which HE gives you. I was apt to do so in some Cases, which prov'd a *great Trial* to me. The LORD is a GOD of infinite *Truth*: And we may rest upon his *Covenant-Faithfulness* in every Promise he gives us: *Heaven and Earth shall pass away, but not one Jot or Tittle of his Word fail*. But yet, when he gives us Promises of providential Deliverances, we are apt to *mistake* either the Time, or Manner of their Fulfilmemt. As God's People of old did, concerning the Manner and Time of the *Messiah's* Kingdom: The Glory of his *second* Coming being often included in the Promise of his *first*. And so sad was the Effect hereof unto them, that because they could not *reconcile* the Providences of God, which attended Christ's first Coming in his Meanness, with the Promis'd and expected Glory of the *Messiah*; they *rejected* the Sent Saviour. And many Instances of the sad Effects of limiting the LORD, in this Regard, might be given out of God's Word. The Promise made to *Jacob*, of the Lord's being *with him*, and *multiplying his Seed*; to *Joseph*, of his *Advancement*; to the *Children of Israel*, of their Deliverance from *Egypt*; to *David*, of the *Kingdom*, &c. were all attended with *seeming* contrary Providences, in their View, which prov'd *very* distressing. And yet, all this while, God was fulfilling his Promises to them, according to the Methods of infinite Wisdom, in such a Way that was most for his *own* Glory, and *their* Advantage. When God makes Promises to his People, they are so *full* and *glorious*, there's such an *Abundance* contain'd in a *few Words*; and they have oft-times such *various* Accomplishments; some *partial* and *initial*, others *complete* and *total*; that 'tis easy for such weak Worms as we, to *mistake*, either the Time, or Manner of the Fulfilment of a Promise. Our God, as a *God of Truth*, is always on his Way, fulfilling his Promises of his People. And yet herein, as a *God of Judgment*, that works gloriously, according to his own unsearchable Understanding; *his Way is* oft *in the Sea, his Path in the great Waters, and his Foot-steps are not known* to his dear Children, *Deut.* xxxii. 4. *Isa.* xl. 28. *Psa.* lxxvii. 19. It becomes us therefore, to *believe*, when we can't *see*; to *adore*, where we can't *comprehend*. And *what we know not now, we shall know hereafter*, John xiii. 7.

3. Learn to *wait* patiently, for the Time of God's fulfilling his Promises; and do not think it *strange*, if you find, as I did, many Deaths to pass over them. When the Lord gives *great Mercies* to his Children, he oft-times finds Work for *all their Graces*: That so his own Name may be glorified, and his People honour'd: Both in the exercising and crowning of every tried Grace. And hereby he makes the Mercy *doubly* sweet to 'em, or *deep-dy'd* in Kindness. For by every new *Difficulty* the Mercy comes thro', it receives another *Dye*, to make its Grace-Colours the *deeper*, and the Glory of 'em so much the more *lasting*. Those Colours that are dy'd in *Grain*, are not so apt to *lose* their Beauty, by being expos'd to the Weather; as those which have a more *slight* Dye. So those Mercies that are won by *much* Faith and Prayer, and brought thro' *many* Difficulties, by the Out-stretched Arm of *Jehovah*; have a *lasting* Glory in 'em; that will abide the scorching Heat of Temptations, transcendently beyond what more *common* Mercies will do. Let us then be willing to *wait*, and *trust* the LORD in the *Dark*: For there shall not *fail ought of the good Things which* HE *hath spoken*, Josh. xxiii. 14. And,

4. Let us learn to put a high *Estimate* upon the Glory reserved for us in the compleat Fulfilment of *all* the Promises. I have told you something of the great Glory I have seen, in God's providential Fulfilment of Promises to me here. And if there is such a Glory in little Salvations; if particular Mercies, and special Deliverances be so sweet to the Saints, even in this Time-State: What will our great, universal, compleat, and eternal DELIVERANCE be! There's no sweet Enjoyment *here*, but what has its bitter Mixture: No Pleasures but what are short-liv'd, and while they last, subject to Mutation. But in *Heaven*, there will be no Sin; and therefore no Sorrow. We shall then want nothing to *compleat our Bliss*, nor be troubled with the least *Fear of losing it*. There will be no Imperfection go *with* us there, nor *follow* after us; and so no *casting out* of *that Inheritance*. There will be no *Death*, to succeed *that Life*; nothing to *obscure* the Glory of *that* Salvation, either in its present Enjoyment, or future Expectation. No more going into *Captivity* then; we shall have *done with Trials for ever*. Let us therefore, with stretched out Neck, look for our *compleat Happiness*, only in that *great Salvation*, which we shall enjoy, when our LORD appears the second Time; which will put us into our eternal GLORY-REST! *Heb.* iv. 9. And from thence we *shall go no more out*, Rev. iii. 12.

F I N I S.

E R R A T A.

[Editor's note. Page and line numbers refer to those of the original pages. In the present transcription, these corrections appear in the running text as bracketed notes, e.g., "had [*sic*, r. was]."]

PAGE 13, Line 9, for *had*, read *was*. p. 19, l. 23, for *raise*, r. *rase*. p. 40, l. 23, for *whither*, r. *whether*. p. 42, l. 3, for *will*, r. *would*. l. 33, for *straitway*, r. *straightway*. p. 55, l. 8, for *delightful*, r. *delightfully*. p. 57, l. 14, for *desired*, r. *desire*. p. 62, l. 2, for *the*, r. *their*. p. 71, l. 1, for *effecting*, r. *affecting*. p. 76, l. 8, for *knew*, r. *know*. p. 94, l. 19, for *Faithfulness*, r. *Fruitfulness*. p. 95, l. 22, for *Enjoyments*, r. *Enjoyment*. p. 126, l. 11, for *'twas inpossible*, r. *was it possible*.

A Brief

ACCOUNT

OF THE

Gracious DEALINGS

OF

G O D,

WITH A

Poor, Sinful, Unworthy CREATURE,

Relating to
Some particular EXPERIENCES of the LORD's Goodness, in
bringing out several little TRACTS, to the Furtherance
and Joy of Faith.

With an APPENDIX, and a LETTER prefix'd on the
Lawfulness of a Woman's appearing in Print.

PART III.

By A. D.

Come and hear all ye that fear GOD, *and I will declare what He*
hath done for my Soul, Psal. lxvi. 16.
And Things which are despised, hath GOD *chosen,--That the*
Flesh should glory in his Presence, 1 Cor. i. 28, 29.
When the LORD *shall build up Zion, He shall appear in his*
Glory.
He will regard the Prayer of the Destitute, and not despise their
Prayer.
This shall be written for the Generation to come: And the People
which shall be created, shall praise the LORD, Psal. cii. 16,
17, 18.

L O N D O N :
Printed by J. HART, in *Popping's Court, Fleet-street*; and sold by
J. LEWIS, in *Patter-noster-row*, near *Cheapside, 1750.*

A Brief

ACCOUNT

OF THE

Gracious DEALINGS

OF

G O D, &c,

HAving in a former little *Tract*, given a brief Account of GOD's Loving-kindness to my Soul, relating to his Work of Grace upon my *Heart*, in a *saving Conversion* to CHRIST, and to my being brought to some *Establishment* in JESUS: And also in *another*, given some Account of the LORD's gracious Dealing [*sic*; r. Dealings] with me, relating to a Train of *special Providences*, attending my *Life*, by which the *Work of Faith* was carried on with *Power*: I shall now in *This*, thro' Divine Assistance, give some farther Account of the glorious Grace of GOD, towards his poor, sinful, Hell-deserving Worm! Relating to,

First. Some particular *Experiences* of the LORD's *great Goodness*, in bringing out several of my little *Tracts*. And

Secondly. The *Answer* of my *Desire and Prayer*, in the LORD's sending some of my *Books* into *America*: To my *Furtherance and Joy of Faith*. The Hints I *chiefly* design to give, relate to,

First. Some particular *Experiences* of the LORD's *great Goodness*, in bringing out several of my little *Tracts*.—And as towards the Close of the *second* Part of GOD's Dealings with me, I mention'd, "The Lord's giving me a Heart and Opportunity, an outward Call, and inward Inclination, to write and publish many little *Tracts*: Which thro' his gracious Assistance, and kind Providence, had been brought out, and dispersed abroad in divers Places and Nations: That HE had given me to hear, that he had *us'd* most of them for the Good of his People: And that I did not doubt, HE would use them *all* to some or other of his dear Children:" I shall now in this *Third* Part, give a few brief hints of what passed between GOD and *my Soul*, with respect to *some* of them. For alas, to my Shame I speak it, as I did not set down what I had from GOD, to encourage me to write and publish *several* of them, I have in a great Measure forgot what HE said unto me! But,

This, thro' Grace, I can say in *general*, that I have purely aim'd at the Glory of God and the Good of Souls, in all the little Pieces I have written and publish'd. That a deep Sense of my own Weakness and Unworthiness, to say any Thing of GOD unto his People, of his Ways and Works towards myself or others, has attended me thro' the Whole of what I have attempted to lisp out, and suffer'd to appear. Many have been the Discouragements I have met with from Satan and my own Heart, about all the Little I have aim'd to do for GOD, as if it would be *fruitless*. And great the Encouragements I have had from the LORD, that my Labour in Him, and for Him, should *not be in vain*. Verily the LORD has allur'd me into his Service, and kindly assisted me in all the little Work, which I as a little Child, have attempted to do in Obedience to my great LORD and MASTER: Which thro' his good Hand upon me, I have been comfortably carried through. And when one and another of my little Pieces have been written, many have been my unbelieving Fears, *Lest they should be useless.* Either that they would not see the Light in Print, or that they would not be own'd by the God of all Grace, by reason of my great Weakness and Unworthiness. But oh, my gracious, faithful GOD, has wrought *Wonders* for me! HE has done for me *more exceeding abundantly than I could ask or think: According to his Riches in Glory by* CHRIST JESUS! *Unto whom be Salvation and Honour, Wisdom and Power, and Blessing, for ever and ever.* Amen.

Thus much in *general*. But as to *Particulars*, alas, I can say but little, of what I receiv'd from the Lord, about bringing out those little *Pieces* which I did not take the *Account of in Writing*.

My design, in those Particulars which I penned, was, To take some Account for *myself*, of what the Lord said unto me about my Books, &c. when He appear'd in his kind Providence, to bring out several of them, and to open a Door for my desired Usefulness. That thro' the Memory of his great Goodness, I might be the more prepar'd to give him the Glory of his Truth and Faithfulness, when I should see all those great Things fulfilled, which in the Greatness of his Grace, He had spoken to me of. Not with a View to *publish* what I wrote, did I engage in this Work; it was only design'd for my own *private Use*. But now the Lord inclines my Heart to prepare it for the *Press*, and graciously acquaints me, that HE will use it to *others*.

And as in the following Particulars, I begin the Account with my *Three Books*, which came out together; and soon after mention, in telling of the great Things which the Lord shew'd me He had done for me, That He had brought out my poor Books, unto *Seven-fold*: I think it best just to give a Hint or two about the first *Four*. Which were these: *A Narration of the Wonders of Grace: In Verse*, &c. *A Discourse on Waking with* GOD, &c. *a Discourse concerning* GOD's *Act of Adoption*. With, *A Discourse on the Inheritance of the adopted Sons of God*. And, *A Sight of* CHRIST, *necessary for all true Christians, and Gospel-Ministers*. These the Lord brought out first; and I woul'd just give a Hint concerning each of them. For the

First, Wonders of Grace, &c. It was wrote upon the Doctrines of Grace, shining gloriously into my Soul, with particular Application; and was first design'd for my own private Use. But after a Time, it appear'd needful to me on divers Accounts to publish it. Many Discouragements I met with in my own Mind, from my Weakness, Unworthiness, &c. But that Word encourag'd my Hope in God, that he would bring it out and make it useful, *And* HE *shall bring forth the Head stone thereof with Shoutings, crying, Grace, Grace unto it*, Zech. iv. 7. I was also much encourag'd as to the Lord's Acceptance of this little Piece, which in Love to his Glory, and for the Good of his People, I cast into the Book-Treasury of the Church; from the *Acceptance of the Widow's Mite*, Luke xxi. 3, 4. As to the

Second, Walking with GOD, &c. It was written in Answer to a Letter from a dear Servant of Christ in the Ministry, who desir'd me to write to him on that Subject. And such was the deep Sense I had of my Unfitness for so great a Work, that I design'd to send him a short Letter, and tell him, He was much mistaken in me, that the Subject was much too great and glorious for such a poor little Worm to say any Thing about it. And so bewailing my Weakness and Unworthiness, to excuse myself from answering his Letter. I said in my own Mind, *Days should speak, and Multitudes of Years should teach* that *Wisdom*, and not such a *Babe* as *I*.

But the Lord gave a Turn to my Mind, by this Thought: "That his Letter was a Call of Providence to engage in the Work." And tho' I had no Ability for it in *myself*, yet the LORD encourag'd me from *his* infinite *All-sufficiency*. The King of *Syria's* sending to the King of *Israel*, to heal *Naaman* of his Leprosy, which he was altogether unable to do, and upon which he rent his Clothes, came into my Mind. With the Prophet *Elisha's* saying to him, *Wherefore hast thou rent thy Clothes? Let him come now to me, and he shall know that there is a Prophet in* Israel, 2 Kings v. 7, 8. From hence the Lord shew'd me, That tho' this Servant of his had sent to me to write on so great a Subject, which I had no Ability for in myself, yet that I need not rend my Clothes as it were, and send him Word, that I could not answer his Request. For as the Prophet *Elisha* said to the King of *Israel*, concerning *Naaman, Let him come now to me, and he shall know that there is a Prophet in* Israel: So said the Lord unto me, "Let him come now unto Me: Bring the Case to ME. Tho' thou hast no Ability to answer the Request that is sent thee; *I* am well able to do it. Bring all thy Wants unto my Fulness: *I* will answer for thee; and he shall know that there is a GOD in *Israel,"* 1 Sam. xvii. 46. By this the Lord strengthned me, to obey the Call of his Providence. And in the Faith of his All-sufficiency, as *Israel's* GOD, as *my* GOD, that would not suffer me to be ashamed, I attempted the Work. And thro his good Hand upon me, was delightfully carried thro' it; and enlarged in my Answer, much beyond what I thought of. And while I was engag'd in the Work, the Lord gave me a Heart-melting Intimation, That it should be *useful to Souls.* From this Word, *Thy Teeth are as a Flock of Sheep, which go up from the Washing, whereof every one beareth Twins, and there is not one barren amongst them,* Song vi. 6. Here our dear Lord, the Bridegroom of the Church, commends the beautiful, useful *Teeth* of his Spouse. By which her *Ministers,* cloth'd with his Beauty and Strength, which prepare her Food, for their Usefulness and Profitableness to the Church, may be chiefly intended. But by *Teeth,* as apply'd for my Comfort in this Work, I understood the *Meditations* of my Heart which I then wrote. By their being as a *Flock of Sheep which are even shorn,* their *Fitness,* thro' the Grace and Power of *Christ,* to prepare *Meat* for his *People.* By their *coming up from the Washing,* their being *sanctify'd* by the *Blood of Jesus* unto this Service. And by their *bearing Twins, and not one barren among them,* their full and extensive *Fruitfulness,* under the divine *Blessing.* Much was I encourag'd from hence, as to this little Piece of Service I was then about. And in some little Time after, the Lord, in his kind Providence, brought out the Book, With respect to the

    Third, Adoption, &c. The Lord having shined into my Heart, to give the Light of the Knowledge of the Glory of GOD in the Face of JESUS CHRIST, with regard to some particular Truths, relating to *God's Act of Adoption,* and to the *Inheritance of the adopted Sons of God*; I was desirous to write what I saw, for the Edification of myself and others. Sweetly was I enlarg'd in the Work; and receiv'd such a Testimony of God's *Well pleasedness* therewith, that fill'd me with Joy, melted my Heart, and humbled me in the

Dust before the *Majesty* of *Divine Grace*. Which shone into my Mind, thro' that Word, *For God is not unrighteous, to forget your Work and Labour of Love, which ye have shewed toward his Name, in that ye have ministred to the Saints, and do minister*, Heb. vi. 10. Oh how sweetly did the Lord testify his *Acceptance*, by this *Word*, of this my little Piece of *Work*, as a Labour of Love, shewed toward *his Name*, and for the Good of *his People!* And how did He point my Eye to the glorious *Recompence of Reward!* Truly, the Lord said so much to me in this one Word, that I knew not how to take it in. I was amaz'd at his infinite Grace, that He should thus regard the feeble Attempts of so weak a Worm, and put it upon his *Righteousness*, not to forget my *Labour of Love* therein! And in due Time, in his infinite Kindness, He brought out for me, this Book also. And as to the

   Fourth, A Sight of CHRIST, &c. My writing of this was occasion'd by a particular Providence. A certain Person I was in Conversation with, having misconstru'd some Expressions of mine, and rais'd a false Report concerning them. Which the Strangers to Christ, and Enemies to his People, gladly receiv'd, and improv'd against others, as well as myself, to further their Opposition to the Cause and People of God, in the Place where I live. Upon which I thought it necessary to set Things in a true Light, and publickly declare to the *wondring World*, and to one that was a *Teacher of others*, who yet knew not what any Person meant, by speaking of *Seeing* JESUS: That CHRIST was to be *seen*. Even *now*, tho' not *carnally*, by the *bodily Eye*, as they misconstru'd my Words, but *spiritually*, by the *Eye of Faith*. And that such a *Sight* of CHRIST, was absolutely necessary for all *true Christians*, and *Gospel-Ministers*, in order to make them *such*. And mightily did the Lord encourage my Heart to engage in this Work, notwithstanding my Weakness, and the Reproaches I might expect to meet with on this Account. I was helpt to believe that it should turn to me for a *Testimony*: According to *Luke* xxi. 13. And such an ineffable Glory I saw, in being a Witness for *Christ and his Truth*, inasmuch as our Lord says, *Whosoever shall confess* ME *before Men, him shall the Son of Man also confess before the Angels of* GOD, Chap. xii. 8. That I could rejoyce, not only to suffer Reproach for the Name of CHRIST, but also to have laid down my Life for his Sake, had He call'd me to it, to bear a Testimony for Him and his Truth in the Earth. Oh, the *Cross of* CHRIST, to take it up in witnessing Work for HIM, was *glorious* in my Eye! And sweetly my Lord carried me thro' this little Piece of Work, and brought it to publick View, to the Glory of his great Grace!

Thus, having prepar'd the Way, I proceed to give the dear Saints, some farther Account of the gracious Dealings of GOD with me, relating to those particular *Experiences* of the LORD's *Goodness*, in bringing out others of my little Tracts: Which I wrote for my *own private Use*. And herein I chiefly regarded the Encouragements which the Lord gave me concerning them, notwithstanding the many Discouragements I met with by various Temptations, from within and without.

In *October*, 1740, my *Three Books* were printed: *vis. New-Birth, Justification* and *Letters*. As to the Two former of these, there was some Appearance of their coming out the last Year: For which I earnestly sought the Lord. But he was pleas'd to delay the Mercy; and there was nothing but Death upon it on every Side, no Manner of Appearance of the Books coming out for near a Twelvemonth.

Under this Providence the Lord humbled me deeply for my Sinfulness and Vileness; which I saw deserv'd this Chastisement: He enabled me to submit to his Will, and be sweetly resign'd to his Sovereign Dispose. Yea, to love, and bless him for what he had done; believing it was most for his Glory, altho' herein he seem'd to work against *me*. Thus he did me Good by his real Delay, and seeming Denial to hear my Prayer.

But lo, The Lord could not hide his Bowels long! All on a sudden as it were, he gave a mighty Turn; a Call of Providence, as we judg'd it, for their Publication; and mightily wrought upon the Heart of my dear Yokefellow to bring them out; and with them a Book of Letters. Did ever any *trust in God*, and were *confounded? Wait for him*, and were *ashamed?* No, he always answers the Faith of his People, and oft-times goes beyond it! He always answers their Prayers, tho' frequently in a Way and Time unexpected; and often doth he do for them, *exceeding abundantly above what they can ask or think!*

Some Time before this, I was under a very deep and humbling *Sense* of my own *Deadness* and *Unfruitfulness to God*. Occasion'd, partly, by what I felt in my own Soul, partly, by some of the dear Saints slighting my Books already extant, and partly, by a Fear that I was of but little Use to those among whom I was conversant. These Things prest my Spirit very much; and I sometimes thought, "That the Lord would not let be in the World long, when my Work for him seem'd to be done."

But I was again encourag'd, and *strengthned in Faith*, from the Consideration of the Lord's Dealing with *Abraham* and *Sarah*, in suffering their Bodies to be both *dead*, before *Isaac* was born: That so it might appear, that he was rather born by the Force of the Promise, than any Efficacy of Nature. From hence I was encourag'd to hope, that the Lord would thus deal with *me*. That tho' all within, and without me seem'd to be *dead*, and no Appearance of *Fruitfulness*; yet that, by the Force of the *Promise*, I should be enabled to bring forth *Fruit unto God*.

This was before my Two Books on *New-Birth*, and *Justification* were written. And a very particular Providence there was, to engage my Mind to write both the one and the other. And Encouragement I had from the Lord with respect to both. To encourage me to begin to write the *New-Birth*, and for Assistance therein, I had these Words: *Go, and I will be with thy Mouth,*—Exod. iv. 12. And, *Thou shalt speak all that I command thee*, Chap. vii. 2. And for Success of the Labour I had *that, God shalt persuade* Japheth, *and he shall dwell in the Tents of* Shem, Gen. ix. 27. And for my Encouragement to write that on *Justification*, I had *this, Cast thy Bread upon the Waters: for thou shalt find it after many Days*, Eccles. xi. 1. And for its Success, I had *these: Behold, I will make thee a new sharp Threshing-Instrument having Teeth: thou shalt thresh the Mountains, and beat them small, and shalt make the Hills as Chaff. Thou shalt fan them, and the Wind shall carry them away, and the Whirlwind shall scatter them: and thou shalt rejoyce in the* LORD, *and shalt glory in the Holy One of* Israel, Isa. xli. 15, 16. *That which had not been told 'em, shall they see, and that which they had not heard, shall they consider*, Chap. lii. 15. *They also that erred in Spirit, shall come to Understanding, and they that murmured, shall learn Doctrine*, Chap. xxix. 24.

Upon this, I wrote both these Books; and they were read by one single Person, for whose Perusal they were principally written. After which, the Lord inclin'd my Heart to desire their Publication; and especially to seek for it, upon some hopeful Appearance thereof, as I have said above. Which tho' the Lord at present seem'd to deny me, yet at length, he granted my Desire, and brought out another Book together with them which I did not then think of. *So gracious was* HE!

And when the Call of Providence for their Publication appear'd, I sought the Lord, that he would tell me his Mind therein. And He was graciously pleas'd to say, *Fear thou not, for I am with thee: Be not dismayed, for I am thy God*, Isa. xli. 10. By which he open'd his Heart to me, and told me, He was *with me* in their Outgoing: That he was *My God*; that all his Fulness was mine, to answer all my Wants: That he was *My God*, to pardon all my Iniquities, and to accept, and bless my Labours. By this

Word also he comforted me, with respect to the Books coming out: *I will be gracious to whom I* will *be gracious, and shew Mercy on whom I* will *shew Mercy*, Exod. xxxiii. 19.

And when the Books were put to Press, and I under some Fears and Discouragements; this Word was apply'd to my Heart, unto much Soul-Sweetness: *I will make of* Thee *a great Nation*, Gen. xii. 2. From whence I was persuaded, That the Lord, who had made me one of *Abraham's Children*, would *bless me with faithful Abraham*; that he would bless *me*, some Way or other, to increase that *great nation of his People*. And this precious Word, the Lord sweetly, and frequently whisper'd to my Soul.

Thus kindly the Lord was pleas'd, by his Promises and Providences, to revive my Hope, that I should yet bring forth Fruit unto Him; after my Dejection at my apprehended Deadness and Barrenness!

Another Instance of God's Kindness to me, in raising me up as it were from the Dead, unto a Life of Fruitfulness, in some Degree, is *this*: He opened a Door for me to write many *Letters* to the *Methodists*; and likewise *blest them* to *many Souls*. Oh, *What shall I render unto the* LORD *for all his Benefits!*

I have hinted before, That some slighted and despis'd me, which was one Cause of my Dejection, and made me fear, that I should be no more useful. But lo, tho' *some* despis'd and rejected; God rais'd up *others* to receive, and even to honour me; and made me, tho' an *Outcast* of the *People*, a *Blessing* unto *them!* When some in *England* slighted my Books, and would *None of me*: God sent 'em *beyond the Seas*: Wrought Marvels by his mighty Hand, for their Disposal, and *there* he would bless them! Not that *all* in *England* despis'd: No; blessed be God, *some* embrac'd, some Souls receiv'd Benefit, and blest the Lord for the Books; even that Remnant which the Lord left me here: Which to *me* was a very great *Mercy*, considering my great *Unworthiness*. And tho' some despis'd me, yet God took Occasion hereby, to commend his Love, in using me to others, so much the more. That Word of late on this Account, has been very sweet to me: *And Things which are* despised, *hath God* chosen, *1 Cor*. 1. 28. I have thought, "It was in some Respect needful, that I should be despised; that the Grace of God in using me, might be the more conspicuous." Oh the Depth of his Mercy and Grace! His Wisdom and Knowledge! How unsearchable are his Judgments! A brutish Man understands them not. God is but making his own Way, in Love and Grace to his Children, when he seems to come forth for their Destruction! When he seems to cast them *off*, it is but in order to commend his Grace the more, in their further *Usefulness! Bless the* LORD, *O my Soul: And all that is within me, bless his Holy Name!* But

Farther, Some Time after the Books were out, the Lord was pleased to draw very near to my Spirit, and to *talk with me* about his *Favour*. He shew'd me what *great Things* he had done for *me*, not only in saving my Soul from *Hell*, but in those great Manifestations of his *Love*, with which he had favour'd me to my own Soul's *Joy*; and also, in those wonderful Favours he had conferr'd upon me, as to my *Usefulness* to *others*. He shew'd me, how he had distinguish'd *me* from most of my *Sex*: That he not dealt with *many*, as he had dealt with *me*; and that he had done all for me *freely*, from his *own Heart*, from the Riches of his own Mercy, and free, sovereign Grace, notwithstanding all my Sinfulness. Oh what a Flood of distinguishing Favour did he let out upon my Soul in those Words: *I took thee from the Sheep-cote from following the Sheep, to be Ruler over my People, over* Israel. (or to *feed* his People: as it is, *Psa.* lxxviii. 71.) *And I was with thee whithersoever thou wentest, and have cut off all thine Enemies out of thy Sight, and have made thee a great Name, like unto the Name of the great Men that are in the Earth!* 2 Sam. vii. 8, 9. The Lord shew'd me, That in his great Grace, he had pardon'd all my great Sins, and brought forth my poor Books, unto Seven-fold, notwithstanding my great Unworthiness! And these last, in the Exuberance of his Love, *Three at once!* He shew'd me, That he had us'd one and another of them; and that he had more Grace in Reserve for me for these last! He sent a Sound of Abundance of Grace into my poor Soul, by that Word, Judah *is a Lion's Whelp; from the Prey, my Son, art thou gone up: he stooped down, he couched as a Lion, and as an Old Lion; Who shall rouse him up?* Gen. xlix. 9. The Grace of this Word was exceeding pleasant to me.

"But, though I, Surely this can't be for *Me!* What is this to *Me?* Judah was call'd a *Lion's Whelp*, because the Regal Dignity was to be in that Tribe: and especially, because CHRIST the King of *Israel* was to spring out of *Judah*. But how is it that this Grace should reach *Me*, that I should be a Partaker of Kingly Power and Dignity?"

Then that Word was brought: *To him that loved us, and washed us from our sins in his own Blood, and hath made us Kings and Priests unto God and his Father*, Rev. i. 6. From whence I saw, That my dear Lord Jesus had not only lov'd me, and wash'd me from all my Sins in his own Blood, and so made me spotless in his Father's Sight; but that he had also made me a

King and a *Priest* unto God; and that in the Royalty of a *Prince with God*, I should prevail over all his and my Enemies.

Then the other Word came in again, with a particular Application to my own Soul: Judah *is a Lion's Whelp; from the Prey, my Son, art thou gone up: he stooped down, he couched as a Lion, and as an old Lion; who shall rouse him up?* From this the Lord shew'd me, what Account he made of me as a Child of his Love, in his dear Son, that he look'd upon me as a *Prince* with him, and that he had given me some *Souls* to take for *him*, by my *Books*, out of the *Enemies Hands*. From the *Prey*, my Son, thou art *gone up!* He shew'd me, that I should *go up*, as it were in *Triumph*, with the *Glory* of the *Prey to Him*. And that I should even *go up* to *Heaven*, triumphing in Grace, to give all the *Glory* to that *Grace*, which had made me useful on *Earth*. He shew'd me likewise, That I had such a Fulness of *Strength* for this Service, in *his* all-sufficient Power and Grace, that I might in Faith, *couch* as a *Lion*, and as an *old* Lion; (that is confident of his Strength) and not be *roused up* from my Resting-Place, thro' Fear of any Enemy, or Disappointment. And that Word was brought to confirm it: GOD *brought him forth out of* Egypt, *he hath as it were the Strength of an Unicorn: He shall eat up the Nations his Enemies, and break their Bones, and pierce them thro' with his Arrows. He couched, he lay down as a Lion, and as a great Lion: who shall stir him up?* Oh the boundless Grace of this Word also! Here I saw, That as GOD brought me forth out of *Egypt*, and had given me Kingly Dignity, Royalty and Power, the *Strength* of an *Unicorn*, I should eat up the Nations my Enemies, I should be successful in my Labours for Christ, I should take the *Prey* for *Him*; notwithstanding my own *Sins*, and the *Sins* of others, and whatever *Opposition* from the Powers of *Hell* might be made against it. And that in the Faith of my *Lord's* All sufficient Grace, I might *couch* as a *Lion*, and as a *great Lion!*

But Oh the Lord by this *Display of Grace*, broke my *Heart* with his *Love*, and melted me into *Tears!* My Soul fell down before him, adoring his *great Grace*, and blessing his *great Name* for it! Bewail'd my *great Sins*, and breath'd after *greater Holiness* than ever! Indeed I was at this Time, so abundantly *satisfy'd with Favour*, so richly *replenish'd with Grace*, that I thought, "If the Lord was to do *no more* for me while in this World, yet that he had already done *so much*, that as a Favourite of Heaven, a special Favourite, I should for ever be under the highest Obligations to love and bless him!" And with the greatest Fervency of Spirit, I put up this Request to the God of all Grace: "That from this Time, he would make me *Holiness to Himself* more than ever!" *Oh my Soul, remember this Loving Kindness of thy God! and what Obligations it lays thee under*!

April 6th, 1741. There was a great *Stir* in my Soul, occasion'd by a deep Sense of my own *Vileness*, and an ardent Desire to *serve* the *Lord Jesus*. At length I resolv'd to go and *tell him* how it was with me: Which I did. And I told the Lord, my *Dear Jesus*, (for with Him in a particular Manner I then had to do) "That I was a *Sinner*, a *chief* Sinner. That if he look'd over all his Children, spread over the Face of the Earth, he could find none like *me*; his Kindness and Grace, and my Sinfulness and Ingratitude being set together. I told him likewise, of my *Unfitness*, and *Unworthiness* to serve him, that I had a longing *Desire* after his Service, and was under a *Necessity* to serve him: That I must serve him, or I should dishonour him, that I must serve him, or I should be ungrateful, slight his Love and pierce him." Then I ask'd him, as the *Prince of Grace*, "Whether he would let a *Sinner* serve him?" I told him *all my Heart*; and how the Case stood with me. "That it was the *Evening* of my Day; that now I could do but *little* for him, but pray'd that I might do *much* in a little."—I told him "Of my *Books*, already brought forth; and pray'd him to take them up, tho' defiled Things, and wash 'em in his Blood, and work by them, and let me serve him by *them*." Pray'd, that he would say to me, with respect to them, *Go, serve me, here and there*;--as he said, *Let there be Light: and there was Light*." And in the Faith of his Love to me, notwithstanding my Vileness, I pray'd him to "*Tell me* whether he would be *gracious* to me in these Regards, and to seal it with a *Kiss*." At which my Soul drew back: Oh thought I, "How can I ask the *Fairest of All-Fairs*, to kiss so *black a Sinner!*" And while I was reasoning Things in my Mind, that Word came in, *According to your* Faith *be it unto you*, Matt. ix. 19. Then I cry'd out, "Lord, I *believe*: I believe thy Grace is sufficient to grant my Desires, that thou delightest to be gracious: and I cast myself upon all thy *Grace*, to *pardon* all my Sins, to *fit* me for thy Service, to *assist* me in thy Work, and to *own* me in the same; to the Glory of Thy and my Father."

Quickly after, that Word came in, *Thou hast ravished my* Heart, *my Sister, my Spouse; thou hast ravished my* Heart *with one of thine Eyes, with one Chain of thy Neck*, Song v. 9. And with it such a Sound of glorious Grace, that melted my Soul, and rejoyc'd my Heart. But yet it was so astonishing, that I found not Room enough to receive it; but said within myself, Surely it can't be *Me!* Surely the Lord can't say so of *Me!* Then follow'd, *Be not* faithless, *but* believing, *John* xx. 27. Then *this, The King is* held *in the Galleries*, Song vii. 5. And with it such a Flow of Grace, that at once refresh'd, and surpriz'd me. I scarce know which was greatest, whether the *Refreshment* to my fainting Spirit, that was ready to faint with Longing to serve Jesus, or the *Surprize* at his Grace, in regard of my Vileness. Indeed it was so *great*, that I knew not how to *take it in*; but was for *arguing it*. Upon which I found some *Withdraw* of the Divine Influence. Then, fearing my Lord was *displeas'd*, I pray'd him, Not to be *angry*, but to *pardon* a Sinner; and told him I could not *stand* before his Anger, but should *die* if HE was angry." Upon this he said, *Only believe*, Mark v. 30.— Then I fell down before him, and said, "Lord, I *believe*, Let it then be according as thou hast said. I give up *Myself*, my *vile Self*, to be *loved* of *Thee*, Oh *Prince of Grace!*" But that He should love such a *black Sinner*, humbled, melted, overcame me, and fill'd my Soul with joyful Wonder. Then I heard this sweet Whisper, *Thou art All-Fair, my Love*, Song v. 7. By which I was pointed, as with a Finger, to the Cause of my Beauty in Christ's Eye; as it lay in his own Love; *My Love!* That as I was Christ's *Love*, as he had fixt his *Heart*, and put his own *Comeliness* upon me; so he call'd me *All-Fair!* Then I *ador'd* the King, the Sovereign Lord of all, that *could love* whom he *would*, that is *gracious* to whom he *will* be gracious, and hath *Mercy* upon whom he *will* have Mercy! But Oh! That the *King*, the King of Heaven and Earth, the *Lord* of all the Creatures in both *Worlds*, that could make *Millions* of Worlds at his Pleasure! Should be *ravish'd, held, captivated* as it were, (with the Strength, the Cords of his own Love) by a *Creature!* by a *Sinner!* It fill'd my Soul with astonishing and delightful *Wonder!* Indeed I found I was able to take in but *little* of this Grace, while in the *Body!* But *rejoycing* in the Royalties, the Glories of my Bridegroom's *Grace*, and *overcome* by the infinite Greatness of his *Love*, I *gave him* my *little Soul*; I *attempted it* at least: and pray'd him to "*Bind me*, and *hold me*, by the Cords of his Love, *fast* unto *Himself for ever!*" And deeply I *mourn'd* before him, for all my Baseness and Ingratitude!

Upon the whole I was persuaded, That I had Christ's *Heart*, and should have his *Hand*. That the *King* was *held* in the *Galleries*; that He would take his *Walks* with me in all the *Paths of Duty*, (in the Outgoings of my poor Books and otherwise) and be *seen* in the Displays of his Grace and Glory, to the Joy of his People, his royal Courtiers! *Oh my Soul, wait thou upon God thy Saviour, for his promis'd Goodness: and thou shalt not be ashamed!*

July 13. Having been under a gentle Chastisement from my gracious Father, a mighty Oppression of Soul, by reason of Sin, a Sense of GOD's Displeasure, and a Fear least he should cast me off, as to Usefulness; I humbled my Soul before him, open'd my Heart to him, and poured out before him all my Trouble. When, in boundless Grace, he was pleas'd to say to me, *Fear thou not, for I am* with thee: (aye, *Still!*) *be not dismay'd, for I am* thy God: *I will* strengthen *thee*, yea, I *will* help *thee, yea, I will* uphold *thee with the Right Hand of my Righteousness*, Isa. xli. 10. By this Word of his Grace, the Lord spoke Pardon, Peace, Deliverance and Salvation to my poor Soul. He let me go *free*, under boundless *Grace*, into his *Service* again! That Word also, under this Trial, was precious to me, *Though ye have lien among the* Pots, *yet shall ye be as the Wings of a Dove, cover'd with Silver, and her Feathers of yellow Gold*, Psa. lxviii. 13. From this I had a Heart-melting Persuasion of the Grace of God towards me, That tho' I had lien among the *Pots*, had been in my own Apprehension, as a *broken Vessel*, cast to the *Dunghill*, stript as it were of all Beauty, Excellency and Usefulness; that *yet* I should be as the *Wings of a Dove*, that *yet* I should mount up in the Service of God, and have a fresh Beauty and Glory put upon me therein!

From the Grace of God in these Words, I was deeply *humbled* under all mine Iniquities, and melted into bitter Mourning; and yet rais'd up into Wonder, Joy and Thankfulness, at that Grace, which let me go *free*, when I might justly have been *destroy'd!* And my Heart was exceedingly set against *Sin*, and drawn out after *Holiness*. And I intreated the Lord, "To let me go forth again into his "Service, under *Blood*, under *Love*, under *Holy Oyl*, to live more to his Glory than ever!" And I doubt not but he heard me. *Salvation to the* LORD!

Quickly after this, he gave me to see in his Providence, That he had not cast me off, that he had us'd me, and still call'd me to further Service. Upon which I fell down before him, and said, "Lord, what, not cast me off *yet!* Ten Thousand *Glories* to the *God of all Grace!*" *Remember this Deliverance, Oh my Soul! And give up thyself to the Lord, to be more entirely* His *than ever!*

Aug. 5, 1741. As I was seeking the Lord for personal Favours, and relative Usefulness; that Word was precious to my Soul, *The* LORD *thy God in the midst of thee is Mighty; he will* save, (from all thy Sins and Fears, and to all thy Desires) *he will rejoice over thee with Joy, he will* rest *in his Love, he will joy over thee with Singing*, Zeph. iii. 17. *Glory be to the Lord for this Grace!*

Aug. 6. As I was seeking the Lord for my Usefulness to Saints and Sinners; it came into my Mind to ask him, "To shew his Grace to the *Uttermost*, in this regard, as far as was *meet* for him to extend it to such a vile, little, worthless *Worm!*" Upon which it was instantly darted into my Mind, "That it was meet for GOD to do what he *will*: That what he *willeth*, is *meet* he should do; because HE willeth it, who is the sovereign Lord of all." Then under fresh Encouragements, I fell down before him, adoring his Sovereignty as *Lord of Heaven and Earth*, and *Lord* of his *own Grace*; and besought him "To extend his sovereign Grace to *me*, the least and last of all Saints, and the Chief of Sinners; since it was *meet* he should shew Favour to whom he *will*." And I cast myself upon his *sovereign Grace*, to be dealt with according to it, as should be most for its own *Glory*. Soon after it came into my Mind, "That my Petitions being put up in *Christ's Name*, would be carry'd in to the *Father.*" And I put them afresh into *Christ's Hands*, so to be. Upon which that Word dropt upon my Heart with much Sweetness, *The* Father *himself* loveth *you*, Joh. xvi. 22. And that, *I* will *be gracious to whom I* will *be gracious*, Exod. xxxiii. 19. And that, *Fear not, for I am* with *thee*, Isa. xli. 10. And that, *He is able to* save *to the Uttermost, them that come unto God by him*, Heb. vii. 25. These sweetly refresh'd my Soul, and reviv'd my Faith in the *Father's*, and *Christ's Love* towards me, with respect to what I was concern'd about. Then that, *If ye will enquire, enquire*: Set my Soul upon further asking the Lord to tell me, "*How gracious* he wou'd be to me." Upon which that Word dropt sweetly into my Soul, *And* HE *shall be for a glorious Throne to his Father's House: and they shall hang upon him all the Glory,—from the Vessels of* Cups, *to the Vessels of Flagons*, Isa. xxii. 23. From whence I saw, That CHRIST was a *glorious Throne* for *me*, as one of his *Father's House*, where, as being made by his *Blood, a King and a Priest to God*, I should, *receiving Abundance of Grace, reign in Life by him*. Then this comforted me: *The Pots in the Lord's House shall be like the* Bowls *before the Altar*, Zech. xiv. 20. For this Grace, I blest the Lord: being persuaded, That *I*, tho' but a *Cup*, should be fill'd with the Wine of the Spirit. And I intreated the Lord, "That since I was but a *Cup*, that could hold, and convey but little, in Comparison with the Vessels of *Flagons*, that therefore I might be fill'd with very *spirituous Wine*, and be in my Measure, like a *Bowl before the Altar*, fill'd with *Wine*, and *dedicated unto God*: and that I might be enabled to hang all the *Glory* of my Cup-Measure upon HIM, who is worthy to bear all the Glory of Cups, as well as Flagons." Quickly after, that Word was apply'd with Power and Sweetness: *I have chosen* Thee, *and not cast* Thee *away*, Isa. xli. 9. From whence, being fully persuaded, that the Lord had chosen *me* to do some *Service* for him, and not cast *me* away, as to *Usefulness*, altho' I was the most unworthy and vilest of all; My Soul was humbled before the Lord, drawn out to love him, and enabled to bless him.

Upon the whole, As my Faith and Hope in *God* were increased; So my Desire after *Holiness* was enlarged. My Soul long'd to live to God, more *intensely* than ever: I saw his *distinguishing Favour*, call'd for *eminent Holiness. Blessed be God for this Visit! Lord, let it be to thy Worm, according as thou hast spoken! And make me, under thy distinguishing Kindness, Holiness to thy Self for ever!*

Aug 7. While I was writing as above, this was suggested to my Mind: "What a *Do* you make about *Usefulness!* What is there in it? It's no such *great Thing.*" To which I answer'd:

"The *Glory of God*, is a *great Thing.*" Again it was suggested:

"You are a *Hypocrite*: because you desire *outward Things.*" I reply'd:

"Be what I *will*, Satan, thou shalt never get me out of the *Hands of Christ.* And I'll desire *outward Things*, (i.e. *Usefulness to others*) for his *outward Glory*; and *inward Things* for his *inward Glory.*"

A few Days ago, this was prest upon me:

"You may be *Great* in this World, have a great Name among the Saints; and yet be *nothing* as it were in the Sight of God: You know how *little* you are. And therefore you need not make such a *Stir* about great *Usefulness*: For you'll quickly be stript of all your *Greatness*, and 'twill be shewn before Men and Angels, what a *little*, insignificant Creature you are." I answer'd:

"*I am little, very little.* But God, by giving me a great *Name* among some of his Children; prepares me for *Usefulness* to them: If they saw me in my own *Littleness*, they would not *regard me.* But God gives me great *Esteem* with them, to serve the Ends of his great *Grace*, in making me *useful* to them. And however *little* I am in *myself*, if I may be *greatly useful* to the *Saints*, I shall rejoice: If God will be *greatly glorify'd*, and his People *edify'd*, by so *little* a Worm, it will be my *Joy.* And tho' I should be stript *naked* of all my *Greatness*, and shewn before *all* in my *Littleness* in the Day of Christ; yet will I *submit* thereto, and even take a Sort of *Pleasure* therein, because God's *great Grace* will be the more *glorify'd*, in working by such a *little Worm*: and therefore I'll go on to serve *Christ* and the *Saints* to the Utmost, however it fares with *me*."

And sometimes I have had such Thoughts pass thro' my Mind, and my *Heart* has been in them: "That if I was to be sent to *Hell* at last, I would do my *utmost* to promote the Kingdom and Glory of Christ, and to *serve* Him and his People in *this World*; and that out of *Love* to *Christ*, and *his Glory*, to the *Saints*, and *their Advantage*."

While I was writing as above, it was suggested to my Mind thus:

"You make a *Do* about your *Usefulness*: What is it? *Others*, far more useful than *you*, make no *Stir* about it." I reply'd:

"Tho' my Usefulness is but *little*, if compar'd with that of other Saints; yet it is *my All*, my *Heart* is in it; it is *All* that *I* can *do* for my Lord."—And that Word was pleasant to me, about the poor Widow that cast in her two Mites: *She hath cast in* All *she had*. And truly I think, if I had ten thousand Times more than I have, CHRIST should have it *All!* If I had the Strength of an *Angel*, I would *serve him* with it. I would *run* about the *Earth* for him; there should not be a *Child* of *his*, but I would bring some *Refreshment* to it, if He would *send me*. *Oh my Lord, thou knowest that these are the Workings of my Heart towards thee. Tho'* Thou *only knowest how little I am in Love to thee; and how little I should do for thee, if thou wast to try me*!

Again, it was said to me, while writing as above:

"How can *that* be? how can *you* love the Kingdom and Glory of Christ, that have *sinn'd* so much against him?" I answer:

"Satan, Tho' I have *sinn'd* grievously, and have done as evil Things as I could; yet I speak the *Truth in Christ, I lie not: My Soul loveth him*!"

I have frequently been tempted, "To say nothing of Christ and his Grace to *others*; because I am such a great Sinner *myself*." Satan has said:

"How can *you* open your Mouth for *Christ*, when you have *sinn'd* so much against him, and are such a *vile* Creature?" I have reply'd:

"I am wash'd in *Christ's Blood*, and forgiven by *Free Grace*; and therefore under the greater *Obligation* to publish its Praises."

Again, I have been tempted. "To cast off the *Service of God*, because I could not do it without *Sin*; but in some respects, were guilty of *more* Sin, the *more* I did for God."

But in the Views of Christ's Blood cleansing me, and my Performances from all Sin, and of his presenting them acceptable to the Father in his own Perfections; I have got the Victory over *this*. God's forgiving Love, has likewise encourag'd me to *fear*, to *serve him*. As has also, The Sufficiency of Christ's Grace, of his Power to enable me for Duty, and strengthen me against Sin.

And I have sometimes found it of Use, to keep down the Power of Sin, and to hold my Heart in an holy Bent against it: To enter a *Protest* against it, when I began any Piece of Service for my Lord: "That if Sin offer'd to disturb me therein, and to rob him of his Glory: I did not *allow* of it; but my very *Soul hated it.*"

Aug. 19, 1741. My Soul was very desirous to have more of my poor *Books* brought out, sent into *America*, and blest unto many Souls. And I sought the Lord for this *Mercy*: and these Words were sweet to me, *He* satisfieth *the longing Soul, and* filleth *the Hungry with Goodness*, Psal. cvii. 9. *And my People shall be* satisfy'd *with my Goodness*, Jer. xxxi. 14. And tho, I had not such a full Satisfaction from them, that I should have the *Mercy*; yet I was directed to take hold of them by Faith as God's Covenant; from, *And take* hold *of my Covenant*, Isa. lvi. 4. Which in some Measure I was enabled to do.

A Suggestion was cast in, while I was seeking the Lord:

"That it was not *meet* for me to ask such *great Things*, because I was so *little*; that it was not *meet* that God should put a *superior Glory* upon the *inferior Members* of Christ's Body."—I reply'd:

"It is meet that GOD should do what He *will*."

And Necessity being upon me, and I very *thirsty*, as well as very *needy*, in the Faith of his boundless *Grace*, I ask'd the Lord to give me the *Mercy* my Soul desired.

And these Words were encouraging to me: *Fear not, for I am* with *thee*, Isa. xli. 10. *As a Prince hast thou Power with God and with Men, and hast* prevailed, *Gen.* xxxii. 28. *The Eyes of the* LORD *run to and fro thro' the Earth, to shew himself* strong *in Behalf of them whose Heart is perfect towards him*, 2 Chron. xvi. 9. *O fear the* LORD, *ye his Saints: for there is no* Want *to them that fear him*, Psal. xxxiv. 9. *Thou hast* ravish'd *my Heart my Sister, my Spouse, thou hast ravished my Heart with one of thine Eyes, with one Chain of thy Neck*, Song iv. 9. *And the Grace of our Lord was* exceeding abundant, *with Faith and Love which is in Christ Jesus*, 1 Tim. i. 14. It was the Love, Grace and Faithfulness of God the Father, and of the Lord *Jesus Christ*, that I apprehended therein, which I hoped would be *exceeding abundant* in granting my Desires, notwithstanding my great Sins and Unworthiness.

Upon the whole, my Soul was encourag'd to *hope* and *trust* in the *Lord* for the Mercy; altho' I had not such a full *Assurance* of it as I could have been glad of. But I was enabled to believe *for it*, to cast myself upon the Grace of God, and of the Lord Jesus Christ *for it*, if consistent with his Glory. And that Word was some Comfort to me, *According to your* Faith, *be it unto you*, Matt. ix. 29. *Oh my Soul*, believe *that thy Faith and Prayer shall not be in* vain: *and* wait *to see which* Way *the Lord will appear, and how kind and gracious he will be!*

Sept. 1, 1741. I receiv'd a Letter from a Friend, the Contents whereof prov'd very trying. And I was much dejected, fearing the Lord would cast me off as to Usefulness. But my dear Lord *Jesus* was pleas'd to manifest his Love sweetly to my Soul, in these Words, of the Spouse, *I am my Beloved's, and his* Desire *is towards me*, Song vii. 10. I was persuaded, that I was my *Beloved's*, that I was Christ's *own*, that his *Heart* was fixt upon me as such; and that no future Changes which might pass over me, tho' they might cast me out of the *Love of Creatures*, should ever separate me from the *Love of* CHRIST. And also, that *his Desire* was towards me; that *whoever* might not desire Communion with me, CHRIST *would*: Yea, *did*, at that very Instant, when I was apt to think, Things look'd as if he would cast me *off*. Which made Christ, and his Love, very *precious* to my Soul; I was fully satisfy'd therewith, and my Heart melted into Tears of Joy and Humility.

Since which, the outward Face of Things appearing still the same, I have been often humbled, and sometimes dejected. But have been much comforted with that Word, *My Beloved is* mine, *and I am* his, Song 2. 16. My Soul has rejoyced in *Christ* as my ALL, cleav'd to him as such, and sweetly have I been satisfy'd with his *Love*. I have earnestly desir'd, "That if the Lord shut up *one Way* of glorifying of him, he would open *another*; that if I might not glorify him by Usefulness to *others*, I might inwardly and secretly, in my *own Soul*, glorify him more abundantly than ever." In which Frame of Spirit, I continu'd till,

Oct. 17. When I receiv'd another Letter from a Friend. And by some Things in it, which I thought look'd as if they would hinder my Usefulness, I was somewhat oppressed in Spirit for a Time. But being willing to *glorify God*, some Way or other, and as Things at present seem'd to work against *me*, I found a Desire to make an entire Resignation of *myself*, and my *dearest Interest*, in being *useful to Souls*, to the Lord's *sovereign Dispose*. I thought on that Word, *Hath* the LORD *as great Delight in Burnt Offerings and Sacrifices, as in* obeying *the Voice of the* LORD? 1 Sam. xv. 22. I thought, "It was *pleasing* to the Lord, to have his People entirely conformed to his *Will*: And that *Holiness*, was a constant *sanctifying of God*, and an entire *Dedication to Him*, in, and under *all Dispensations*." Upon which, my Soul was drawn out to *sanctify the Lord*, and to *dedicate myself* to him, in *that* I was at present under. And the rather had I a Desire to do this, now Things seem'd to work *against me*, that I might *glorify him the more*, and shew a *more disinterested Love*. I thought, "There might be somewhat of *Self*, to prompt me to love and bless the Lord, when he apparently wrought *for me*; but if I did this, when he seem'd to work *against me*, I should *honour* and *please* him the more, and more answer the Character of a *Friend of God*. As he styled his Servant *Abraham*, who without Hesitation, at his Bidding, *offer'd up his only Son*." And therefore I fell down before the Lord, humbled myself on Account of my *Vileness*, acknowledged that he needed none of *my Services*, and that he would be righteous, if he was to cast *me off*, as to Usefulness: Yea, that he would be so, was he to deal with me according to what I was in myself, if he sent me to *Hell*. And I gave up myself, and my dearest Concern into his Hands, after this Manner: "Lord, I am wholly *Thine*: Do with me as thou *pleasest*. I make an entire *Resignation* of all that concerns me to thy *sovereign Dispose*. Wound me, smite me where, and how *thou pleasest*; only get thyself *Glory*, and give me Grace to *glorify thee in all*, and do with me just as *thou wilt*." And I found a delightful *Satisfaction*, in pleasing and glorifying GOD, in blessing him for his Works, and in rejoycing with him in them; and in that I might do so in the *darkest Dispensation*.

Quickly after, those Words dropt sweetly upon my Heart, *Seeing thou hast not withheld thy* Son, *thine* only *Son from* ME, *By my* SELF *have I sworn saith the* LORD,—*That in Blessing I will bless thee, and in Multiplying I will multiply thee*, Gen. xxii. 12,—17. In which the Lord testify'd his *Well-pleasedness* with me, in *resigning* my hoped for, and desir'd *Usefulness*, to be wholly at *his Dispose*. And likewise assur'd me, that he would make me *fruitful*. With both which I was sweetly delighted, and enabled, with Humility and Joy, to hope in the Lord.

Thus profitably did the Lord exercise me by the Trial! Thus sweetly did He mix Light and Darkness, Joy and Sorrow! And I had a Desire kept up in my Soul to *glorify him*, altho', as to the present Appearance of Things, I seem'd to be cast out of his Sight; and was apt to say, at times, with the Church, *My Strength and my Hope* (as to Usefulness) *is perished from the*

LORD, *Lam.* iii. 18. Thus under various Frames, but mostly resign'd to the divine Will, I went on till,

Oct. 21, 1741. WHEN reading *John* xi. 25. *Jesus said unto her, I am the Resurrection and the Life: he that believeth in me, tho' he were dead, yet shall he live*: I was much drawn out to *believe in Christ* for a *renewed Life of Usefulness*. And tho' at present all Things round about me seem'd to be *dead* in this regard, yet I had a Soul-strengthening View of my Lord's Fulness, as the *Resurrection* and the *Life*. I saw an infinite *Ability* in HIM, to raise me from the Dead, unto a Life of Service. And being encourag'd by his gracious, faithful Promise, Tho' he were *dead*, yet *shall he live*: I *believed on him*, for the Fulfilment of it to *me*. That he would *open* to me fresh Opportunities to serve him, as *Rivers in high Places. I believe on him*,for the free and full Forgiveness of all my Sins, which render'd me unworthy of his Service; for fresh Flows of divine Favour; for all the Assistances, inward, and outward I stood in need of; and for all Success consistent with his Glory. And I was verily persuaded, that my dear Lord, would again appear for me in these Regards.

And in the Evening, I saw much *Glory* in his *Service*, and on his *Servants* that were honour'd to *serve him*. Was much *humbled* under a Sense of my own *Vileness*, and *Ingratitude* to the Lord, and *Unfitness*, to serve him. That Word much humbled me, *Can ye drink of the Cup that I drink of? and be baptiz'd with the Baptism that I am baptized with?* Mark x. 38. "Ah, thought I, what can *I* do or suffer for *Christ*, in Comparison of the Doings and Sufferings of *those* whom he highly honours!" And after much working of Heart with *Desire*, and some Degree of *Fainting*, to do *something* for him, altho' I was the least and last of *all*, and could neither *do* like his *great Servants*, (one of which I had particularly on my Heart) nor expect to be *honour'd* like *them*: the Lord broke in sweetly with this Word, *Fear not, for I am* with thee:—*be not dismayed, for I am* thy God, *Isa.* xli. 10. In which the Lord spoke very comfortably to my Heart. "Fear not, said He, for I am *with* thee, even *Thee*: Be not dismayed, for I am *Thy God*." Oh what a sweet Emphasis did he put upon the Word *Thy! Thy God!* In this the Lord spake two Things to me. 1. That he was *my God*, even *mine*; altho' I was so far behind his *other Servants*, which I saw him love and honour so much; and that from the same Grace, he would love, and use me, even *me*. 2. That tho' I could not do that *Service* for him which others did; yet that in what he would enable me to *do*, I had *himself*, as *my God*; that all in *him*, as the God of all Grace, was *mine*. And I *knew* it was the Voice of GOD. I *felt* his Power on my Heart. And was more fully convinced that it was *his*, in that I could not, tho' but a few Moments after, make such an *Impression* upon my own Soul, nor regain, by thinking over the *Word*, what I *felt* when HE spake it to me. It was so *sweet*, that I wanted the Impression to be *lasting*. But the Lord is a Sovereign; and keeps the Seal of his Love in a Promise, by the Holy Ghost, upon the Hearts of his Children, for a longer, or shorter Season, just as it *pleaseth* him. When HE *speaks*, he speaks like HIMSELF, with Majesty and Efficacy, worthy of GOD! And often he speaks so much Grace to his People, unto so much Soul-Sweetness, in *one Word*, that will take *many* of theirs to *tell it out*, and never can it be fully done.

However, by his saying to me, I am *Thy God*, he let me know that he was *mine*, that he was so, unto those *Ends of Grace*, for which I *thirsted*, and was almost ready to *faint*. That as he had a glorious CAUSE carrying on in the Earth, in which my Heart delighted, he would, as *My God*, love, and honour *me*, to have a *Finger* in it, that I should some Way or other promote it. By which he humbled and melted me, and rais'd me up into Faith, Joy and Thankfulness. I fell down before him, "Acknowledg'd myself to be the Chief of Sinners, and pray'd him to magnify his Grace, and its exceeding Riches, in dealing with me according as he had spoken." And I was fill'd with *Wonder*, that he would be thus *gracious* to such a *vile Sinner!* That Word was *sweet* to me, *Will God in very deed dwell with Men on Earth?* 2 Chron. vi. 18. My Soul cry'd out, will GOD in very Deed love and own *vile me! That* also rais'd my Wonder, *Shall Sarah that is ninety Years old bear?* Gen. xvii. 17. Shall I, that am as it were *dead*, be *fruitful!* Then *that* comforted me, *Is any Thing too hard for the* LORD? Chap. xviii. 14. And then *these, A little one shall become a Thousand, and a small one a strong Nation:—For in my Wrath I smote thee, but in my Favour have I had Mercy on thee*, Isa. lx. 10,—22. And this Word also was *sweet* to me, *I will be merciful to their Unrighteousness, and their Sins and their Iniquities will I remember no more*, Heb. viii. 12.

Upon the whole, my Soul was much strengthned in Faith, that my God would appear for me again; and was drawn out to love the Lord, and to have Evil. *Wait, O my Soul, upon thy God, who will again appear to thy Joy.*

Oct. 22, 1741. While I was writing as above, this was suggested to my Mind:

"And what are you the *better* now for your Promises? What have you *got* by them? You have had *Words* before; but what have they *brought forth?* Can you give a single Instance of any Fruit?"

But my Mind being much imprest with somewhat I had just before heard; and I unwilling to leave writing till I had finish'd the Account: I was not so much at Leisure to attend the Temptation, nor to answer it as to other Times. I was in some Degree wounded by it; and in some Measure enabled to resist it, and to hold fast my Confidence in God, and his faithful Word. But the Intention of my Mind being on another Thing, *that*, at present, engross'd my Thoughts. But,

Oct. 23. In the Review of the above Temptation, I was troubled that my Spirit was no more *edg'd* against the Tempter; and that I had not for *God's Honour*, borne a more vehement Testimony to the Faithfulness of his Word, and against the Father of Lies.

And now, O Satan, since thou didst ask me, "What I was the *better* for God's Promises?" I answer:

"*Much every Way*. They are my *Gain*, my *Treasure*, the *Bonds* which God has given me to bind Himself to be *mine* forever; and to do *great Things* for my Soul." Dost thou ask me, "What I have *got* by the Promises?" I answer:

"I have got *all* by them that I can *desire*. Even the *God* of all Grace in *Christ*, to be my eternal LOT; and all the *Grace* that is in him, to be laid out all manner of Ways, in *Kindness* towards *me*, thro' *Christ Jesus*, according to the Infinity of his *Wisdom*."—Dost thou ask me "What the Promises given me have *brought forth?*" I answer:

"A *Life full* of Mercies, of Supports, Comforts, Deliverances, of marvellous Salvations, and amazing Favours, ever since I have *known the Lord*, or rather been *known of Him*; has been the glorious *Fruit* of the many, the great, the exceeding great and precious *Promises* which he hath given me."—And dost thou call upon me to "Give a single *Instance* of the *Fruit* of the Promise?" Take for Answer:

"All that wonderful Train of *Providences*, of gracious *Appearances*, which attended my Removal from *N---n*, to *W---h*; and from *W---ea*, again to *W---h*. Wherein I saw all the *Promises* the Lord had given me, *fulfilled*; motwithstanding the many *Deaths* which pass'd over them, and *Clouds* with which for a Time they were obscur'd; and that *there had not failed ought of all the good Things which the* LORD *had spoken*."

"And as to the Promises the Lord has *now* given me, I *know* they were from *him*, I *know* his sweet, his all-efficacious *Voice*. There's none can speak *like Him!* And be it *known* unto Thee, O Satan, in the Lord's Strength, and for his Honour, I will *believe* his *Promises* to be true and faithful, like *Himself*, the true and faithful GOD; chiefly, because they are *His*, and because I have *experienced* them to be so. And I will *wait* upon my GOD, accounting *him*, both *able* and *faithful* who hath promised; for all promis'd Mercies in his own Time and Way, altho' ten Thousand Deaths should pass over them. For he will not *leave me, nor forsake me*: nor suffer a *Jot* or *Tittle* of his *Word* to *fail*. *Here*, in JEHOVAH I *trust*; and I shall not be *ashamed*."—*All Love and Glory for ever be to his most high and holy Name*!

Oct. 24, 1741. A Letter from a Friend. In which I saw much of God's Kindness to *me*. Which rejoyced, humbled, melted me down before the Lord. It was the *Dawn* of another *Day* in Providence, after the dark *Night* that had been upon my Mind was over, which strengthned my *Faith* in the Promise. Or rather brought the Grace of the Promise nigh to my spiritual *Sense*. And I earnestly desir'd, That whether I was *afflicted*, or whether I was *comforted*, it might be for *God's Glory*. That I might not rejoyce in any Favour shewn to *me*, merely for my *own Sake*, but chiefly, that hereby *God* might have the more *Glory*. I long'd to love GOD for *Himself*, and every Thing else, the most delightful, for *his Sake*. I long'd to be *loyal* to CHRIST, to live upon *him*, as my ALL, in the *Enjoyment*, as well as in the *Want* of sensible Comforts, and instantly, to ascend with the Glory of all to *him*.— *Live, O my Soul, upon thy Lord's Sweetness, whenever he gives thee any Joy in, and Refreshment thro' the Creatures! Rejoyce not in the Creature, nor thy Comfort therein, separate from Christ; but let* HIM, *thy Beloved, that Mass, that Bundle of* SWEETNESS, *engross thy whole Heart! So shalt thou be satisfy'd as with Marrow and Fatness; and not overmuch lifted up with smiling, nor cast down with frowning Providences.*

And remember, When thou hast a joyful Day, a Night of Sorrow may quickly succeed it. And when it's Night with thee, that a Morning of Joy will shortly appear. When thou mournest, let it not be as one without Hope: For God will help thee, right early. And when thou rejoycest, let it be with Trembling: lest thou shouldst rejoyce in any Thing below thy GOD, *rob him of his Glory, and provoke him to grieve thee. For such is his Jealousy for his own Glory, and thy Happiness, that he keeps a strict Eye over thy Heart, lest it steal out from Him, to any other Object. And if it does, from his Love, he'll reclaim thee by a Rod, and perhaps a sharp one too, in his fatherly Displeasure. Watch thy Heart therefore, and pray, and labour, that thou mayst serve the* LORD *with Fear, with filial Reverence, as a dear, an obedient Child. And when and where thou failest, wash by Faith in the*

Blood of Christ, that Fountain set open for Sin, and for Uncleanness. Confess thy Transgression unto the LORD, *and he, as thy Father, will forgive the Iniquity of thy Sin. Thus walk before thy God continually; living upon Him as thy* ALL, *and unto Him as thy* END. *Delighting in his All-Sufficiency, and revering his Authority: In both which, let Him be* Thy God. *And thus walk on with him, thro' Light and Darkness, Day and Night, until that Day comes on, when thy Sun shall no more go down. Until thou art got out of the Reach of Sin and Satan, and beyond all Danger of God's fatherly Anger, into* Immanuel's *Land of Love and Life: Where the* LORD *will be thine everlasting* Light: *And the Days of thy Mourning shall be* ended! Lord Jesus, *say* Amen! *So shall it be!*

Oct. 29, 1741. As I was seeking the Lord, that he would open a Way for my farther *Usefulness*, in other of my *Books*: It dropt sweetly on my Mind. "That Christ had prevailed to open the Book, and to loose the seven Seals." Quickly after, I read *Rev.* v. and was much delighted with Ver. 5, 6, 7.— *Behold the Lion of the Tribe of* Juda, *the Root of* David, *hath prevailed to open the Book, and to loose the seven Seals thereof. And I beheld, and lo, in the Midst of the Throne, and of the four Beasts, and in the Midst of the Elders stood a Lamb, as it had been slain, having seven Horns, and seven Eyes, which are the seven Spirits of God sent forth into all the Earth. And he came and took the Book out of the Right Hand of him that sat upon the Throne.* The Comfort I received from it for myself, *This*: "That my dearest *Jesus*, as *King* upon the *Throne*, had prevailed in the Virtue of his *Blood*, as the *Lamb once slain*, to take the *Book* of his *Father's Decrees*; to take up all the *Grace*, written for *me* therein. And to *loose the seven Seals*; that he had an absolute *Power* given him over all Creatures and Things, unto all the *Ends* of Grace: Or to remove in *Providence*, all the *Lets* which impede and obscure *purposed Grace*," And the Perfection of his *Wisdom* and *Power* to accomplish all *God's Designs*, much delighted my Soul. While I view'd him as the *Lamb* in the *midst of the Throne*, having *seven Horns, and seven Eyes*, the *seven Spirits of God* (the Holy Ghost in his seven-fold Operations, to be) *sent forth into all the Earth*. And in the Faith hereof, I pray'd him "To look on the *Book*, and to work for me on *Earth*, according to what was written for me in *Heaven*. To make visible in his gracious Providence, the secret Purposes of Grace, recorded in that Book which he had prevailed to take out of the Father's Hand."—*O my Soul, wait thou upon thy all-wise and all-powerful* Lord, *to open for* Thee *the seven-sealed Book! And remember, whatever* Instruments *he may please to use in this Work, that it is* Himself *is the great* Agent: *who once dy'd for thee on the Cross, and now lives for thee on the Throne! Wait to see the Wonders of his Love, and to give him all the Glory!*

Oct. 31. Upon some Stirrings of *Sin* in my *Soul*, I was much *oppressed in Spirit*, with my Hellish Baseness, and Unkindness to my *Lord*; and some Degree of Fear lest my Sins should separate me from Communion with him in *Love*, and oblige him to cast me off, as to *Service*. My Heart was ready to *break*, I knew not what to do, but I fell down before him, and as I could, bewail'd my Wretchedness, confess'd I was a *Sinner*, a *chief* Sinner, that I *deserv'd* to be cast *away*, yea, into the hottest *Hell*; that there was no *Help* for me but in Himself, the mighty SAVIOUR; that I *fled* to his *Cross*, and *hung* upon him for all *Salvation*. I told him, "I was *grieved*, and pained at *Heart* for my Baseness to him; and I cast myself at his *Feet*."—But still my *Pressure* remained. Until it was suggested to me, "That the *greater Sinner* I was, and the *greater* my *Iniquities* were, the more I should *honour Christ*, as the *great* SAVIOUR, if I *believed on him* for *my Salvation.*"

Upon this, being somewhat *rais'd in Spirit*, and enlarg'd with Desire to *glorify him*, I fell down before him again, and *confess'd* my Vileness: "That I was the *vilest Sinner* that ever came to him; but that for *his Honour* as the *great* SAVIOUR, I *believed on Him* for *all Salvation*." And this I did with a Sort of *holy Pleasure*. Not at my *Vileness; no*, that was my exceeding *Grief*. But that hereby, the *Glory* of the *Saviour* would be the more advanced, by my *believing* on him for *Salvation*, and by his *saving* of me to the *Uttermost*. But *still* my Burden was not wholly *gone*. The Weight of *Sin* made my *Heart sink* within me, altho' I knew the *Rock* was beneath me. Oh my Ingratitude and Unkindness to my loving Lord, *pressed my Soul down*. And a Crowd seem'd to stand in my Way to oppose my coming to him, and *forbid* my intreating his Favour: suggesting, "That he *would not*, or *could not* love me, or at least, that it was not *meet* for him so to do." But that Word dropt on my Mind, *The Kingdom of Heaven suffereth Violence, and the Violent take it by Force*, Matt. xi. 12.

Upon which I fell down before the Lord again, and told him, "I was a *leprous Sinner, full of Leprosy*, overspread with the *Plague of Sin*, from the *Head* even to the *Foot*; and pray'd him as the *great High-Priest over the House of God*, in the Virtue of his great *Sacrifice*, to *pronounce*, to make me *clean*, from Sin in its Guilt, Filth and Power. I pray'd him to *love me*, to make me *like him*, and to let me *serve him*. I *claspt about him*, and said, *I will not let thee go*."

Soon after, this Word came in, *If Heaven above can be measur'd, and the Foundations of the Earth searched out beneath, I will also cast off the Seed of* Israel *for all that they have done*, saith the LORD, *Jer.* xxxi. 37. The infinite *Grace* of it comforted me. But Oh, all that I had *done* against my gracious *Lord*, pierc'd me to the *Soul*. Then this Word was apply'd sweetly, *Be it unto* Thee, *even as thou* wilt, *Matt.* xv. 28. By which the Lord granted my *Requests*, and I was enabled to believe that he would *love me, vile me*, make me *like him*, and let me *serve him*. Which gave me sweet, solid *Soul-Rest*. But still my Burden was not *quite* taken off. There was something between *me* and my *Lord*. (Perhaps some Degree of secret Suspicion, that he could not delight in such an unlovely Creature) Then he said, *Thou hast* ravish'd my Heart, *my Sister, my Spouse, with one of thine Eyes, with one Chain of thy Neck*, Song iv. 9. By this he *shed abroad his Love* abundantly in my *Soul*, he *pour'd it* into my *Heart*, he told me, that he *lov'd me*, that he *delighted* in me as his *own*.

Then I fell down before him; was melted into Tears of Love, Joy and Praise: I ador'd his Grace; and pray'd him to let a *black Sinner kiss his Feet*. Now my Joy was *full*. I had found my *Lord*, and his *Love*, which was *better* to me than *Wine! Better* than *Life!* Then that Word dropt sweetly on my Heart, THOU *art more glorious and excellent than the Mountains of Prey*, Psal. lxxvi. 4. Before this, that Word had been a sweet Support to me, *The* Lame *take the Prey*, Isa. xxxiii. 23. And now my dear Lord had opened his Heart to me, and told me *Himself* was *mine* in *Love*; and my Joy was *full*: Oh how precious, how exceeding precious was CHRIST to *me!* I told him, "That I lov'd *Himself* more than all his *Gifts*; that if it was possible for me to enjoy the *Favours* my Soul desir'd, as to the external Part of them, without *Himself*, his *Heart*, his *Love*, I could not be *satisfy'd*. That *Himself* was my ALLL, and himself in *them*, in the Royal Grants he had made me, made *them* precious to my Soul." Oh how *sweet* was *Christ* and his *Love* to *me!* How did my Soul *delight* in, and *cleave* unto *Him in Love!* I hated *Sin* intensely, and pray'd against it most earnestly. *Remember, O my Soul, the Loving-Kindness of the* LORD *to Thee! Watch against Sin, and labour to walk worthy of his infinite Love!*

Nov. 12, 1741. As I was seeking the Lord, that Word dropt upon my Heart, *Then was I in his Eyes as one that found* Favour, Song vii. 10. In which I heard an encouraging Sound of Free-Grace, That *I* should find *Favour* with the Lord, with regard to *Usefulness*. And a sweet Remembrance of that wonderful *Favour* which I found with my dear *Lord Jesus* in

Time past, was brought to my Mind. When under a special Providence, he admitted me into *Bosom-Communion* with him in *Sion*, in answer to my Desires and Prayers, in such a Manner that I was abundantly *satisfy'd* with his Goodness, and took up my *Rest* in his Favour, as in the *Midst of Delights*. And I was drawn out to intreat I might find the same *Favour* with him, as to *Usefulness*. I had a deep Sense of my own Unworthiness, and I told my dear Lord, "That I was very *thirsty* and *needy*, but came unto Him in the *Faith* of his *Grace*, as being *full of Grace, a Well of Life*, infinitely enough to *satisfy* all my Desires; that I pleaded nothing but *Grace*, and intreated him not to send a *Sinner away empty*." I was *pained* with Desire after Christ and his Love, after Himself in Love. I wanted his *Heart's Delight* to be in me, and his *boundless Favour* to flow out upon me, in making me *fruitful* and *useful*. And tho' I was such a *black, unlovely Sinner*, yet since he had *lov'd* me, and *dy'd* for me, I pleaded the *Strength*, the *Sovereignty* of his Love, who can *command* his Loving Kindness, and be *gracious* to whom he *will*. I cast myself at his *Feet*, as *Ruth* at the *Feet* of *Boaz*, and intreated him to *spread his Skirt over me*; and found sweet Liberty to move him to it with *this*: That he was my *Kinsman*, my *near*, my *nearest Kinsman*. That in his infinite Grace, he had made Himself of *Kin* to me, tho' a poor *Stranger*, that he had took my Nature, dy'd for me, and betroth'd me to Himself: And therefore I pray'd him to *do the Kinsman's Part*, to spread his *Skirt* over me, and *satisfy* me with all that *Favour* which my Soul long'd for.

And these Words were sweet to me: *Your Heart shall live that seek GOD*, Psal. lxix. 32. I saw, there was Grace *enough* for me in *God in my Saviour*, and that in any *other*, there could not be enough. And I had a sweet Persuasion, that my Heart should *live*, in seeking Him; that he would flow out upon me as a Well of living Water, to my full Supply. This likewise delighted me, *I, even I am he that comforteth you*, Isa. li. 12. Oh thought I, "There's none but He has *Grace* enough to do it!" This Word also was brought, *The* LORD *thy God in the* Midst *of thee is Mighty; he will* save, *he will* rejoyce *over thee with Joy: he will* rest *in his Love, he will* joy *over thee with Singing*, Zeph. iii. 17. Precious was this to my Soul. But some Degree of Fear I found, lest I should not be so highly favour'd. From which that Word deliver'd me, *Be not* faithless, *but* believing, *John* xx. 27. Then I took in the Grace of the other sweetly, and believed, That the LORD *my God*, my dear *Lord Jesus*, my royal *Bridegroom*, had lov'd and chosen *me*; that he was in the *midst* of me, that he *dwelt* in me as in his Palace. That in his mighty Love and Power he would *work* for me. Yea, that I was his *Heart's Delight*; that he would rejoice over me with *Joy* and *Singing*, and complacently *rest in his Love*. Likewise, this was sweet to me, *The* LORD *God will make my Feet like* Hind's Feet, *Hab*. iii. 19. I was persuaded, I should *leap* over Difficulties, and *walk upon my high Places* in his Service. This Word also was precious to me, *Thou shalt be called* Hephzibah,—*and thy Land shall be married*, Isa. lxii. 4. Hence I saw, That I should be the LORD's *Delight*, that I should be *married* to him, appear to be so, under bright Displays of his infinite *Favour*, as my Royal *Bridegroom*. Oh this *Grace* fill'd me with Wonder and Adoration, that I should be the LORD's *Delight*, and find such *Favour* with him, who had deserv'd to be an Object of his *Wrath* forever! Sweetly it *melted* my Soul, *humbled* me for my Vileness, and made me *long* after Holiness. *Bless the* LORD, *O my Soul! Believe thy Bridegroom's Grace: and wait for the Time when thou shalt be in his Eyes, as one that has found* Favour.

Nov. 16, 1741. As I was writing my *Letter to the Saints, on the Duty of Love*; this was much imprest upon my Mind:

"That it would rise up in Judgment against me and condemn me; by Reason of my little Love to them: And therefore I had better desist, and say nothing about it." But I was enabled to answer the Tempter *thus*:

"If hereby I can *serve Christ* and the *Saints*, I am willing to be *condemn'd*. I shall not be condemned as to my *Person*, and if I should be as to my *Actions*, yet if the *Glory of Christ* may be hereby the more advanced, and the *Saints* reap any *Advantage*, I will write it notwithstanding. I write it as a Rule to *myself*, as well as *others*. And as to *teach others*, and not *do* the same Things *myself*, is an aggravated *Sin*; so I desire to *watch*, and that hereby I may be the more *quickned* to the Obedience of *Love*. And besides, it is the *Will of my Lord*, that I should write it; and *Necessity* is laid upon me so to do."

And that word was much upon my Mind, *Necessity is laid upon me; yea, Wo is unto me if I preach not the Gospel*, 1 Cor. ix. 16. I saw from hence, That as the Apostle *Paul*, was laid under a *Necessity* to preach the *Gospel*, and *Wo* would have been unto him if he had not done it. So *Necessity* was laid upon me to write this *Letter*. As the Lord had reveal'd his *Mind to me*, that I should do it, answer'd all my *Objections* against it, and sweetly drew my Soul into a *Resolution* to engage therein, by many Texts of Scripture some Time before. So that I was persuaded, That tho' I was as mean as a *Barley-Cake*, (by which *Gideon* was represented) yet that tumbling into the Host of the Lord's Enemies, I should *smite them*, and do some Service for him, and his dear Children by this Performance. And as my Heart had been sweetly melted under the infinite, condescending Grace of Christ, in telling me, "That he had *Need* of me for this Work:" upon which I had said to him, "Then, *Lord Jesus*, take *me, O Prince of Grace!* Take *me* thy poor *Colt*, the *Foal of an Ass*, and ride forth in the Majesty of thy Love as the King of *Sion*, bringing *Salvation* to thy *People*, by the meanest and most despicable of all *Thine*; and *Thou* shalt have all the *Glory!*" And as I had said thus to Christ; I could not go *back*; but thought myself under a *Necessity* to go on with my Work in writing this Letter; and that *Wo* would be unto me if I did not.

And that Word also comforted, melted and encouraged my Heart to proceed herein, *As a Father pitieth his Children; So the* LORD *pitieth them that fear him*, Psa. ciii. 13. From whence I saw, That tho' I was a poor, weak, imperfect Creature in *Love*, yet in as much as I desir'd to serve my *Father* herein, and to encourage his dear *Children* so to do; he would not deal with me in the Wrath of a terrible *Judge*, but have Compassion on me in the Bowels of a *Father*. And this Word also was sweet to me, *For he that in these Things serveth Christ, is acceptable to God*, Rom. xiv. 17. I was hence persuaded, That the Work I had begun, was a Piece of *Service* for my Dear *Lord*, and *acceptable* to *God* my *Father*. And hence was strengthned to proceed in it. *Oh my Soul, Watch thou in all things, that thou doest not act contrary to that Duty of Love which the Lord hath taught thee, and enabled thee to point out to others!*

As soon as I began to write as above, This was darted in upon me:
"You are a *Tell-Tale*"—To which I answer:
"Satan, I am *Christ's*: I will be for *Him*; and *tell* of *his* Love and Grace, and of *thy Devises* to hinder his Service, and the rising Glory of his Kingdom."

Nov. 20, 1741. As I was beginning to transcribe my Letter, *Hints of the Glory of Christ*: &c. This was much imprest upon my Mind:
"That my Labour would be in *vain*: That I was labouring in the Fire for very *Vanity*. That the Lord did not *love me*, nor *chuse me* for this Work. As I might *see*, in as much as it had not yet been of Use to the Person for whom I immediately wrote it. And that therefore I had better desist."—To which I answer'd:
"Tho' it hath not as *yet* been of Use to him; perhaps it *may be*. And as the Lord call'd me to write it at first, if it should not be of Use to *him*,

perhaps it may to some *others*. God may *cross Hands*; and lay his Hand of Blessing hereby, upon some that were not in *my Thoughts*. As he has done in other Instances; and therefore I'll write it again. I'll take it for *my Lord*; and let *Him* do what he *pleaseth* with it."

In the Evening, My Soul was much drawn out to seek the Lord, "That he would make me *useful*, and bring out the *Letter* I had begun to transcribe, and my *other Books*." As one destitute of all *Creature-Help*, I cried unto him in the *Faith* of *his* infinite All-Sufficiency, "That HE would bring Salvation to me by his own Almighty Arm. That He that made all Things by a Word of his Mouth, would speak the Word, and thereby give me the Desires of my Heart." And *believing* his infinite *Grace*, I cast all my *Wants* upon him, *Myself* and all my *Concerns* at his Feet, to be dealt with according to his *Sovereign Grace*, as should be most for its *own Glory*. And I had a sweet *Persuasion*, That the Prince of Grace, *would not, could not*, send me away *empty*.

And in the Night, these Words dropt sweetly on my Mind, *And I appeared unto* Abraham, *unto* Isaac, *and unto* Jacob, *by the Name of* God Almighty, *but by my Name* JEHOVAH, *was I not known unto them*, Exod. vi. 3. *And the Angel of the* LORD *appeared unto him in a Flame of Fire, out of the midst of a Bush: and behold the Bush burned with Fire, and the Bush was not consumed.—And the* LORD *said, I have surely seen the Affliction of my People which are in* Egypt, *and have heard their Cry, by reason of their Task-Masters: for I know their Sorrows. And I am come down to deliver them,--Come now therefore, and I will send* Thee *unto* Pharoah, *that thou mayst bring forth my People the Children of* Israel *out of* Egypt, Chap. iii. 2,—7, 8,—10. *Therefore behold, I will allure her, and bring her into the Wilderness, and speak comfortably unto her. And I will give her her Vineyards from thence, and the Valley of* Achor *for a Door of Hope*, Hos.ii. 14, 15. And, *when the Time of the Promise drew nigh,*—Moses *was born*, Acts. vii. 17,—20. From whence I was taught,

I. That it is God's usual Way, when he designs *Mercies* for his People, and is pleas'd to make *Promises* thereof, To appear unto them by the Name of *God Almighty*, in his own Almightiness, his All-sufficiency to *fulfil* his Promise; to encourage their Faith and Trust in him.

II. That between God's *making* and *fulfilling* of his Promise, between his People's trusting in him *for*, and enjoying *of* promis'd Mercies; there are often very *great Deaths* pass over them: As there did upon those Promises made unto the Seed of *Abraham*, when they were in *Egypt*.

III. That when the Lord's People are brought into the *Wilderness*, into Affliction, it is HE that brings them there. He doth not *send*, but *bring* them, *allure* them into the Wilderness. *When he putteth forth his own Sheep, he goeth before them, and they follow Him*; because they *know* his sweet, alluring *Voice*.

IV. That when God's People are in the Wilderness, *Himself* is *with* them there. He doth not *leave* nor *forsake* them, but *dwells in the Midst of the Bush*, when it is *all on Fire*, to keep it from being *consumed*.

V. That the Lord will do his People *good by Affliction*; he will *speak comfortably* to them *in it*, and give them *Advantage by it*: He will give them their *Vineyards* from a barren Wilderness while they are in it, and the *Valley of Achor*, of Trouble, for a *Door of Hope* out of it.

VI. That all the Afflictions of God's People while in the Wilderness, are well *known* to him, and taken *Notice* of by him: He *knows* their Sorrows, and *hears* their Groanings.

VII. That as certainly as the Lord appears to his People by the Name of *God Almighty*, to encourage their Faith and Hope in his Promise; so surely will he be known unto them, when the Time of the Promise comes on, by his Name JEHOVAH, as a *Covenant-keeping, Promise-fulfilling* GOD. As the great I AM, that is unchangeably the *same*, of *one Mind*, and infinitely *strong* in performing what he hath spoken. And,

VIII. That when the Time of the Promise draws nigh, God is never at a Loss for *Instruments*, for *Ways* and *Means* to fulfil his Word. He will raise up some *Moses* or other, and say unto him, *Come now, and I will send Thee to my People*, to bring them out of their present Misery and Confinement, unto that Glory and Enlargement which I have promis'd them.

From all these Things I was instructed and comforted, enabled to hope in God, and wait for him, for promis'd and desir'd *Usefulness*. And in the general, I was helpt to *rejoyce* in the *Lord*, and to be *fearless* of *Tribulation*; since the God of my Salvation would be *with* me in it, and *deliver me* from it. *Bless the* LORD, *O my soul, for his Goodness in preparing thee for Trials! And if he brings thee into the Valley of the Shadow of Death; Fear no Evil, since He is with thee, and will bring thee thence, into the Light of Life.*

Dec. 6, 1741. My Soul was much drawn out in the Morning, in seeking the Lord, "That he would have *Mercy on me*, with respect to *Usefulness*." And immediately I receiv'd a Letter from a Friend that gave me a delightful Account, That the Lord had made me of *Use* to comfort and strengthen *his*

Soul. I receiv'd it as an *Answer of Prayer*; and saw how particularly the Lord had answer'd some of my Cries. My Heart was melted, humbled, and fill'd with Joy and Wonder. I fell down before the Lord, lov'd, ador'd, and prais'd him as I could. *Glory be to his Name for this Mercy!*

In the Evening I lov'd and bless'd the Lord *again*, for the Mercy receiv'd; and pray'd him to let me *serve him more abundantly*. I *long'd*, I *thirsted*, and was ready to *faint* to serve him. I had a very great *Sense* of my own *Sinfulness*, and *Unworthiness* of the Mercy; and I intreated my dear *Lord Jesus*, "That he would not be *angry*, that such a *vile Sinner*, asked such an *Abundance of Grace!*" I told him, "That if his Grace was not *infinite*, I *could not, durst not ask*. But since it was *boundless*, without *Limits*, and I so very *thirsty* and *needy*; I pray'd him not to send me away *empty*." And instantly that Word came in, with a Soul satisfying Sweetness, Thou *shalt be* filled, *Matt*. v. 6. *Thou*, notwithstanding thy Vileness, thy great Wants, and vast Desires, shalt be *Filled*. I took it as my *Lord's Bond: Believ'd* his *Grace*, that I should be *satisfy'd* with his *Goodness*; and sweetly entred into *Rest*.

In the Night Season, I was *very thirsty again*, and *long'd exceedingly* to *serve* my dear *Lord Jesus*, in *feeding his Sheep and Lambs*. Upon which a Question was started in my Soul: "Thou art so exceedingly *desirous* to *serve the Lord; What* hast thou to serve him *with? See*, What hast thou *got?* What canst thou *do* for him? At this I was somewhat *abashed*.

But the *Loaves* and *Fishes* came into my Mind; when the Lord had Compassion on the Multitude, design'd to feed them, and said to his Disciples, *How many Loaves have ye? Bring them hither unto me*. Mark vi. 38. Matt. xiv. 18. The Disciples were for *sending the Multitude away*, knowing they had but *five Loaves and two Fishes*: Nothing, in Comparison, to feed them. But our Lord *blest*, and *brake*, gave them to the *Disciples*, and the Disciples to the *Multitude; and they did all eat and were filled; five Thousand Men, beside Women and Children, and twelve Baskets full of Fragments were taken up*. This was a great Encouragement to my Faith. I thought, "I had *three Books*, (my last *Three*, which came out together, my Mind was upon) and tho' I had *but* Three; yet the *Lord Jesus* could feed *three Thousand* thereby, if I brought them unto *Him*." The *Woman* also that had the *bloody Issue* that *touch'd the Hem*, of the *Lord's Garment* for healing; upon which he said, *Virtue is gone out of me*, Luke viii. 46. dropt upon my Mind, and I was much encourag'd from hence. That if, I prest thro' the *Crowd*, and *touch'd* the *Hem* of my *Lord's Garment*, *Virtue* should come *out of him*. Which I was *enabled to do*. I came to *Christ* with my *three Books*, and laid hold by *Faith*, on his compleat *Righteousness*, for free Forgiveness, and full Justification, for Blessings, even the *Blessing* of *Abraham*, to come down upon *me*, particularly that Part of it: *Thou shalt be a Blessing*. I *believed* on my dear *Lord Jesus*, for a *Blessing* to come down upon *me*, and my *poor Books*, for the *feeding of Thousands*; that I by *them*, might be a *Blessing* to *Thousands* of his Children. Then these Words came in: *And he that sat upon the Throne, said,—It is done*, Rev. xxi. 5, 6. They entered my Heart, in the Majesty and Glory of GOD, as a *Royal Grant* from the *Prince of Grace* on his Throne, of that *great Request*, which *I*, a vile *Sinner*, had asked; and abundantly *satisfy'd* my Soul. Now I had *enough*. From *this*, and the other Promise in the Evening, (*Thou shall be filled*: And, *It is Done!*) my Desires were sweetly *satisfy'd*. Oh, *my Lord*, herein and hereby, *spake like Himself!* I *knew* his *Voice, ador'd* his *Grace, admir'd and believ'd* his *Word*.

But as I was not instantly melted into Tears of Joy, as at some Seasons, I was tempted to question whether it was the *Lord*, that spake to me. But I believ'd his *Word*; and had a humbling Sense of my *Hardness of Heart*, and of his *boundless Grace* to such a *vile Wretch!* I thought the God of all Grace, might well be said to be *Good and Kind, to the Evil and Unthankful*. Not that I was *altogether* unthankful: My Soul lifted up itself with all the Strength it had, to thank and bless the Lord for his Kindness. But because I was not so much *melted*, nor raised in *Praise*, as I would or should, I had a deep Sense of my *Unthankfulness* for such *great Grace*.

Then these Words came in, *I will be merciful to their Unrighteousness, and their Sins and their Iniquities I will remember no more*, Heb. x. 12. *Then shall ye remember your own evil Ways, and your Doings which were not good, and shall loath yourselves in your own Sight,—When I am pacify'd towards thee for all that thou hast done*, Ezek. xvi. 63. and xxxvi. 31. These *melted* me into *Tears*. Then these came in: *Behold the Bridegroom cometh*, Matt. xxv. 6. *The Voice of my Beloved! behold, he cometh, leaping upon the Mountains, skipping upon the Hills*, Song ii. 8. Oh, *these* melted my Soul down, and fill'd me with Wonder, Love and Joy. I was persuaded, That my Lord was *coming*, and as a *Bridegroom*; that having lov'd and wash'd me from my Sins in his own Blood, he came leaping over those Mountains, and skipping upon the Hills in his *mighty Love*, to *marry me to Himself*, to hold Communion with me as his *Bride*. But Oh, how I *blush'd* at my own Blackness, *admir'd* his Love, and *ador'd* his Grace to such a vile

Sinner! And greatly my Soul long'd, in all holy Conversation and Godliness, to go forth to *meet* the Bridegroom.—*Bless the* LORD, *O my Soul, for this Visit; and wait to see which Way the Bridegroom cometh, what Speed he will make, and what great Things his great Love will do for thee! For verily there shall be a Performance of those Things which have been told thee from the Lord.*

Dec. 7, 1741. As soon as I rose, that Word dropt sweetly on my Heart, *God having raised up his Son Jesus, sent him to bless you, in turning away every one of you from his Iniquities,* Acts iii. 26. It was first sweetly apply'd to my own Soul. I was taught from it, 1. That the Grace or Kingdom of God in the Soul, consisted in turning it away from its *Iniquities.* And, 2. That the Soul's *Turn* from Iniquity, was a *Blessing,* God's Blessing to it thro' his Son *Jesus,* the sent *Saviour.* It was very sweet to *me,* That God should send his *Son Jesus,* to *bless me,* with the *Forgiveness* of Sins, and under pardoning Grace, with a saving *Turn* from *Sin* unto *God:* In the Enjoyment, and Service of Whom, all Happiness consisteth.—And the Word bearing in upon my Mind with a more than *ordinary* Power; I thought, Surely there was something *extraordinary* at Hand. And presently my Thoughts were turn'd to *others,* thus: "Who knows but God is about, even this Day, to bless some Souls in turning them from their Iniquities, thro' his Sent Son Jesus, by me as an Instrument, in Something of mine, that is either wrote, or printed?"

And this Impression increas'd upon me: *That So it was.* And these Words came in, *Thus shall it be done to the Man whom the King* (the King of Grace and Glory, as it was apply'd to *me*) *delighteth to honour,* Esth. vi. 11. *Since thou wast precious in my Sight, thou hast been honourable, and I have loved thee: therefore will I give Men for thee, and People for thy Life,* Isa. xliii. 4. (Give the [*sic*; r. thee] *Souls,* for thy Life of Joy) *Rise,* Peter; *kill and eat,* Acts x. 13. (By which, the Refreshment *Peter's* Soul should have, in the Conversion of the *Gentiles* by his Ministry, was intended: And what I should have in the Conversion of some *Souls,* was intimated to *Me*) *Lo, this* is *our God, we have waited for Him, and He will save us: this is the* LORD, *we have waited for Him, we will be glad and rejoice in his Salvation,* Isa. xxv. 9.

These *humbled* my Soul before the *Lord,* and *adoring* his *Grace,* I was for *bewailing* my own *Wretchedness.* But the Lord called me to *Rejoyce,* and to rejoyce with *Him.* And that Word dropt on my Mind, *Sing unto the* LORD *a new Song, for he hath done marvellous Things: his Right Hand, and his Holy Arm hath gotten Him the Victory*, Psa. xcviii. 1. Then I attempted my Duty, ador'd and prais'd the Lord the King; and pray'd him, "That if he had this Day gotten himself the Victory in any Sinners Hearts, by so vile a Worm; that Himself would take all the Glory: That he would Ride on prosperously in the Majesty of his Grace; and enable me to give him the Glory due to his Name." I rejoyced in and with him, and prais'd him as I could: And especially rejoyced in the Prospects of that Day, when I should praise him perfectly, and eternally. I sung the xcviii Psalm, the two last Verses of the cxiii, and the cxlvi. under gracious Influences of the Holy Ghost: And an Heart-Melting Intimation, That I should have a *New Song put into my Mouth*: Such an One, for the Conversion of Souls, as I never had yet. That the Lord would make me, tho' a poor *Barren* Creature, to *keep House*, and be a *Joyful Mother of Children*. That tho' *poor and needy*, he would thus lift me from the *Dust*, and out of the *Dunghil*, to *set me among the Princes of his People*. And that I had the *God of* Jacob *for my Help: Who made Heaven, Earth and Sea; which keepeth Truth for ever: which executeth Judgment for the Oppressed, which giveth Food to the Hungry.* And greatly I rejoyced, that the LORD *Looseth the Prisoners, Openeth the Eyes of the Blind, Raised them that are bowed down, Loveth the Righteous, saveth Strangers, Fatherless and Widow*: And shall *Reign for Ever, as My*, as *Sion's God—Praise the* LORD, *O my Soul! And remember* this Day. *Perhaps thou mayst hear of God's Loving Kindness towards thee hereon, even in this World. But if not, expect it in that to come. And adoring thy Lord's Grace, walk humbly, and thankfully before him all the Days of thy Life, until thou shalt praise* him *in the Heights. And let Sin be the abominable Thing which thy Soul hateth. Remember what high Obligations, Boundless Love, has laid thee under! God hath not dealt with many, as he hath dealt with Thee! Dissolve, O my saved Soul, under the Heart Melting Influence of God's Love! Of that Love which has saved thee again and again: sav'd thee in various Ways; and sav'd thee from such Depths of Misery, to such Heights of Glory! Praised be the* LORD's *great and glorious Name for Ever. And let the whole Earth be filled with his Glory!* Amen, *and* Amen!*

---

*The Reader is desir'd to take Notice, that the Account given in the last Paragraph, I took down as Matter of *Experience*, for a Memorandum of *that Day*, not knowing but in this World, I might hear of the Lord's Goodness, in converting some Soul, by something I had written, even on *that very Day*.—But as I hadn't yet

Dec. 10, 1741. This Morning, soon after I awak'd, I had a painful *Feeling* of the Working of *Sin* in my Soul, an humbling *Sense* of the God-provoking *Nature* thereof, and a delightful *View* of GOD's boundless *Love*, thro' a crucify'd JESUS, in its *infinite Overflowings* and *glorious Triumphs* over all my *Sins*. Quickly after, this Word came into my Mind, *Whereby are given unto us exceeding great and precious Promises; that by these you might be Partakers of the Divine Nature*, 2 Pet. i. 4. It was *sweet* to my Soul; tho' I thought I understood but little of the *Grace of it*. But thus much I conceiv'd of it. That by the exceeding great and precious *Promises* of God to his People, and especially *That, I will be to them a God*: They were made Partakers of the *Divine Nature*. 1. In that they are made Partakers of the *Holy Ghost*; in that *He*, the *Third Person* in God, who is GOD by *Nature*, who hath all the Essential Glories of the *Godhead* in him, *Personally* dwells

---

heard of this, I was in doubt about inserting it in this *Third Part* of my Printed Account; lest any should think I pretended to a *Spirit of Prophecy*, or immediate and infallible *Inspiration*. Any yet I was loth to omit it; not knowing but its *Publication*, might be the *Means* of my hearing of the Lord's Appearance on that Day; if this little Piece should fall into the Hands of any Person that the Lord hath wrought upon by any of my poor Writings at that Time, who might be thence induced, for the Glory of God and my Joy, to *acquaint me therewith*.—And as one of the Children which God hath given me by what he hath enabled me to write, informs me upon my Enquiry, that her first being bro't to venture upon Christ for Salvation was about *that Time*, tho' She can't tell the *Day* precisely; I think it best to insert *her Account*: As from thence it seems probable to me that her Conversion might be on *that very Day*, tho' She can't exactly *remember it*. She writes thus:

"As to what you desire me to tell you, when I was first enabled to *believe*, from *reading of your Book of Letters*, I cannot be exact to a *Day*. But I believe it was about *that Time*. At that Time I was in *Great Distress*, as I had been for above a Year: And often, in *Reading*, when I was ready to give *all up*, I then felt a *Power to believe in Christ*, and *cast myself upon him* as a *perishing Sinner*: From what *Encouragement* you give to *such*."

N.B.: This Book of Letters, was my First Vol. And one of those *Three Books* that came out together: By which the Lord told me, that I should take *some Souls for Him*, as a *Prey*, out of the Hands of Sin and Satan. And this Friend's being bro't to *believe in Christ thereby*, at a *Time*, as She said in another Letter, when She *tho't that there was no Mercy for her*: May serve as a Confirmation in *Providence*, that the Encouragement given me concerning these Books by the *Promise*, was *indeed from the* LORD.

in *them*. 2. In that, by the indwelling Presence of the *Spirit* in the Saints, the GOD of all Grace and Glory, dwells in *Them*: or, That the *Father* and the Son, dwell in the Saints by the *Spirit*, and manifest the Glories of the *Godhead* in their *Souls*. And 3. In that, while the Three-One GOD *dwell* in the Saints, and *display* the Glories of the Divine Nature in their Souls by the Spirit, *They* are *changed* into the same *Image*: Or, have the moral, communicable Perfections of God, stampt upon their Souls. Which gives them a begun *Fitness* to enjoy and glorify God, or to live delightfully, and obedientially, under the rich, replenishing Influence, the sweet, enkindling Beams of Divine Glory: of all the boundless Perfections and infinite Glories of the *Godhead*, casting their Rays thro' *Christ* upon the *Saints*, in Grace and Providence, all manner of Ways. This in general I apprehended by the Saints being said to be made Partakers of the *Divine Nature*. And that they might particularly be said to be *Partakers* hereof, in that, *they*, with *Christ*, in *their* Measure, *partake* of the same *Spirit*, with which *He* is immeasureably *filled*: And as Heirs of GOD, and Joint-Heirs with CHRIST, have a joint *Participation* with *Him*, of this Glorious INHERITANCE. And therefore the *Promises*, the Grants, the Settlements of Grace, by which they are made Partakers of such great, such excellent Glory, must needs be *exceeding Great and Precious!*

And by this word, *Whereby* are given unto us—my Thoughts were led back to the preceding Verse. And I saw it related unto his *Divine Power*; and was to be understood *Thus*: That God by his Divine Power had given unto us exceeding great and precious Promises; that by these we might be Partakers of the Divine Nature. Upon which I was somewhat at a Loss to see, *How* the Promises were given by *Divine Power*. "The *Promises*, thought I, are surely rather, The Gift of *Divine Grace*, than of Power."

Quickly after, The Lord sweetly shew'd me, That it was the *Power of his Grace*, that was intended thereby. And that therefore, when he made known his Ways of Grace to *Moses*, and made all his Goodness, in the Wonders of his Love, to pass before him, he proclaim'd his Name, as *The* LORD, *the* LORD *God*: JEHOVAH, JEHOVAH ELL: *The Strong God: Merciful and Gracious, Long-suffering, and abundant in Goodness and Truth*, Exod. xxxiv. 6, &c. JEHOVAH, JEHOVAH *the Strong* GOD: This the Lord sets *first*, before *Merciful and Gracious*, &c. To shew, That it is as the *Strong* GOD, from the *infinite Strength*, of the Love, Mercy and Grace of his own *Nature*, that all the *Promises* and *Declarations* of his Mercy and Grace, are made, and performed, to the most unworthy, miserable and provoking *Sinners*.

And so *Moses understood it*. And therefore when pleading with God that he would pardon his sinful, provoking People *Israel*, he puts in Mind of his Power: *And now, I beseech thee*, says he, *let the Power of my Lord be great, according as thou hast spoken, saying, The* LORD *is Long-Suffering, and of great Mercy, forgiving Iniquity, and Transgression:—Pardon, I beseech thee, the Iniquity of this People, according to the Greatness of thy Mercy,—* Num. xiv. 17, 18, 19. He pleads the Greatness of God's *Power*, that it might be extended, manifested, shewn forth in the Greatness of his Pardoning *Mercy*: or, for *great Pardon* to be extended, according to the *great Power* of his *Mercy*.

But Oh, how *glad* was *I*, to see the exceeding great and *precious Promises of God, all given by his Divine-Power, the Infinite Power* of his Grace, that so by *These*, as *thus* given, I might be made a *Partaker* of the *Divine Nature! Here* I saw all the *Promises* stand *secure*, firm and stable, in the Infinite *Strength* of that *Grace*, which gave them. And what a firm Foundation was laid herein, for my Faith and Hope to *rest on*, and expect all Promis'd *Grace*, and particularly with respect to my *Usefulness*, notwithstanding all my Unworthiness and Provocations: Since the *Grace of the Promise*, had the Infinite *Strength of Jehovah* in it; was *given*, and should be *performed*, by the Infinite *Strength* of his Invincible, Irresistible, and All-Conquering *Grace!* Oh *This* suited *Me*, such a wretched Sinner, well! How did it *humble*, and *delight me*, to see, That God could *love* whom he *would*, and be *gracious* to whom he *would!* That all his Love, Mercy, Long-suffering, and abundant Goodness, had the *Infinite Strength* of the GOD-HEAD in them.

And as I saw I could *understand* but *little*, what it was to be *made a Partaker of the Divine Nature*; a Motion was made in my Soul, "To ask the Lord to give me an experimental *Knowledge* thereof, a *Taste of it, a Feeling Possession of Himself*." Which I did. And blessed be his Name, while I was speaking, He heard.

While I was adoring *God*, and the Infinite Strength of his *Grace* in the *Promise*, thro' his crucify'd *Son*; casting Myself *upon it*, and praying to be dealt with according *to it*, and particularly with respect to *Usefulness*; and that I might have *Himself*, his *Love*, his *Heart* therein: The Lord drew *very near* my Spirit, and said, "Thou *hast* ME. *It is done*, "*Thus shall it be done to the Man whom the King delighteth to honour*."—But Oh, how I was *humbled* under my own Vileness, *bewail'd* my Wretchedness, and *ador'd* his Grace, That not only granted my *Requests*, and *honour'd* me, but *delighted* to honour *Me*, the *vilest of Sinners!* I saw, That it was every Way like *Himself*, JEHOVAH ELL, the *Strong* GOD, *Merciful and Gracious!* Oh how I *hated Sin*, and *pray'd* for its *Destruction! Long'd* to see *my God at Home*, as He *is*, and to love and serve him *perfectly!* I *ador'd his Grace*, and tho' I could not *praise him* according to his *excellent Greatness*, I offered up a *Mite*, all my *Soul* could give, in the *Name of Jesus*. And I prayed him for *his Sake*, to be *Gracious to me*. Then this came in, *The Father Himself loveth you*. And under the sweet Influence of *his Love*, I *lov'd him* again, I hated *Sin*, and lothed *myself* because of it. My Heart made a *Noise* within me as it were, because of my Unkindness and base Ingratitude to the *God of Love!* And I pray'd him "To *pardon* and *subdue* mine Iniquities, and to love me into *Likeness* to him, and *Fitness* for his Service, and every Way display his *Grace* towards me, for the *Glory* of *his own Name*." Then he said, *Be still:—I am thy* GOD. By which he spoke to me *all the Grace* that I wanted, and laid me to *Rest* in his *own Bosom*. Then that Word delighted me, *He bringeth out their Host by Number: He calleth them all by Names, by the Greatness of his Might, for that he is strong in Power, not One faileth*, Isa. xl. 26. I saw, That as he brought out the Stars by Number, called them all by Names, and kept them from *failing* in their *Course*, by the *Greatness* of his *Might*, as the *God of Nature*; so he bringeth out the Host of his *People*, calleth them all by *Names*, and keeps them from *failing* in their *Course*, in that *Work*, that *Sphere* he had allotted them, by the *Almightiness* of his *Grace*; and that Thus he would deal with *Me.—Oh, What shall I render to the LORD for all his Benefits! My Soul, Trust thou in the LORD, and wait on Thy GOD continually! Surely thou hast nothing else to do, but, in all holy Obedience, to love and adore the God of Love! Let this be thy Life Below; till that which is in part is done away, and swallow'd up of perfect Love, and Endless Life Above! Lord Jesus, say* Amen.

Oct. 18, 1742. Having sought the Lord, I began to write my *Letter to the believing Negroes*: But it was suggested to my Mind: "That the Lord had not *sent me* about that Work."—Upon which, my Heart being much drawn out towards them, I sought the Lord again: "That if He had any Thing to send to those his Children by *Me*, He would signify his Mind, and give me a Message." And the Lord was graciously pleased to say: *Go,—and I will be with thy Mouth*, Exod. iv. 12. And, *The Companions hearken to thy Voice: cause Me to hear*, (or as Mr *Durham* renders the Word, and as it was brought to me, cause ME to be *Heard*) Song viii. 13. By which Words the

Lord *encourag'd* me to engage in the Work, *satisfy'd* me of his Presence with me therein, and informed me what I should say; That *Himself* should be the *Subject* of my Discourse, that I should cause *Him* to be *Heard*. And blessed be his Name, He carried me comfortably through it.

But when I was got towards the Close, my Bowels yearn'd towards the poor *Negroes* that were yet in *Unbelief*; and I know not how to wind up, without saying somewhat to *Them*. But here again I was told: "That I was not *call'd to it*, that it would be in *vain* to say any Thing, and that I had better leave *them* quite out."—But that Word, in seeking the Lord, was some Encouragement to me: *That he that ploweth should plow in Hope, and that he that thresheth in Hope, should be Partaker of his Hope*, 1 Cor. ix. 10. Upon which I engaged in the Work.

But not finding that Liberty therein which my Soul desired, I was again tempted to leave that Part out of the Letter. Upon which I sought the Lord again to know his Mind. And as in the former Part I was *enlarged* beyond my Expectation, and much *straitned* in the latter; I brought the *Whole* before the Lord, and *shew'd Him the Work*: And ask'd Him to tell me, "If He would have me send it in *Writing*, to those few Persons which I had in my Eye when I first began, or in *Print*, that it might be useful to *others*, with *them*: And also, If He would have the *last Part* left *out*, or the *Whole sent*."—And while I blessed the Lord, for the Assistance of his Spirit, wherein I was enlarg'd, and humbled myself before Him, wherein I was straitned: He was graciously pleas'd to *accept the Whole*, and particularly satisfy'd me about *that Part*, whereof I was in *Doubt*. These Words were apply'd with Power and Sweetness to my Soul: *He that goeth forth and weepeth* (by which the last Part was particularly glanc'd at) Psal. *bearing precious Seed, shall doubtless come again rejoicing, bringing his Sheaves with him*. cxxvi. 6. *God hath chosen Things which are not, to bring to nought Things which are: That no Flesh should glory in his Presence*, 1 Cor. i. 28, 29. *There is none like* That, *give it* ME, 1. Sam. xxi. 9.—This filled me with *Wonder* at infinite *Condescension*, that the great GOD, should *regard* the weak Attempts of his feeble Worm to serve Him; and call for his *own Word*, wrapp'd up as it were in my *Weakness*, as his *chosen Sword*, to be given into his *Almighty Hand*, to fight his Battles and gain his Victories.

Then this Word came in: *The Lord hath* Need *of him*, Luke xix. 34. That is, of the *Whole* of this my weak Service in *Print*, as it was then apply'd to *me*. Then follow'd, *Rejoice greatly, O Daughter of Zion; shout, O Daughter of Jerusalem: Behold, thy King cometh unto thee: He is just, and having Salvation, lowly, and riding upon an Ass, and upon a Colt the Foal of an Ass*, Zech. ix. 9. Oh this abundant *Grace*, this *Lowliness*, this infinite *Condescension* of *Zion's* King, That he should say, He had *Need* of my weak Service, and would *Ride* thereon in the Triumphs of his Love, bringing Salvation to his People! It melted me, Humbled me in the Dust, and raised me into Love, Joy, and Thankfulness.

Then these Words came in, to raise my Wonder and Adoration, *Will God in very Deed dwell with Men on Earth? behold Heaven, and the Heaven of Heavens cannot contain Thee; how much less this House which I have built?* 2 Chron. vi. 18.—*O Thou that inhabitest the Praises of* Israel, Psal. xxii. 3.—Oh, thought I, "It was infinite Condescension in the great JEHOVAH, to dwell in that *magnificent Temple* which *Solomon* built; but how much more is it *so*, that He should dwell in my *feeble Praises!* Will GOD in *very Deed* dwell with *Me*, in my weak Praises, as in his *House*, displaying his *Glories* there," Then my Heart was struck with a delightful Sense of the *Love of God* towards me herein; and sweetly it was shed abroad in my *Heart* by the *Holy Ghost*, in that Word, *And the* LORD *had* Respect *unto* Abel, *and to his* Offering, Gen. iv. 4. Oh, I saw, That *Christ loved me*; and that in Love to my *Person*, He accepted my Offering, my Service, my feeble Work! And *much* it affected my Soul, that my Dear Lord *Jesus* should thus *acquaint me* with his Grace; and *strongly* my Heart was attracted to *love Him* again, to Love *Himself*, and his *Work*, his *People*, &c. for *his Sake*.—Then I wanted to know the *Father's* Mind concerning me, and my present Service; and sweetly *his Love* flow'd in upon my Heart, from these Words: *The Son can do nothing of Himself, but what He seeth the* Father *do*, Joh. v. 19. And, *The* Father *Himself* loveth *you*, Chap. xvi. 27. And then the *Love* of the *Spirit* likewise, was let in upon my Soul, from *These Three are One*, 1 Joh. v. 7. Oh the Love of the *Three-One* GOD, which I then beheld! I saw, That the *Father* lov'd me in Christ, that *Christ* lov'd me from the Father, and the *Spirit* from both. And that *God in Christ* was *Well-pleased* with my *Person*, and *accepted* my *Service!* And that it was the *Mind* of the *Three-One* GOD, to be *Gracious* to me therein! Oh the sweet, Soul satisfying, Heart-melting Fellowship, which I then had with *God in Love!* My Soul was humbled before the LORD, for all my Unkindness, Ingratitude, and base Selfishness; enlarg'd to praise and adore Him as the God of Glory, the God of all Grace in Christ; and long'd to be at Home, that I might love, adore, and praise Him, perfectly and for ever! Oh surely, This was a *Foretaste of Heaven*, an *Earnest* of *that Bliss!* Then these Words came in, in the *Majesty of* JEHOVAH: *The* GOD *of Glory thundreth*, Psal. xxix. 3. *He maketh Lightnings with Rain, and bringeth forth the Wind out of his Treasures*, Jer. x. 13. *He stood and measured the Earth: He beheld,— and the everlasting Mountains were scattered, the perpetual Hills did bow*, Hab. iii. 6. *The Sea saw [it] and fled, and* Jordan *was driven back. The Mountains skipped like Rams, and the little Hills like Lambs. What ailed thee, O [thou] Sea, that thou fleddest? Thou* Jordan, *that thou wast driven back? Ye Mountains, that ye skipped like Rams; and ye little Hills like Lambs?* Psal. cxiv. 3, 4, 5, 6. By These I had a sweet *Intimation*, and conceiv'd a delightful *Hope*, That GOD would display *his Glory*, by and through *my feeble Work*: That He would *thunder* from *Sinai's* Mount upon secure Sinners; and make *Lightnings* with *Rain*, enlighten their Minds in the Knowledge of CHRIST, and refresh their Souls with the Showers of his Grace; and bring forth the *Wind* of his *Spirit* out of his upon Dry-boned Sinners *Treasures*, unto their Conviction and Consolation, their Life and Joy. And that He would do this as the GOD *of Glory*: with such a *Majesty*, that every Way becomes his *Great* BEING! And that all *Opposition* should *flee* before Him! That the *Sea* of Nature-Corruption, should *see* Him, and *flee*, and the over-flowing *Rivers* thereof, and be *driven back*. That the *Hearts* of *Sinners*, firm as *Mountains* in their Opposition to God, should *bow*, shake, and tremble, and skip like *Rams* and *Lambs* at the *Presence* of the LORD, this LORD of GLORY!—Upon this, my Soul ador'd the *Majesty* of JEHOVAH, and my Heart made *Melody* to Him with Thanksgivings for all his Grace: In that Word, which was precious to me, *He exalteth the Horn of his People, the Praise of all his Saints, even of the Children of Israel, a People near unto Him. Praise ye the* LORD. And also, this Verse, which came sweetly into my Mind, tun'd my Heart to the Musick of Praise:

> Ye People, Bless the LORD,
> And lift his Glory high:
> Your Praise in Songs record;
> For GOD is ever Nigh!

Oh my Soul, remember the Kindness of thy GOD to thee at this Time: how He accepted thy feeble Work, and gave thee sweet Intimations of his using it. And though, weak as it was, thou thoughtest again and again, Surely the LORD *hath not Chosen This; Surely He will not Work by This:' Yet encourag'd by Him, Wait thou upon Him, to see how his own Arm will bring Salvation, to the eternal Glory of his Power, in thy Weakness! And, Lord, let it be unto thy Worm, according to thy Word!* Amen.

Feb. 9, 1742-3. My *Second Volume of Letters* was put to the Press. Before I began, the last Summer, to take the Copies of these Letters, I thought to take no more; not seeing which Way to dispose of the Books. But having wrote a pretty many Letters to be sent to my Friends at one Time, I found my Heart inclin'd to take the Copies of them. But yet, as I had no Prospect of *Printing them*, I was under a prevailing *Unwillingness* to engage in the Work. And was for arguing it with the Lord, and telling Him, "That I would gladly go about the Work, if it might be for *His Glory*: But I fear'd it would be *Labour in vain.*"—Then He said unto me, *What is that to Thee? Follow thou me,* Joh. xxi. 22. By which the Lord kindly rebuk'd me, instructed me into my Duty, and sweetly drew me to engage in the Work, at *his Bidding*; and to leave it entirely to his *sovereign Dispose*, to do what *He pleased* with it. And as soon as *I* was made willing to go about the Work, He said, for my Encouragement therein, "Did ever any trust in God and were confounded?" *Thou hast ravish'd my Heart my Sister, my Spouse,* Song iv. 9. And, *The Lord hath need of them,* Mat. xxi. 3. Then joyfully I took those Copies, and presented them to the LORD. And sweetly has He drawn me to, and carried me thro' the Work, in taking the rest of the Copies, to compleat this *Volume.* And lo, as soon as it was finish'd, my gracious God, in his kind Providence, call'd for its *Publication.—Learn, O my Soul, To obey the Lord, whenever He calls thee forth into any Piece of Service for Him; altho', like Abraham, thou should'st go out, not knowing whither thou goest: For a goodly Heritage will thy Lord give thee!*—I come now to give some Hints of,

Secondly, The *Answer* of my Desire and Prayer, in the Lord's sending some of my *Books* into *America*: To my *Furtherance and Joy of Faith.*

And as the Lord wrought great Desires in my Soul, and enabled me to put up earnest Supplications, that some of my poor Books might be sent into that Part of his Earth: (As I have already said, in my Note, *Aug.* 19, 1741.) And also gave me to hope in his Word, That the *Lion of the Tribe of* Judah, had *prevailed to open the seven-sealed Book*; that *Christ* had *prevailed*, and would *prevail*, to open for me his Father's *Purpose*, in Relation thereto, in Providence, (As *Oct.* 29): So, when the *Time of the Promise drew nigh*; my dear *Husband*, having Thoughts of going into *America* on another Account, which he judg'd to be a Call of Providence, He resolv'd to print and take many of *my Books with him.* Did ever any *seek the* LORD in *vain? Trust in* GOD, and were *confounded?* Or *wait for* HIM, and were *ashamed?* No; All the Lord's Suppliants, his Dependents and Expectants, shall say, *Lo, this is our* GOD, *we have waited for Him, and* HE *will* save us: *this is the* LORD, *we have waited for Him, we will be glad and rejoice in his* Salvation!

And as when my *Second* Volume of Letters, last mention'd, was to be printed; and other of my Books soon to follow, which were to be sent into *America*; I had some *Fears* of the Difficulties, Dangers, and Trials, that might attend their Publication: I thence sought the Lord, to give me some Encouragement from Himself about them, and as to this Book in particular, that was just *then* coming out. And He was pleas'd to say to me, *Fear not ye;—for ye seek* JESUS, Mat. xxviii. 5. This gave me sweet *Peace* in attempting the *Work*, and strengthened me to hope for a *good Event.* I was also further encouraged from this Word, *For the Merchandize of Wisdom is better than the Merchandize of Silver, and the Gain thereof than fine Gold*, Prov. iii. 14. From hence I was taught, That it was my Duty to *venture out*, in *this Work for* GOD, in the Face of all Dangers and Difficulties that might attend; in Hope of that *Gain* in the Glory of God, and the Good of his People, which my Soul desir'd; and which is so far superior to *that*, for which this World's *Merchants* run such *Hazards*, and make such *large Adventures.* And by this Word also, the Lord strengthned and encourag'd me: *He that goeth forth and weepeth, bearing precious Seed, shall doubtless come again with Rejoicing, bringing his Sheaves with him,* Psal. cxxvi. 6.—*Oh my Soul, Be thou like the* Husbandman! *Go forth in thy Work for God, to comfort and exhort thy Brethren by the Word of the Lord, in the Face of Storms: For, bearing precious Seed, thou shalt come again with Rejoicing, bringing thy Sheaves with thee. Thou shalt find a rich Account of thy Seeds Time Labours, in the blessed Fruit thereof, to thy own and others Joy in this World, and an Harvest of endless Glory, in that to come! Prosper thou, O* LORD, *this Work of my Hands!*

April 29, 1743. The last Week, My Pamphlet, *A brief Account of the gracious Dealings of GOD with a poor, sinful, unworthy Creature, Relating to the Work of Grace on the Heart, in a saving Conversion to* CHRIST, &c. Part I. was put to the Press. As was soon after the IId Part. I had much Work, much Writing, &c. upon Hand the last Week; by which I was in some Sort diverted from that particular *Seeking of the Lord*, for some Intimation of his Mind, about the Publication of this little Tract, which I had been wont to observe with respect to my others already published. And as soon as I had finish'd the Work of the former Part of this Week, and my Mind was a little unbended from it; this Thought was darted in: "That I had not *sought God*, about the Publication of this little Piece." Which laid me under Guilt for my Neglect, Concern for that Dishonour which I had done to God thereby, and Discouragement, lest it should be useless. Not that I did not seek God at *all*; for in a more *general Way*, I did. I ask'd his Direction about it, and his Blessing upon it, and dedicated it to Him. But thro' Hurry, I did not so *particularly* seek Him, as I ought to have done, I went, as to its Publication, upon a more *general Persuasion*, that it was *God's Mind* it should come *out*. Which arose from that sweet Encouragement which He gave me at first to write it, and also from that which I receiv'd, when I sought the Lord about the Publication of my last *Book of Letters*. For, as I said, it was not *that Book* only, but all the *other* which were design'd to be brought out, and dispos'd of with it, that I had in my *Thoughts*, when I was under some *Fears*, as to the *Difficulties* which might attend their *Publication*, sought the *Lord* about it, and receiv'd gracious Encouragement from *Him*, to proceed in the *Work*, and *trust* the same with Him. But not having sought God, nor receiv'd any Intimation from Him, about this little Piece in *particular*; I humbled my Soul before Him, confest and bewailed my Sin, and pray'd Him to tell me something of his Mind.

And while I was before Him, He instantly and sweetly, broke in upon my Heart with this Word: *Thou art my Servant,—in whom I will be glorified*, Isa. xlix. 3. By which he testify'd his gracious *Acceptance* of my feeble Work, and Design to *use it*; that He would account Himself *glorify'd*, and get Himself *Glory* thereby. And sweetly this Grace melted my Heart, humbled me in the Dust before Him, and rais'd up my Soul to praise and bless Him. And I admir'd his forgiving Love, and said, with the Prophet, *Who is a* GOD *like unto Thee, that pardoneth Iniquity, and passeth by the Transgression of the Remnant of his Heritage? He retaineth not his Anger for ever, because He delighteth in Mercy!* And these Words also brake in, with Power and great Glory: *And the Woman fled into the Wilderness, where she hath a Place prepared of God, that they should nourish her there. And to the Woman were given two Wings of a great Eagle, that she might fly into her Place:—where she is nourished—from the Face of the Serpent*, Rev. xii. 6, 14. From which the Lord gave me a sweet Hint, *Where* my poor Books were to be *us'd*, even in the *American* Wilderness; that there I had a *Place* prepared of God, *Father, Son* and *Spirit*; that there were *Two Wings*, a Fulness of *Power*, given me to fly into *that* my Place, and that there I should be *Nourish'd* from the Face of the Serpent; who by his Rage, forc'd me out of *England*. And sweetly that Word dropt upon my Heart, *And* there *will I nourish thee*, Gen. xlv. 11. I read the Scriptures, and precious they were to me; and especially the Account given of the *Woman*, the *Church*, Rev. xii. as it was then apply'd to my own *Person* and *Case*. And from hence I was taught, 1. That whenever the *Woman*, the *Church*, or any of her *Seed*, appearing in the *Glory of Christ*, and adorn'd with the *Doctrine* of the *twelve Apostles*, doth labour to bring forth any *Fruit unto God*, the *Dragon*, the *Devil*, is *wroth*, and stands ready to *devour it*. 2. That the Dragon's Rage against the Woman, may be so *great*, as to force her thereby, to *flee* from him into the *Wilderness*. 3. That when this is the Case, even *there* She hath a *Place* prepar'd of GOD, where She shall be fed and nourish'd. 4. That for this her Flight into the Wilderness, She hath *Two Wings*, a Fulness of *Power* given her. 5. That when the Woman is got into her Place in the Wilderness, even *thither* will the Dragon go after her, casting *Water* out of his Mouth like a *Flood*, to cause her to be *carried away* of the Flood. And 6. That in this Case, the *Earth* shall help the Woman; that tho' the Dragon thus pursues and persecutes the Woman, She shall not be *destroy'd* and *swallow'd up* by him, but shall have suitable, seasonable, and sufficient *Help*. And oh how sweet and encouraging were these Things unto *Me!*

Long have I look'd upon my poor *Books* as my *Children*, by which I hop'd to serve and glorify GOD. And having conceiv'd Hopes that the Lord would bring them out, and use them; when the Time drew nigh, I have *cried, travailing in Birth, and pained to be deliver'd*. And when opprest with Fear that they would not come forth, and so all my Labour be in vain; the Lord has comforted me with this Word, "Shall I bring to the Birth, and not cause to *bring forth?* Saith the LORD." And when any of them have been brought out, and I have been ready to think, that one, and another of them would be the *last*; the Lord hath said unto me, "Shall I cause to bring forth, and *shut the Womb?* (Shall I do this, and no more for thee?) Saith *thy* GOD." By which He has sweetly encourag'd me to hope in his Mercy; and upon me it has been, according as I hoped and trusted in HIM. For most of my poor Books are now brought forth, and all the rest are coming out. *Oh what a Good, Gracious, Wonder-working, and All-performing* GOD, *have I!*

But, Oh! the *Dragon* had been *wroth* with me, and made some of the *Friends* of CHRIST to be the Channels of his Rage, and from *England*, with my poor Books, he forceth me to flee.—"But my Soul, be not dismayed:

Since GOD is *for thee*, Who can be *against thee?* See, *yonder*, in the *Wilderness*, thy GOD hath prepared thee a *Place*, where HE will *nourish* thee from the Face of the Serpent! And he hath given thee of the freest Grace, *two Wings* of a *great Eagle*, the *Grace* and *Power* of thy Dear *Lord Jesus*, who bears and carries thee as on *Eagle's Wings*, and *Faith* and *Love* from him: Upon which, soar thou aloft, and *fly* from the *Face of the Serpent*, into thy *prepared Place*. And tho' some of thy *Mother's Children* are angry with thee; be not overmuch *grieved*, for it is the *Serpent's* Rage against CHRIST, which *They* vent against *Thee*. Thy Lord, takes all the unkind Treatment which *thou* meet'st with, as done to *Himself*. And as *He* in the Days of his Flesh, when despis'd and rejected in one Place, departed to another: and has bid *thee*, when persecuted in *one City*, to flee unto *another*; So, take thy *Wings*, the Wings of *His* Grace and Providence, and of *thy* Faith and Love, which He hath given thee, and flee yonder unto thy *Place*. Thou hast a Place there, tho' none *here*. And there thy Lord will skreen and nourish thee from the Serpent's Rage. And don't wonder, if the Dragon should cast Water out of his Mouth like a Flood *after thee*; nor be dismayed thereby: For the LORD GOD will and *help thee*, that *right early*: and never suffer thee to be destroy'd by the Serpent's Rage. — And remember what He said unto thee, even this Day, '*I have chosen Thee*, and not cast *Thee* away? I will make all my *Goodness* pass before thee, and I will proclaim the Name of the LORD before thee; and will be gracious to whom I *will* be gracious,' Exod. xxxiii. 19. which he spake concerning a *particular* Service. And, 'I will make of *Thee* a *Great Nation*,' Gen. xii. 2. By which He hinted thy more *general* Usefulness. Which with Joy and Wonder made thee cry out, LORD, What, *Still!* Hast thou more Grace in Reserve for me *Still!* What bless me, and work by me *Still!* Ten Thousand *Glories* to thy *great Grace!* Upon which He answer'd, 'I will *never* leave thee,'—*Then, Oh my Soul, Love the* LORD, *hope in* HIM, *and wait for the God of thy Salvation! And thou Shalt see Him as thy Wonder-working And Covenant-keeping* GOD!"

A Hint I would just give, as to the 2d Part of my *Brief Account of the gracious Dealings of* GOD, *Relating to a Train of special Providences attending Life*. This, as I said, was not put to Press quite so soon as the other. I wanted Time to revise it, *&c*. But as both are but one continued Account of the Lord's Dealings with me; which were both as it were coming out together; I take that gracious Promise which the Lord gave me for the 1st Part, *Thou art my Servant—in whom I will be glorify'd*: to extend also to the 2d Part.

THUS, I have given some Account of the Lord's gracious Dealings with me, most of which I took for myself; relating to several of my little *Tracts*, which in his kind Providence He has brought out for me: To my *Further-ance and Joy of Faith* in *Him*, as my Prayer-hearing, Promise-fulfilling, and All-performing GOD.

What farther I have had from God about my poor Books, which through Hurry I did not write down, I can't give much Account of. But sweetly has He encourag'd me to write and publish them *all*. And the Number of my little Pieces, which the great Grace of my God has brought out for me, are as follow.

I. *A Narration of the Wonders of Grace, in Verse*, &c.

II. *A Discourse on Walking with GOD*: &c.

III. *A Discourse concerning GOD's Act of Adoption: And another on the Inheritance of the Adopted Sons of* GOD.

IV. *A Sight of* CHRIST, *absolutely necessary for all true Christians, and Gospel-Ministers*: &c.

V. *A Discourse on Justification*: &c.

VI. *A Discourse concerning the New-Birth*: &c.

VII. *Letters on spiritual Subjects, and divers Occasions*: &c. VOL. I.

VIII. *A Letter to all the Saints, on the general Duty of Love.*

IX. *A Letter to the Reverend Mr John Wesley: In Vindication of the Doctrines of Absolute Election, Particular Redemption, Special Vocation, and Final Perseverance.*

X. *Some Thoughts about Faith in* CHRIST. *Whether it be requir'd of all Men under to Gospel? To prove that it is.*

XI. *A Letter to the Negroes, lately converted to CHRIST in America.*

XII. *Letters on spiritual Subjects, and divers Occasions*: &c. VOL. II.

XIII. *Letters sent to an Honourable Gentleman, for the Encouragement of Faith.* VOL. I.

XIV. *A Letter to such of the Servants of* CHRIST, *who may have any Scruple about the Lawfulness of printing any Thing written by a Woman*: &c.

XV. *Letters to the Rev. Mr. J. Wesley: Against Perfection.*

XVI. *Meditations and Observations upon the eleventh and twelfth Verses of the sixth Chapter of Solomon's Song.*

XVII. *Brief Hints concerning God's Fatherly Chastisements: Shewing their Nature, Necessity, and Usefulness; and the Saints Duty to wait upon God for Deliverance, when under his Fatherly Corrections.*

XVIII. *The Hurt that Sin doth to Believers*: &c.

XIX. *A Brief Account of the gracious Dealings of* GOD, *with a poor, sinful, unworthy Creature. Relating to the Work of Divine Grace on the Heart, in a saving Conversion to* CHRIST, *and to some Establishment in Him.* Part I.

XX. *A Brief Account of the gracious Dealings of* GOD, *with a poor, sinful, unworthy Creature. Relating to a Train of Special Providences attending Life, by which the Work of Faith was carried on with Power.* Part II.

XXI. *A Letter to all Those that love CHRIST in Philadelphia: To excite them to adhere to, and appear for, the Truths of the Gospel.*

What I had from the Lord to encourage me, with respect to the most of these, has been particularly mention'd. And most of the rest, which came out as it were together, were included in that general *Encouragement*, which I receiv'd from the *Lord*, when I sought Him about the Publication of my second *Book of Letters* For as I have hinted, it was not *that Book* only, but *others* also, which came out with it, that I had in my Thoughts, when I sought the Lord; and the Encouragement I receiv'd from Him, extended to them *all*. But I would just give a Hint or two as to *Three* of them in *Particular*. Which are,

First, The *Letter to the Rev. Mr John Wesley: In Vindication of the Doctrines of Absolute Election*, &c. When I began this Letter, I design'd to send it to him in *Writing*. But being enlarg'd beyond my Expectation, as I wrote much more than I at first purpos'd, and as I had some Doubt, whether he would have Patience to *read it*, and thence, some Fear, that it might be of *little Use*: I spread the Case before the Lord. And intreated Him to tell me, If He would have me send the Letter to Mr. *Wesley* in *Writing*, for his own Use only; or in *Print*, that others might see it together with him? And the Answer I receiv'd from the Lord, was this: *Bind up the Testimony, Seal the Law among my Disciples*, Isa. viii. 16. By which I was fully satisfy'd, that it was *God's Mind*, I should *print it*. That thereby, I should bear a publick *Testimony* for Him and his Truths before *All*; and thus as it were *seal the Law*, the *Doctrines of his Word*, which thro' his Assistance in that Letter, I had been vindicating. The Lord cast a particular *Shine* upon this Part of the Word, *Among my Disciples*. He pointed to it as with a Sun Beam, which made his Mind perspicuous to me. "*There*, as if the Lord should say, *there*, among *my Disciples*, let this Testimony be. *They* shall have it. Bind up the Testimony, seal the Law, make it sure *among them*." And for its Usefulness, sweetly the Lord encourag'd me by this Word, *Many shall run to and fro, and Knowledge shall be increased*, Dan. xii. 4.

Secondly, Thoughts, about Faith in CHRIST: *&c.* This, which was first design'd for *private Use*, and wrote for the Perusal of a Friend, when the Lord made it evident to me, that to bear Witness for Him and his Truth, it was my Duty to *publish it*; I had some Fears, from my own Weakness, *&c.* lest it should not be of that Use which he desir'd, lest the dear Children of God, should not regard me. But sweetly the Lord encourag'd me, from that Word, *I have graven Thee upon the Palms of my Hands,* Isa. xlix. 16. By which I had a Heart-melting Discovery of the Love of Christ to *Me*, even to *Me*, with Relation to this little Piece, and an Assurance given me, that He would *use it* to some of his People. That for this Service, He had *graven me* upon the *Palms of his Hands*. That as sure as He dy'd for me on the *Cross*, as his precious *Hands* were there *pierc'd for me*; as He had the quickest Remembrance of his *Death*, and pleaded the Efficacy thereof on his *Throne* above; so surely, in his infinite Love to me, and as a Fruit of his Death, He would *use this little Piece*, to some of his *People*: In the Publication of which, I singly aim'd at *his Glory*, in bearing Witness for *Him* and his *Truth* in the Earth. And,

    Thirdly. The *Letter to those that love* CHRIST *in Philadelphia, to excite them to adhere to, and appear for, the Truths of the Gospel*: This Letter, I had some Thoughts of sending in *Manuscript*, and of getting a Friend to read it to several of Those, who in a Letter of his, he had mention'd to me, that were drawn off from the Truths of the Gospel. But as I thought it might be more extensively useful, if I sent it in *Print*; I sought the Lord about it. And in great Grace, He said for my Encouragement, *Surely I will be with thee,* Judg. vi. 16. By which He assur'd me of his Presence and Blessing, in the Outgoing of this little Tract. And tho' I thought other of the Lord's Servants, were far more fit to engage in this Service, than *poor me*; and from a deep Sense of my own Weakness and Unworthiness, said in my Heart, "Who or what am *I*, that *I* should engage in this "Affair?" Yet that Word mightily encourag'd me, *She put her Hand to the Nail, and her Right Hand to the Workman's Hammer,* Judg. v. 26. From hence the Lord shew'd me, That the weaker the Instrument was, that attempted his Service; the more Himself, the Almighty Agent, would be glorified in working by it. And then, tho' under the deepest Sense of my own Weakness, yet, leaning on an Almighty Arm, from a Heart fir'd with Love to the Glory of God, I attempted the Work. And full was the Assurance, and precious the Consolation which the LORD gave me, that His Presence should be with me, from that Word, *And with the last, I am* HE, Isa. xli. 4. Oh the ineffable

Sweetness of this Word! It suited me well; it solv'd all my Doubts and Difficulties. I thought myself to be the Least and Last of *all*. But, "Fear not, said the LORD: For, *With the Last, I am* HE. I *am* with thee: I *will* be with thee. Fear not engaging in the Work, because of thy own Weakness; Since my Omnipotence is engag'd for thee. Since *I*, the Great I AM, the All-sufficient GOD, am with *thee*, a poor, little, insufficient *Worm*."—Most sweetly then, in the Faith of infinite Grace, Power, and Faithfulness, being engag'd for me, of the Great JEHOVAH's being *with me*, tho' the *least* and *last* of *all*; I wrote and publish'd this *Letter*. Which is the last of my little *Tracts*, that, thro the gracious Dealings of GOD with unworthy *me*, are *extant*. For all which, and the Use that He has made, and will make of them, for his own Glory and the Good of his People, I *bless* his *great Name*, and shall *praise* his *Grace for ever*. O may those that *fear* GOD, *magnify the* LORD *with me!* Great are the Things with He hath *done* for me! Great are the Things which he hath *spoken* concerning me! And lo, HE hath said unto me, *I will not leave thee, until I have done that which I have spoken to thee of. For the Mouth of the* LORD *hath spoken it*, Gen. xxviii. 15. Isa lviii. 14.

And *still* I am persuaded, that the Lord has *more Kindness* in *Reserve* for me. And I hope in his Mercy, that other of those little *Fragments*, which at His Bidding I have *gather'd up*, will not be *lost*; but that in his good Time, they also shall be *brought forth*, by his own All-gracious, and Almighty *Hand*: To the Glory of his Name, and the Good of his People.

Concerning this poor, broken, brief Account of the LORD's gracious Dealings with me, even this *Third Part*, which was at first design'd for *my own Use*; He hath inclin'd my Heart, and greatly encourag'd me to prepare it for *Press*. When I had some Thoughts about it, I sought the Lord, to know if *He would have me do it*; and receiv'd a secret Hint, that I should, from these Scriptures: *He established a Testimony in* Jacob, *and appointed a Law in* Israel, Psal. lxxviii. 5. *Her Children arise up, and call her Blessed*, Prov. xxxi. 28. From the former, I had a Glance of GOD's *Mind*, that He would have me prepare the *Account* I had taken, of his gracious Dealings with *me*, for the *Press*; and leave it as a publick *Testimony* of his *great Goodness*, among his *People*. From the latter, I reciev'd a sweet Hint, that it might be a useful and acceptable *Provision* for the *Children* of the *Church*: Which drew out my Desires that it might be so, and in some Measure inclin'd my Heart to engage in it. But as I was not fully persuaded about it, I sought the LORD for further Satisfaction, before I could engage therein. And especially, as I wrote it for *myself*, and had some Fears, that it might not be so fit for Usefulness to others. Inasmuch as therein, I did not address them, but the LORD, and my *own Soul*, upon the Notes which I took of his gracious Dealings with *me*, and the Outgoings of my Heart towards *Him*. And soon after, these Words dropt sweetly into my Mind, *And there shall come forth a Rod out of the Stem of* Jesse, *and a Branch shall grow out of his Roots. And the Spirit of the* LORD *shall rest upon Him, the Spirit of Wisdom and Understanding, the Spirit of Counsel and Might, the Spirit of Knowledge, and of the Fear of the* LORD: And shall make Him of quick Understanding in the Fear of the LORD, *and he shall not judge after the Sight of his Eyes, nor reprove after the Hearing of his Ears. But with Righteousness shall He judge the Poor, and reprove with Equity, for the Meek of the Earth*, Isa. xi. 1, 2, 3, 4. From hence I had a Heart-melting Discovery, that the Lord would *have me* prepare my Notes for the *Press*, and that HE would *use them*. That my Dear *Lord Jesus*, who humbled Himself to become a *Rod* out of the Stem of *Jesse*, and a *Branch* out of his *Roots*, to sympathize with his People in their low Estate; that HE upon whom the Fulness of the Spirit rests, as my exalted King, would *judge with Righteousness*, and *reprove* thereby *with Equity* for *me*. That HE, by the Publication of what passed between *Him* and *me*, about my *Books*, would for *me* reprove with *Equity*, those unjust *Censures*, which had been pass'd by Some. As if in the Publication of my Books, I had done what I was not *call'd to*, and therein sought *myself*, and outward *Gain*. And precious was this Hint to me, That my dear Lord *hereby*, would set Things in a true *Light*: would *judge*, or plead my Cause, *with Righteousness*, and *reprove with Equity*. And oh how sweet were these Words to me: *For the Meek of the Earth!* But still, notwithstanding this Part of its Usefulness, for the *Conviction of God's People*, and so, for the *Glory of his Name*, which the Lord hinted to me; I much wanted to know, if it might be useful for the *Refreshment* of some *poor Souls*. And to satisfy me in this, which I so much desir'd, the Lord brought that Word, *Then shall the Lambs feed after their Manner, and the waste Places of the fat Ones, shall Strangers eat*, Isa. v. 17. Oh this delighted my Heart, that the *Lambs of Jesus* should be *fed* hereby: And that what *full Souls* passed over, the *Poor* and *Hungry* should gather up. And then follow'd this Word, with great Power, *And the People which shall be created, shall praise the LORD*, Psal. cii. 18. And when I look'd it, the preceding and following Words were very precious to me. As ver. 16, 17. When *the* LORD *shall build up Zion, He shall appear in his Glory. He will regard the Prayer of the Destitute, and not despise their Prayer*. Oh how exceeding applicable did these Words appear to my Case! With respect to those glorious Discoveries of Himself which the LORD had made unto me, in relation to that Work about which my Heart had been engag'd, for the Edification of his People by my poor Books! And also with respect to those glorious Grants that He had given me, in answer to my Prayer, which as one *destitute* of all *Creature Help*, I had put up unto *Him!* And thus the following Verses also. *He looked down from the Height of his Sanctuary: From Heaven did the* LORD *behold the Earth: To hear the Groning of the Prisoner, to loose those that are appointed to Death; To declare the Name of the* LORD *in* Zion, *and his Praise in* Jerusalem, Ver. 19, 20, 21. Oh how sweetly did these Verses *agree*, with the Account which I had taken of the LORD's gracious Dealings with *me!* And then, from the former Part of the 18th Verse, how abundantly was I satisfy'd of my *Duty*, in preparing it for the *Press: This* shall *be written for the Generation to come!* And from the latter Part of it, how abundantly was I delighted with the happy *Effect*, the *Glory of God*, beheld in the Glass of the Promise: *And the People which shall be created, shall* praise the LORD! Oh how fit, how sweet, how glorious, was this *Word* unto *me!* A *Word in Season, how good is it!*

Having then, this Satisfaction of my Duty, and Hope of its Success; I gladly began the Work. And shall now commit the Whole unto the GOD *of all Grace. Who is Able to do* for his dear *Children*, by this broken *Account* of his *gracious Dealings* with *me* his *weak Worm, more exceeding abundantly than I can ask or think*: To his endless Praise, thro' JESUS CHRIST. *To Whom be Glory and Dominion for Ever and Ever.* AMEN.

APPENDIX.

WHEREAS in this *Third* Part of my brief Account of GOD's Loving-Kindness towards me, in bringing out my little *Pieces*, to the Number of *Twenty-One*; I have hinted what I had from GOD about their *Publication*: I shall now give in this appendix,

First, Some *farther Account* of the *Lord's Goodness*, in bringing out divers *other* of my poor *Manuscripts*; and also some Hints of that great *Encouragement* which the Lord gave me to present them to *publick View*.

Secondly, Answer to an *Objection* that may be made against the Lord's Grant of my Desire in *special Favour*, in sending my Books into *America*: From that great *Trial* which followed upon it in the *Loss of my dear Husband by Sea*. And

Thirdly, Close, with a Word or two of *Use.*—I am to give,

First, Some *further Account* of the *Lord's Goodness*, in bringing out divers *other* of my poor *Manuscripts*; and also some Hints of that great *Encouragement* which the Lord gave me to present them to *publick View*. And in order hereto,

As in this *Third* Part of my brief Account, I have mention'd that earnest *Desire*, which the Lord wrought in me, to have some of my *Books* sent into *America*; and the *Hope* I had in his *Word*, that *there* my GOD would *use* them: I *begin* this farther Account, with my *Husband's* going into *America*. That *undesired Way*, being God's *appointed Mean*, by which he granted my *Desire*, in that Respect, and fulfilled his own *Promise*, and did for me therein, *more exceeding abundantly than I could ask or think*. As my dear Husband, apprehending it his Duty to go thither on another Account, brought out *all my Books*, I then had by me in MS. and took with him a great *Number* of them; which the Lord *blest* to *many Souls.*—*Praise* to my good GOD, who in this Regard heard my *Prayer!*

Aug. 17, 1743. My dear *Husband* went from Home, in order to embark for *America*. At which Time, the Lord most kindly granted my Desire, and abundantly satisfy'd me with his Favour, in bringing out *all my Books*, that I had by me, even *all my Manuscripts*, except some *few Letters, Glory be to his great Name!*

Some Time after my Husband was gone, the Lord gave me Opportunity to write many *Letters* to his dear Lambs, who desir'd to hear from me. And I found my Heart inclin'd to take the *Copies* of them. But as I could see no

Way how any more of my *Books* should be brought out and dispos'd of; I was at a Loss, if it was my Duty to take them, or not; and loth to labour in vain, to take Copies of Letters which might not come out, or be of any farther Use. Yet I desir'd to *serve Christ* as much as ever, tho' I was in Doubt, if I could serve him by taking those Copies: And looking up to the Lord for Direction, He said unto me, *Leave thy Fatherless Children* with ME: *I will preserve them alive*, Jer. xlix. 11. I had long look'd upon my *Books*, as my *Children*: And by this Word the Lord encourag'd me to go to Work again, and leave the Copies of Letters I might after take, with *Him*, unto his *Care*, and for Him to glorify Himself thereby, as HE *pleased*.

And about this Time, I had some pleasant Thoughts, "of committing every of the Books I might after write, into the Hands of CHRIST, as a small Gift, or Legacy, for his weak Children." And I was much delighted to think, "That in his infinite Grace, He would accept my little Mites, which given *by Him*, He had inclin'd my Heart to offer up *unto Him*; and that He would *see to it*, that they were not *lost*, and bring them *out*, that his weak Children might not lose their *Right*."—LORD JESUS, *of thy Royal Grace, accept the* Goat's Hair, *what Thou gavest* [*sic*; r. givest] *to, and shall willingly be offer'd by, thy most weak, unworthy Worm, towards building thee a Sanctuary!*

Oct. 1, 1744. I sought the Lord, about bringing out a *Third* Book of *Letters*. And He satisfy'd me that it was his Mind it should come out, by this Word, which He brought to my Heart with Power and Sweetness, *O my Dove, that art in the Clefts of the Rock, in the secret Places of the Stairs, let me see thy Countenance, let me hear thy Voice; for sweet is thy Voice, and thy Countenance is comely*, Song ii. 14. "Look forth (said the Lord) in this Piece of Service for ME, let Me therein hear thy Voice; for sweet is thy Voice unto *Me*, and thy Countenance is comely." And whereas I was under a humbling Sense of my own Vileness, my dear Lord, sweetly cheer'd my Heart, by giving me to see Myself *in the Clefts of the Rock*, secur'd in his Wounds; and that by Virtue of his All-cleansing *Blood*, He could, He did, call me *His Love, his Dove, his Undefiled*; notwithstanding all my Defilement in Heart and Ways. Which melted me into Humility, Love and Thankfulness.—And then being satisfy'd that it was the Lord's *Mind*, that I should publish a *Third* Book of *Letters*, I ask'd Him which should come out *first*; as I had more than one by me. And He said. Judah *shall go up*, Judg. i. 2. By which He pointed to that which my Thoughts were first upon. Which was a Collection of Letters, sent to the Reverend Mr. *Whitefield* and his *Friends*. For as *Judah* was the *Regal* Tribe, I was pointed thereby to those Letters sent [to] that dear Servant of Christ, Mr *Whitefield*, and to several of his *Brethren* in the *Ministry*; who were as *Princes* among God's People: *These*, said the *Lord, shall go out first*. Upon which I fell down before Him, and gave up the Book, and what the LORD had given me to bring it out, as an Offering unto HIM, to build up his People, his spiritual *Temple*; as *David* offer'd of what the Lord had given him, towards the building of his material *Temple*. And most kindly, for *Jesus Sake*, the Lord accepted it. And sweetly apply'd that Word to my Heart, which He sent to his Servant *David, He will make thee an House*, 2 Sam. vii. 11. By which the Lord assur'd me, "That He would *use this Book*, that He would bless it to his dear Children, and make me fruitful thereby."—And with respect to what I offered, which the Lord had given me to bring it out, He assur'd me that I should receive *an Hundred fold in this World, and in the World to come, Life everlasting*. And as in some Sort, it was as it were my *All*; the Lord encourag'd me to hope that He would give me *more*, to bring out some of my other Books for Him, from that Word, *Now He that ministreth Seed to the Sower,—multiply your Seed sown, and increase the Fruits of your Righteousness.—That you always having all Sufficiency in all Things, may abound to every good Work*, 2 Cor. ix. 8, 10.

Oct. 8. Having sought the Lord, on other Accounts, I again ask'd Him to give me some Word about this Book of Letters, as above. And He said unto me, *Go to my Brethren, and say unto them, I ascend unto my Father and your Father, and to my God and your God*, Joh. xx. 27. By which the Lord again encourag'd me to publish it. But as the Word did not come with so much Power, as at some Times; I was a little inclin'd to Heaviness. But by that Word, the Lord rais'd me in some Measure, *He that goeth forth and weepeth, bearing precious Seed, shall doubtless come again with Rejoicing, bringing his Sheaves with him*, Psal. cxxvi. 6. And then these Words came in, *Rejoice in the Lord always; and again, I say, Rejoice*. Phil. iv. 4. *As sorrowful, yet always rejoicing, as poor, yet making many rich, as having Nothing, and yet possessing all Things*, 2 Cor. vi. 10. By which I had a sweet Intimation of the Lord's *using* this little Book, and of the Ground that I had to rejoice in the *Lord again*, on this Account; notwithstanding the Scriptures I had this Day to encourage me, came not with such Power, as at some Seasons.—*Oh my Soul, be thou like the Angels of the* LORD, *Hearkning to the Voice of his Word, when He doth but whisper to thee, and speaks not so loud as at other Seasons. And thankfully receive the*

Refreshment which thy Lord gives, when He comes down upon thee as the Dew and the small Rain, as well as when He waters thee with the great Rain of his Strength. And wait for the Fulfilment of all his Promises. For as the Lord assur'd thee this Day, concerning what He gave thee about this Book, There shall not fail ought of all the good Things which the LORD *hath spoken.*

June 12, 1745. The Lord brought out my *Third* Book of *Letters*: At the Close of which He inclin'd me to add a *Letter on the Being and Working of Sin in a justified Man,* &c. and another *Letter on the Duty and Privilege of a Believer to live by Faith; and to improve his Faith unto Holiness.* And to encourage me to hope, that the Lord would *use* this Book, (brought out) He gave me these Words: *Feed thy Kids beside the Shepherds Tents,* Song. i. 8. *Thou makest the Outgoings of the Morning and the Evenings to rejoice,* Psal. lxv. 8. By the first, the Lord gave me to hope that I had some *Souls* (some *Kids*) given me to be *fed* by the *Book,* in the several Places where it might be sent. And by the latter, I was persuaded, that the Lord would *bless* both the *former* and the *latter Parts* of the Book.

July 7, 1746. BEFORE this Time, the Lord gave me to hear, that He *had* blest my *last Book,* to some Souls in several Places. *Glory* to my All-gracious, my infinitely faithful, and All-performing GOD!—And now the Lord inclin'd my *Heart,* and gave me *Ability* to put to the Press *Two* other Books, viz. *A Postscript to a Letter on the Duty and Privilege of a Believer to live by Faith,* &c. (which was at the End of the Book published last Year). To which was added, *A Caution against Error, when it springs up together with Truth; in a Letter to a Friend*; and *Some of the Mistakes of the* Moravian Brethren, *in a Letter to another Friend.* And with this Book, to feed my dear Lord's tender Lambs, He inclin'd my Heart to bring out a *Fourth* Book of *Letters.*

The *Postscript* I had long desir'd to write, but was providentially prevented, chiefly by other Work of God, which called for present Attention. When I thought at first of writing it; I desir'd to know the Lord's Mind, "If He would have me go about it." And He signify'd his Approbation thereof, and the Reward that I should receive therein, by that Word, apply'd with Power and Sweetness to my Heart: *For God is not unrighteous to forget your Work of Faith and Labour of Love, which ye have shewed towards his Name, in that you* have *ministred to the Saints, and do minister,* Heb. vi. 10. By the Word *have* ministred to the Saints, the Lord pointed my Eye to the *Letter* I had published; and by the Word *do* minister, to the

Postscript which I was inclin'd to add to that Letter: And by the first of these Words, He signify'd his Acceptance of what I *had* already *done*; and by the latter, his gracious Approbation of what I then *inclined to*, and the blessed Fruit which should attend that Labour. Upon which, in the Lord's Name and Strength, *I began the Work*.

But thinking I should be more fully *fit* for it, in some Respects, after I had heard further from a *Friend*; I thought it best to *wait* a little, altho' I had then some *Leisure* for the Work. But my waiting prov'd *fruitless*, as to the Particulars which I thought of.—And I afterwards saw, that I thereby yielded to a *Temptation*; in neglecting, while I had a *little Time*, the *present Work* which the Lord encourag'd me to engage in. And as I was for some Time providentially prevented from proceeding therein, (altho' by other Parts of the Lord's blessed Work which he gave me to do) I fear'd my God was *displeas'd* with me, for not *improving* those present Moments which He gave me for that Service; and knew not, if He would ever let me do it. There was at Times, a Desire on my Heart after the Work; but I sometimes found I had lost my *Spirit* for it, and often fear'd that it would be *useless*, if I then attempted it; but however, I had no *Time* for it.

After this, I was *ill*, and thought thus: "If the Time of my Dissolution was near: What would I do for *Christ*, before I am taken up to be *forever with the Lord?*" And that Word was brought to my Mind, *Well done thou good and faithful Servant; enter thou into the Joy of thy Lord*. And instantly, glancing upon that Work which I had left *undone*; [I] thought, "That my Lord could not call me, *Good and faithful Servant*; because I had neglected doing that which He set me about."—Upon which, as I was griev'd for my Neglect, and fear'd, if I should attempt the Work now, it would be Fruitless; I bewail'd my Negligence before the Lord, acknowledg'd his Righteousness, if He should never let me do that Piece of Service; plainly told him how Things at present stood, and humbly ask'd Him, "If, notwithstanding, He would have me attempt it?'—And, forgiving my Iniquity, He most graciously said unto me, *Open to* ME, *my Sister, my Love, my Dove, my Undefiled: for my Head is filled with Dew, and my Locks with the Drops of the Night*, Song v. 2. This Scripture the Lord apply'd to me a little Time before, about the same Thing, and he was now again pleas'd to speak to my Heart therein. By the first Clause, *Open to* ME, *&c.* my kind lord, with most endearing Language, call'd me to engage afresh in the *Work*, which I had so long neglected. And by the latter Part of the Verse, *For my Head is filled with Dew*, &c. He led my Thoughts to those inclement Distillations of *Error*, which had fallen upon his *Head*, (his *Government*, to the Injury of several of the doctrinal Truths thereof) in that *Night* which had pass'd over a Part of his People which I was concern'd for. And strongly, thro' my Lord's Hand upon my Heart, *my Bowels were moved for Him*, afresh to engage in *that Part* of his *Service*. As by this, and many other Scriptures, He satisfy'd me, It was his *Mind* that I *should*— Which fill'd my Heart with Wonder at his Grace, that He should permit me to attempt it *now*, after so *long a Time!* And tho' in some Sort I had lost my Strength, yet the Lord said unto me, *Fear thou not, for I am with thee: be not dismayed, for I am thy God: I will strengthen thee, yea, I will help thee, yea, I will uphold thee with the Right Hand of my Righteousness*, Isa. xli. 10. And to comfort me at last, He said, *There shall not an Hair of your Head perish*, Luke xxi. 18. By this Text my Lord told me, That I should lose *Nothing*, none of the desir'd *Fruit* of my Labour, tho' I had neglected the Work *so long*.—And truly the Lord so over-ruled my Delay, that during the Time of it, I was more fully acquainted with those *Errors*, which I was to bear *Witness against*, and prepar'd me to *answer* the Objections made against his *Truths*.—Fill'd now with Hope in God, Dependance on Him, and Resolution for him, I design'd to attempt the Work.

But straightway after this I fell *sick*, and was laid aside for some *Weeks* from the desired Service of my dearest Lord. Many Promises he gave me for my Comfort, some of which seem'd to foretel my *Recovery*. And in the Lord's good Time, he was pleas'd to *redeem my Life from Destruction*, to strengthen me in Soul and Body, and to carry me comfortably thro' the Work. *All Praise to his glorious Name!*

To this *Postscript*, as I said above, I added the *Letter, A Caution against Error*, &c. Many Words I had to encourage me to send this Letter in writing at first, to the Person to whom it was writ. Some of which are inserted in a *Postscript* at the *End* of it. And this Word also encourag'd me about it, *Thou art my Battle-Ax and Weapons of War*, Jer. li. 20.

And as to the other *Letter* added, *Some of the Mistakes of the Moravian Brethren*; It was written at first, in answer to the Request of a particular Person, who desir'd me to inform him, "Wherein I thought the *Moravians* were *mistaken*." And tho' I was not so free at first to engage in this Work, as in some others, it being of a controversial Nature; yet the Lord inclin'd me, for the Glory of his Name, and the Good of Souls to attempt it, and with much Evidence to the Truth, and sweet Pleasure in it, He carry'd me thro' the Work. But when I had wrote it, having other Work upon Hand, I was not free to take the *Copy* of it, until the Lord brought this Scripture to my Mind, *He that hath my Word, let him speak my Word faithfully: What is the Chaff to the Wheat? saith the* LORD, Jer. xxiii. 28. The Lord's Voice to me herein was this: "Have I given thee *my Word* in this letter: And wilt thou not *speak it*, write, preserve, and communicate the same? Wilt thou be *unfaithful?* What is the *Chaff* of *Error*, to the *Wheat* of *Truth?* My Truth is *valuable*: Wilt thou not *speak it?*" The Lord also brought to my Mind, That wicked and slothful Servant, who hid his Lord's Money in the Earth; and what was said unto him, *Thou oughtest therefore to have put my Money to the Exchangers, and then at my Coming I should have received mine own with Usury*, Matt. xxv. 27. From this the Lord said unto me, "It is *my Money, my Truth*, which I have given thee in this *Letter*, to trade with: It is not *thine*, to do what *thou* pleasest with it, to hide it at *thy Pleasure*. Thou oughtest to put *my Money* to the *Exchangers*, to communicate it to my *People*, that at my *Coming* I may receive mine own with Usury." From these two Scriptures, the Lord fully convinc'd me that it was my Duty to *copy out* the *Letter*; and my Spirit was laid under such Awe, by the *one Talent* that was taken *away* from the slothful Servant, and given to him that had *Ten*; that I durst do no other. I thought, "If I did not put my Lord's Money to the Exchangers, if I did not speak his Word faithfully; He might justly *take it from me*, and use me *no more* to any of his People." And from that Clause, "Receive mine own with *Usury*," I was encourag'd to hope, that if I was found in my Duty, my dear Lord would have *Glory*. Upon which my Heart was fully inclin'd, and sweetly drawn to this little piece of Work. And the Copy I took at the Lord's Bidding, and laid it at his Feet, to do what *He pleased* with it.

Soon after, the Lord shew'd me, how *good* He was to me, in persuading me to *take the Copy*. For the *Original* being sent to the Person for whom it was writ, he and others being displeas'd with it, as it oppos'd their Errors; it was resolv'd among them, That it should never be *seen more* by any Person. "It is not *fit* to be seen:" said one of them. So that, if I had not had the *Copy*, the Witness which the Lord enabled me to bear for his Truth in that *Letter*, would have been as it were entirely *lost*.

And when the *Postscript* to my Letter publish'd the last Year, was written; it appear'd to me very *needful*, to add that Letter, *A Caution against Error*, &c. and this, *Some of the Mistakes of the Moravian Brethren*, to that Postscript: Which for the Glory of God, and the Good of his People, I accordingly *did*.

And before I put this *Book*, and the Book of *Letters* to the Press, I sought the Lord for his *Blessing* upon them. But while I was before Him, I and such a Sense of my Vileness, and Unworthiness of the great Favours which my Soul desir'd, that I thought, "It was in some Sort enough for *me*, to be honour'd to *aim* at God's Glory, in any little Thing I did; if He should please to take *no Notice* of it, and not to make *any Use* of it," I thought, "What am *I*, that I should be so earnest for my Books being *blest!*" Tho' most surely I desir'd this for the Glory of God and the Good of Souls. But under a deep Sense of my own Unworthiness, I cast my poor Books, as Mites of Duty, in Love to his Glory, at the Royal *Feet* of the *Prince of Grace*, to be dispos'd of as to Usefulness, according to his *sovereign Pleasure*. And instead of a Word to comfort me, that He would *bless them*, which I at first desir'd; I *trusted* the *Books* in the *Lord's Hands*, with sweet Submission and a pleasureable Satisfaction, that He should glorify Himself thereby, just as HE *pleased*.—In a little Time after this, that Word was brought to Mind, with an encouraging Sound of glorious Grace, *If any Man serve* ME, *Him will my Father honour*, Joh. xii. 26. By which a *Blessing* upon the Books was hinted to my Faith and Hope.—Soon after, that Word was apply'd to my Heart, *I will surely do thee Good*, Gen. xxxii. 12. And this, *For I will not leave thee until I have done that which I have spoken to thee of*, Chap. xxviii. 15. Which pointed my Eye to the Word I had before, *If any Man serve Me, Him will my Father honour*, and further encourag'd my Faith and Hope, for a *Blessing* upon these poor Books.—About this Time also, the Lord apply'd many Promises to me, as a Child of *Abraham*, that were made to him the Father of the Faithful. Frequently that, *I will make of thee a great Nation*, Gen. xii. 2. The latter Part of the Verse, also, the Lord was pleas'd to apply, *And I will make thy Name great, and thou shalt be a Blessing*. And also that Promise made to *Jacob*, Gen. xxviii. 14. which was thus brought to me, *I will spread thee abroad, to the West and to the East, and the North, and to the South*. And that Word also the Lord apply'd to me some little Time before, *By Myself have I sworn, That in Blessing I will bless thee, and in multiplying I will multiply thee*, Gen. xxii. 16, 17. And some of the Promises apply'd, seem'd to look as if there would be Opposition made by some, as I thought, against one of the Books. *These: I have made thee an Iron Pillar, and brazen Walls,—And they shall fight against thee, but they shall not prevail against thee: for I am with thee, saith the* LORD, *to deliver thee*, Jer. i. 18, 19. *Whosoever shall gather together against thee, shall fall for thy Sake,—And every Tongue that shall*

rise against thee in Judgment, shalt thou condemn, Isa. liv. 15—17. And,
Thou shalt *drink, and make a Noise as thro' Wine, and devour, and subdue
with Sling-Stones*, Zech. ix. 15.—And most certainly, by inward Temptations, I was set upon, Not to publish the *Postscript*, &c. I thought Satan
seem'd to be in a Rage at me.—*But fear not, O my Soul, Since the Lord
hath said,* "I am with thee: be not dismayed, for I am thy God." *Wait thou
on thy God continually, to see his promis'd Goodness, in the Land of the
Living; and to give Him the Glory of all his Grace.* GOD *is a Refuge for
thee: Flee unto Him to hide thee. Walk humbly with thy God; and, All his
Goodness* (according to his Promise) *He will make to make to* [*sic*] *pass
before thee.*—"Blessed be the LORD God of *Israel*, from Everlasting, and
to Exerlasting [*sic*; r. Everlasting], *Amen*, and *Amen*.

Aug. 10, 1746. As I was desiring a Blessing on the *Postscript*, &c. that
Word was bro't to my Mind, *Thou hast the Dew of thy Youth*, Psal. cx. 3.
From this I had a sweet Persuasion, That *Christ* had receiv'd the *Holy
Spirit*, for some of his *People*, to be distill'd upon them thro' *that Book*.
And in the Evening, my Heart was much drawn out to ask for a *Blessing* on
both the Books: That the *Postscript*, &c might be blest, for instructing and
confirming some of the weak and wavering Saints in the Truth; and for the
Reduction of some of those fallen into Error. And that the *Book of Letters*
might be blest, for the Feeding of many of my dear Lord's tender Lambs;
and for the Conversion of some Soul, or Souls, to Christ. And soon after,
these Words came in, *The* LORD *shall open unto thee his good Treasure, the
Heaven to give Rain unto thy Land*, Deut. xxviii. 12. And, *I will do this
Thing also that thou hast spoken*, Exod. xxxiii. 17. By these I was encourag'd to hope, that my Requests were granted; and I pray'd the Lord to
fulfil those his good Words unto *me*. And soon this Word came in with
much Power, and Heart melting Sweetness, *Can a Woman forget her
Sucking Child, that She should not have Compassion on the Son of her
Womb? Yea, they may forget: Yet will not I forget thee, saith the* LORD.
*Behold, I have graven thee upon the Palms of my Hands, and thy Walls are
continually before Me*, Isa. xlix. 15, 16. By which my Lord assur'd me, that
He could not, would not *forget me*, but grant my Desires, and abundantly
satisfy me with his *great Goodness*; as He had dy'd for me on the Cross, to
grant me the Blessings I desir'd from his Throne. And with sweet Freedom
I drew near to my dear *Lord Jesus*, as his *Sucking Child*, and pray'd Him to
draw out the *Breast*, and let me *milk out and be delighted* with the *Abun-*

dance of his Love, Life, and Glory. And believing in him, and thankful to him, *I rejoiced in his* Word, *as one that had found great* Spoil.

With these Two Books, that Postscript and 4th Book of Letters, the Lord brought out also my *Two Letters on Baptism*. As from some Occurrences in Providence, it seem'd to me, that these Letters might be of present Use, and that it was my Duty to print them; I sought the Lord about their Publication, and for his Blessing thereon. And most kindly my Lord said unto me, *There will I give thee my Loves*, Song. vii. 12. These Words appear to be spoken by the *Spouse* to *Christ*; but he was pleas'd to apply them as *his Words* to my *Soul*: And by them said unto me, "*There*, in that *Path of Duty*, will I *give thee my Loves*: My *Blessing* upon these Mites of Service, and my *Heart-Love* therein." By which my Lord satisfy'd me, that it was his *Mind* I should publish them, sweetly drew me to this my *Duty*, and melted my Soul down with his infinite *Grace*. These Words also, the Lord sweetly apply'd to my Heart, *I will pour my Spirit upon thy Seed, and my Blessing upon thine Offspring: And they shall spring up as among the Grass, and as Willows by the Water-courses. One shall say, I am the* LORD'*s: and another shall call himself by the Name of* Jacob: *and another shall subscribe with his Hand unto the* LORD, *and sirname himself by the Name of* Israel, Isa. xliv. 3, 4, 5. Hence the Lord persuaded me, that he would pour his *Spirit* upon his *People*, and his *Blessing* upon his *Offspring*, and upon those of them in particular, which he had given *me*, to be useful to, by these my poor *Letters*; and that hereby some should be encourag'd to *follow him*, to his Glory, in his solemn Ordinance of *Baptism*, and therein profess that they were, and dedicate themselves to be, the LORD's.—Glory to the GOD of Promise! *Thy Words were found, and I did eat them, and thy Word was unto me the Joy and Rejoicing of mine Heart.*

April 19, 1747. My *Letters on Baptism, Postscript*, and both my last *Letter-books*, the Lord hath now given me to hear, That he hath *blest them* for the *Good of Souls*.—O what a good *God*, a kind *Father*, a bounteous *Master*, have *I! Who* (in Grace) *is a God like unto Thee, who pardoneth Iniquity, and passeth by the Transgression of the Remnant of his Heritage! Who is a strong* LORD *like unto Thee, and to thy Faithfulness round about thee!*

April 23, 1747. I sent my Letter to Mr. *Cudworth* to the Press, which is a *Reply* to his *Answer* to my *Postscript*. I thought when I publish'd that little Piece, I should meet with *Opposition*, by some of the Promises given me. And when I *did*, it was no Surprize to me; but what the Lord said unto me before, encourag'd me, and enabled I was to plead his *Promise* with him. I thought when I had read his publick *Answer* to my Postscript, which was very sophistical, there seem'd to be a Call of Providence for my *Reply*, in Vindication of the Truth, against the Errors which he advanc'd. But as this would call me off from other Work, and as I don't natively delight in Controversy, the Prospect of it was not naturally pleasing to me. But upon my receiving his little corrupt Piece, fitted to entangle Souls, the Lord said unto me, *Rise up my Love, my fair One, and come away*, Song ii. 10. By which he seem'd to call me inwardly to engage in this Work of *Reply*. And again, the Lord said to me, *Open thy Mouth for the Dumb, in the Cause of all such as are appointed to Destruction*, Prov. xxxi. 8. By this Scripture the Lord hinted to me my Duty, to assert and vindicate his Truth, for the Help of those of his dear Children who might be *ensnar'd*, or *oppressed* by this little erroneous Piece, and not know how to extricate, or *speak for themselves*; And likewise to open my Mouth in the *Cause of all his Saints*, who by this little corrupt Piece *are appointed to Destruction*: All those being deem'd therein, *Natural Men*, who have and plead for, *Holiness in themselves*. And upon reading this sophistical little Piece, the Lord further encourag'd me to Reply, by this Word, *Fear thou not, for I am with thee: be not dismayed, for I am thy God: I will help thee, yea, I will strengthen thee, yea, I will uphold thee with the Right Hand of my Righteousness*, Isa xli. 10. And by that Word also, *Inasmuch as ye have done it to the least of these my Brethren, ye have done it unto me*, Matt. xxv. 40. By the former of these, the Lord assur'd me of his *Help*, of sufficient *Assistance* for this Service. And by the latter, my Lord's infinite *Grace*, in his *Acceptance* of this Service, as done to *Himself*, was signify'd to me; as my Heart was sweetly enlarg'd thereby, to engage therein, for the Good of some of the least of his *Brethren*. For before this, I had some Discouragement arose in my Mind, from a Thought, "That it would not be of *general Use*." But, Oh, when my Lord said, *Inasmuch as ye have done it to the* least of these my Brethren, *ye have done it unto* ME; it was *enough*. If HE would take this poor little Piece of controversial Work, as done to his great SELF, altho' it should be of Use only to some *few* of the very *least* of his *Brethren*, I found it an All constraining *Motive* to engage therein; and esteem'd my Lord's *Acceptance* of my poor little Work, as my *exceeding great Reward*. And towards the very *least* of his *Brethren*, with Desire after their Relief and Advantage, *my Bowels were moved*.

Thus, encourag'd by the Lord, and trusting in him, I began the Work; and thro' his Power and Grace, was comfortably carried thro' it. And when finisht, I sought the Lord for his Blessing upon its Publication, and to say somewhat to me about it. And that Word he apply'd to my Heart, *And ye shall be Witnesses unto* ME, Act. i. 8. And that Word, a little Time before, the Lord set with Power on my Heart, about its Publication, *I am with thee*, Isa. xli. 10. By these my gracious Lord assur'd me, to my Joy, that in this little Piece of controversial Work, I should be a *Witness* unto HIM; that his *Presence* was with me in its *Out-going*; and encourag'd me to *hope* for his *Blessing* thereon. Lord, *Remember thy Word unto thy* unworthy Worm, *upon which thou hast caused me to hope!*

June 21, 1747. I sent my *Fifth* Volume of *Letters* to the Press. When I was about to send it, I thought it my Duty to seek the Lord for his *Blessing* thereon, and to say somewhat to me for my *Encouragement* about it. But as I was under various Trials, and Heaviness of Spirit, by a pressing Sense of my own Sinfulness, I thought I was not *fit* to pray to the Lord. Nevertheless I *attempted* my Duty. And these Words were brought to my Mind, *Thine Iniquity is taken away, and thy Sin purged. And I heard the Voice of the* LORD, *saying, Whom shall I send, and who will go for Us?* Isa. vi. 7, 8. By the former Verse, the Lord rais'd my Spirit, and deliver'd me from the Burden of Sin. And I thought, if the Lord had took away mine *Iniquity*, and purged my *Sin*; I might intreat him to *send me* forth, by this little Book, to do some *Service* to his People. And while by the latter Verse I heard the Voice of the Lord, saying, *Whom shall I send, and who will go for Us?* I said, as the Prophet, *Here am I, send me.* I was encourag'd by this, *Whom shall I send,* and *who will go for Us?* to hope that the Lord had some *Service*, to be done for his dear Children, by my poor little Book; and humbly intreated him, to *send me*, thereby to do it: that his *Blessing* might attend this my feeble Attempt for his Glory and the Good of his People. Next, that Word came to my Mind, *For we are unto God a sweet Savour of Christ, in them that are saved, and in them that perish*, 2. Cor. ii. 15. From hence I had a Heart-melting Persuasion, that in this little Book, I should be *unto God a sweet Savour of Christ*. And I admir'd his infinite Grace, that any Service of so vile a Creature, should be acceptable to him thro his dear Son. That He should thus have *Respect* to the Lispings of a *Babe*, concerning the Glory of his Great *Son*, unto this my poor *Offering*, thro' the Sacrifice of *Christ*, having made my *Person accepted* in Him the *Beloved*: As God had *Respect* unto *Abel*, and to his *Offering*. And much *Glory* I saw in the *Service of God*, and was drawn out to *love*, and *desire it*, as his *Honour* was not only thereby *advanced*, but also his *Heart delighted*. but still I wanted to know if the Lord would please to bless my poor Book to his *Children*. And that Word he sweetly brought to my Heart, *Let us eat and be merry*, Luk. xv. 23. By which the Lord hinted to me, that He would make a *Feast* for some of his dear *Children* by my poor Book, and that *He* would rejoice with *them* therein. And some farther Satisfaction therein I wanted, or rather , Communion with God in Love, with respect hereto, and I pray'd my dear Lord, to give me a Word from his *sweet Mouth*: And He said unto me, *And the Roof of thy Mouth like the best Wine for my Beloved, that goeth down sweetly, causing the Lips of those that are asleep, to speak*, Song. vii. 9. By which he assur'd me, that my *Palate*, or spiritual *Taste* of his Truths, as manifest in my little Book, should be as the *best Wine* for *his Beloved*, that goeth down *sweetly*, causing the Lips of those that are *asleep*, to *speak*: To delight, and awake to Love and Praise, his *sleeping Children*. And a Sense of the *Father's Love*, of the *Son's*, and of the *Spirit's Love* towards me herein, in thus using this little Piece for the Good of God's People, melted my Heart, and rais'd me to admire his infinite Grace, to so vile a Worm. The Language of my Heart was, "*Lord*, why *me!* why *me*, that *Thou* shouldst be thus *gracious* to *sinful me!*" Upon which my Lord said, *Thou art all fair, my Love, there is no Spot in thee*, Song iv. 7. Which further melted and delighted my Soul, and gave me a sweet View of the *Love of Christ* towards me, of his having *wash'd* me from my *Sins* in his *own Blood*, ador'd me with his *Righteousness*, and that in his infinite Grace, he dealt with me as one that was *all fair* in his *own Beauties*. But farther, I desir'd, that my dear Lord would please to bless my poor Book for the Conversion of some *Soul*, or *Souls*, if agreeable to his and his Father's Will. And these Words being brought to my Mind, gave me some Hope that He would do this Thing also, for which I had spoken: *I have chosen thee, and not cast thee away*, Isa. xli. 9. *Fear not*, O Jacob, *my Servant, I will pour my Spirit upon thy Seed, and my Blessing upon thine Offspring.—One shall say, I am the* LORD'*s: and another shall call himself by the Name of* Jacob: *and another shall subscribe with his Hand to the* Lord, *and sirname himself by the Name of* Israel, Chap. xliv. 3, 5.—*Wait, O my Soul, to see how thy God, will shew forth the exceeding Riches of his Grace, in Kindness towards thee, thro' Christ Jesus!*

May 9, 1748. Having Thoughts of sending my little Pieces to the Press, *Hints of the Glory of Christ, as the Friend and Bridegroom of the Church*;

and *Thoughts on the Lord's Supper*: I intreated the Lord to give me some Word to *encourage* me, if he would have them *published*. And this Word first came to my Mind, *Feed my Lambs*, Joh. xx. 25. And as I was under Discouragement from my own Weakness, Sinfulness, and Unworthiness, the Weakness of my poor little Pieces, and some Fears and Temptations, lest they should *not be useful*, for the Glory of God and the Good of Souls; my Heart seem'd to *draw back*. But these Words were brought to encourage me, *O my Dove, that art in the Clefts of the Rock, in the secret Places of the Stairs, let me hear thy Voice, let me see thy Countenance; for sweet is thy Voice, and thy Countenance is comely*, Song. ii. 14. *He that overcometh, and keepeth my Works unto the End, to him will I give Power over the Nations: (And he shall rule them with a Rod of Iron: as the Vessels of a Potter shall they be broken to Shivers) even as I received of my Father*, Rev. ii. 26, 27. Which sweetly persuaded me, that it was the *Mind of Christ*, to *hear my Voice*, in the Publication of these *two* little *Pieces*; and also gave me some Encouragement as to *others* I desir'd to publish: And made it plain, that it was my Duty to *overcome by Faith*, my Fears and Discouragements, and to keep the *Lord's Works*, unto the *End*, the *Work* that he gave *me to do*, in Writing and Printing, for his Glory, and the Good of Souls: And that my Labour should *not be in vain in the Lord*. This Word also enocurag'd me, *I will make of thee a great Nation*, Gen. xii. 2. And this likewise, with Heart-melting Power was brought to my Mind, *I have chosen thee, and not cast thee away*, Isa. xli. 9.—With respect to the largest of these little Pieces, I was under some Discouragement, as I thought it had not been so useful to the Person to whom I sent it in MS. as I wished. But to encourage me concerning that, and its Publication; (and other such like Things, wherein I had, or might attempt any Thing for the Glory of God and the Good of Souls, and not instantly see a wish'd Effect, and my Desires fulfilled as to particular Persons and Things:) this Word was bro't, *If the Son of Peace be there, your Peace shall rest upon it; if not, it shall turn to you again*, Luk. x. 6. The Hint I receiv'd, was this: "That I ought to wish well *to*, and seek the *Good of Souls*, for the *Glory of God*; and if my Attempts, according to his *revealed Will*, were according to the Purpose of his *secret Will*, as to the Persons and Things I *aim'd at*; He would *succeed them*: If *not*, my *Peace*, my *Labour of Love*, should turn unto me again; not as being in *vain* in the *Lord*, but as *accepted* by him, and to be *rewarded* of him: Or, that He would *esteem* of my weak *Attempts* of Duty, in Love to his Glory, as if I had thereby *done something* for his Honour, and the Good of

Souls."—Else, I saw, that many of the *Labours*, of some of the *Servants of Christ*, yea, even of the *Son of God*, in the Days of his Flesh, would have been in vain. As under Discouragement, some of the great Servants of Christ, have been ready to say. But well our glorious Lord, knows how to *sympathize* with every Servant of his, great or small, that is *tried* in this Regard; in that *He Himself*, on Account of the little Success of his Ministry to the *Jews*, was *tempted in this Point like as we are*, tho' *without Sin*. But in the Foreview of it, he is brought in thus speaking, *Then I said, I have laboured in vain, I have spent my Strength for Nought, and in vain*, Isa. xlix. 4. But the reading of what our Lord adds, which encourag'd HIM, was at this Time strengthening and sweet unto *me: Yet surely my Judgment is with the* LORD, *and my Work with my God. And now saith the* LORD, *that formed me from the Womb to be his Servant, to bring* Jacob *again to him, Tho'* Israel *be not gathered, yet shall I be glorious in the Eyes of the* LORD, *and my God shall be my Strength*, Ver. 4, 5.—Thus was I encourag'd to put my little Pieces to the Press.—*O my* GOD, *succeed my weak Labours, and do for me exceeding abundantly, more than I can ask or think!*

June 6, 1748. I sent my *Sixth* Volume of *Letters* to the Press. And upon seeking the Lord for some *Encouragement* as to its Publication, He was pleas'd to persuade my Heart, that He was *with me* therein as *my God*: and that I should be unto *Him* in that Service, a *sweet Savour of Christ*: And upon intreating him for a *Blessing* thereby upon precious Souls, He said unto me, in the Infinity of his Grace, *Thou hast* prevailed, Gen, xxii. 28. Oh, *what shall I render to the* LORD *for all his Benefits!*

Aug. 12. I sought the Lord, to know if he would please to have the *Appendix* I had written to my Pamphlet, [*Some Thoughts about Faith in Christ*: &c.] published. And by the following Scriptures brought to my Mind, I was persuaded and satisfy'd, that it was the *Lord's Will*, that it should appear in Print. *Now they have known that all Things whatsoever thou hast given Me, are of Thee. For I have given them the Words which thou gavest Me, and they have received them*, Joh. xvii. 7, 8. The Hint I receiv'd from hence was this: That as our great *Lord*, gave his *Disciples*, the *Words* which his Father gave him, which they *received*, and whereby they *knew* that all Things which his Father gave him, which he had declared to them, were of *God*: So that *I*, his poor *Worm*, after the Example of my great *Lord*, should be faithful in declaring to my *Brethren*, the Things which he had given unto *me*; and that thro' his Blessing thereon, they might *know* the Things (and this of the Command of Faith given to all Men in the Gospel, as being one of those) that the Father gave to Christ. Then this Word came in, *Now He that ministreth Seed to the Sower, increase the Fruits of your Righteousness*, 2 Cor. ix. 10. From whence I was instructed, That as the Lord had *ministred* to me some farther *Light* into this his *Truth*, I ought to *sow it*, in its *Publication*, that thro' his Blessing thereon, there might be a farther *increase* of Light among his People. This Word also, gave me some Pleasure, *And might perfect that which is lacking in your Faith*, 1 Thes. iii. 10. I thought if the Lord would please to *use* what I had written, to help the *Faith* of any [of] his Servants in this *Particular*; how great a *Blessing* it would be to me! And while my Heart was thus working to the Lord's People, this Word dropt on my Mind, *He that in these Things serveth Chirst, is acceptable to God*, Rom. xiv. 18. A Thought of *serving Christ*, in what I had written, sweetly inclined my Heart to its Publication. And that Word came in with Sweetness, *And where I am, there shall also my Servant be*, Joh. xii. 26. And what our Lord spake of himself, and of the Work which the Father gave him to do, encourag'd me to publish what I had written: *I must work the Works of him that sent me, while it is Day: the Night cometh when no Man can work*, Joh. ix. 4. But still I wanted, and intreated the Lord to speak to me concerning this Work, in some Word, with greater Power, unto fuller Satisfaction, and Heart-melting Influence. Upon which he said, *Thou art* Gilead (an *Heap of Witness*) unto ME, Jer. xxii. 6. Which sweetly melted my Heart, and fill'd me with joyful Wonder at his infinite Grace, to a Creature so unworthy, to a Sinner so vile; and made me cry out, *Lord, why me! Why me! How is it that thou shouldst be thus gracious unto me!* I admir'd and ador'd his boundless Love and Grace, in which he *dy'd* for me, not only to save me from *Hell*, and to bring me to *Heaven*; but also, that he might employ me in his *Work*, while in my Time-State. And that he should herein do so *much* for me, give me so *many* little Pieces to bring out for Him, and then in his infinite Condescension, account me herein, as an *Heap of Witness* unto HIM! And falling down before him, I blest his Name, that as a God Hearing Prayer, he had given me so full an Answer. And I gave him my little *Self*, in all my little *Service*, as the *Purchase* of his *Blood*, and pray'd him to pardon, and accept me in this Thing I had just finisht, and that he would make it a Blessing to his dear People.—And to comfort me concerning its Weakness, this Word was given me, *That Thou givest, they gather*, Ps. civ. 28. And concerning its Useful-ness, this Word, *The* LORD *shall increase you more and more*, Psal. cxv. 14.

Remember, O Lord, *the Word to thy* Worm, *upon which thou hast caused me to hope!*

Aug. 13. I was troubled, that thro' Hurry I had not so fully sought the Lord, as I should, before I sent my *Sixth* Volume of *Letters* to the Press; and likewise, that I did not write down the Encouragement I then had from the Lord, till some Time after, when I did not fully remember all that he said to me. And my Spirit was much prest with a Sense of my *Sin*, in neglecting the same, and of that great *Loss* I might sustain thereby; in that if I had been more earnest with God in Prayer, and had waited upon him in a more particular Manner for the good Words of his Grace, I might have receiv'd a greater Blessing, with respect to that Book. And in the midst of my Dejection, a Thought came into my Mind, "That it was not too late *now*, the Book was not finisht, and the Lord was a God merciful and gracious, I might seek him for a Blessing on it *still*."—But oh how it reviv'd me to think, that there was yet *Room* for me to *seek God*, before the Book came out!—With joyful Haste, I fell down before the Lord, humbled myself for my Sin, and took Hold on his Covenant, wherein he has said, *I will be merciful to their Unrighteousness, and their Sins and their Iniquities I will remember no more*. And I pray'd him, as *The* LORD, *the* LORD *God, merciful and gracious, forgiving Iniquity, Transgression and Sin, slow to Anger, and abundant in Goodness and Truth*, to extend his infinite Grace, over all my abounding Sin, in granting me a *Blessing now* on this poor Book, for the Glory of his own Name, and the Good of his dear People. And while I was before him, He was graciously pleas'd to say to me, *And the Roof of thy Mouth like the best Wine for my Beloved, that goeth down sweetly, causing the Lips of those that are asleep, to speak*, Song vii. 9. Which sweetly melted my Heart, while I receiv'd it as a full Answer of my Prayer, from the God of all Grace, that he would *bless* this poor *Book*, to his dear Children. For I had intreated my *great Lord*, to bless it to his *tender Lambs*, to instruct, revive and comfort them thereby, as their various Cases required: and likewise to make it a *Blessing* to every *Soul* that might read the Book; and particularly I desir'd the *Conversion of Souls* thereby. But as I thought the Word did more peculiarly respect the Edification of the Saints, which the Lord promis'd me by that Book; I thank'd and blest him for such a gracious Answer to my Request in *that Regard*; and earnestly I pray'd him to grant a Blessing of *Life* thereby, upon some *dead Sinners*, and to give me some Word of Encouragement as to this. I was directed to cast myself upon my Lord's Grace, for the Grant of my Desires, to be dealt with by sovereign

Grace, as should be most for its own *Glory*. And soon after, this Thought came into my Mind, "That as I had appealed unto *Grace*; unto *Grace* I should *go*." And some Degree of Encouragement and Rest it gave to my Heart. But I found such an Earnestness of Spirit, that I knew not how to let my *Lord go*, except he *blest me*, in converting some Souls by my poor Book, and gave me some Word to encourage me about it. I pleaded the Infinity of his Grace, the Immensity of his Fulness, that he would not be the *poorer*, if he *granted* my Desire, nor the *richer* if he *deny'd* my Request; and pray'd him as the *God of Compassions*, not to send a needy, thirsty *Soul*, away *empty*. I ask'd him, "If it would not be to his endless *Praise* by Men and Angels, if He glorify'd his *Grace*, in thus working such a little, vile, unworthy *Worm!*" And tho' I desir'd to ask with Submission to his Will, yet I knew not how to be deny'd. "Oh, thought I, my Lord *can*, he *can* be thus *gracious* to me; He is *Able* to *do this*." And while my Heart was thus working, He said unto me, *I* will *make of* Thee *a great Nation*, Gen xii. 2. No sooner almost had I said, My Lord *can*, He *can*; but He said, I *will*; I *will* make of *thee* a *great Nation*. Which melted, and delighted my Heart. That Word also came in, *Thus shall it be done to the Man whom the King* delighteth *to honour*, Esth. vi. 9. O this Word, *Delighteth*, that the Lord should *delight* to be *gracious* unto *me*, affected me much. And as I had ask'd the Favour I requested of the *Father*, in the Name of *Christ*, and was thinking that my Lord would intercede for me, this Word came in, *We* have *the Mind of Christ*, 1 Cor. ii. 16. Which led me to the Promises he had given me, and persuaded me, that he *had* therein spoke his *Mind*; and that it was indeed his *Design* to bless this poor Book, for the Good of Souls, for the Edification of his Saints, and gave me Hope for the Conversion of Sinners thereby. Upon which I ador'd and blest him, and pray'd him to *remember his Word, upon which he had caused me to hope,—Oh my Lord, satisfy a longing, waiting Soul, with thy great Goodness; To the Praise of the Glory of thy Grace!*

May 10, 1749. I sought the Lord about the Publication of my *Seventh* Volume of *Letters*: And He was pleas'd to say to me, with respect to this Service, I *have* chosen thee, *and not* cast thee away, Isa. xli. 9. *Whatsoever thy Hand findeth to* do, *do it with thy* Might, Eccles. ix. 10. And, *Be stedfast, unmoveable, always abounding in the* Work of the Lord, *forasmuch as ye know that your Labour is not in* vain *in the Lord*, 1. Cor. xv. 58. By these Words, I was directed and excited to publish this Volume, and my Duty and Privilege therein, were sweetly hinted to me: For which I gave Thanks. And

I intreated my dear Lord, to grant his *Blessing* upon this little *Piece*, for the *Feeding of his tender Lambs*, and the *Conversion of Souls*; and to give me some Word to *encourage* my Faith and Hope therein. And He was pleas'd to say, *I will give* Men *for* thee, *and* People *for* thy Life, Isa. xliii. 4. By this I was caus'd to hope, that the Lord would give me some Souls to be useful to, by this Book, for the Life of my Joy to Him. But something farther I wanted my Lord to say to me, about his granting me his Blessing on this my weak Labour. And by these Words he was pleas'd to raise my Faith and Hope, Prov. x. 21. Isa. liv. 1, *&c.* Chap. lx. 1, 3. And to assure me thereof, by, *I will not* fail thee, *nor* forsake thee, Josh. i. 5. And, *In blessing*, I will *bless thee, and in multiplying* I will *multiply thee*, Gen. xxii. 17. And that Word, with a sweet Soul-melting Power, dropt on my Mind, *Thou hast ravished my Heart, my Sister, my Spouse, with one of thine Eyes, with one Chain of thy Neck*, Song iv. 9. This Word came in while I was seeking for a Blessing on my poor Book; and I tho't, that it was a glorious Reward of my feeble Work, if my Lord's *Heart* was pleas'd therewith, and delighted with my Faith and Love therein. But I pray'd him, if He took *Pleasure* in this poor *Work*, that he would *bless it unto Souls*. And most graciously by the former Words, he granted my Desire, and assur'd me of my Request.— After this, I intreated my dear *Lord Jesus*, to speak to my *Heart*, and to tell me the Thoughts that were in *His*, that very Instant, concerning my Person and Work, as wash'd in his Blood, and cloth'd with his Beauties, and to seal his Love with a Kiss. Humbled I was, under a deep Sense of my Unworthiness of so high a Favour; but I pleaded the Freeness and Exuberance of his Grace, to the chief of Sinners. And the *Lord of Glory*, from his exalted Throne at God's Right Hand, in infinite Condescension granted my Petition, and cast his Royal *Favour*, upon vile, unworthy *me!* He said unto me, *Thou art* all-fair, my Love, *there is* no Spot in thee, Song iv. 7. By which my Lord assur'd me of my *Beauty* in *his Eye*, and *Interest* in *his Heart*. And then He added, *How much better is* thy Love than Wine! *and the Smell of thine* Ointments *than* all Spices! Ver. 10. Which amazing Words of infinite Grace, spoke to my Heart with a sweet Soul-melting Efficacy, humbled me in the Dust before him, for my poor, low, *little Love to him*, and rais'd me into Wonder, Joy and Praise, that my *great Lord*, should thus *regard* and *delight* in it, and by an amazing *Stoop* of infinite *Favour*, thus graciously *acquaint me*, that my weak imperfect *Love*, was to Him, *better than Wine!* and the Smell of mine *Ointments* than *all Spices!* That my unworthy *Person*, and this my poor *Service*, as cleansed by *his* Blood, and array'd with his Beauties, were his *Heart's Delight!*—And as I had asked a Blessing on my poor Book of the *Father*, in the Name of Christ; my Lord assur'd me of *his Grace*, likewise, in the Grant of it, and of the *Father's* being of the same Mind with *Him*, in what he had said unto me: By that Word, my *Father* and *I* are *one*, Joh. x. 30. *Who is a God like unto Thee, that pardoneth Iniquity, and passeth by the Transgression of the Remnant of his Heritage. Let thy Mercy O* LORD *be upon me, and thy Blessing on this my poor Work, according as I trust in Thee!*

    June 29, 1749. Having Thoughts of sending to the Press my second Volume of *Letters* to an *Honourable Gentleman*; I sought the Lord for his *Direction and Blessing*; and that he would please to speak to my Heart in some or other of the precious *Words* of his Grace. And the Lord bro't this to my Mind, *Feed thy People with thy Rod,—let them feed in* Bashan *and* Gilead, Mich. vii. 14. By which I had a sweet Hint, That God the Father, had granted to his *Son Jesus*, to *feed* his *People* with his *Rod*, or *Governing Power*, by his own precious *Truths*, in my poor little *Book*; and that thereby they should feed as upon *Bashan* and *Gilead*, the High *Mountains* of *Israel*. By this my *Duty* to bring it out, and my *Privilege* therein, were hinted to me. For which I *blest the Lord*, and intreated him to *bless the Book*, for the *Edification* of the *Saints*, and the *Conversion* of some *Sinners*. Then this Word came in, *God is able to make all Grace abound towards you*, 2 Cor. ix. 8. *Grace*, suited my great *Unworthiness*, and *all* Grace, my extensive *Desires of Usefulness*, unto Saints and Sinners, and encourag'd my Hope as to both. And for both, I cast *myself* upon this *All-Grace*, or *All-sufficient Grace*, to be dealt with thereby, as should be most for the Praise of its own *Glory*. These Words also, the Lord spake to me, *Lovest thou* ME?—*Feed my Lambs*, Joh. xxi. 15. *Inasmuch as ye have done it to the Least of these my Brethren, ye did it unto* ME, Matt. xxv. 40. *The Lord sent a Word into* Jacob, *and it hath lighted upon* Israel. By which my Love to Christ, and Desire to feed his Lambs, were *drawn out*, and a sweet Persuasion *given me*, that the Lord would *feed* them by my poor *Book*, that he thereby sent a *Word* unto them, that should *light* upon them; and that what I desired to do for *them*, He would take as done to *Himself*. His gracious *Acceptance* of this my weak Labour, was likewise signify'd to me by that Word, GOD *accepteth thy Works*, Eccl. ix. 7. And as I desir'd to do much for my *Lord*, by this little *Book*, while, to exalt his Grace, *He* did much for *me* as to its *Usefulness*: He said unto me, *What wilt thou that I shall do unto thee?* Luk. xviii. 32. Upon which the Language of my Heart was, "Lord, take the Book into thy own Hand, and feed thy Lambs, and convert some Soul, or Souls, thereby." Then He said, *Be it unto thee even as thou wilt*, Matt. xv. 28. *Thy Faith hath saved thee, go in Peace*, Luk. vii. 50. And as for the Grant of my Request, I *hoped in his Word*; So I long'd to have his *Love shed abroad in my Heart*, and that he would tell me the present Thoughts of *his Heart*, concerning *me* and my poor *Work*, if He *lov'd* and *delighted* therein. Which great Favour, I asked of the *Lord*, and that He would speak like *Himself*, unto Heart-melting Influence. And tho' my dear Lord had said so much to me, yet if He spake not thus *again* to me, I knew not how to be *satisfied*. And as for a small Moment, He seem'd to *hide Himself* from me, I mourn'd my *Vileness* and *Unworthiness*, and pleaded his *Grace*. Then this came in, *Thou art ever with me, and all that I have is thine*, Luk. xv. 35. It was as if my Lord had said, "If I don't manifest myself to thee so fully at this Time, at some Seasons, thou hast an entire and eternal Interest in ME, and *my Fulness*." This stay'd my Heart; but yet I wanted my Lord's manifested Love. Then He said unto me. *There will I give thee my Love*, Song vii. 12. The Words again, of the *Spouse to Christ*, my Lord took, and made them *his own* to *me*; and thereby assur'd me, That *there*, in *that Service*, He would give me *His Loves*, the various Displays, and Flows, of his infinite *Favour*, in *blessing* my poor *Book*, for the Good of Souls: For which I humbly gave Thanks. But still, I wanted a farther Opening of his *Heart*, and knew not how to go from Him, unless He drew *near*, and spake with greater Power to my Soul. My Spirit *grieved*, and as it were *dy'd* for want of his Favour. Then, in his boundless Grace, my Lord *drew nigh*, and said, *I am come into my Garden, my Sister, my Spouse; I have gather'd my Myrrh with my Spice, I have eaten my Honey comb with my Honey, I have drank my Wine with my Milk: Eat, O Friend, drink, yea, drink abundantly, O beloved*, Song v. 1. And by these All gracious Words, spoke to my Heart with a Soul-melting Power and Sweetness, I was abundantly *satisfy'd*. I had what I *wanted*, my *Lord*, and his *Love*: I had Him in Communion, and his Love in Enjoyment. And Oh How I admir'd his *Grace*, that He should call *me*, his vile Worm, His *Sister*, his *Spouse!* That He should assure me of his Delight, his present Delight, in my Person and Service, that He had *eaten* and *drank*, and made Himself a *Feast*, as it were, upon his *own Provisions*, in his unworthy Worm, and my poor Work! And that from the Delight He took herein, He would likewise feast his *Favourites*, and say, *Eat O Friends, drink, yea drink abundantly, O beloved!*—Then I fell down before Him, ador'd and blest him for this sweet, this full, Answer of Prayer; humbled myself at his

Foot, for my Vileness and Unworthiness; lamented my Unprofitableness, that there were so little in me and my poor Service, to delight my Lord's Heart; and pray'd him to extend his Grace, according to his Word.—*Lord, say,* AMEN. *And let me say, with thy Saints and Angels,* HALLELUJAH! *To* HIM *that sits upon the Throne, and to the* LAMB, *be Blessing and Honour, and Glory and Power, forever and ever.* Amen!

July 17, 1749. I sought the Lord about copying for the Press *Short Notes on the Love of Christ,* from Eph. iii. 19. And by these Words was excited thereto, *Every Scribe which is instructed unto the Kingdom of Heaven, is like unto a Housholder, that bringeth forth out of his Treasure Things new and old,* Matt. xiii. 52. *And at our Gates are all manner of Pleasant Fruits, new and old, which I have laid up for Thee, O my Beloved,* Song vii. 13. *I have chosen you, and ordained you, that you should go and bring forth Fruit, and that your Fruit should remain,* Joh. xv. 16. *Whatsoever thine Hand findeth to do, do it with thy Might,* Eccles. ix. 10. *These are also Proverbs of* Solomon, *which the Men of* Hezekiah *King of* Judah *copied out,* Prov. xxv. 1. *Lovest thou* ME?—*Feed my Lambs,* Joh. xxi. 15. These Words encourag'd me to *copy out* what I had written of the *Love of Christ,* &c. with some small *Additions,* which I purpos'd to place at the End of a little Piece, I had Thoughts of Reprinting. But as I was under a humbling Sense of my own Vileness, Unworthiness and Weakness, and the little I had said, or could say, on so great a *Subject,* I wanted the Lord to say something farther to me, to assure me it was my *Duty* to take the Copy I had Thoughts of, in order to its Publication: And by that Word, apply'd to my Heart, I was fully satisfied, *This shall be written for the Generation to come: and the People which shall be created, shall praise the* LORD, Psal. cii. 18. For which humbly and joyfully I gave Thanks.—*O my Lord, of thy condescending Grace, go with me into, and carry me thro' the Work, to thy Praise! Do Good in thy good Pleasure thereby unto some of Thine! And say of thy little Worm, among the rest of thy better Children, and greater Servants,* I am glorified in them!

Aug. 3, 1749. Having copied my *Notes on the Love of Christ,* as above, and Thoughts of adding them to my little Piece, *The Hurt that Sin doth to Believers,* which I had a Desire to Re-print; as when first printed, I chiefly design'd it for *England,* and almost all the Copies were, by Mistake, sent into *America,* when my dear Husband went: I sought the Lord for his Direction and Blessing. And while I was before him, this Word dropt on my Heart, with great Power and Sweetness, *Yea saith the Spirit,* Rev. xiv. 13.

By which I receiv'd an Intimation, as to their Publication, and the Lord's Blessing thereon. O this, *Yea, saith the Spirit!* melted my Heart, humbled me before the Lord, and engag'd me to praise him: To give Thanks to the *Father*, who sends the Spirit in Christ's Name; to the *Son*, who dy'd and lives, that He might send him; and to the *Holy Ghost*, who comes as sent, who would come, and bless these weak Labours, of his vile, unworthy, Hell deserving *Worm!* I took the Words, as a *Grant* of that *Blessing*, my Soul *sought*: Which I tho't extended to the *Whole* of what I desir'd to publish, in this Piece.—But I wanted the Lord to say somewhat to me in *particular*, to the former and the latter Parts, of this intended Book. And for the former Part, *The Hurt of Sin*, and *The Word of Intreaty*, at the End of it, He was graciously pleas'd to hint both my Duty and Privilege in its Publication, by that Word, sweetly apply'd to my Heart, *Wash one another's Feet*, Joh. xiii. 14. And by this also, my Lord's Pleasure with my feeble *Attempt*, notwithstanding my *Unworthiness*, was signify'd to me. And as I was praying for his Blessing upon this, and the latter Part, *Notes on the Love of Christ*, He said unto me, *Because I live, ye shall live also*, Chap. xiv. 19. By which I was sweetly persuaded, that because *Christ lives* for me at God's Right Hand, I should *live also*; Rejoice for the Consolation, which He would minister to his dear Children, by what I had written, of his *Knowledge-passing Love*, which my Heart pray'd for. And for a Blessing on the *Improvement* thence made, to poor *Sinners*, I likewise pray'd. And soon that Word dropt on my Heart, *The Dead shall hear the Voice of the Son of God; and they that hear, shall live*, Joh. v. 25. By which I was encourag'd to hope, that my Lord would speak *Himself* by his *own Truths*, in the feeble Lines I had written, to the Hearts of some *dead Sinners*. And that Word also was bro't to my Mind, *The* LORD *was with* Samuel, *and did let none of his Words fall to the Ground*, 1 Sam. iii. 19. Which gave me Hope, that the Lord would bless the *Whole* of what He gave me to say for Him in this *Book*. And as I was humbled before him, under a Sense of my Littleness and Vileness, and told the Lord, "That I was not a *Samuel*, one of his *Prophets*, or *great Servants*; but one of the *least* and *last*, and *worst* of his Children:" He said unto me, *I have chosen* thee, *and not cast* thee *away*, Isa. xli. 9. As to *Usefulness*, in this poor *Book*; as I took it. Which melted my Heart, and I pray'd him to exalt his Grace, to work by it, for the Glory of his great Name, and secure to Himself all the Praise. Then that Word was bro't *O* Naphtali, *satisfy'd with Favour, and full with the Blessing of the* LORD: *possess thou the West and the South*, Deut. xxxiii. 23. By which a sweet

Hint was given me, of the *Grant* of all that *Blessing* on my poor *Book*, that my Soul *desir'd*; to my full Satisfaction with *Favour*, and Possession of that happy wondrous *Lot* assign'd me. And soon after, that Word dropt on my Mind, *Behold, I and the Children which the* LORD *hath given me, are for Signs, and for Wonders in* Israel; *from the* LORD *of Hosts, which dwelleth in Mount Zion*, Isa. viii. 18. Which fill'd my Heart with a precious abiding *Savour*, of the wondrous *Grace* of *God*, cast upon *Christ*, his *First born Son*, and thro' Him upon all his *Junior Brethren*, his *given Children*; and so upon *me* the Lord's *little One*, in relation to *Christ* with respect to this, my *little Service*. O how *sweet* was it, is it to me, That in all the wondrous *Grace*, cast upon *me* thro' *Christ*, in all my Work appointed, and Success granted, I *share* the same *with* HIM! That I am *with* HIM, in my *proper Sphere*, in my *little Measure*, for a *Sign*, and for a *Wonder*; (of infinite Kindness, of omnipotent Favour:) *from the* LORD *of Hosts, which dwelleth in Mount* Zion!—AMEN! HALLELUJAH!

THUS have I given some Account of the Lord's Loving-kindness towards me, in bringing out *Twelve* more of my little *Books*; and also hinted what I had from HIM, to *encourage me* in their *Publication*.—From which I hope, my dear Friends in Christ, will see how *greatly the Lord lov'd me*, in bringing out my *little Pieces*; and be able to judge of my *Motives* to appear in *Print*; and also hence be induced to form similar Ideas concerning those few *more*, that may yet see the Publick Light. As what I may have from God about Those, I don't at present think to publish. And to shew the complete Number of my Books now extant, I shall add the latter to the former, with their Names, as they came out in Order.

XXII. *Letters on Spiritual Subjects, and divers Occasions: sent to the Rev. Mr. George Whitefield, and others*, &c. VOL. III.

XXIII. *A Postscript to a Letter lately published, on the Duty and Privilege of a Believer, To live by Faith, and to improve his Faith unto Holiness*: &c.

XXIV. *Letters on Spiritual Subjects, and divers Occasions*: &c. Vol. IV.

XXV. *Brief Hints concerning Baptism*: &c.

XXVI. *A Letter to Mr William Cudworth: In Vindication of the Truth, from his Misrepresentations:—Being a Reply to his Answer to the Postscript of a Letter lately published*: &c.

XXVII. *Letters on Spiritual Subjects, and divers Occasions*: &c. VOL. V.

XXVIII. *Hints of the Glory of Christ, as the Friend and Bridegroom of the Church: From the Seven last Verses of the Fifth Chapter of Solomon's Song*: &c.

XXIX. *Thoughts on the Lord's Supper*: &c.

THESE Books were dispersed in *England*; and the most if not every one of these, with the former, which before, and together with them, were here dispersed abroad; The Lord hath now given me to *hear*, that they have been much *blest unto some Souls*. And I trust they *are blest*, and *shall be blessed* in *Time to come*. Even in *England*, my good GOD, had greatly blest my poor Writings, before any of my Books were sent into *America*: Tho' I had not so full a Knowledge of it *then*, as hath been given me *since*; and was under Discouragement, from the *Opposition* I met with from *some*, and fearing the Books were of but little *Use to others*.—But the Lord *wrought for me*, tho' it was *out of my Sight*, and brought it to my View, when I had most *Need* of the Consolation.—And since I heard of the Lord's using my *former Books*, for the Instruction and Comfort of some Souls, and for the Conversion of *others*; I think the *latter*, have been more *extensively blest*, for the Edification of *Saints*, for the Relief and Refreshment of our dear Lord's *tender Lambs*. O marvellous *Grace*, to a Creature the most *unworthy!* Unbounded, All-surmounting *Mercy*, to a *Sinner* deserving the utmost *Misery!* Thus in *England* hath the Lord my Father, shewn the *exceeding Riches of his Grace, in Kindness towards* me *thro'* Christ Jesus!—Nor was *England* a Place large enough, to answer the vast Designs of *his* Loving Kindness to unlovely *me*; but to *other Nations*, and even to *America*, must my Books be *sent*, and there also *blest!* O wondrous *Lot*, assign'd me in surprizingly *Free*, and *Infinite Favour!* For' tho' *less than the least of all Saints*, and the *chief of Sinners*: So *great* hath been the Grace of GOD towards me! So *great* hath been his promis'd Goodness, his Covenant Faithfulness! And *still* his infinite *Kindness*, is to *me* extended, and in it He hath spoken of *great Things* concerning me, for a *great while to come! Praise* to that *Grace*, which *reigns thro' Righteousness, by* Jesus Christ *our* Lord!—I am to give,

Secondly. Answer to an *Objection* that may be made against the Lord's Grant of my Desire in *special Favour*, in sending my Books into *America*: From that great *Trial* which follow'd upon it, in the *Loss of my dear Husband by Sea*. For,

As in this *Third* Part of my brief Account, I gave a Hint of the Lord's sending my Books into *America*, as an *Answer of Prayer*; and of his engaging my Heart to *trust in Him*, and fearless, *venture* into *this Service for Him*, in the Face of Difficulties: From those Words. *Fear not ye; for ye seek* JESUS: And, *The Merchandise of Wisdom is better than Silver, and the Gain thereof than fine Gold*: Hence, as it pleas'd God to exercise me with so great a *Trial* as the *Loss of my dear Husband by Sea*, in his Return Home: Some may be ready to think and say,

Obj. That if the Lord had granted my Desire in *special Favour*; and call'd me to venture in this Service for his *Honour*: Surely the *End*, would not have been so *dark* and *trying*: The *Event*, having in it, rather the Face of a *Rebuke*, than the least Aspect of *Favour*.—To this therefore, I think it my Duty to make some *Reply*. And to set Things in the same *Light*, in which they appear to *me*, let it be observed by way of *Answer*, in General:

Ans. 1. That my dear Husband's going into *America*, was not *desired*, nor *sought for*, by *me*, nor was his going thither, on Account of *my Books*, but on *other Accounts*; and his *Design* to take the Books with him, was *after* he had *determined* his Voyage. So that my great Trial in the Loss of my dear Yokefellow, was *not* occasion'd, *principally*, by *my Books* being sent into *America*: Tho' it followed thereon consequentially.—But if it *had*; no just Argument could thence be drawn, That the Lord had not granted my Desire in *special Favour*, nor call'd me to venture in this Service for his *Honour*, Because,

Ans. 2. The *Judgments of God* are a *great Deep*: *No Man knoweth either Love or Hatred, by all that is before them*: Whilst, *All Things come alike unto all*. So that GOD's *Way* being in the *Sea*, and his *Path* in the *great Waters*, his *Footsteps* are (at Times, to his dearest Favourites) *not known*. And,

Ans. 3. The *Estimate* of God's *special Favour*, or of his *fatherly Displeasure*, in his various Dispensations towards his dear Children, is not to be taken merely from the outward *Face of Things in Providence*; but rather from the inward *Effect* of those Dispensations upon their Souls.— Great Trials, are not always the Fruit of great Sins, nor a Token of God's great Displeasure, but are sometimes an Indication of his great Favour. As is clear in the Case of *Job*, whom the Lord singled out in special Favour, to be an eminent Instance and Example of *suffering Affliction and of Patience*, to GOD's *Honour*, in supporting him *under the Trial*, and bringing him *out of the Furnace*, as *Gold seven Times refined*, and to *Job's* special *Advan-*

tage, present and eternal. So that, if *great Trials*, are blest to God's People, to exercise their *Graces*, and to prepare them for their *Crown*, they may, they ought to be, esteemed by them, as Tokens of his *special Favour*. And so, the greatest temporal *Loss*, may prove to Wisdom's Merchants, the greatest *Gain*, both spiritual and eternal: And can be no *Argument*, against the Grant of their Desires in peculiar *Favour*, nor against their being call'd of GOD to venture in any Piece of Service for his *Honour*; whatever *Trial* may attend their *Labour*.—But, more particularly,

Though, No Affliction that befalls the Saints in a Way of Duty, can be any just Argument against the Lord's special Mercy; yet Satan and Unbelief, are not wanting to make such *Suggestions*, when the dear Children of God are under *trying Dispensations*. And thus I must confess, that my Soul-Enemies, tho' in the main mightily restrained, yet at Times, under my great Trial, have said unto me, "*Where is thy God?* If thou hadst *found Grace in his Sight as* his *special Favourite*, would he have dealt *thus with thee? Is this the End*, of thy *trusting in God?* &c." To which when most oppress'd, I was enabled to reply thro' Grace, "No; this is not the *End*: My GOD, is but on his *Way*, in special Favour, to do me *Good*, by this *great Trial*. Tho' he now veils his Face in a *Cloud*, he will again bring me forth to the *Light*, and I shall behold his *Righteousness*. But, whatever my GOD doth with me; HE will be *glorify'd*; and *that* shall be *my Joy*, &c."

I have no Doubt, of God's sending my Books into *America*, as an *Answer* of my *Prayer*, nor that he did this of *special Favour*. And in that he did it by Means of my dear *Husband's* going thither, who dispers'd them abroad in such *Numbers*, as no other Person either could or would; my GOD herein, hath not only *answered*, but far *exceeded*, my Desires, Faith and Hope. O how small would have been my Portion of Favour, if God had granted my Request, in the Way I wish'd, and sent only a *few of the Books*, to be dispers'd by a *Friend* that went thither, as I *desired*; to what it *was*, when the Lord answered my Prayer in his *own Way*, and did for me therein, according to the infinite Grace of his *own Heart!*—By the Way, then, How *good* is it, to refer all our Petitions, for Manner, Measure, and Time of Answer, to the Wisdom and Grace of the God of Compassions: Who delighteth to do for his People, *exceeding abundantly above all that they ask or think!*—Great was the Goodness of my GOD towards me, in sending my Books by my dear *Husband*, in that unthought of, undesired *Way*; in carrying him and them safe over the great Waters; in preserving his Life till they were spread abroad, and till he could inform me, "That many dear Friends desir'd to be remembred to me most kindly, and that he would acquaint me, that the Books had been *blest to their Souls*, and they made to *bless* GOD, that they ever saw them:" Which was, and is, my present *Consolation*, and will be my eternal *Joy*, to the endless *Glory* of infinite *Grace!*

And as my dear Husband, aim'd at the Glory of God and the Good of Souls, in his going into *America*; and in his Work, which he did there, and likewise had the Satisfaction to see his Desires in part accomplished: So likewise, he had the Pleasure to see, and to acquaint me, "That *his Labours* in the *Gospel of Christ*, were *blest* for the Edification of *Saints*, and for the Conversion of some *Sinners*, not less than *Eleven or Twelve Souls.*" This he inform'd me of with the deepest Humility, under a Sense of his great Unworthiness, and with the highest Wonder at the exceeding Riches of God's Free Grace, in thus working by his Ministry. And this was to *me*, a very great *Joy*; and made the Pain of Absence more easy. Yea, I thought, when I had this News, "That I could freely give him up to the *Lord's Service*, if he should call for his very *Life* to be spent in it; and that I should lose my *Pain* for his Absence, in the *Pleasure* of my Lord's Glory, by his Presence where such blessed Work was to be done by him."—And as the Lord wrought this Disposition then in my Heart; So when he was pleas'd thus actually to *try me*, it was brought to my Thought. And thro' his Grace with my Spirit, I was still of the *same Mind*, and sweetly the Lord drew me into Resignation to, and Acquiescence with, his *good Pleasure*.

But notwithstanding this, my *Trial* was very *great*; not only *personally*, but *relatively* consider'd, with respect to the *Church*. I had not only lost my dear *Husband*, but the Church also had lost its *Pastor*. I gave a Hint in the *Second* Part of my Brief Account, of that great *Love* to the *People*, and *Concern* for their *Good*, which the Lord wrought in my Soul, when he first brought me amongst them, from the Promises he gave me concerning them.—And by his applying that Word to my Heart, *He sent before them* Moses, *and* Aaron, *and* Miriam: I was persuaded that the Lord had some Work for *me* to do among them. And thus, a *natural Care* for their *State*, possessed my Heart. And this Love and Care being continu'd, was heightned, by their being left destitute, having *none* to care for them. *Their* desolate Case, made *my Heart* desolate.

Great were my Trials, with respect to the *Church* during my dear Husband's *Absence*, who was providentially detained from us, much longer than he thought of or designed. For while he was absent, many of our Members dy'd, others were providentially remov'd, and the Auditory much decreased, &c. This melancholy Aspect, greatly *try'd me*, as it did also my dear *Husband*, who would fain have return'd to us much sooner, but was prevented. But the Lord did me *great Good*, by my *great Trials*. Blessed be his holy Name, he hereby exercis'd and increas'd my Faith and Love, Hope and Patience, and every Grace. So that I would not have been withont [*sic*; r. without] my *Afflictions*, which were attended with such blessed *Fruits*. Believing, I rejoiced, that the Lord led me the *right Way*, to a *City of Habitation*. And as my God enabled me to bring a little *Glory to* HIM, under my Griefs, my *Joys* therein, were *unspeakable!* I lov'd the *Glory of God*, I rejoiced in it, far above *all Things*. But the low Estate of the Church, lay very near me. This put me upon crying to the Lord most earnestly, for my dear Husband's *Return*, and that the Lord, in an eminent Manner, would *return with Him, and build up the Tabernacle of* David, *which was fallen down* amongst us. I pray'd, I wrestled with God, I could not, would not, let him go, without a Blessing. And he said unto me, repeatedly, *I know thee by Name; and thou hast found Grace in my Sight*: And, *Thou hast prevailed*. Innumerable were the Promises that the Lord gave me; which greatly reviv'd, and mightily supported me. I liv'd amidst promis'd Grace, I trusted Divine Faithfulness. And whenever my Heart fainted, some Word or other, as a spirituous Cordial, was given me. And fain, very fain, would I have seen the Promises fulfilled in my dear Husband's safe *Return*, and his abundant *Usefulness*. I could see no Way like *this*, for the Glory of God, and our Joy. And therefore thought, "That if the Lord *comforted me on every Side*, (as he said he would) surely he would return my dear Husband, and work eminently by him." But GOD's *Thoughts* and *Ways*, were as *high* above *my Thoughts*, and the *Ways* which *I* drew out for him to work in, *as the Heavens are above the Earth!*

Thus for several Years was I carried on. Promises supported me, Providences try'd me. And a Spirit of Supplication, with earnest Expectation for GOD, were kept up in my Soul. I cry'd to him, believ'd in him, lov'd him, long'd for him, and patiently referring the Time of his Appearance for me, to his sovereign Pleasure, and cheerfully, for his Honour, I waited for him. And every Spring and Fall, when I had Hopes of my Husband's Return, my Trial was renewed by repeated Disappointments.—And when *I* last expected his coming, according to his Purpose, I had many Scriptures brought to my Mind on a certain Day, and part of the next, with Power and great Glory: and that in particular, *Lo, this is our God, we have waited for him, and he will save us: this is the* LORD, *we have waited for him, we will be glad, and rejoice in his Salvation*, Isa. xxv. 9. Whence I thought, "Perhaps this may be the Time of my dear Husband's landing." But again I thought, "Surely it cannot, as the Wind is contrary." And while I was reasoning thus in my Mind, those Words came in, *My Thoughts are not your Thoughts, neither are your Ways my Ways, saith the* LORD. *For as the Heavens are higher than the Earth, so are my Ways higher than your Ways, and my Thoughts than your Thoughts. For as the Rain cometh down, and the Snow from Heaven*, &c.. Isa. lv. 8, 9, 10, 11. Upon which, I knew not what to think, more than this, "That God's Word, should be fulfilled in his own Way." And wait I did, to see how the Lord would work.—And as divers of the Promises seem'd to bespeak the Church's Deliverance near, and that, *Thou shalt arise and have Mercy upon* Zion: *for the Time to favour her, yea, the set Time is come*, Psal. cii. 13. I rejoic'd in Hope of promis'd Glory.—But soon, amidst all the Brightness that shined upon my Spirit, that Word was brought, *Who is among you that feareth the* LORD, *that obeyeth the Voice of his Servant, that walketh in Darkness and hath no Light? let him trust in the Name of the* LORD, *and stay upon his God*, Isa. l. 10. This I knew not how to take: Having had so many Promises of *Light*, that such a Word should come in, which seem'd to foretel *Darkness*. But I thought, "Perhaps the Lord might open this to me more hereafter."

And lo, from that Time, when I look'd for Light to surround me *suddenly*, Darkness cover'd me *speedily*. The *Fleet* came, with which I expected my *Husband*, but *He* was not with it; nor any *Letter* from him, (as I us'd to have when he was prevented coming) nor *Account* of him, had I by it.—This *try'd me exceedingly*; as from the Time I waited earnestly and constantly, in hopes to see, or hear from him, or of him, and could hear Nothing, for near *Six Months* afterwards.—During this Time of Trial, the Lord supported, and variously exercised me. I walk'd in *Darkness*, indeed, and had *no Light* in Providence; but enabled I was to *trust in the* LORD, and to *stay upon my* GOD, in the Faith of his Promise: That I should yet see his Faithfulness, in fulfilling his Word according to his own Mind: And I hop'd it might be in the Way that I desir'd; *viz.* in my dear Husband's safe *Return*, after so long an *Exercise*. Various Temptations at Times press'd hard upon me, but exceeding great and precious Promises were given to support me; and I counted my God *able* and *faithful* who had *promised*; and for *his Honour*, labour'd thus to set to my Seal, *That* HE *is true: Believing to see the Goodness of the* LORD, *in the Land of the Living*.

At length, it pleas'd my kind Lord, to grant my Desire of a *Letter.*—But oh! the *News* it brought: Instead of my dear Husband's safe *Return*, I heard of his *Death*, and that he was *cast away* in his Passage home, by the *foundering of the Ship!* How *grieving* was this to Nature! How *trying* to my Faith and Hope! The real *Loss* of my *dear Yokefellow*; the seeming *Denial* of my *earnest Prayers*; and the *Failure* of my *Expectation*, as to his Return, which I hoped might have been included in God's never-failing Promises, with the *Distress* of the *Church*, occasion'd thereby; came all upon me at *once*. And *Satan* and *Unbelief* with their usual *Insults*, would fain have *triumph'd over me*. And doubtless, prest with such *Weights*, I should have sunk in *deep Waters*, if I had not been mightily *Underpropped*. But, Glory to the *Eternal* GOD! *Underneath were the Everlasting Arms!* I received *Mercy*, and fainted *not*, in the *Day of Adversity*; but was enabled to stand my Ground for GOD, and in Faith to resist the *Enemy*. And the Lord in tender Pity, *restrained* the Power of Darkness, and blest me with the Light of *Promise*, that I might endure the Gloom of *Providence*. So far as the Trial had the Face of *Rebuke*, I was humbled for my Unworthiness and Vileness, justify'd GOD in his Dispensations, as holy, wise, and good. My Heart clave to him. I lov'd, ador'd, and blest him in all. And amidst my Sorrows, in my greatest Depressions, I rejoiced, that whatever *fell*, God's *Glory*, by all would *rise*. I lov'd the Glory of God above *all Things*; I earnestly long'd actively to *glorify him in all*; and with my utmost Strength, attempted to give him *Praise*. I dreaded Nothing so much, as casting *Dishonour* upon my *good* GOD, by any unmeet *Dejection of Spirit*, when cast by Providence into the *Depths of Trial*. And blessed be the Lord my own God, that I was enabled to think and speak well of HIM, under *all* and to rejoice in HIM as my ALL: And in Hope of the Light of *Glory*, when the Vail of *Darkness*, should be taken off the Face of *Providence*, and I see it clearly, in a full Consistency with the *Promise*. And mean while, To give my GOD a *little Glory* by the *Trial*, Oh, it was Joy in Sorrow, Ease in Pain, Life in Death, to my Spirit! I accounted *this* as my *Gain*, a Gain so *great*, that no Loss of mine could *equalize*, or was worthy to be *compared with it*: Yea, my very *Loss*, as a subservient *Means*, to this great *End*, was esteemed by me a Sort of *Gain*. Thus my good GOD, supported, instructed, and counsell'd me. For

Once in particular, when I was thinking on my Trial, "That in Itself, and Circumstances, it was the *greatest* I ever met with": This was suggested to my Mind, "That if this was the *greatest Trial* I ever met with; if I would

love, adore and bless my GOD under it, now he seem'd thus to rebuke me;
I should give him a *greater Glory*, than I ever gave him." And this, of the
Glory of GOD, took my Heart exceedingly, and drew away my Soul after it.
I rejoiced at a Thought, of *glorifying* GOD *in the Fires*; and lost my Pain, in
the sweet Pleasure. I rejoiced at my given Opportunity, to give Glory to my
great and good GOD. I look'd upon this as my *Work*; and long'd to engage
in it in good Earnest.—And while I was thus exercis'd, the Lord shined into
my Heart, to give the Knowledge of his Glory in the Face of Christ, in this
Trial: He opened *another Prospect* of it to me, and shew'd me, That I rather
mis called this Affliction, when I nam'd it *Rebuke*, and ought to account it
a *Favour*, and an *Honour* cast upon me, that I was call'd by such a *Trial*,
and enabled by *Grace*, to give the Lord such a *Glory*, as without it I could
not have given him. And thus I saw, That *Sufferings* to the *Saints*, and *this*
to *me*, was a *Gift* of God's *special Love*, for the *Sake of Christ*, that *on the
Behalf of Christ, it was given me, not only to believe on him, but also to
suffer for his Sake*, Phil. i. 29. This also was farther clear'd to me, from
Mar. x. 30. *But he shall receive an Hundred-fold mow in this Time, Houses,
and Brethren, and Sisters, and Mothers, and Children, and Lands, with*
Persecutions; *and in the World to come eternal Life.* Peter said to our *Lord,
Lo, we have left all, and have followed thee*, Ver. 28. *And* Jesus *answered
and said, Verily I say unto you, There is no Man that hath left House, or
Brethren, or Sisters, or Father, or Mother, or Wife, or Children, or Lands,
for my Sake and the Gospel's, But he shall receive*, &c. Ver. 29, 30. Here
our dear Lord assures his Followers, that they should be no *Losers*, but
Gainers, by whatever they had *forsaken* for *Him*, and his *Gospel's Sake*,
that now in *this Time*, they should receive an *Hundred-fold*, and in the
World to come eternal Life. And among their *Receivings* here, as Royal
Gifts of his *special Favour*, he puts in *Persecutions*. Strange! That
Persecutions should be put into the *Reward* of those, who had *forsaken all
for Christ's Sake*. But *thus, thus* Troubles and Afflictions, are cast upon the
Favourites of Heaven, that have left any Thing for Christ's Sake, To give
them the present Bliss, under Efficacious Grace, of *Opportunities to glorify
God*, and our *Lord Jesus Christ*, by their *Sufferings*; that this also may be
unto *their Glory*, for the Advancement of their *Crown*, when HE appears!
Oh rich *Reward*, of forsaking *All* for *Christ's Sake!* Ineffable *Gain*, of that
Loss!   Thus, in General and Particular, I have attempted to set Things in
the *same Light*, in which they appear to *me*: In order to shew, That the
Lord's sending my Books into *America*, was the *Answer* of my *Prayer*, in

special Favour: And also, That as I was call'd to *trust the Lord*, and to *venture* in this Service for his *Honour*; So my *Gain* was unspeakably *great* thereby, to my exceeding *Joy*, notwithstanding my great *Trial* and *Sorrow*, in the *Loss* of my dear *Yoke-fellow*: Yea, to shew, That my great *Loss*, over-ruled by Grace, for the Glory of God by *me*, and for my Glory in *Him*, was my ineffable *Gain!* And this I have done,

1. For the Vindication of *God's Honour*: The Honour of his Grace and Faithfulness, as a GOD *hearing Prayer*, and *keeping Covenant*. And

2. For the *Advantage* of his *dear Children*: To remove any *Objection*, or Cause of *Stumbling*, from the tender Lambs of Christ, which might be cast in their *Way*, while viewing the Lord's gracious Dealings with *me*, from that great *Trial*, with which he was pleas'd to *exercise me*. And these *Ends* I chiefly had in *view* in this appendix.

And as my Trials respected, not only *Providences*, but also *Promises*; I have one Thing more, that for the Glory of God and the Good of his People, I would give some Hints about. *This*:

That it pleaseth God at Times, to fulfil his Promises to his People, not by the Gift of those *very Things*, or in those *very Ways*, which they *desir'd*, and perhaps *expected* from the Promise: But by Things, of in Ways, which HE, in his infinite Wisdom and Goodness, sees *better*.

Of this I have had abundant Experience, in these my late Trials. To instance in one Particular.

About a Fortnight before I heard of my dear Husband's Death, while I was waiting with a *Who can tell* but God may be gracious to me, in his *safe Return?* Had almost lost *Hope* of it, but knew not how the Lord might *appear*, tho' every Thing then look'd very *dark* and *trying*: That Word, with great Power, came into my Mind, *Pursue*; *for thou shalt surely recover all*, 1 Sam. xxx. 8. This Word, I knew not how to take. I thought it very improbable, that my Husband should be return'd, and my Desire thereby granted, in the Deliverance and Prosperity of the Church. But I ask'd the Lord, "If there was yet room for me to hope for so great Favours?" And I was directed to cast myself upon the Grace, Power and Faithfulness of GOD, to fulfil his Promise as should be most for his own Glory in my Salvation. Then that Word came in, *Go thy Way, and as thou hast believed, so be it done unto thee*, Mat. viii. 13. And these likewise, Ps. xii. 5. *For the Sighing of the Needy, now will I arise, saith the* LORD, Isa. xlii. 13, 14. *The* LORD *shall go forth as a mighty Man, he shall stir up Jealousy like a Man of War: He shall cry; yea, rore; he shall prevail against his Enemies. I have long*

Time holden my Peace, I have been still and refrained myself: now will I cry like a travailing Woman, I will destroy and devour at once. From these Words I was persuaded, that the Lord would *surely* and *speedily* appear for me, to answer my Faith and Hope, in promis'd Deliverance; notwithstanding the Triumphs of my spiritual Enemies over me, in the Depths of my Distress, while in Providence the Lord hid his Face. And by the former, *Pursue, for thou shalt without Fail recover all*: I was directed to go on by Faith and Prayer, in the *Pursuit* of promis'd Mercies, and assur'd that I *should recover all*; as it were out of the Hand of the Enemy; tho' at Times I was ready to give up all for *lost*, as if my Hope was *cut off*, and carried away by adverse Power. And being thus strengthned by these Promises, I waited for their Fulfilment; and knew not then, but the Lord might perform his Word, in that very *Way*, and by that very *Person* which I desir'd; *viz.* by returning my dear Husband in Safety, and by Blessing his Ministry for the Church's Prosperity: Tho' at that Time, nothing appear'd but the contrary.

And blessed be my good GOD, he speedily fulfill'd his Word, and answer'd my Prayer, in giving me to hear of my husband. And tho' it was of his *Death*, by which my Hope was cut off as to his *Return*, and so as to his *Usefulness*, who was the *Person* that I wish'd, and hop'd the Lord would work by: (And which I then was apt to call the *very Thing* that I sought; but have since seen, that the *main Thing* I sought the Lord for, was the *Prosperity of the Church*; and that my dear Husband's *Return*, and *Usefulness*, were but the *Means*, I wish'd to have the *Thing* I desir'd accomplish'd by: For,) Yet, the Lord's *Promise*, did not *fail*, nor did what I hop'd for *from it*, come to *Nothing*. My Hope (what I hop'd for) in his *Word*, was *Gladness*: Or, the Matter of my *Joy*, in its *Accomplishment*. For tho' the Lord did not give me the main *Thing* I desir'd, by my Husband's *Return*, he gave it me in another *Way*, which HE thought *better*, by another *Minister*, brought to reside amongst us, and dispense his *Gospel* to us; and some *Reviving* by his Ministry he blest us with. The Lord *lov'd* my dear Husband into his own Bosom, *lov'd* the Trial of his Death to me and the Church, and *lov'd* another Minister to us in his Room: All which, infinite Wisdom and Goodness saw *better*, more for God's Glory and our Advantage, than if Things had been as I *wish'd*, and *hop'd for*.—And as when God gives Mercies and Comforts to his People, he sometimes gives them in *Parts*: And reserves to himself a Liberty to bestow what *Trials* with them, HE pleaseth, to answer the Ends of his Wisdom and Grace: So, tho' the Mercy I desir'd, was at first given but in part, and various Trials attended, while this Minister *resided* with us, and after he had done *ministring* to us; yet the *Lord appear'd for us.*—That Promise, before I heard of my Husband's Death, was apply'd for Comfort to my Heart, *I will settle you after your* old Estate, *and will do* better *unto you than at your* Beginning, Ezek. xxxvi. 11. From this I was persuaded, that the Church should enjoy a *Pastor*, and be blest with the Administration of *special Ordinances*, &c. and that therein, under a rich Descent of Divine Influence, the Lord would do *better* unto us than at our *Beginning*: And fain would I have *had*, yea, was apt to *think*, my dear *Husband* might be the very *Person* and *Instrument*, design'd by the *promis'd Grace*. But tho' Providence shew'd, that *He* was not the Person, nor yet that other *Minister*, intended in the Promise: Yet the Lord, to fulfil his Word, appear'd gloriously, as a GOD *hearing Prayer*, at a Time of our *great Necessity*, in providing *another Person*, a *choice Minister*, for us, and giving him into the *Bosom of the Church*. Whose Ministry being *blest* unto us, we requested him to take the *Pastoral Care of us*: To which the Lord, of his infinite Mercy, *inclin'd his Heart.*—And tho' the Church is yet in a low Estate; we hope to see the *Plummet* in the Hand of *Zerubbabel*, in the Hand of *Christ*, the King of *Sion*, that *again* he *will build us, and* we *shall be built*: And with Expectation for GOD, who hath promis'd to do *great Things*, we wait to see, How much *better* the Lord will do unto us, than at our *Beginning!*—And in divers Respects, I see already, how much *better* it was, for God's Glory, and the Good of his People, that HE took his *own Way*, in working Deliverance for us, according to his Promise, than if he had wrought in *that Way*, which I most earnestly *desired*.

Thus, *Pursuing*, in the Paths of Duty, promis'd Mercy, *I have surely recover'd*, and *shall recover all. All* that the *Lord intended* in the *Promise*, and *all*, in *Substance*, that *I desir'd*, and *hop'd for*, from the Word of the Lord: Tho' not in that *very Way*, and by that *very Person* which I *wish'd*, and in some Sort *expected*; but in *others*, that *God saw better*, and in and by which, I trust, HE will far *exceed* my Expectation: Fulfilling his Promises, and my Desires, in *doing for me*, according to the Immensity of his Wisdom and Goodness, and the Eternity of his Truth and Faithfulness, *more exceeding abundantly than I could ask or think!**—From hence then I shall

---

*N.B.: The Reader is here desir'd to review the Instruction given me in the Night of Nov. 20, 1741. For doubtless the Lord intended more in the Truths he taught me by those Scriptures then apply'd to me, than what at that Time I appre-

Thirdly, Close this appendix with a Word or two of *Use*. And

1. Let the dear Saints be *cautious*, when God applies Promises to comfort them in their Distresses, which foretel their Deliverances; How they draw out *Ways*, and fix *Times*, for GOD to *walk*, and *work in*: As He often *performs* his Word, *answers* their Faith and Prayer, *fulfils*, and even *exceeds* their Desires, in granting them, not those *very Things*, or not in those *very Ways*, which they most earnestly *wish* and *expect*, but in *others*, which for his Glory and their Good, are *far, far, better*. 'Tis true, our good God, doth

---

hended.—My Instruction and Comfort then given, were rather general, than *particular*, viz. "That the Lord would open the Way for my desired Usefulness according to his Promise. And that tho' I might meet with Trials before the Fulfilment of the Promise, yet when the Time of it came, I should be deliver'd out of them."— But now, having the Light of Providence, to irradiate the Promise, I humbly think, That the Lord design'd me a farther Usefulness, than what at that Time I explicitly desir'd: That he intended Promises which should be afterward given me, as well as those that were then apply'd: That the Time of the Promise, respected both: That the Trials I might meet with between the giving and fulfilling of the Promise, had likewise a double Aspect: And that the Deliverance, and the Deliverer, then hinted, were various in their Intendment, and distinct in their Accomplishment.

The Usefulness which I then chiefly sought, was that I earnestly wish'd for by the bringing out of my Books, the sending them abroad, and particularly in *America*. The Promises then given me chiefly respected this. The Trials I was first to meet with, related to the Delay of the Books coming out, it being from that Time near two Years, ere Providence open'd a Way for their being printed. But when the Time of the Promise, in that Respect, drew nigh, lo, my GOD brought them out, as it were all at once. And an unthought of Instrument, my dear Husband, the Lord employ'd, to disperse them in *America*.

But my farther Usefulness, which the Lord also intended, did particularly respect this poor little Church, for which I all along was much concerned. The Promises which the Lord gave me after my Husband's Departure, chiefly respected their Prosperity, which I most earnestly sought for. The Trials I met with relating to the Church, occasion'd by my Husband's long Stay, and the Delay of the Answer of my Prayers, were very great, a Wilderness indeed; into which the Lord brought, and in some Sense allur'd me: And fitly was this my State resembled by the Bush on Fire, and not consumed. But when the Time of the Promise respecting the Church, drew nigh, the Lord in boundless Mercy and infinite Faithfulness, rais'd up a Deliverer, and wrought Deliverance, by sending the Minister he had provided; and whom he gave to be our Pastor.—Thus in both Respects, was I satisfy'd with the Lord's promis'd Goodness, and my Trials in both, were blest for my Advantage.

many Times perform his Promise, answer our Faith and Hope, and abundantly satisfy our Desires, by granting us the *very Things*, in those *very Ways*, that we *request* and *expect*: As in my *Second* Part of Brief Account, *&c.* page 34, *&c.* But as he doth not *always* do thus; it is safest to wait for the Explication of the *Promise*, in *Providence*, before we draw any positive *Conclusions*, as to the particular *Manner* and *Time* of its Accomplishment.

2. Let the *Heirs of Promise*, judge the GOD of *Promise*, both *able* and *faithful*, to *fulfil* his gracious Engagements: For not a Jot or Tittle of his Word shall *fail*. If he visits us not in *that Way* which we *wish*, or *expect*, he will come in *another* and *better*. Whatever *fails*, God's *Promise* shall not *fail*, nor any Part of the *Grace* of it, be *unaccomplished*. And much it is for God's Honour, and our Joy, that we set to our Seal, *That* HE *is true*. And that, while promis'd Mercies are depending, we frequently say in Faith and Hope, *The Strength of* Israel, *will not* lie, *nor* repent: *Hath* HE *said, and will he not* do it? *Or, hath* HE *spoken, and will he not* make it good? For thus *believing*, there shall be a *Performance* of those Things, which are *told us from the Lord*. And hence,

3. Let us learn, the *Blessedness of Those*, who *trust in the* LORD *at all Times*, and *pour out their* Hearts *before* HIM, who as their GOD, *is a* Refuge *for them*: For, *They shall* praise *the* LORD, that seek him. *Their Heart shall live, that* seek GOD. *For the Eyes of the* LORD *run to and fro thro' the whole Earth, to shew Himself* strong, *in behalf of* them (in fulfilling his Promises and working Deliverances for *them*) *whose* Heart (in respect of *Trust*) *is* perfect *towards him*—*Now unto* HIM *who* hath done, and is *able* to *do for me*, and all his *Suppliants, exceeding abundantly above all that we ask or think, according to the Power that worketh in us, Unto* HIM *be* Glory *in the* Church *by* CHRIST JESUS, *throughout all Ages, World without End!* Amen.

P O S T S C R I P T.

Feb. 21, 1749. I sought the Lord, to know if He would please to have my *Third* Part of *Brief Account* put to the Press, having finisht its *Appendix.* And by these Scriptures sweetly apply'd to my Heart, I was persuaded it was his Mind that it should. *Fear thou not, for I am* with thee; *be not dismayed, for I am* thy God, Isa. xli. 10. From this I had a sweet Hint, That the Lord would be *with me* in its Out-going, as my GOD. Which fill'd me with Heart-melting Wonder, that the Lord should be *with me*, and *my* GOD *still*, notwithstanding my Unprofitableness. *Lovest thou* ME?—Feed my Lambs, Joh. xxi. 15. By this my dear Lord call'd for this little Piece to come out, put it upon *my Love to him, to feed his Lambs* thereby, and gave me a pleasing Hint, That this Blessing should attend my Labour. *Thou art* Gilead *unto* ME, Jer. xxii. 6. That is, An *Heap of Witness* unto HIM, in this *Service*, and an *Healer* of the Spirits of his People, as it was then apply'd with Heart-melting Power unto *me*. And as I had some Fears, lest by its Publication, any should *think of me* more *highly* than is *meet*; or any reflect upon me, for presenting to *publick View*, while *I was living*, what passed between God and my Soul in *private*: These Scriptures were brought, *I have made thee an Iron Pillar, and brazen Walls: Be not dismayed at their Faces, lest I* confound *thee before them*, Jer. l. 17, 18. *Whosoever therefore shall be* ashamed of ME, *of him shall the Son of Man be* ashamed, *when he cometh in the Glory of his Father, with his holy Angels*, Mar. viii. 38. These laid my Spirit under an holy Awe, pointed my Eye singly to the Lord, and made me in some Sort regardless of Men. This Word likewise came in, to excite me to publish it now, and to hint it to me as Duty, *She hath done what She* could, Ch. xiv. 8. That Text also encourag'd me, *This* shall be written *for the Generation to come: and the People* that *shall be created*, shall praise the LORD, Ps. cii. 18. And, *The Lord hath* Need of him, Mar. xi. 3. By this my Heart was sweetly melted, at the infinite Condescension of my Lord's Grace, that He should say, HE had *Need* of this my poor Service!—O *my dear* Lord Jesus, *drawn by thee, of* thine own *I* give thee! *And with it, my* little Self. *Wash thy vile Worm, and my polluted Service in thy precious Blood, cloth me with thy Beauties; take my feeble Work, into thine Almighty Hand, get Thyself* Honour *thereby; and let thy most unworthy Worm have the* Bliss, *with all thy Saints and Angels, to give thee* endless Praise!—*Say*, Lord Jesus, *yea, thou* dost *say, Be it unto* thee, *even as thou* wilt!

F I N I S.

E R R A T A.

[Editor's note. Page and line numbers refer to those of the original pages. In the present transcription, these corrections appear in the running text as bracketed notes, e.g., "*Dealing* [*sic*, r. *Dealings*]."]

PAGE 3, Line 14, for *Dealing*, read *Dealings*; p. 66, l. 31, for *the*, r. *thee*; p. 80, l. 21, after *fled*, r. *Jordan*, before *and* [Editor's note. The preceding "correction" is confused. Dutton's text should be corrected to the text of Psa. 114:3 in the 1611 KJV.]; p. 105, l. 31, for *gavest*, r. *givest*; p. 111, l. 29, for *thought*, r. *I thought*; p. 119, l. 1, for *Exerlasting*, r. *Everlasting*; p. 132, l. 7, after *any*, r. *of.*

A

LETTER

To such of the

SERVANTS

OF

CHRIST,

WHO

May have any Scruples about the Lawfulness of
PRINTING any Thing written by a Woman:

TO SHEW,

That BOOK-TEACHING is *private*, with Respect to
the *Church*, and permitted to *private Christians*; yea, commanded to Those, of *either
Sex*, who are Gifted for, and Inclin'd to engage in this Service.

By   *A. D.*

LONDON:

Printed by J. HART in *Poppings-court, Fleetstreet*; and
Sold by J. LEWIS, in *Bartholomew-Close*, near
West-Smithfield; and E. GARDNER, at *Milton's-
Head* in *Gracechurch-Street*, 1743.

[*Price One Penny*]

A

L E T T E R

To such of the Servants of *CHRIST*, who have any Scruple
about the Lawfulness of PRINTING any Thing written
by a Woman: A Friend and Servant of Theirs, sendeth
Greeting.

Honour'd Brethren,

HAving heard that some of you have objected against my appearing in
Print; as if it was contrary to the revealed *Will* of God: I thought it my Duty,
meekly and humbly to offer to your Consideration, what is satisfactory to
my own Soul in this regard: And,

First, I beg Leave to assure you, that my Design in publishing what I
have written; was only the Glory of God, and the Good of Souls. This *End*
I know you approve of. And that the *Means* I have made Use of to attain it,
is Lawful and Right, will be evident, if you consider,

Secondly, That my appearing in Print, is not *against* any of the Laws
of Christ in the sacred Records. These I highly value, and desire ever to
obey with the greatest Delight. It is not against *that*, 1 Tim. ii. 12. *But I
suffer not a Woman to Teach, nor to usurp Authority over the Man, but to
be in Silence.* Nor yet against *that*, 1 Cor. xiv. 34, 35. *Let your Women keep
Silence in the Churches: for it is not permitted unto them to speak; but they
are commanded to be under Obedience, as also saith the Law.* It is plain
from these *Texts*, that it is a Publick Authoritative Teaching in the Church,
that is here forbidden unto *Women*: And that it is in this regard only, they
are commanded to be in Silence. And *Printing* is a Thing of a very different
Consideration.

For tho' what is printed is published to the *World*, and the Instruction
thereby given, is in this regard *Publick*, in that it is presented to every ones
View: Yet it is *Private* with respect to the *Church*. *Books* are not Read, and
the Instruction by them given in the *public Assemblies* of the Saints: But
visit every one, and converse with them in their own *private Houses*. And
therefore the Teaching, or Instruction thereby given is *private*: and of no
other Consideration than that of Writing a private *Letter* to a Friend, or of
having private *Conference* with him for his Edification. And this is not only
permitted to all the Saints, of whatever Sex they be, But,

Thirdly, It is *commanded*, Rom. xiv. 19. *Let us therefore follow after the Things which make for Peace, and Things wherewith one* (any one, Male or Female) *may edify another.* If it is the Duty of *Women* to seek the *Edification* of their Brethren and Sisters; then is it their Duty to use the *Means* of it, whether it be in speaking, writing, or printing: Since all these are *private*, and proper to the *Sphere* which the Lord has allotted them. Thus any Believer, Male or Female, that is gifted for, and inclin'd to publish their Thoughts in Print, about any Truth of Christ, for the private Instruction and Edification of the Saints; is *permitted, yea, commanded* so to do. And unless *Women* were excluded from being *Members* of Christ's mystical Body, *their Usefulness*, in all due Means, ought not to be hindred. Since it is declar'd, that *from Christ the Head, the whole Body, fitly joined together, and compacted by that which every Joint supplieth, according to the effectual Working in the Measure of every Part, maketh Increase of the Body, to the edifying of it self in Love*, Eph. iv. 16. If the *whole Body*, from Christ the Head, has Nourishment ministred to it, by that which *every Joint* supplieth, even those weak ones, of the *Female* Sex; then must *they* have some *Way* of communicating what they receive from Christ, to the rest of their Fellow-members. And if it should be said, *this ought to be in private Converse*: I must beg Leave to add, and in *Printing* too. For this is one *Way* of private Converse with the Saints: Only it is a more *extensive one*, of talking with *Thousands*, which otherwise could not have been spoke with, nor can ever be seen *Face to Face in the Flesh*. And is it the worse on this Account? Nay, surely, this *kind* of Communion with the Saints, in regard of the *Numbers* it extends to, is far preferable to that of *personal* Communion, because of its *narrow Bounds*: and yet it is as *private*. But,

Fourthly, As private Instruction is the *Duty of Women* as well as Men; so we have an *Example* thereof, *Acts* xviii. 26. Where we are inform'd that *Aquila and Priscilla took unto them*, even an *eloquent Apollos, a Man mighty in the Scriptures, and Expounded unto him the Way of God more perfectly*. And *this* of communicating ones Mind in *Print*, is as *private*, with respect to particular *Persons*, as if one did it particularly unto every one by *himself* in ones *own House*. There is only this *Difference*: The one is communicating ones Mind by *Speech*, in ones *own* private House: The other is doing it by *Writing*, in the private House of *another* Person. Both are still *private*. And to this *last*, there needs not the *publick* Authority of Christ in his Church; (as there does for Preaching) because this is not *publick*, but *private* Teaching. That which is exhibited in *Books*, can never be prov'd to be *publick* Teaching, unless the Books were *design'd* for the Instruction of *publick* Assemblies, and are accordingly *read* in them.

Once more, since *Women* are *allow'd* the Liberty of the *Press*, and some have us'd it about *Trifles*, and as it is to be fear'd under the Dictates of Satan, to the Propagation of his Kingdom: Shall none of that *Sex* be suffer'd to appear on *Christ's Side*, to tell of the Wonders of his *Love*, to seek the *Good* of Souls, and the Advancement of the Redeemer's *Interest?*—Surely, I look upon the *Opposition* made hereto, to be an *Artifice* of Satan, to hinder the rising Glory of Christ's Kingdom, and the Knowledge of Him, spreading itself over all the Earth. And therefore the Children of Light should beware of this Wile of the Prince of Darkness. For Satan never has been, nor will be wanting to *oppose* the Lord's Servants, of whatever *Sex, Rank,* or *Age* they be. He always has had, and will have something to *object* against them, under one specious *Pretence* or other, if possible to hinder their *Usefulness.* Either he will say, They are *unfit* for such a Work, or *unworthy* of it, that they are *arrogant and assuming,* that they *take too much upon them,* and *run before they are sent*; or one thing or other, he will always have to *object,* as a *Reason* why they should be *disregarded. Christ,* the Head of the Church, when as the Father's Servant, he came to finish the Work which he had given him to do on the Earth, was thus *treated* by Satan. And thus it *far'd* with those which he set *first* in the Church, the *Apostles.* And so had it *been* with all his *Ministers* ever since. And so great is the Devil's *Rage* against *Christ,* that he will not let *any,* even the least and last of all, that appear for *Him,* go *free,* without shooting his *Arrows* at them. And he never wants *Instruments* to spread his *Insinuations.* Yea, so *wilily* doth he work, that he sometimes gets indiscernibly into the *Lord's Servants* themselves, and causeth them to *oppose* one another in the *Service* of their great *Master.* Thus he got into *Peter,* when he dissuaded our Lord from going thro' with the great Work of Redemption, which his Father gave him to do: Upon which he said unto him, *Get thee behind me Satan,* Mat. xvi. 23. And thus, no doubt, under *his* Influence, the Disciples had *Indignation* against the Woman who pour'd the Box of precious Ointment upon Christ's Head; and said unto her. *To what purpose is this Waste? For this Ointment might have been sold for much, and given to the Poor.* To whom our Lord reply'd:—*Why trouble ye the Woman? For she hath wrought a good Work upon me.*—*Verily I say unto you, wheresoever this Gospel shall be preached in the whole World, there shall also this that this Woman hath done, be told for a Memorial of her,* Matt. xxvi. 7, &c.

From hence it is evident, That the Servants of Christ themselves, when under the Influence of Sin and Satan, may with Indignation *oppose* one another in his Service, for those good Works, which the Lord himself will own and honour. And therefore we had need to *watch* over our own Spirit, and against the Suggestions of Satan: lest we oppose the Honour and Interest of our dear Lord, and step aside into the Service of his grand Enemy, before we are aware.—And however *weak* any Servant of Christ is, or his Performances may be, yet ought he not therein to be *despis'd* of those who are, or esteem themselves to be *strong*. Since the Lord hath not *despised the Day of small Things*. If any Person is fully persuaded in his own Mind, from the Word and Spirit of Christ, that it is his Duty to engage in any Piece of Service for God; it is sufficient Warrant for him so to do. Nor ought he to be judged and condemned by his Fellow-Servants; since in this Affair, *to his own Master he stands or falls*. Nor can any Person justly say, that such a Performance will be useless to *all*; which is of no Benefit to *him*. For evident it is, that *Gifts*, whether greater or lesser, are to be *us'd*, and were not given in *vain*: And that the Exercise of those Gifts, which may be of little or no Use to *some*, are of great Service to *others*.—Let us therefore *improve* all the Talents given us; and whether we have received Gifts for publick or private Instruction, let us *use* the same, nothing doubting, but our Lord of his infinite Grace, will crown our Labours with the promis'd and design'd *Success*.

Imagine then, my dear Friend, when my *Books* come to your *Houses*, that I am come to give you a *Visit*; (for indeed by *them* I do) and patiently attend to the Lispings of a *Babe*: Who knows but the Lord may ordain *Strength* out of the Babe's Mouth? And give you a Visit *Himself*, by so weak a *Worm*, to your strong Consolation? It is all one to Omnipotence, to work by Worms, as by Angels. And remember, that the more contemptible and weak the *Instrument* is that the Lord *works* by, the more it commands the Glory of his *Grace*, and the Excellency of his *Power*.

But yet, if after all that has been said, any of you are not *willing* to have Communion with me in this *Way: The Will of the Lord be done!* There is *another* Way in which I shall, thro' divine Assistance, endeavour to have *Communion* with you, and seek your *Good*: And this is by *Prayer* unto God for you. For as *for me to live is Christ*; so while I live in the Flesh, it is my earnest Desire, some Way or other, to serve *Him*, his *Interest and People*: And when in any Respect, or Degree I can do it, I think my self *happy*.— Thus wishing all Peace and Prosperity: I am,

Gentleman and Brethren,

Your most affectionate,

Humble Servant,

In our Glorious L O R D,

A. D.

F I N I S.

INDEX